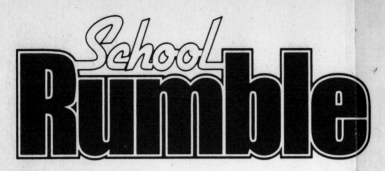

School Rumble

11

Jin Kobayashi

TRANSLATED AND ADAPTED BY
William Flanagan

LETTERED BY
HudsonYards

BALLANTINE BOOKS • NEW YORK

School Rumble volume 11 is a work of fiction. Names, characters, places, and incidents are the products of the author's imagination or are used fictitiously. Any resemblance to actual events, locales, or persons, living or dead, is entirely coincidental.

A Del Rey Manga/Kodansha Trade Paperback Original

Published in the United States by Del Rey Books, an imprint of The Random House Publishing Group, a division of Random House, Inc., New York.

DEL REY is a registered trademark and the Del Rey colophon is a trademark of Random House, Inc.

Publication rights arranged through Kodansha Ltd.

First published in Japan in 2005 by Kodansha Ltd., Tokyo.

ISBN 978-0-345-50562-0

Printed in the United States of America

www.delreymanga.com

9 8 7 6 5 4 3 2 1

Translator and adapter: William Flanagan
Lettering: HudsonYards
Cover Design: David Stevenson

Honorifics Explained

Throughout the Del Rey Manga books, you will find Japanese honorifics left intact in the translations. For those not familiar with how the Japanese use honorifics and, more important, how they differ from American honorifics, we present this brief overview.

Politeness has always been a critical facet of Japanese culture. Ever since the feudal era, when Japan was a highly stratified society, use of honorifics—which can be defined as polite speech that indicates relationship or status—has played an essential role in the Japanese language. When addressing someone in Japanese, an honorific usually takes the form of a suffix attached to one's name (example: "Asuna-san"), is used as a title at the end of one's name, or appears in place of the name itself (example: "Negi-sensei," or simply "Sensei!").

Honorifics can be expressions of respect or endearment. In the context of manga and anime, honorifics give insight into the nature of the relationship between characters. Many English translations leave out these important honorifics and therefore distort the feel of the original Japanese. Because Japanese honorifics contain nuances that English honorifics lack, it is our policy at Del Rey not to translate them. Here, instead, is a guide to some of the honorifics you may encounter in Del Rey Manga.

-san: This is the most common honorific and is equivalent to Mr., Miss, Ms., or Mrs. It is the all-purpose honorific and can be used in any situation where politeness is required.

-sama: This is one level higher than "-san" and is used to confer great respect.

-dono: This comes from the word "tono," which means "lord." It is an even higher level than "-sama" and confers utmost respect.

-kun: This suffix is used at the end of boys' names to express familiarity or endearment. It is also sometimes used by men among friends, or when addressing someone younger or of a lower station.

-chan: This is used to express endearment, mostly toward girls. It is also used for little boys, pets, and even among lovers. It gives a sense of childish cuteness.

Bozu: This is an informal way to refer to a boy, similar to the English terms "kid" and "squirt."

Sempai/Senpai: This title suggests that the addressee is one's senior in a group or organization. It is most often used in a school setting, where underclassmen refer to their upperclassmen as "sempai." It can also be used in the workplace, such as when a newer employee addresses an employee who has seniority in the company.

Kohai: This is the opposite of "sempai" and is used toward underclassmen in school or newcomers in the workplace. It connotes that the addressee is of a lower station.

Sensei: Literally meaning "one who has come before," this title is used for teachers, doctors, or masters of any profession or art.

Onee-san/Onii-san: Normally older siblings are not called by name but rather by the title of older sister (Onee-san) or older brother (Onii-san). Depending on the relationship, "-chan" or "-sama" can also be used instead of "-san". However, this honorific can also be used with someone unrelated when the relationship resembles that of siblings.

Obaa-san/Ojii-san: Japanese grandparents are called by their titles rather than by name. Grandmothers are called "Obaa-san" (or "Obaa-sama" to imply added respect and distance, or "Obaa-chan" for more intimacy). Likewise grandfathers are called "Ojii-san," "Ojii-sama," or "Ojii-chan."

-[blank]: This is usually forgotten in these lists, but it is perhaps the most significant difference between Japanese and English. The lack of honorific means that the speaker has permission to address the person in a very intimate way. Usually, only family, spouses, or very close friends have this kind of permission. Known as *yobisute*, it can be gratifying when someone who has earned the intimacy starts to call one by one's name without an honorific. But when that intimacy hasn't been earned, it can be very insulting.

Cultural Note

To preserve some of the humor found in *School Rumble*, we have elected to keep Japanese names in their original Japanese order— that is to say, with the family name first, followed by the personal name. So when you hear the name Tsukamoto Tenma, Tenma is just one member of the Tsukamoto family.

School Rumble 11

Jin Kobayashi

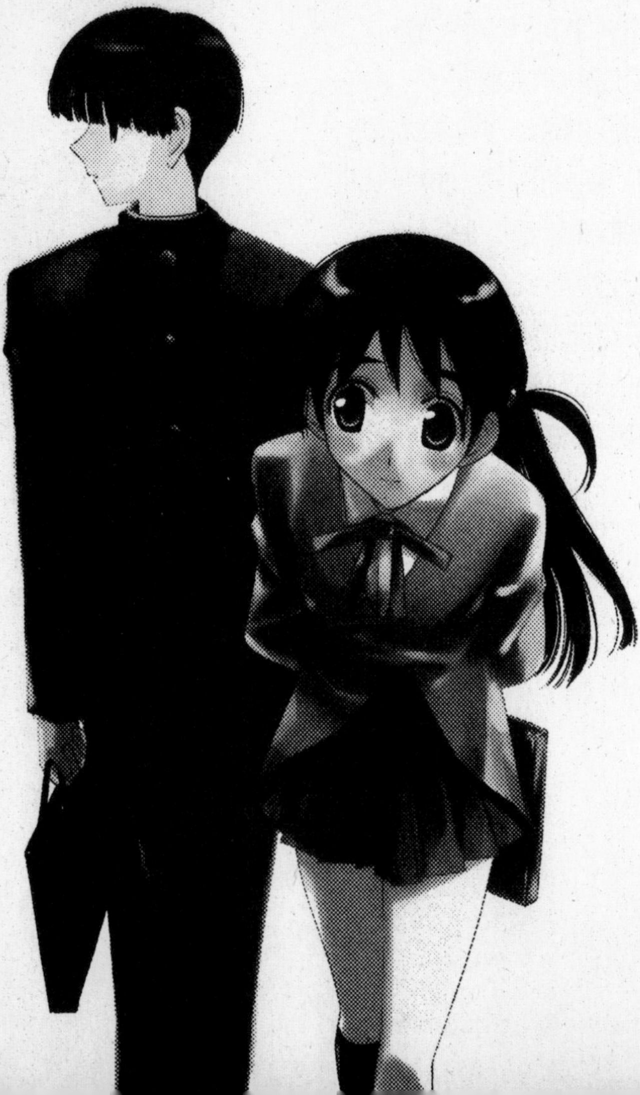

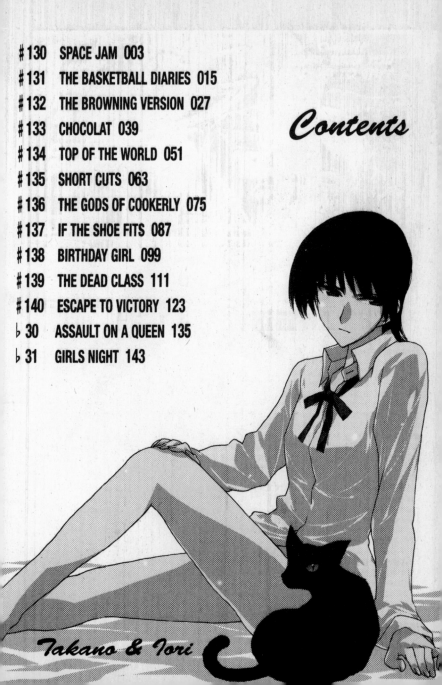

Contents

Takano & Iori

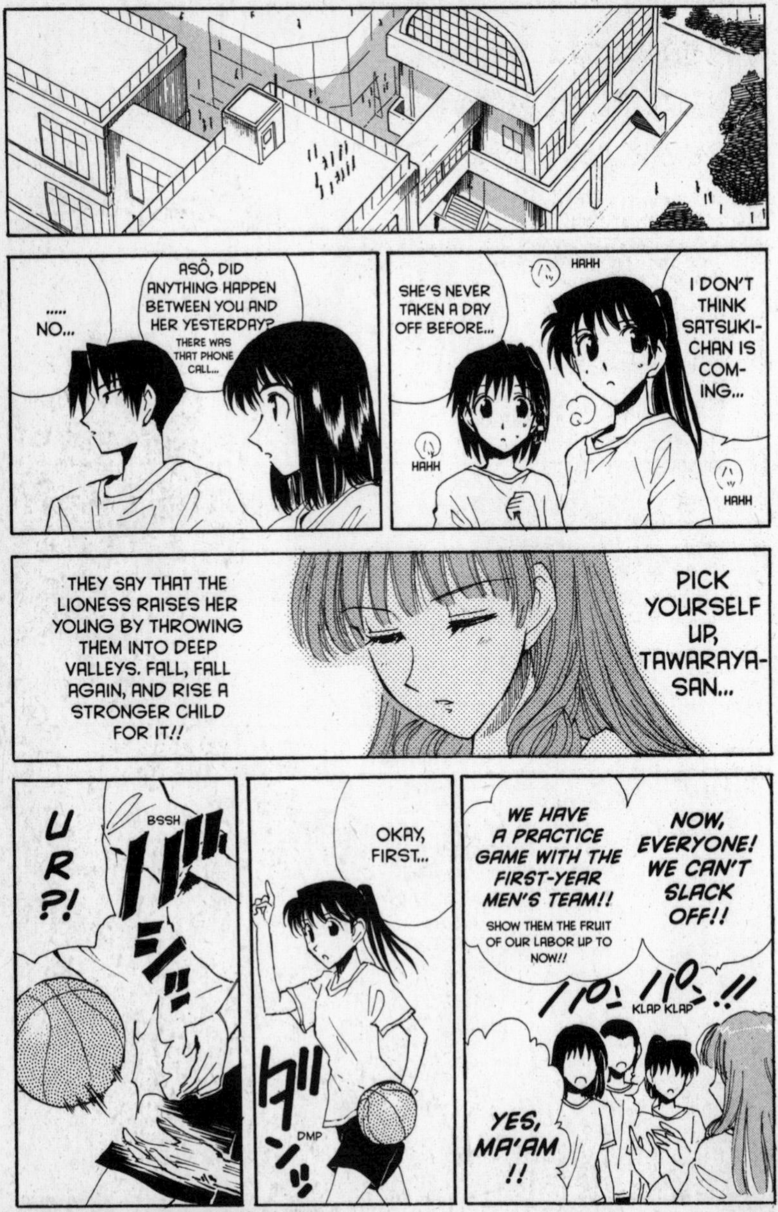
HAHH
I DON'T THINK SATSUKI-CHAN IS COMING...
SHE'S NEVER TAKEN A DAY OFF BEFORE...
HAHH
HAHH
ASÔ, DID ANYTHING HAPPEN BETWEEN YOU AND HER YESTERDAY?
THERE WAS THAT PHONE CALL...
..... NO...
PICK YOURSELF UP, TAWARAYA-SAN...
THEY SAY THAT THE LIONESS RAISES HER YOUNG BY THROWING THEM INTO DEEP VALLEYS. FALL, FALL AGAIN, AND RISE A STRONGER CHILD FOR IT!!
NOW, EVERYONE! WE CAN'T SLACK OFF!!
WE HAVE A PRACTICE GAME WITH THE FIRST-YEAR MEN'S TEAM!!
SHOW THEM THE FRUIT OF OUR LABOR UP TO NOW!!
KLAP KLAP
YES, MA'AM!!
OKAY, FIRST...
DMP
BSSH
UR?!

#130 SPACE JAM

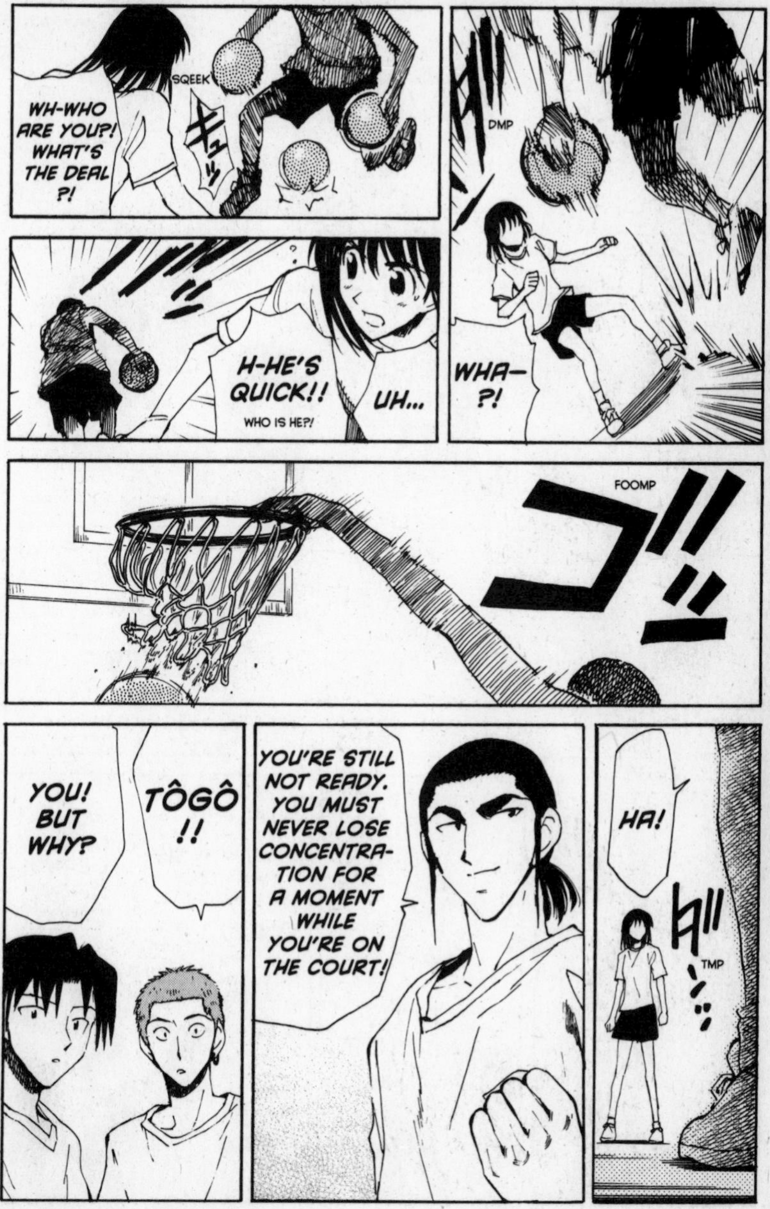
DMP
WHA— ?!
SQEEK
WH-WHO ARE YOU?! WHAT'S THE DEAL ?!
UH...
H-HE'S QUICK!!
WHO IS HE?!
FOOMP
HA!
TMP
YOU'RE STILL NOT READY. YOU MUST NEVER LOSE CONCENTRATION FOR A MOMENT WHILE YOU'RE ON THE COURT!
TÔGÔ !!
YOU! BUT WHY?

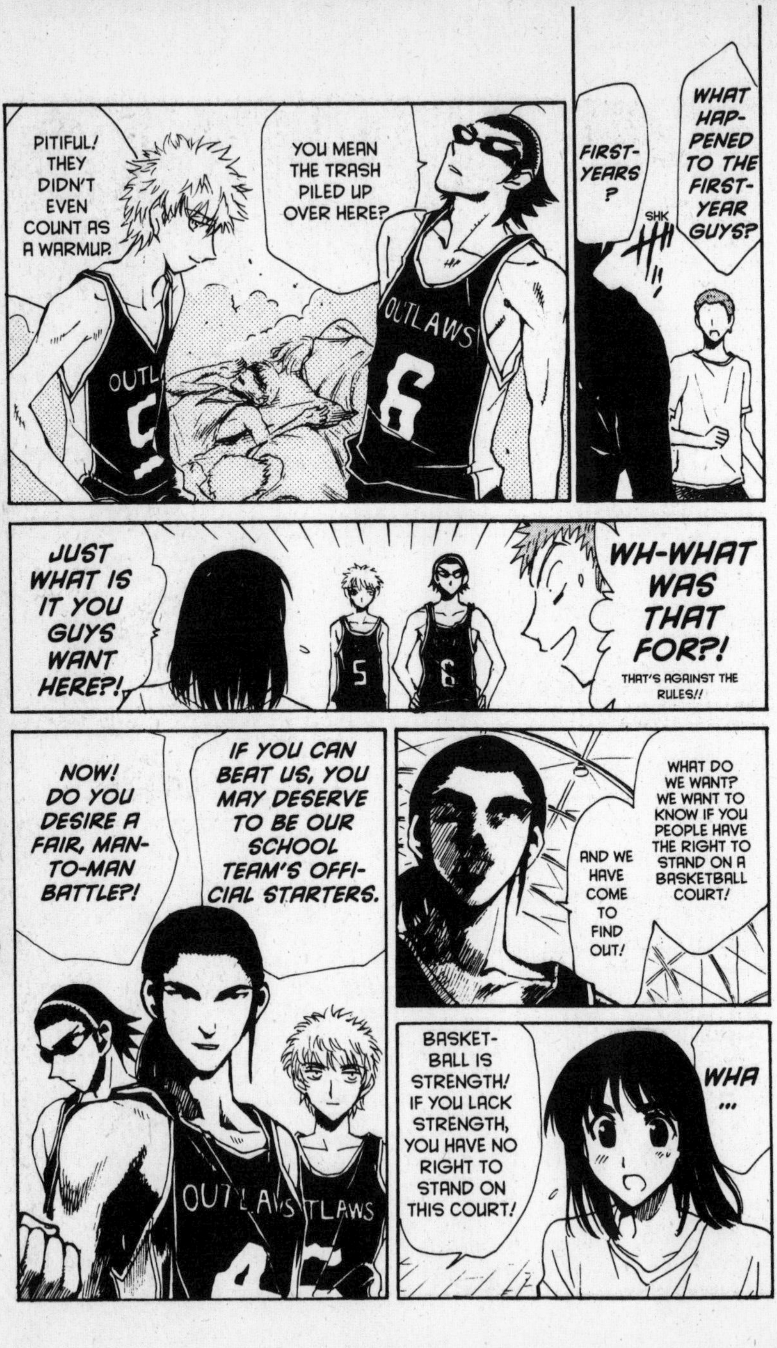
WHAT HAP-PENED TO THE FIRST-YEAR GUYS?
FIRST-YEARS?
SHK
YOU MEAN THE TRASH PILED UP OVER HERE?
PITIFUL! THEY DIDN'T EVEN COUNT AS A WARMUP.
WH-WHAT WAS THAT FOR?!
THAT'S AGAINST THE RULES!!
JUST WHAT IS IT YOU GUYS WANT HERE?!
WHAT DO WE WANT? WE WANT TO KNOW IF YOU PEOPLE HAVE THE RIGHT TO STAND ON A BASKETBALL COURT!
AND WE HAVE COME TO FIND OUT!
WHA...
BASKET-BALL IS STRENGTH! IF YOU LACK STRENGTH, YOU HAVE NO RIGHT TO STAND ON THIS COURT!
IF YOU CAN BEAT US, YOU MAY DESERVE TO BE OUR SCHOOL TEAM'S OFFI-CIAL STARTERS.
NOW! DO YOU DESIRE A FAIR, MAN-TO-MAN BATTLE?!

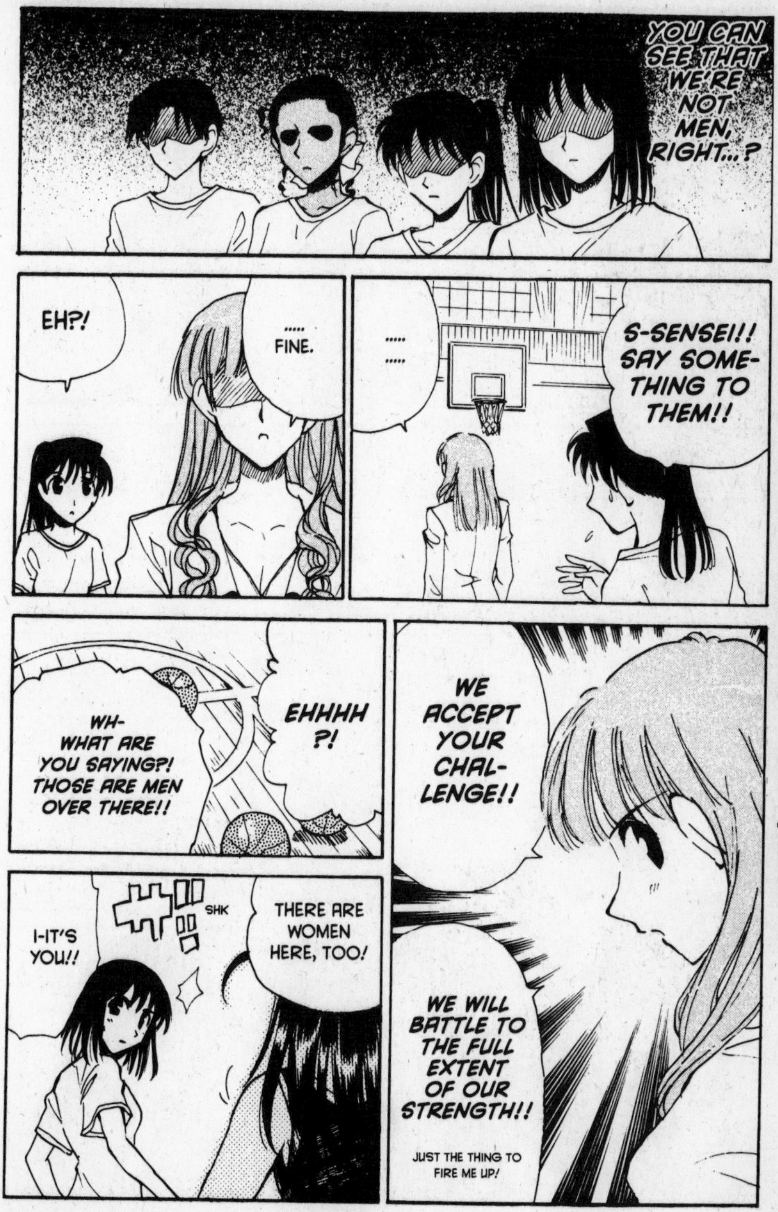
YOU CAN SEE THAT WE'RE NOT MEN, RIGHT...?
S-SENSEI!! SAY SOME-THING TO THEM!!
......
......
..... FINE.
EH?!
WE ACCEPT YOUR CHAL-LENGE!!
WE WILL BATTLE TO THE FULL EXTENT OF OUR STRENGTH!!
JUST THE THING TO FIRE ME UP!
EHHHH?!
WH- WHAT ARE YOU SAYING?! THOSE ARE MEN OVER THERE!!
THERE ARE WOMEN HERE, TOO!
SHK
I-IT'S YOU!!

Anegasaki Tae: Pulled Right Along in Misimpressions.

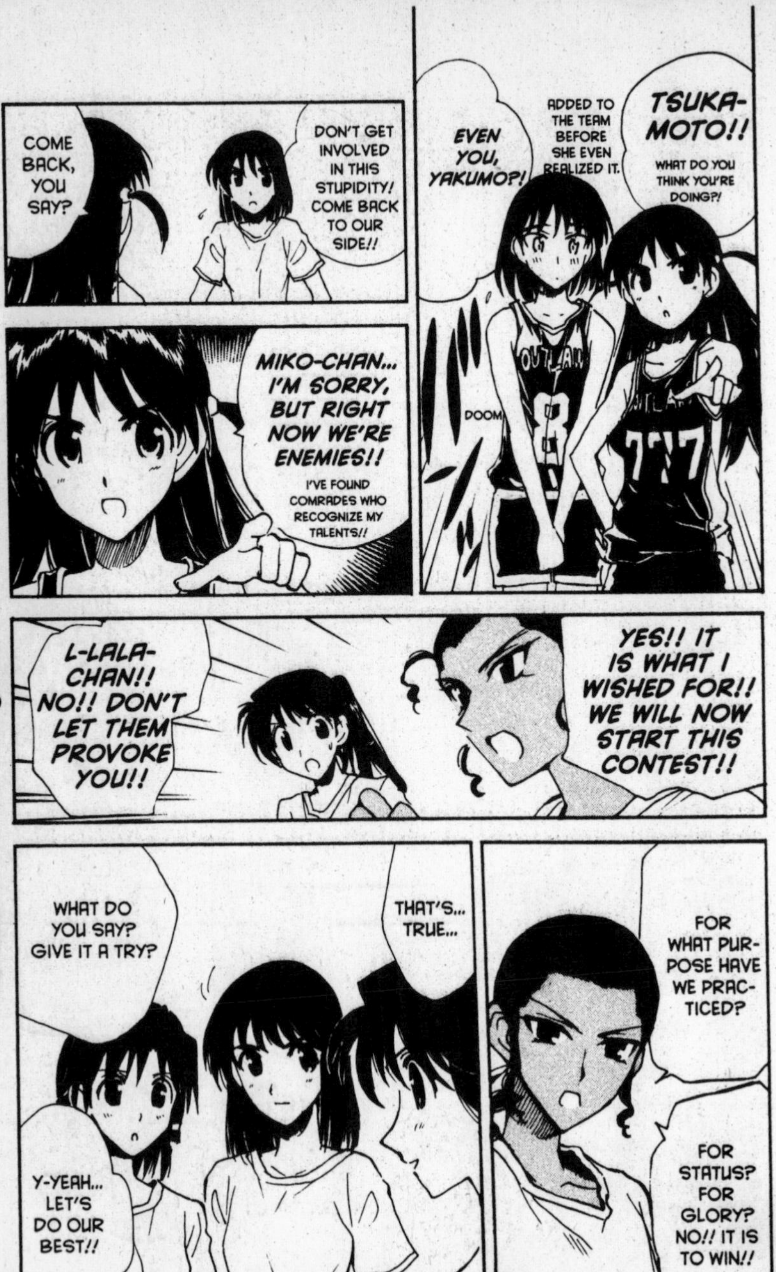
TSUKA-MOTO!!
WHAT DO YOU THINK YOU'RE DOING?!
ADDED TO THE TEAM BEFORE SHE EVEN REALIZED IT.
EVEN YOU, YAKUMO?!
DOOM
DON'T GET INVOLVED IN THIS STUPIDITY! COME BACK TO OUR SIDE!!
COME BACK, YOU SAY?
MIKO-CHAN... I'M SORRY, BUT RIGHT NOW WE'RE ENEMIES!!
I'VE FOUND COMRADES WHO RECOGNIZE MY TALENTS!!
YES!! IT IS WHAT I WISHED FOR!! WE WILL NOW START THIS CONTEST!!
L-LALA-CHAN!! NO!! DON'T LET THEM PROVOKE YOU!!
FOR WHAT PURPOSE HAVE WE PRACTICED?
FOR STATUS? FOR GLORY? NO!! IT IS TO WIN!!
THAT'S... TRUE...
WHAT DO YOU SAY? GIVE IT A TRY?
Y-YEAH... LET'S DO OUR BEST!!

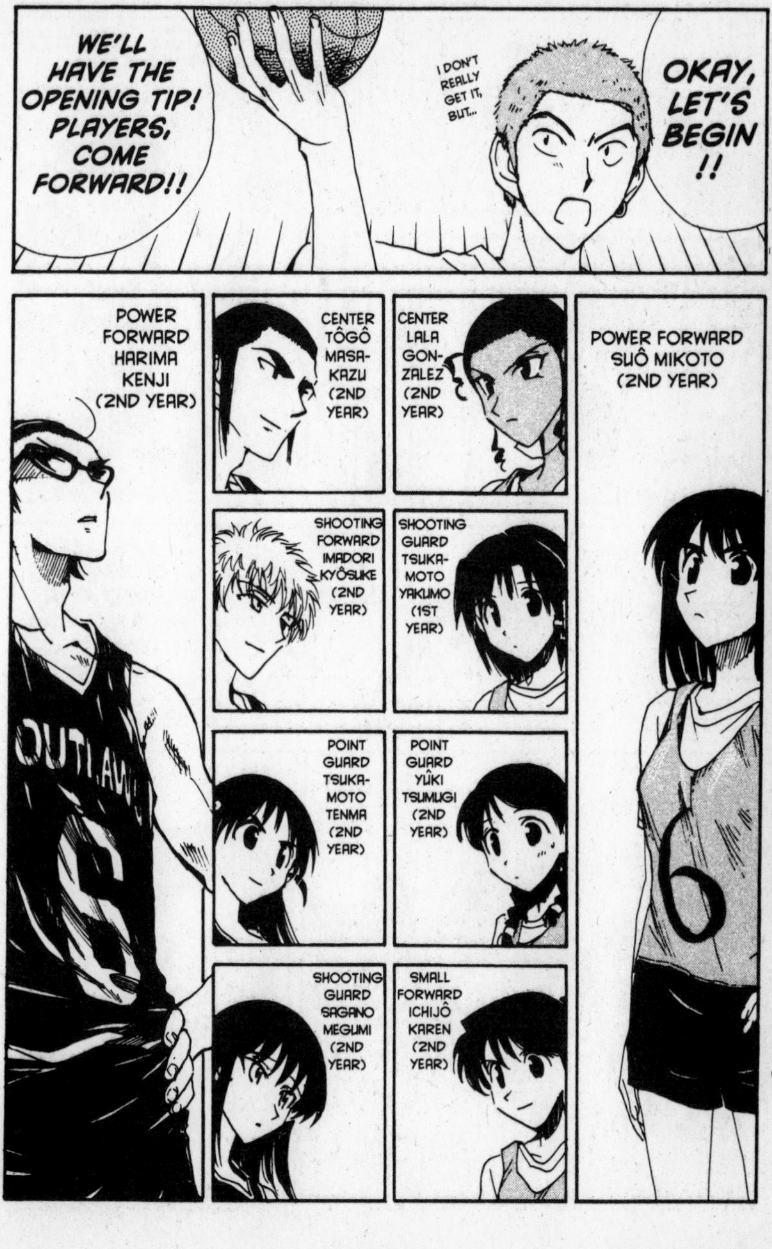
OKAY, LET'S BEGIN!!
I DON'T REALLY GET IT, BUT...
WE'LL HAVE THE OPENING TIP! PLAYERS, COME FORWARD!!
POWER FORWARD SUÔ MIKOTO (2ND YEAR)
CENTER LALA GONZALEZ (2ND YEAR)
CENTER TÔGÔ MASAKAZU (2ND YEAR)
SHOOTING GUARD TSUKAMOTO YAKUMO (1ST YEAR)
SHOOTING FORWARD IMADORI KYÔSUKE (2ND YEAR)
POINT GUARD YÛKI TSUMUGI (2ND YEAR)
POINT GUARD TSUKAMOTO TENMA (2ND YEAR)
SMALL FORWARD ICHIJÔ KAREN (2ND YEAR)
SHOOTING GUARD SAGANO MEGUMI (2ND YEAR)
POWER FORWARD HARIMA KENJI (2ND YEAR)
OUTLAW

Sorry for the Sudden Change, but Manager Yûki Tsumugi Stands In as a Player.

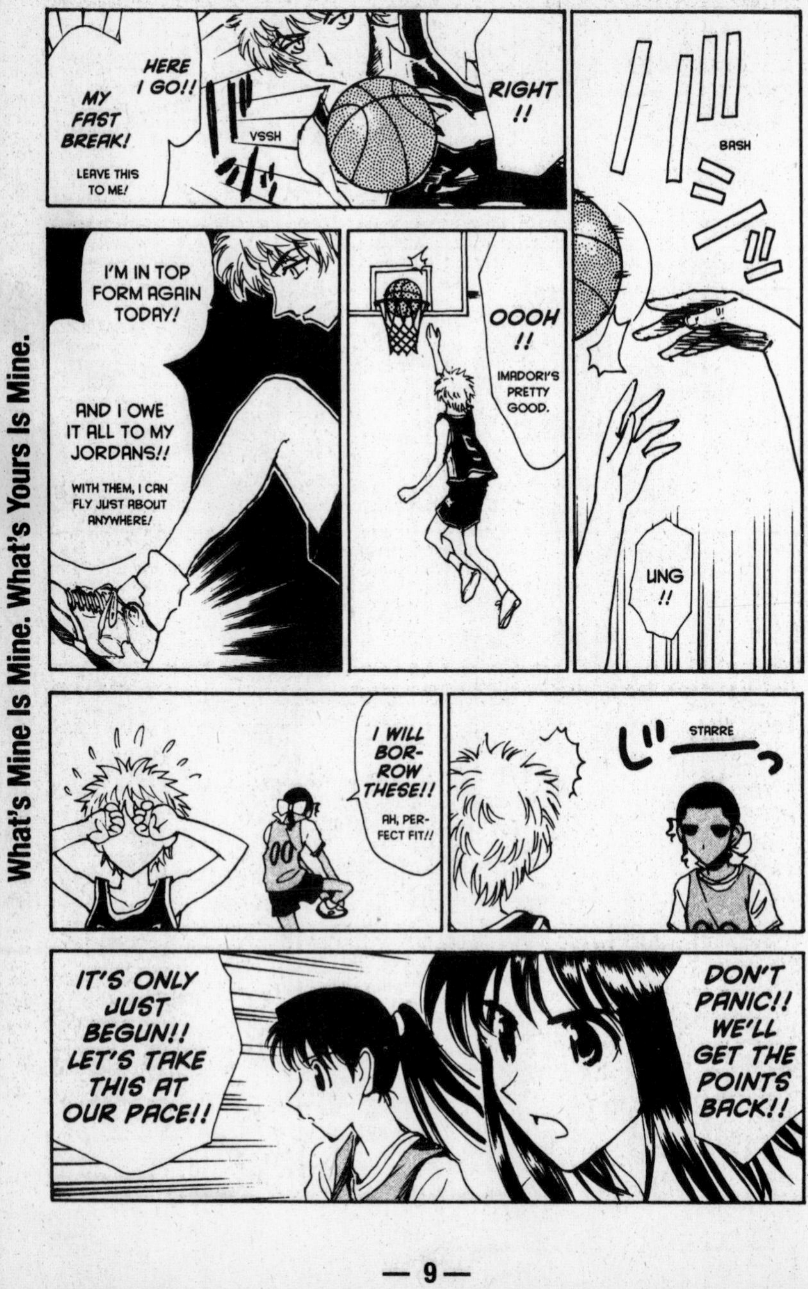
BASH
UNG !!
RIGHT !!
HERE I GO!!
MY FAST BREAK!
VSSH
LEAVE THIS TO ME!
OOOH !!
IMADORI'S PRETTY GOOD.
I'M IN TOP FORM AGAIN TODAY!
AND I OWE IT ALL TO MY JORDANS!!
WITH THEM, I CAN FLY JUST ABOUT ANYWHERE!
STARRE
I WILL BOR-ROW THESE!!
AH, PER-FECT FIT!!
DON'T PANIC!! WE'LL GET THE POINTS BACK!!
IT'S ONLY JUST BEGUN!! LET'S TAKE THIS AT OUR PACE!!

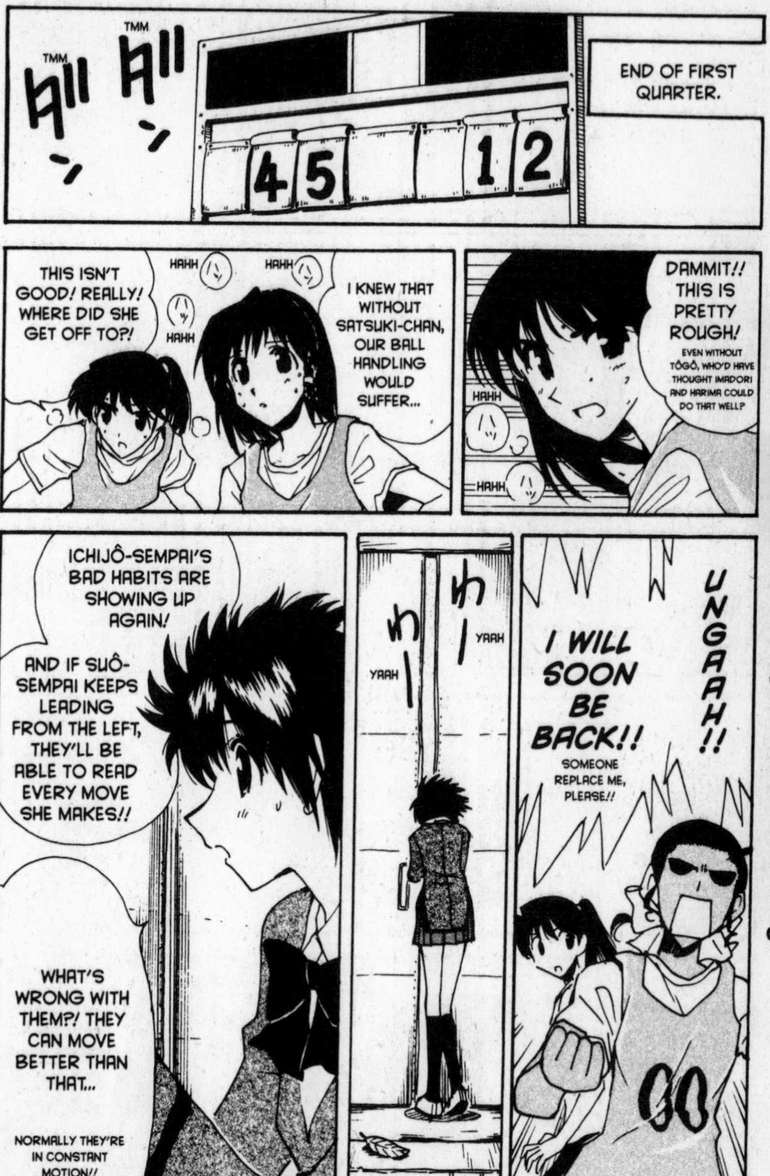
END OF FIRST QUARTER.
TMM
TMM
45
12
DAMMIT!! THIS IS PRETTY ROUGH!
EVEN WITHOUT TÔGÔ, WHO'D HAVE THOUGHT IMADORI AND HARIMA COULD DO THAT WELL?
HAHH
HAHH
HAHH
I KNEW THAT WITHOUT SATSUKI-CHAN, OUR BALL HANDLING WOULD SUFFER...
HAHH
THIS ISN'T GOOD! REALLY! WHERE DID SHE GET OFF TO?!
HAHH
UNGAAH!!
I WILL SOON BE BACK!!
SOMEONE REPLACE ME, PLEASE!!
YAAH
YAAH
ICHIJÔ-SEMPAI'S BAD HABITS ARE SHOWING UP AGAIN!
AND IF SUÔ-SEMPAI KEEPS LEADING FROM THE LEFT, THEY'LL BE ABLE TO READ EVERY MOVE SHE MAKES!!
WHAT'S WRONG WITH THEM?! THEY CAN MOVE BETTER THAN THAT...
NORMALLY THEY'RE IN CONSTANT MOTION!!

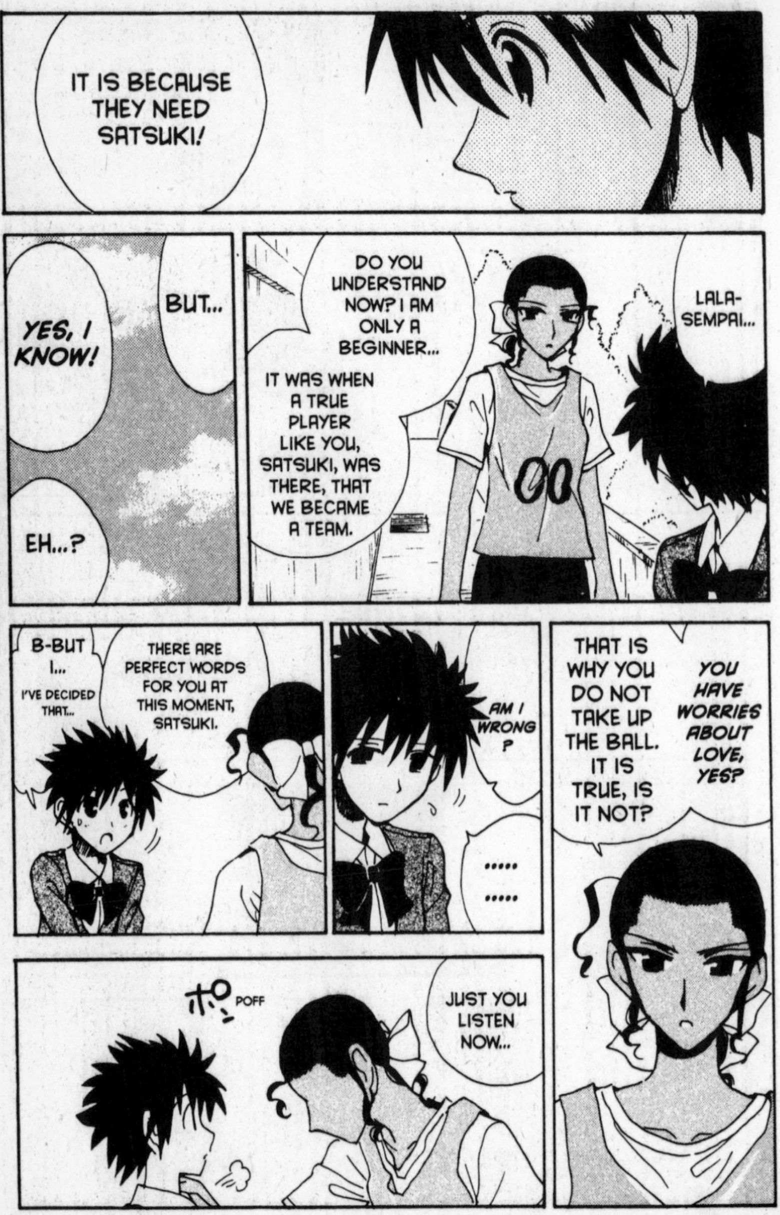
IT IS BECAUSE THEY NEED SATSUKI!
LALA-SEMPAI...
DO YOU UNDERSTAND NOW? I AM ONLY A BEGINNER...
IT WAS WHEN A TRUE PLAYER LIKE YOU, SATSUKI, WAS THERE, THAT WE BECAME A TEAM.
BUT...
YES, I KNOW!
EH...?
YOU HAVE WORRIES ABOUT LOVE, YES?
THAT IS WHY YOU DO NOT TAKE UP THE BALL. IT IS TRUE, IS IT NOT?
AM I WRONG?
....
THERE ARE PERFECT WORDS FOR YOU AT THIS MOMENT, SATSUKI.
B-BUT I...
I'VE DECIDED THAT...
JUST YOU LISTEN NOW...
ポ POFF

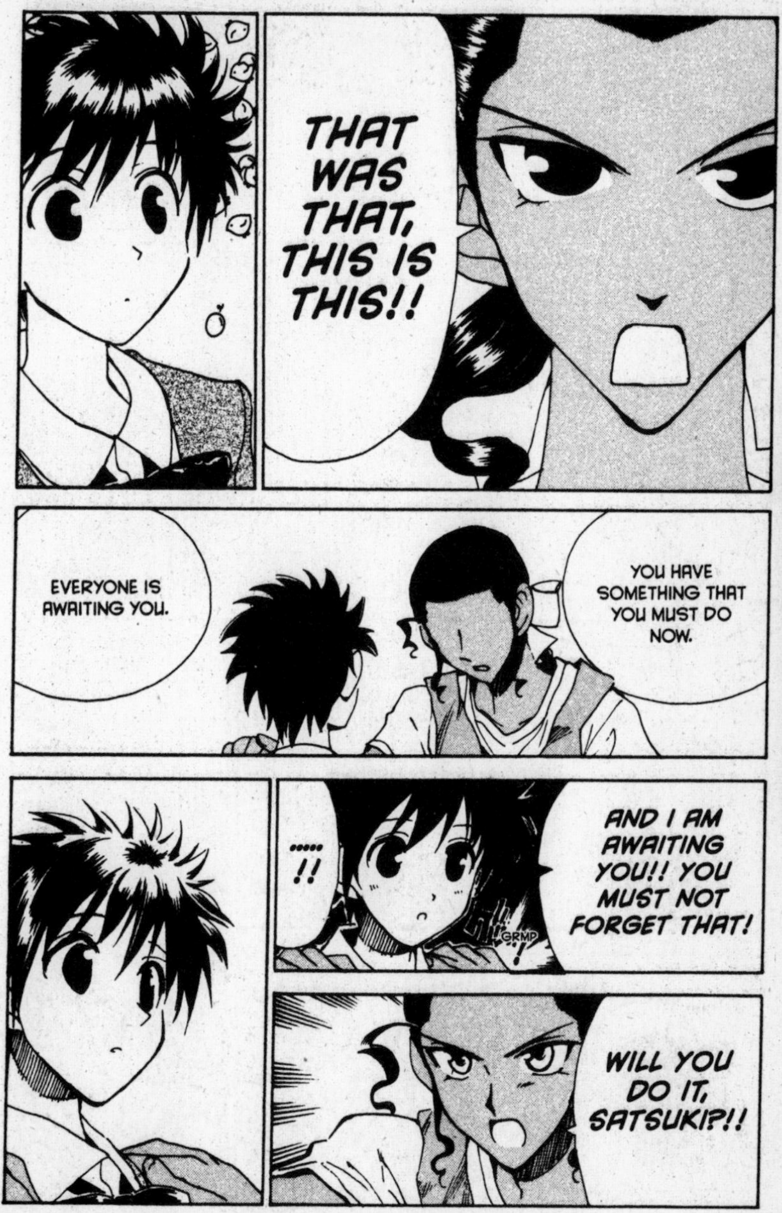
THAT WAS THAT, THIS IS THIS!!
YOU HAVE SOMETHING THAT YOU MUST DO NOW.
EVERYONE IS AWAITING YOU.
AND I AM AWAITING YOU!! YOU MUST NOT FORGET THAT!
GRMP
……!!
WILL YOU DO IT, SATSUKI?!!

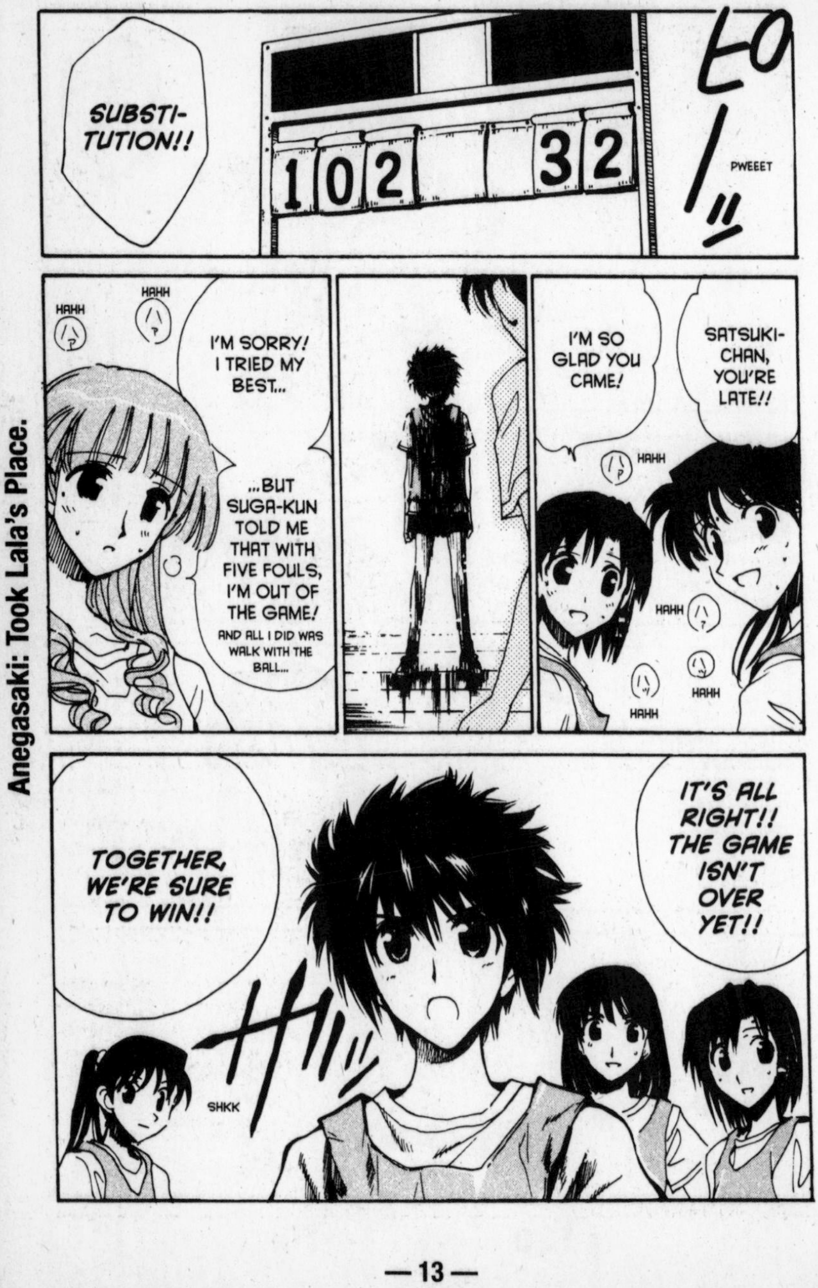
PWEEET
SUBSTI-TUTION!!
102 32
SATSUKI-CHAN, YOU'RE LATE!!
I'M SO GLAD YOU CAME!
HAHH
HAHH
HAHH
HAHH
I'M SORRY! I TRIED MY BEST...
...BUT SUGA-KUN TOLD ME THAT WITH FIVE FOULS, I'M OUT OF THE GAME!
AND ALL I DID WAS WALK WITH THE BALL...
HAHH
HAHH
IT'S ALL RIGHT!! THE GAME ISN'T OVER YET!!
SHKK
TOGETHER, WE'RE SURE TO WIN!!

Anegasaki: Took Lala's Place.

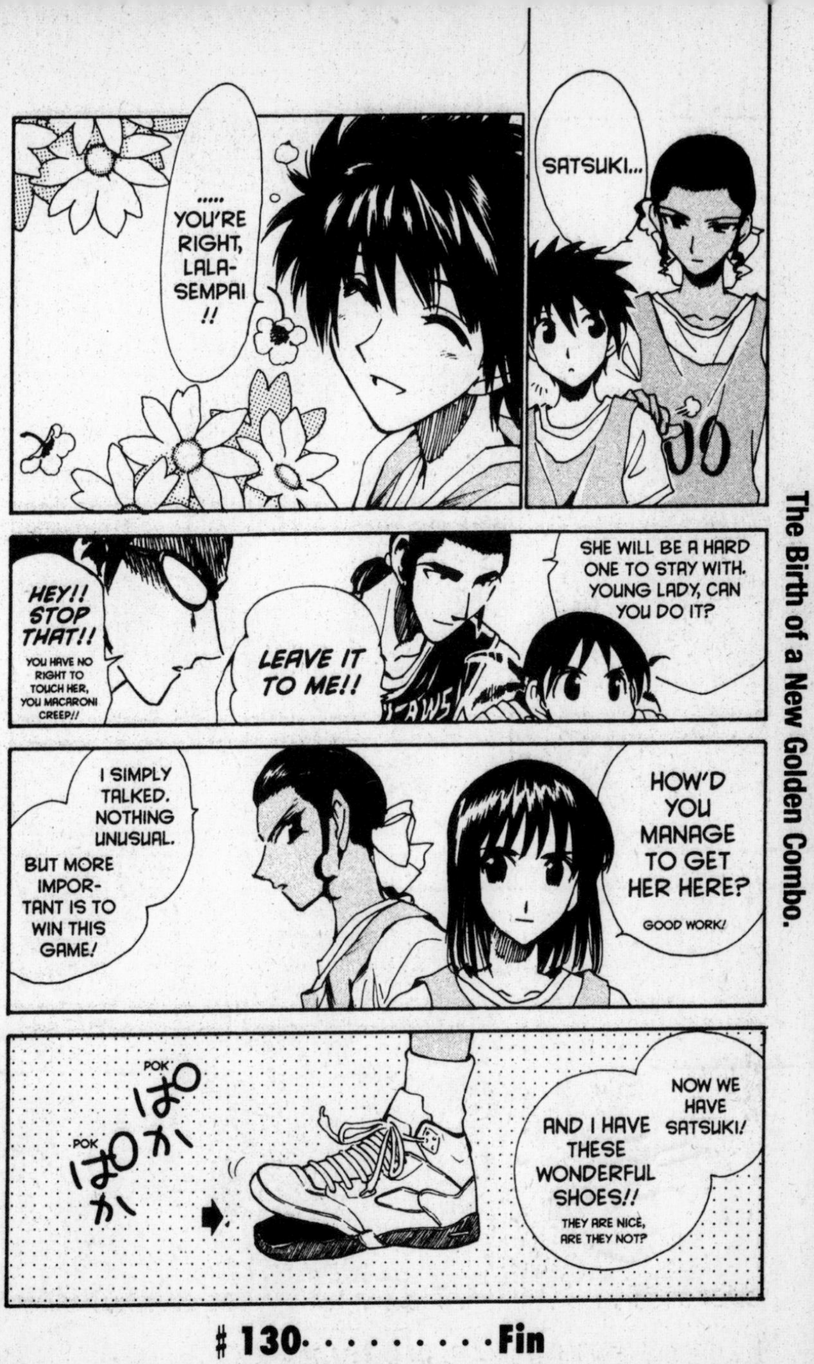
SATSUKI...
..... YOU'RE RIGHT, LALA-SEMPAI !!
SHE WILL BE A HARD ONE TO STAY WITH. YOUNG LADY, CAN YOU DO IT?
LEAVE IT TO ME!!
HEY!! STOP THAT!!
YOU HAVE NO RIGHT TO TOUCH HER, YOU MACARONI CREEP!!
HOW'D YOU MANAGE TO GET HER HERE?
GOOD WORK!
I SIMPLY TALKED. NOTHING UNUSUAL.
BUT MORE IMPOR-TANT IS TO WIN THIS GAME!
NOW WE HAVE SATSUKI!
AND I HAVE THESE WONDERFUL SHOES!!
THEY ARE NICE, ARE THEY NOT?
POK ぱか
POK ぱか

The Birth of a New Golden Combo.

 # 130· · · · · · · · ·Fin

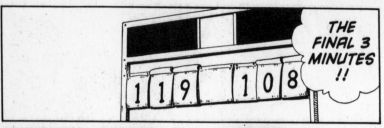

119 108
THE FINAL 3 MINUTES!!
...... UM...
WH- WHAT'LL I DO...?
DITHER
DITHER
YAKUMO!! PASS!! PASS TO ME!!
OVER HERE!!
H-HARIMA-SAN, PLEASE TAKE IT FROM HERE...
RIGHT!! I'VE GOT IT, LITTLE SISTER-SAN!!
WHOOSH
SHNT
DMP
NICE SHOT!!
SHUMP
I-I'M SORRY, NEE-SAN... YOU WERE BEING COVERED, SO...
R-REALLY? SO YOU DID THE UNEXPECTED, HUH?
THAT'S YAKUMO, LOOKING OUT FOR ME!!
TSK! HARIMA'S PLAYING SOME STRONG OFFENSE!!
I CAN'T BELIEVE HIS STAMINA!!

#131 THE BASKETBALL DIARIES

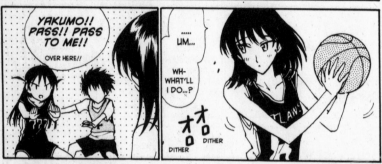

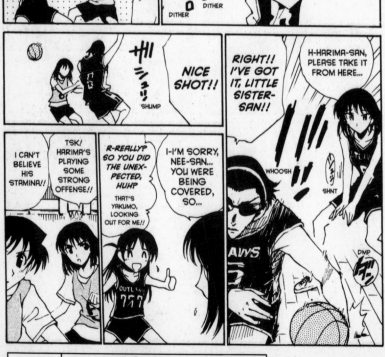

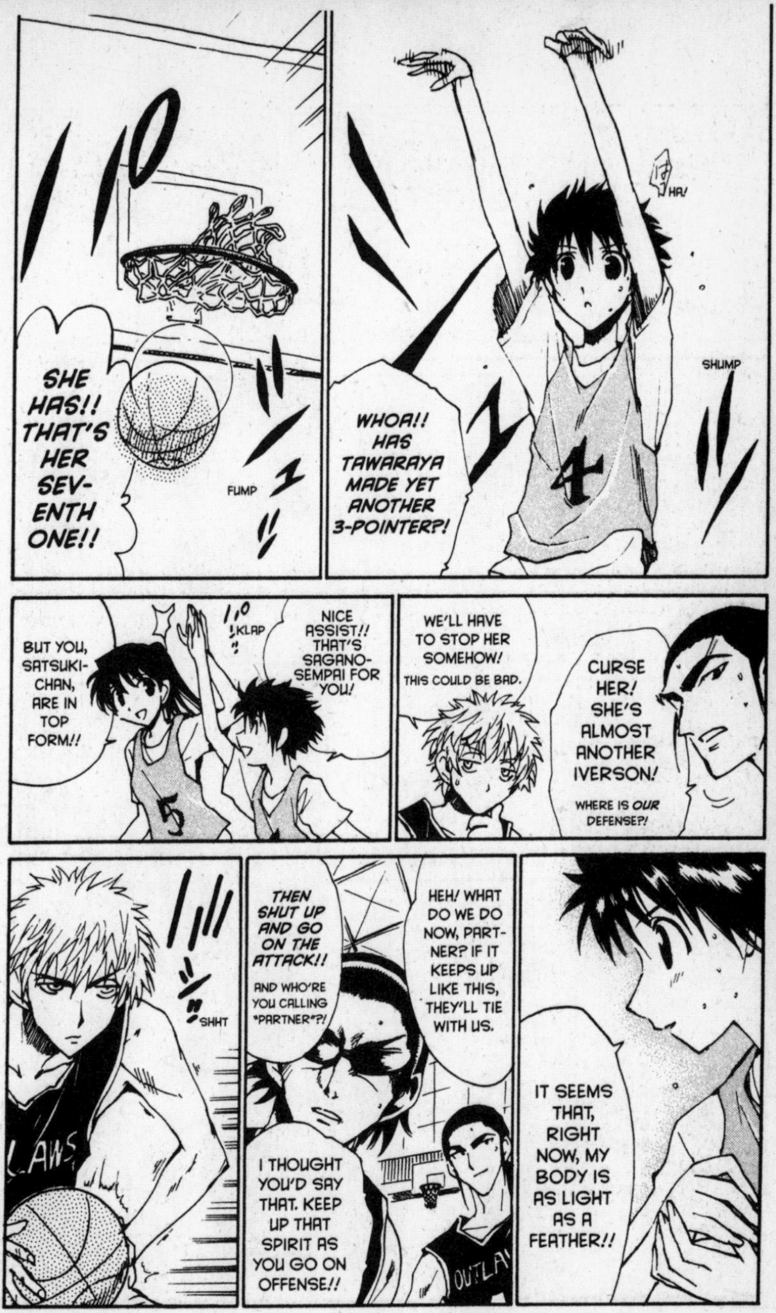
HA!
SHUMP
WHOA!! HAS TAWARAYA MADE YET ANOTHER 3-POINTER?!
FUMP
SHE HAS!! THAT'S HER SEV-ENTH ONE!!
CURSE HER! SHE'S ALMOST ANOTHER IVERSON!
WHERE IS OUR DEFENSE?!
WE'LL HAVE TO STOP HER SOMEHOW!
THIS COULD BE BAD.
NICE ASSIST!! THAT'S SAGANO-SEMPAI FOR YOU!
KLAP
BUT YOU, SATSUKI-CHAN, ARE IN TOP FORM!!
IT SEEMS THAT, RIGHT NOW, MY BODY IS AS LIGHT AS A FEATHER!!
HEH! WHAT DO WE DO NOW, PART-NER? IF IT KEEPS UP LIKE THIS, THEY'LL TIE WITH US.
THEN SHUT UP AND GO ON THE ATTACK!!
AND WHO'RE YOU CALLING "PARTNER"?!
I THOUGHT YOU'D SAY THAT. KEEP UP THAT SPIRIT AS YOU GO ON OFFENSE!!
SHHT

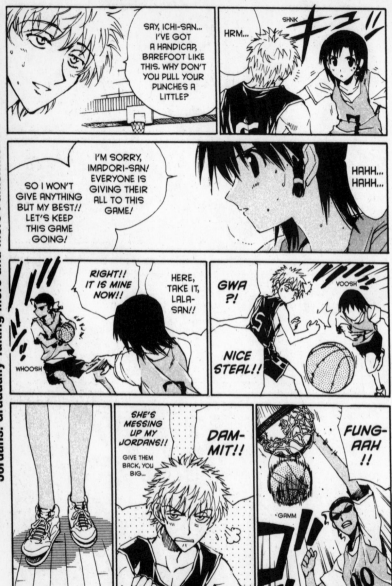

Jordans: Gradually Taking More and More Punishment.

SHNK
HRM...
SAY, ICHI-SAN... I'VE GOT A HANDICAP, BAREFOOT LIKE THIS. WHY DON'T YOU PULL YOUR PUNCHES A LITTLE?
HAHH... HAHH...
I'M SORRY, IMADORI-SAN! EVERYONE IS GIVING THEIR ALL TO THIS GAME!
SO I WON'T GIVE ANYTHING BUT MY BEST!! LET'S KEEP THIS GAME GOING!
VOOSH
GWA ?!
NICE STEAL!!
HERE, TAKE IT, LALA-SAN!!
RIGHT!! IT IS MINE NOW!!
WHOOSH
FUNG-AAH !!
GAMM
DAM-MIT!!
SHE'S MESSING UP MY JORDANS!!
GIVE THEM BACK, YOU BIG...

Tôgô's Stock: Skyrocketing.

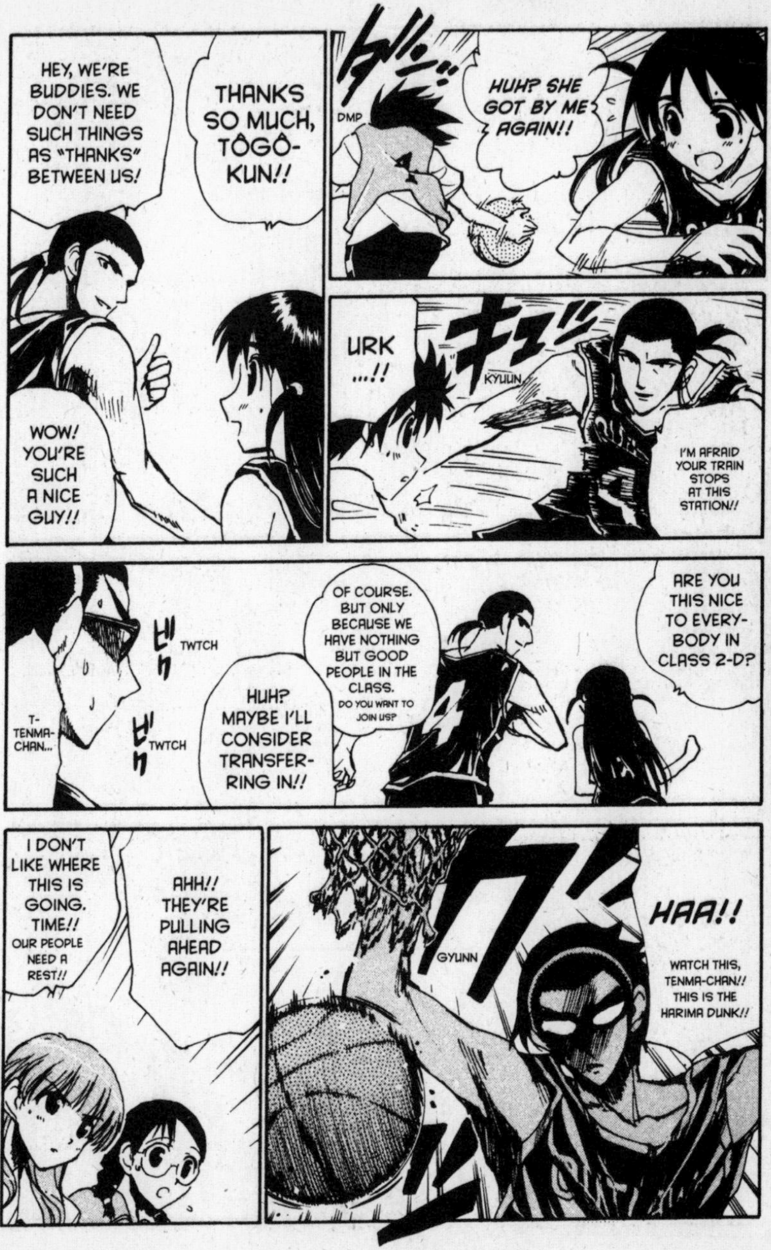
HUH? SHE GOT BY ME AGAIN!!
DMP
KYUUN
URK ...!!
I'M AFRAID YOUR TRAIN STOPS AT THIS STATION!!
THANKS SO MUCH, TÔGÔ-KUN!!
HEY, WE'RE BUDDIES. WE DON'T NEED SUCH THINGS AS "THANKS" BETWEEN US!
WOW! YOU'RE SUCH A NICE GUY!!
ARE YOU THIS NICE TO EVERY-BODY IN CLASS 2-D?
OF COURSE. BUT ONLY BECAUSE WE HAVE NOTHING BUT GOOD PEOPLE IN THE CLASS.
DO YOU WANT TO JOIN US?
HUH? MAYBE I'LL CONSIDER TRANSFER-RING IN!!
TWTCH
TWTCH
T-TENMA-CHAN...
HAA!!
WATCH THIS, TENMA-CHAN!! THIS IS THE HARIMA DUNK!!
GYUNN
AHH!! THEY'RE PULLING AHEAD AGAIN!!
I DON'T LIKE WHERE THIS IS GOING. TIME!!
OUR PEOPLE NEED A REST!!

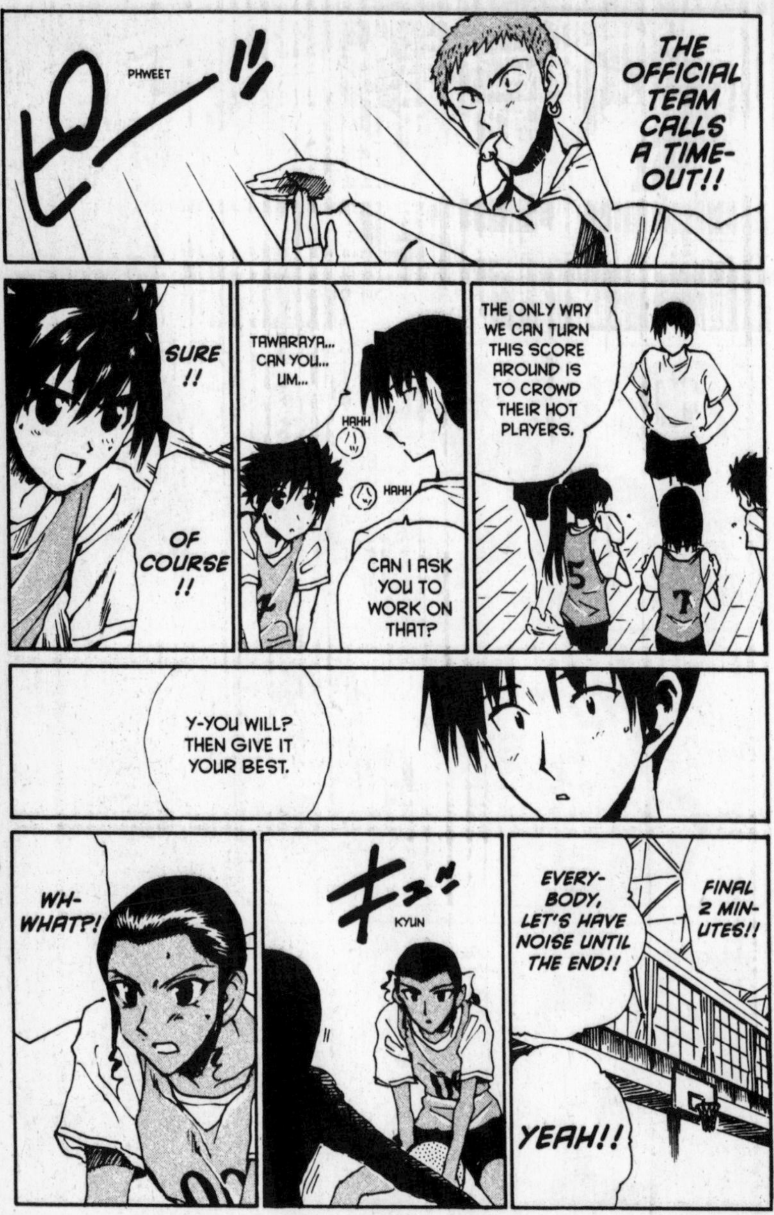
THE OFFICIAL TEAM CALLS A TIME-OUT!!
PHWEET
THE ONLY WAY WE CAN TURN THIS SCORE AROUND IS TO CROWD THEIR HOT PLAYERS.
TAWARAYA... CAN YOU... UM...
HAHH
HAHH
CAN I ASK YOU TO WORK ON THAT?
SURE !!
OF COURSE !!
Y-YOU WILL? THEN GIVE IT YOUR BEST.
FINAL 2 MIN-UTES!!
EVERY-BODY, LET'S HAVE NOISE UNTIL THE END!!
YEAH!!
KYUN
WH-WHAT?!

Lala vs. Tenma History: 2 Matches, 2 Lala Wins.

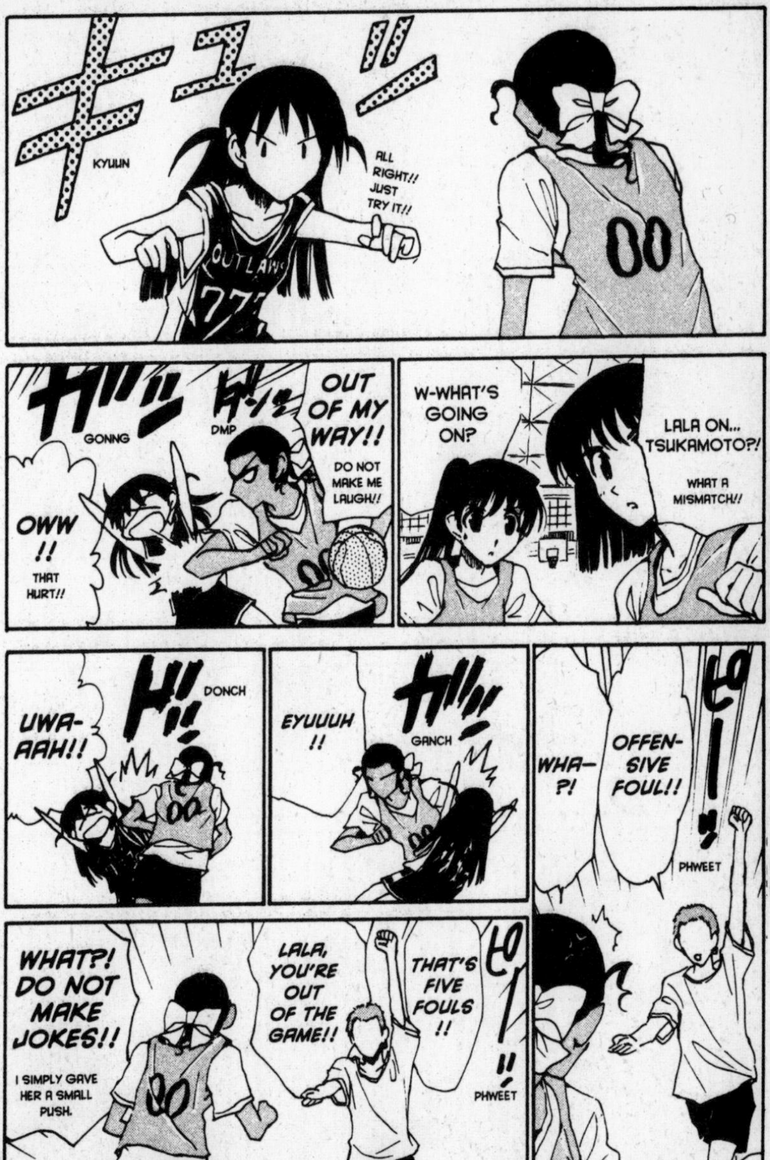

KYUUN
ALL RIGHT!! JUST TRY IT!!
W-WHAT'S GOING ON?
LALA ON... TSUKAMOTO?!
WHAT A MISMATCH!!
OUT OF MY WAY!!
DO NOT MAKE ME LAUGH!!
DMP
GONNG
OWW!!
THAT HURT!!
OFFEN-SIVE FOUL!!
WHA-?!
PHWEET
EYUUUH!!
GANCH
DONCH
UWA-AAH!!
THAT'S FIVE FOULS!!
PHWEET
LALA, YOU'RE OUT OF THE GAME!!
WHAT?! DO NOT MAKE JOKES!!
I SIMPLY GAVE HER A SMALL PUSH.

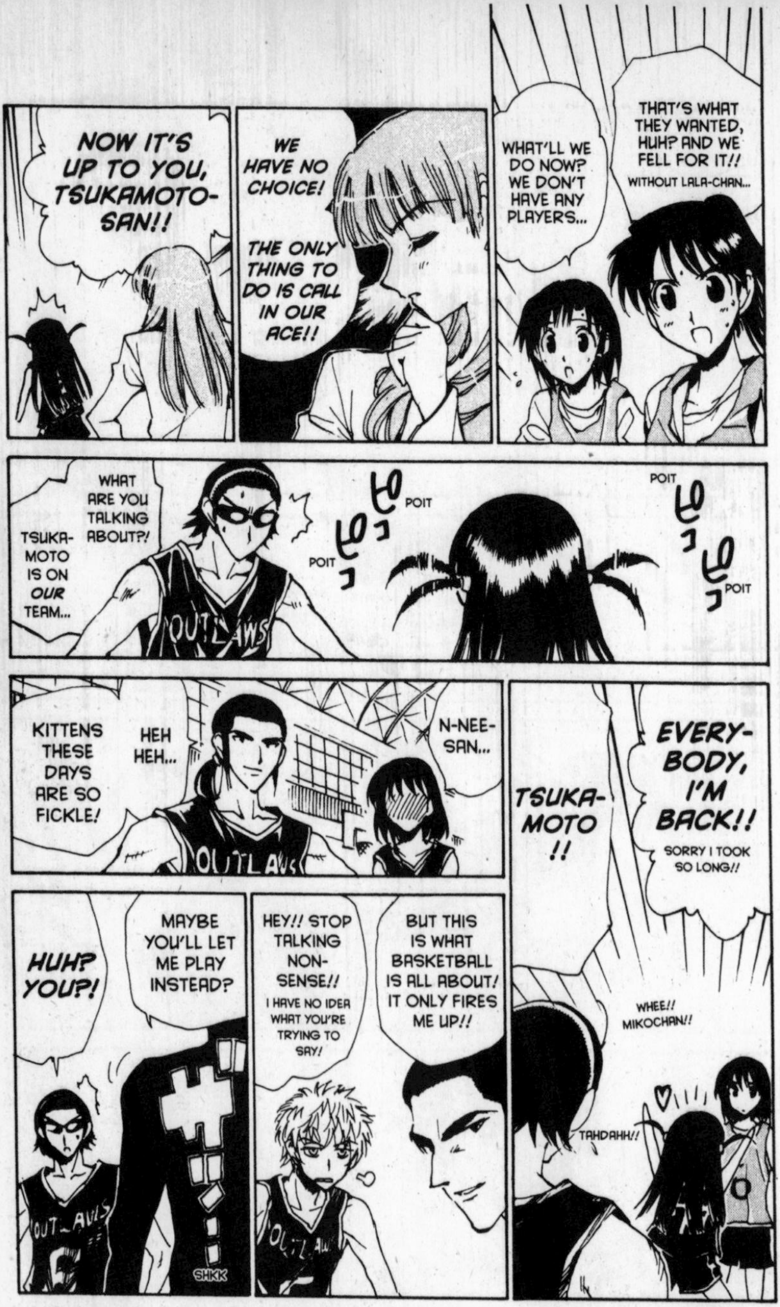
THAT'S WHAT THEY WANTED, HUH? AND WE FELL FOR IT!!
WITHOUT LALA-CHAN...
WHAT'LL WE DO NOW? WE DON'T HAVE ANY PLAYERS...
WE HAVE NO CHOICE!
THE ONLY THING TO DO IS CALL IN OUR ACE!!
NOW IT'S UP TO YOU, TSUKAMOTO-SAN!!
POIT
POIT
POIT
POIT
WHAT ARE YOU TALKING ABOUT?!
TSUKAMOTO IS ON *OUR* TEAM...
EVERYBODY, I'M BACK!!
SORRY I TOOK SO LONG!!
TSUKAMOTO!!
WHEE!! MIKOCHAN!!
TAHDAHH!!
N-NEE-SAN...
HEH HEH...
KITTENS THESE DAYS ARE SO FICKLE!
BUT THIS IS WHAT BASKETBALL IS ALL ABOUT! IT ONLY FIRES ME UP!!
HEY!! STOP TALKING NONSENSE!!
I HAVE NO IDEA WHAT YOU'RE TRYING TO SAY!
MAYBE YOU'LL LET ME PLAY INSTEAD?
SHKK
HUH? YOU?!

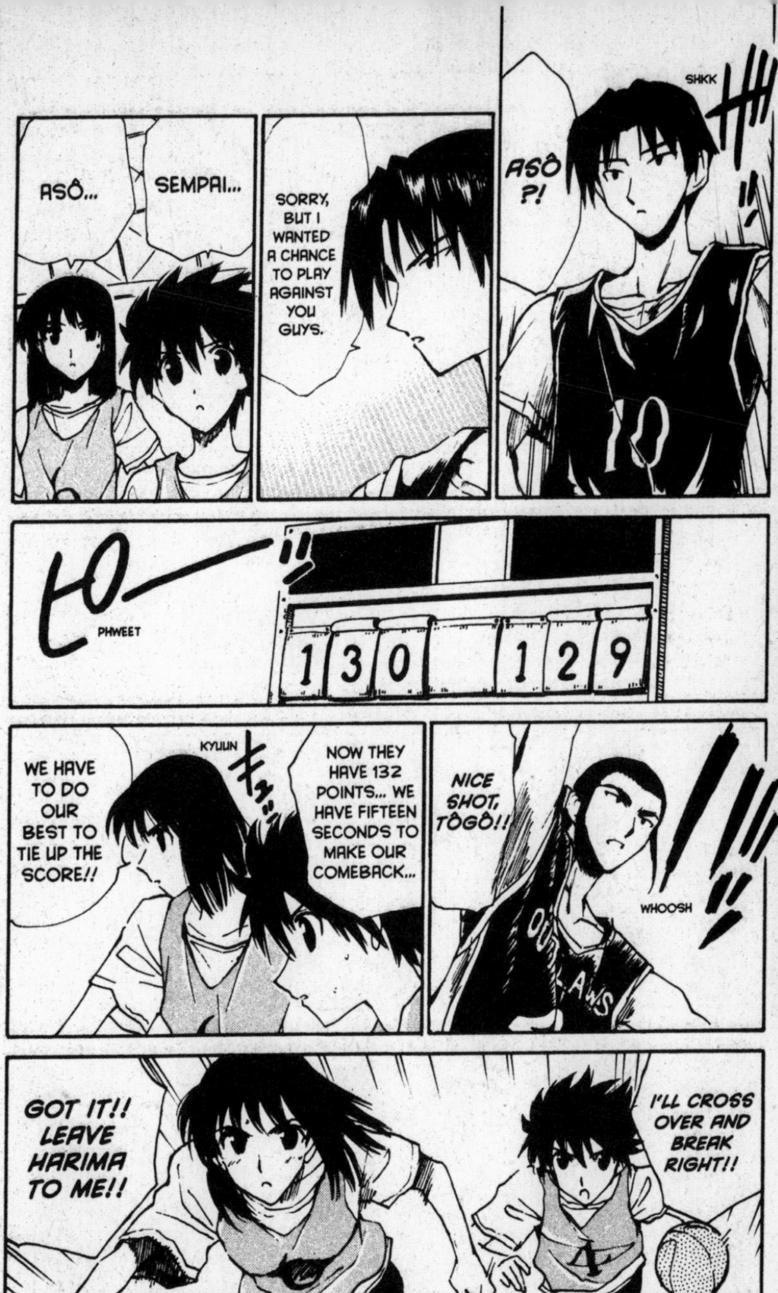
SHKK
ASÔ ?!
SORRY, BUT I WANTED A CHANCE TO PLAY AGAINST YOU GUYS.
SEMPAI...
ASÔ...
130 129
PHWEET
WHOOSH
NICE SHOT, TÔGÔ!!
NOW THEY HAVE 132 POINTS... WE HAVE FIFTEEN SECONDS TO MAKE OUR COMEBACK...
KYUUN
WE HAVE TO DO OUR BEST TO TIE UP THE SCORE!!
I'LL CROSS OVER AND BREAK RIGHT!!
GOT IT!! LEAVE HARIMA TO ME!!

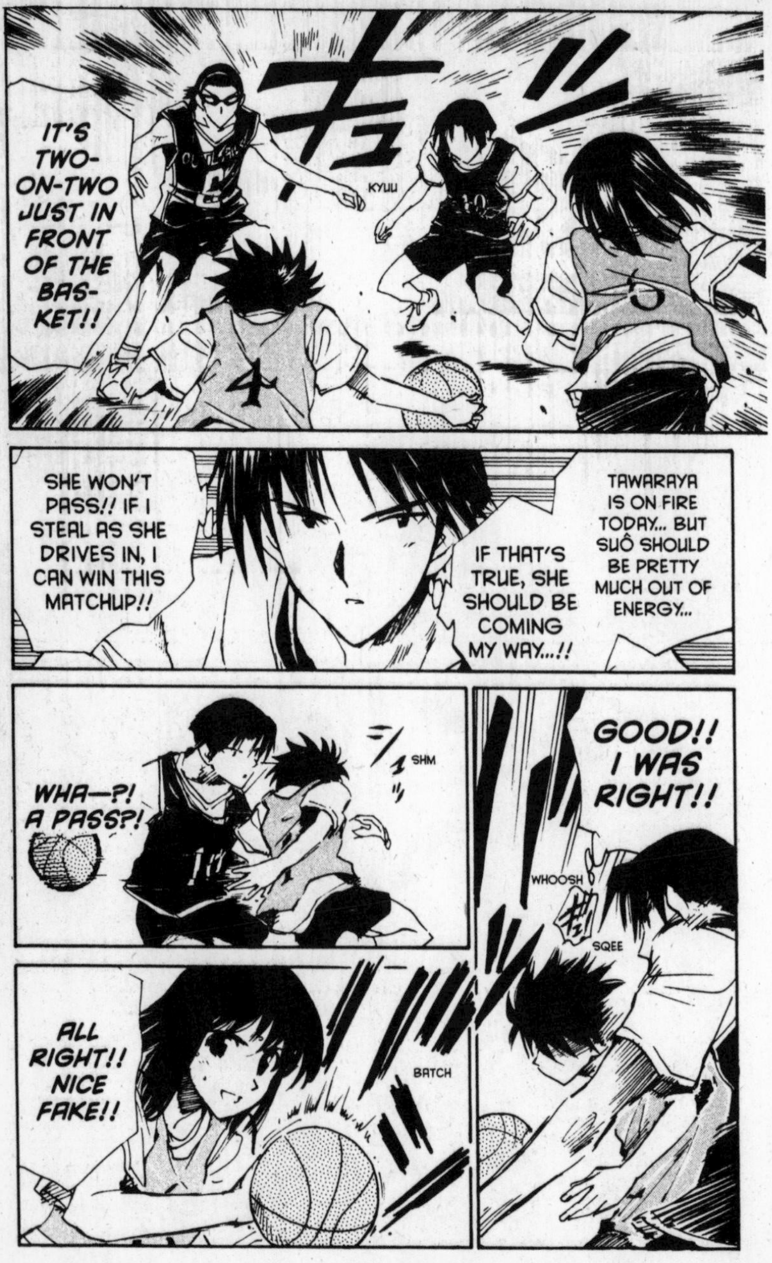
KYUU
IT'S TWO-ON-TWO JUST IN FRONT OF THE BAS-KET!!
TAWARAYA IS ON FIRE TODAY... BUT SUÔ SHOULD BE PRETTY MUCH OUT OF ENERGY...
IF THAT'S TRUE, SHE SHOULD BE COMING MY WAY...!!
SHE WON'T PASS!! IF I STEAL AS SHE DRIVES IN, I CAN WIN THIS MATCHUP!!
GOOD!! I WAS RIGHT!!
WHOOSH
SQEE
SHM
WHA—?! A PASS?!
BATCH
ALL RIGHT!! NICE FAKE!!

Mr. Cool and Mr. Fool: First Teamed in Pool Hockey.

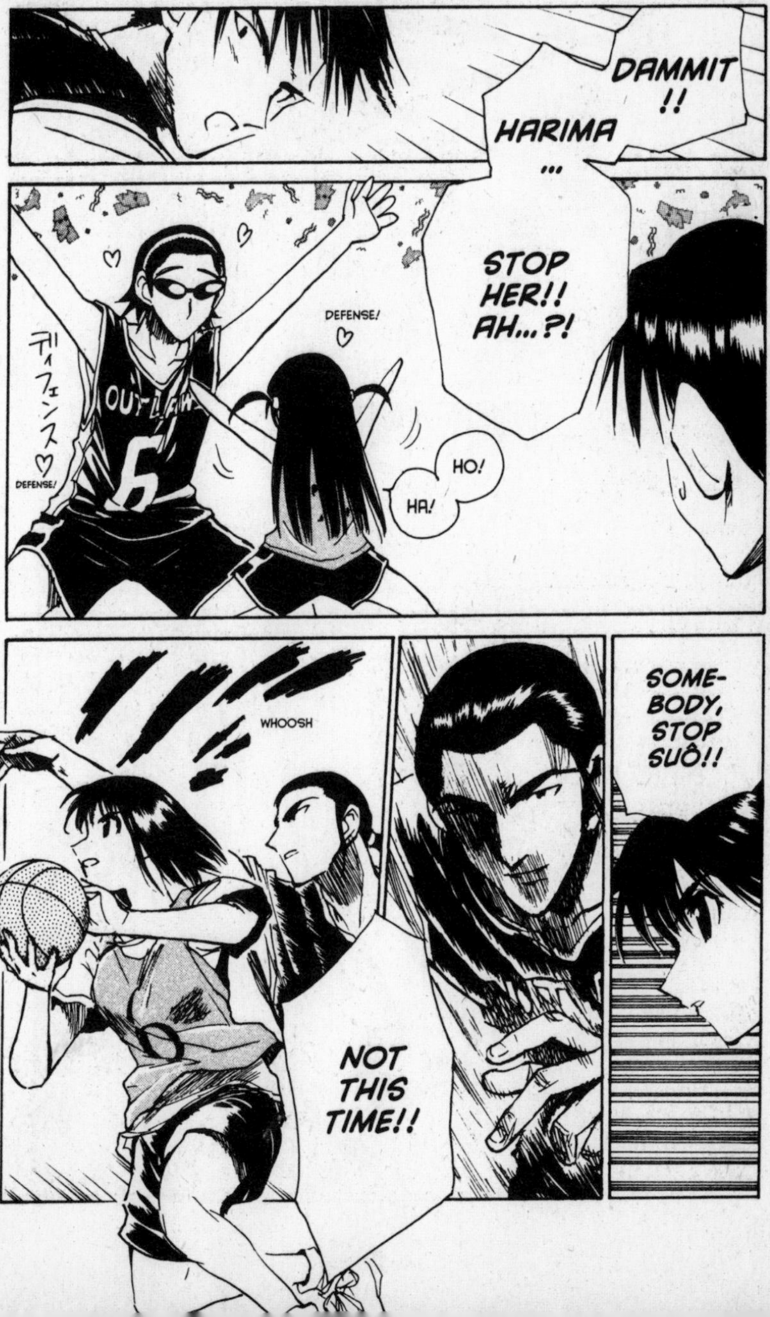
DAMMIT!!
HARIMA... STOP HER!! AH...?!
HO!
HA!
ディフェンス♡
DEFENSE!
DEFENSE!
SOME-BODY, STOP SUÔ!!
WHOOSH
NOT THIS TIME!!

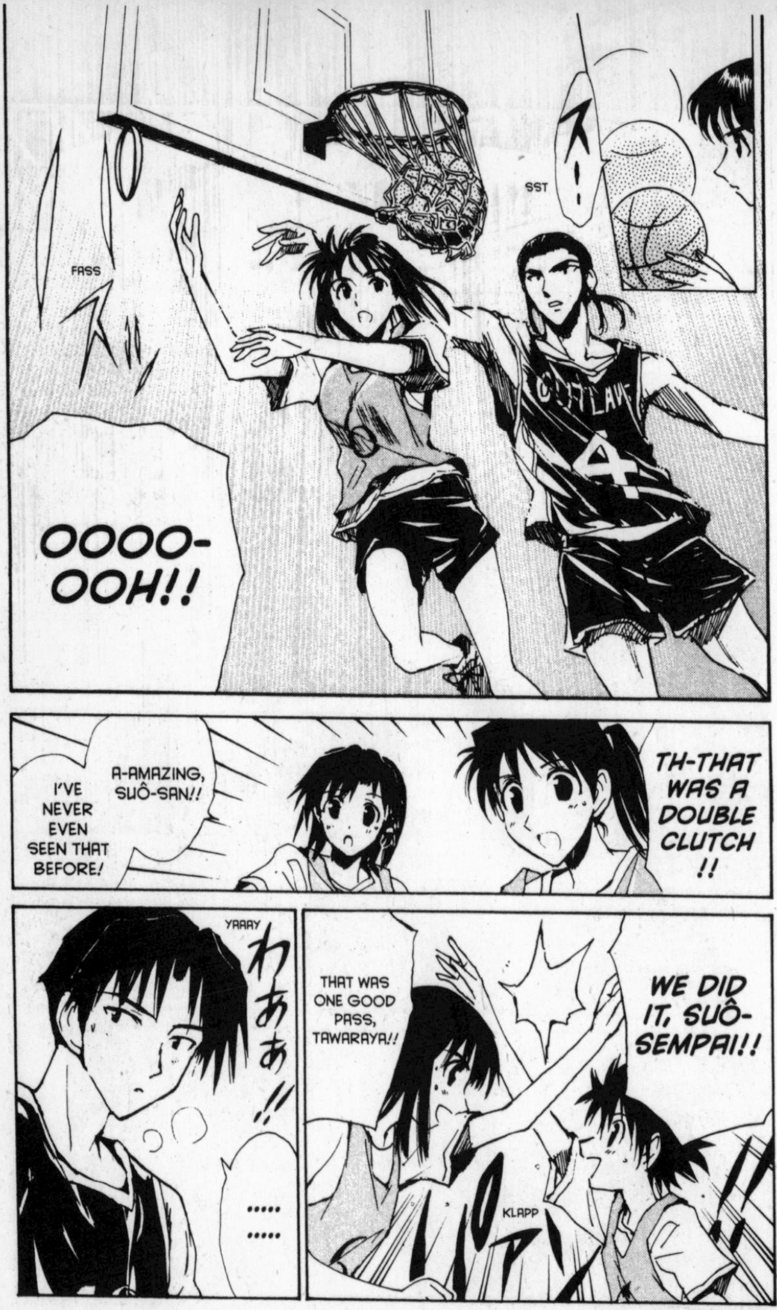

SST
FASS
OOOO-OOH!!
TH-THAT WAS A DOUBLE CLUTCH !!
A-AMAZING, SUÔ-SAN!!
I'VE NEVER EVEN SEEN THAT BEFORE!
WE DID IT, SUÔ-SEMPAI!!
THAT WAS ONE GOOD PASS, TAWARAYA!!
KLAPP
YAAAY
わああ!!
......
......

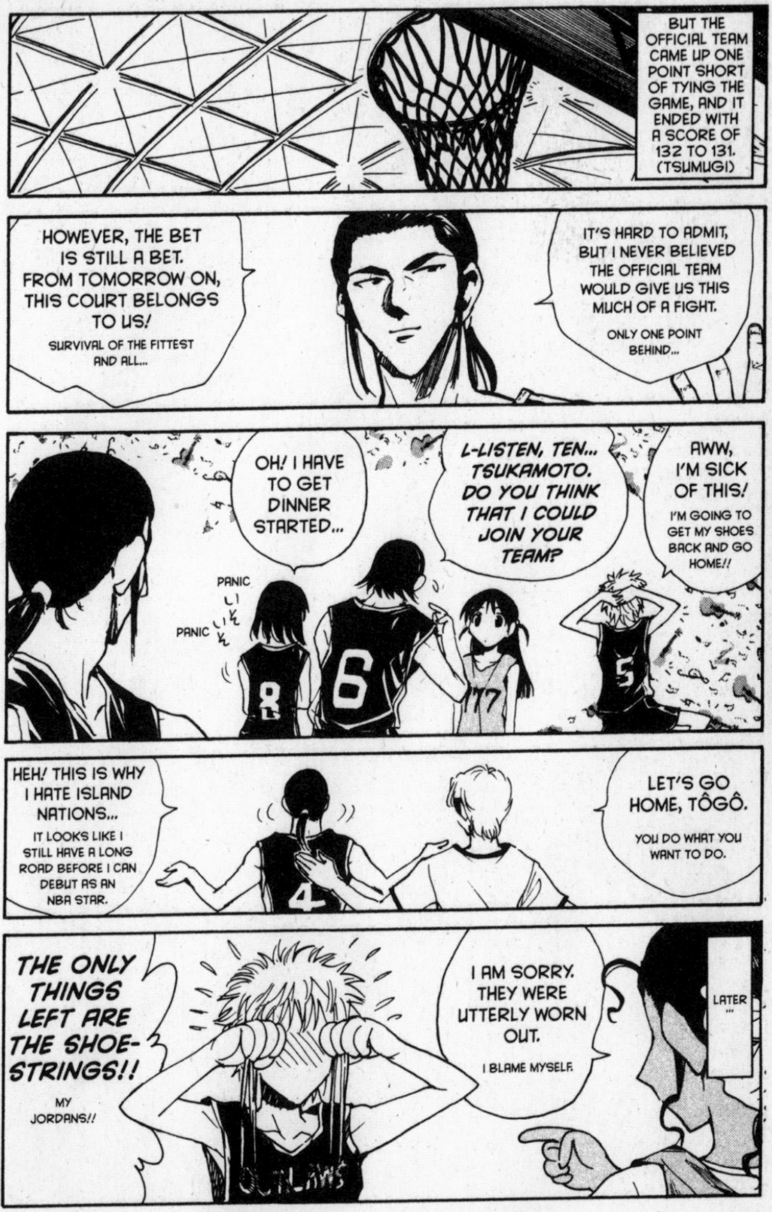
BUT THE OFFICIAL TEAM CAME UP ONE POINT SHORT OF TYING THE GAME, AND IT ENDED WITH A SCORE OF 132 TO 131. (TSUMUGI)
IT'S HARD TO ADMIT, BUT I NEVER BELIEVED THE OFFICIAL TEAM WOULD GIVE US THIS MUCH OF A FIGHT.
ONLY ONE POINT BEHIND...
HOWEVER, THE BET IS STILL A BET. FROM TOMORROW ON, THIS COURT BELONGS TO US!
SURVIVAL OF THE FITTEST AND ALL...
AWW, I'M SICK OF THIS!
I'M GOING TO GET MY SHOES BACK AND GO HOME!!
L-LISTEN, TEN... TSUKAMOTO. DO YOU THINK THAT I COULD JOIN YOUR TEAM?
OH! I HAVE TO GET DINNER STARTED...
PANIC
PANIC
LET'S GO HOME, TÔGÔ.
YOU DO WHAT YOU WANT TO DO.
HEH! THIS IS WHY I HATE ISLAND NATIONS...
IT LOOKS LIKE I STILL HAVE A LONG ROAD BEFORE I CAN DEBUT AS AN NBA STAR.
LATER...
I AM SORRY. THEY WERE UTTERLY WORN OUT.
I BLAME MYSELF.
THE ONLY THINGS LEFT ARE THE SHOE-STRINGS!!
MY JORDANS!!

Imadori: Went Home Barefoot.

 # 131 · · · · · · · · · Fin

Several days after the game…

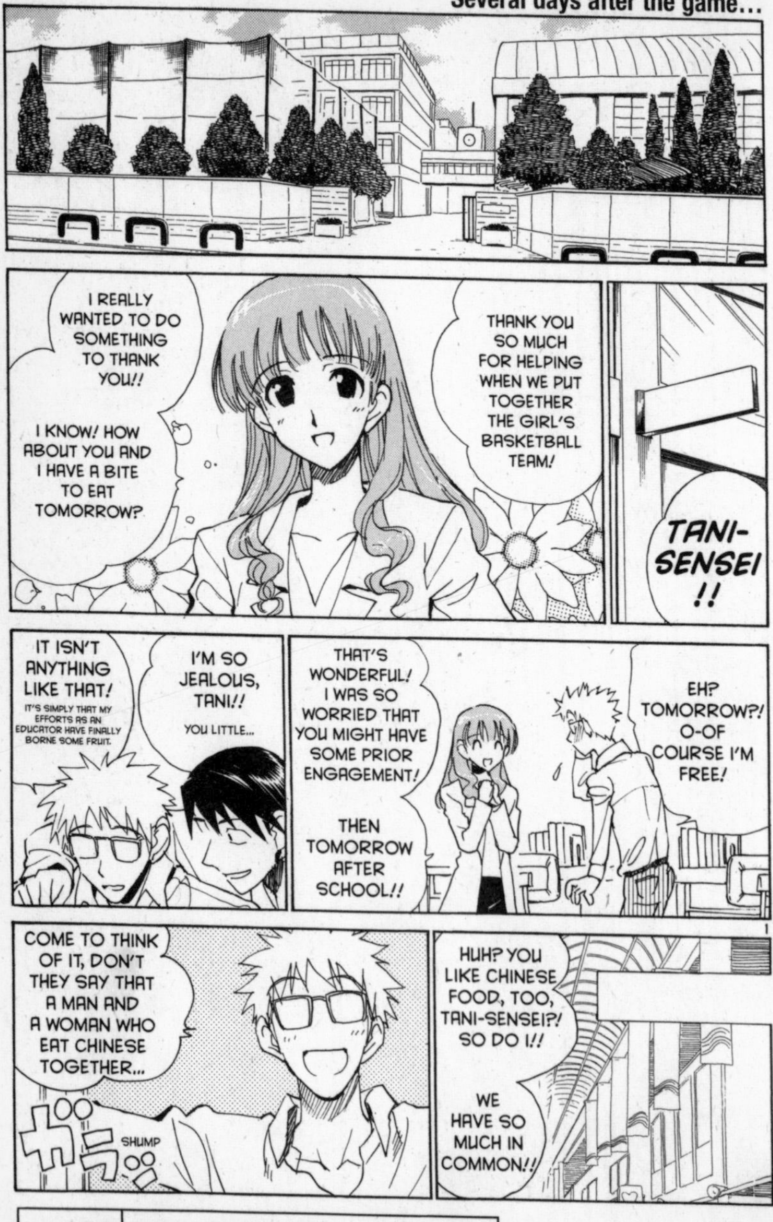

TANI-SENSEI!!
THANK YOU SO MUCH FOR HELPING WHEN WE PUT TOGETHER THE GIRL'S BASKETBALL TEAM!
I REALLY WANTED TO DO SOMETHING TO THANK YOU!!
I KNOW! HOW ABOUT YOU AND I HAVE A BITE TO EAT TOMORROW?
EH? TOMORROW?! O-OF COURSE I'M FREE!
THAT'S WONDERFUL! I WAS SO WORRIED THAT YOU MIGHT HAVE SOME PRIOR ENGAGEMENT!
THEN TOMORROW AFTER SCHOOL!!
I'M SO JEALOUS, TANI!!
YOU LITTLE...
IT ISN'T ANYTHING LIKE THAT!
IT'S SIMPLY THAT MY EFFORTS AS AN EDUCATOR HAVE FINALLY BORNE SOME FRUIT.
HUH? YOU LIKE CHINESE FOOD, TOO, TANI-SENSEI?! SO DO I!!
WE HAVE SO MUCH IN COMMON!!
COME TO THINK OF IT, DON'T THEY SAY THAT A MAN AND A WOMAN WHO EAT CHINESE TOGETHER...
ガラッ
SHUMP

132 THE BROWNING VERSION

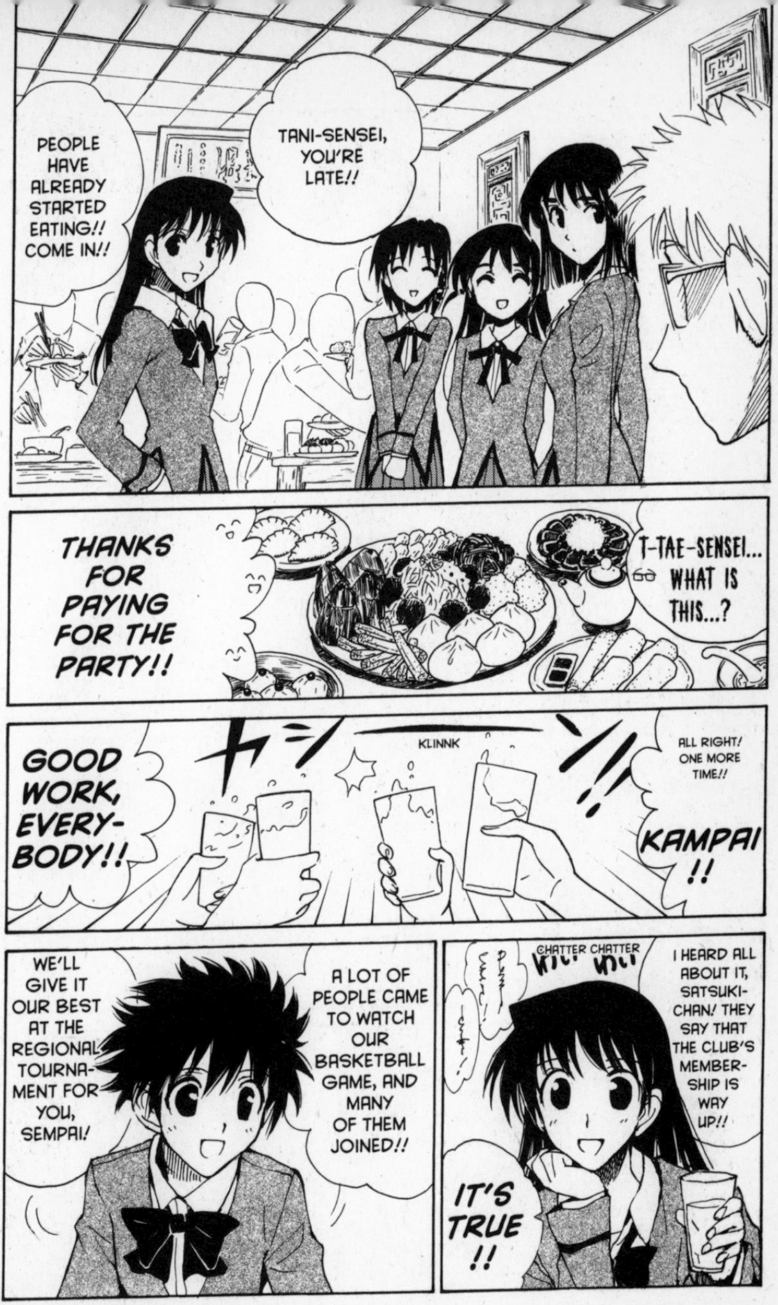

TANI-SENSEI, YOU'RE LATE!!
PEOPLE HAVE ALREADY STARTED EATING!! COME IN!!
T-TAE-SENSEI... WHAT IS THIS...?
THANKS FOR PAYING FOR THE PARTY!!
ALL RIGHT! ONE MORE TIME!!
KAMPAI !!
KLINNK
GOOD WORK, EVERYBODY!!
CHATTER CHATTER
I HEARD ALL ABOUT IT, SATSUKI-CHAN! THEY SAY THAT THE CLUB'S MEMBERSHIP IS WAY UP!!
IT'S TRUE !!
A LOT OF PEOPLE CAME TO WATCH OUR BASKETBALL GAME, AND MANY OF THEM JOINED!!
WE'LL GIVE IT OUR BEST AT THE REGIONAL TOURNAMENT FOR YOU, SEMPAI!

Takano Akira: Before We Knew It, She Was Our Director of Public Affairs. (Yûki)

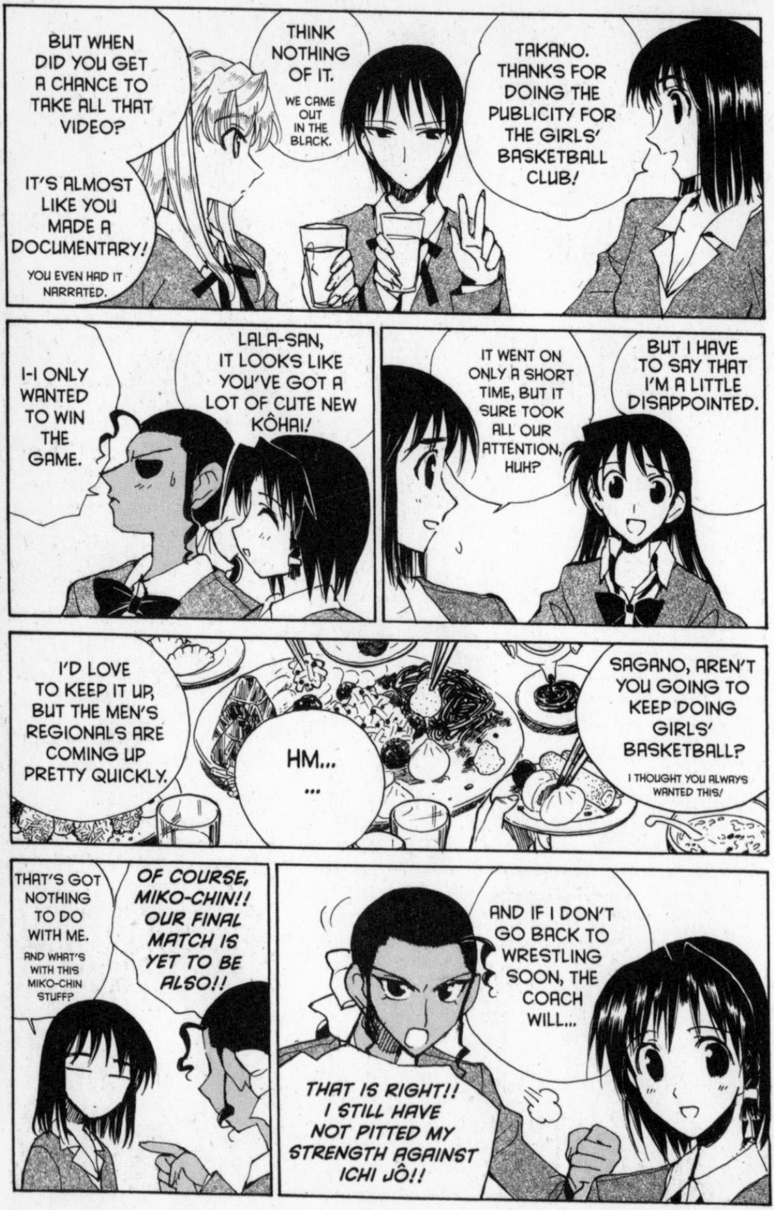
TAKANO. THANKS FOR DOING THE PUBLICITY FOR THE GIRLS' BASKETBALL CLUB!
THINK NOTHING OF IT.
WE CAME OUT IN THE BLACK.
BUT WHEN DID YOU GET A CHANCE TO TAKE ALL THAT VIDEO?
IT'S ALMOST LIKE YOU MADE A DOCUMENTARY!
YOU EVEN HAD IT NARRATED.
BUT I HAVE TO SAY THAT I'M A LITTLE DISAPPOINTED.
IT WENT ON ONLY A SHORT TIME, BUT IT SURE TOOK ALL OUR ATTENTION, HUH?
LALA-SAN, IT LOOKS LIKE YOU'VE GOT A LOT OF CUTE NEW KÔHAI!
I-I ONLY WANTED TO WIN THE GAME.
SAGANO, AREN'T YOU GOING TO KEEP DOING GIRLS' BASKETBALL?
I THOUGHT YOU ALWAYS WANTED THIS!
HM... ...
I'D LOVE TO KEEP IT UP, BUT THE MEN'S REGIONALS ARE COMING UP PRETTY QUICKLY.
AND IF I DON'T GO BACK TO WRESTLING SOON, THE COACH WILL...
THAT IS RIGHT!! I STILL HAVE NOT PITTED MY STRENGTH AGAINST ICHI JÔ!!
OF COURSE, MIKO-CHIN!! OUR FINAL MATCH IS YET TO BE ALSO!!
THAT'S GOT NOTHING TO DO WITH ME.
AND WHAT'S WITH THIS MIKO-CHIN STUFF?

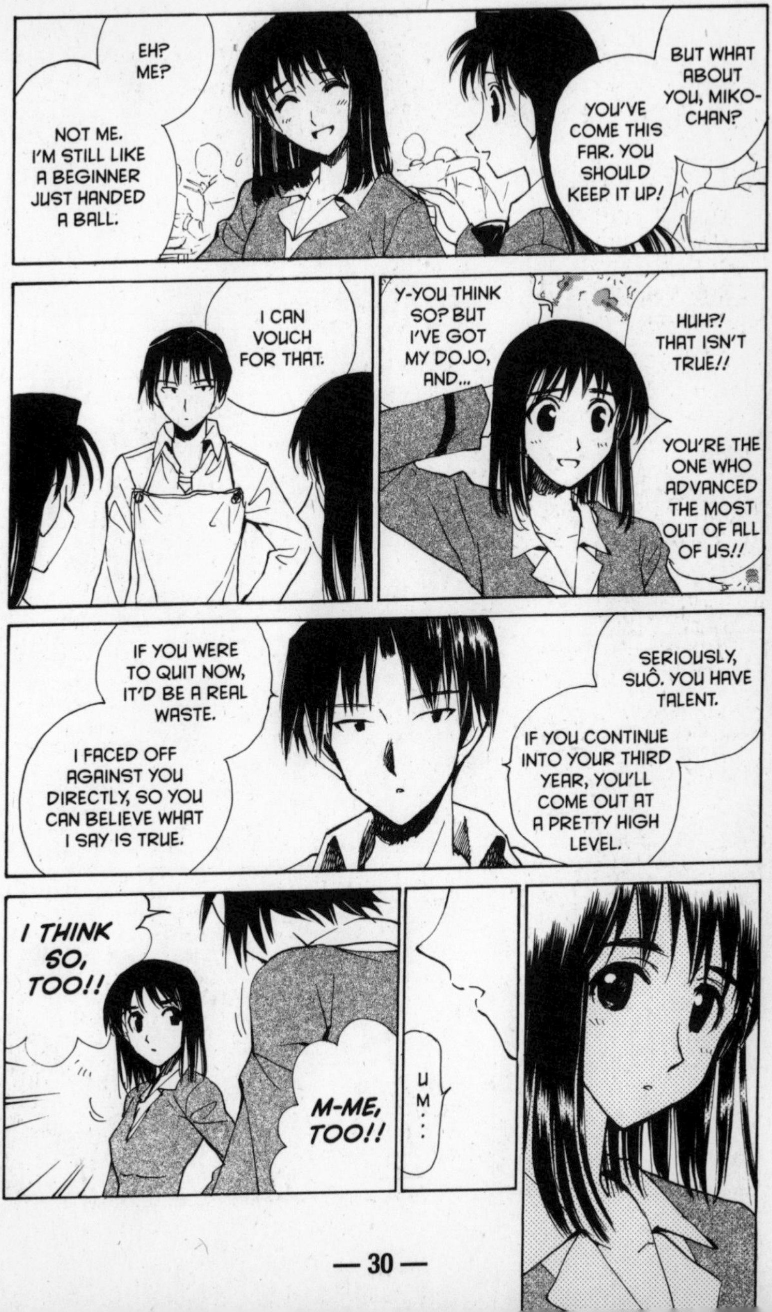
BUT WHAT ABOUT YOU, MIKO-CHAN?
YOU'VE COME THIS FAR. YOU SHOULD KEEP IT UP!
EH? ME?
NOT ME. I'M STILL LIKE A BEGINNER JUST HANDED A BALL.
HUH?! THAT ISN'T TRUE!!
YOU'RE THE ONE WHO ADVANCED THE MOST OUT OF ALL OF US!!
Y-YOU THINK SO? BUT I'VE GOT MY DOJO, AND...
I CAN VOUCH FOR THAT.
SERIOUSLY, SUÔ. YOU HAVE TALENT.
IF YOU CONTINUE INTO YOUR THIRD YEAR, YOU'LL COME OUT AT A PRETTY HIGH LEVEL.
IF YOU WERE TO QUIT NOW, IT'D BE A REAL WASTE.
I FACED OFF AGAINST YOU DIRECTLY, SO YOU CAN BELIEVE WHAT I SAY IS TRUE.
UM...
I THINK SO, TOO!!
M-ME, TOO!!

Asô Hiroyoshi: Presently Working for the Mei Li Restaurant.

She Has Many Friends Who Feel the Same Way, So...

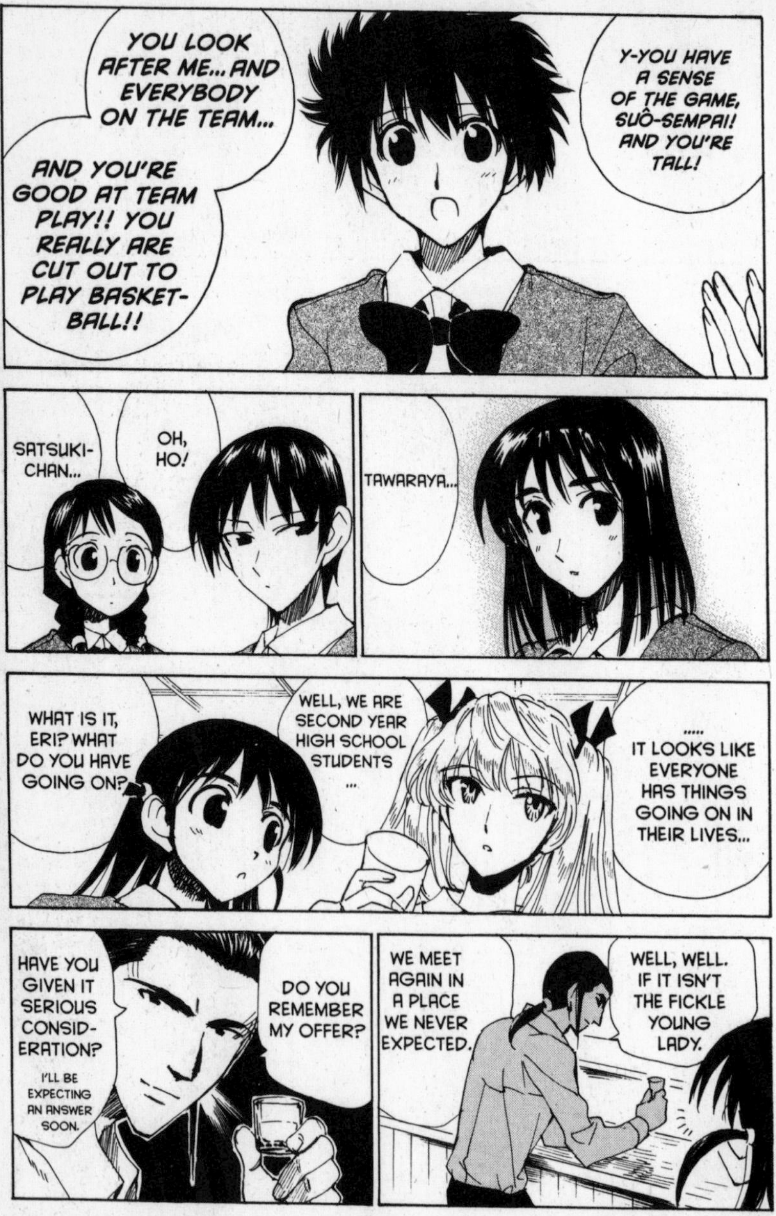
Y-YOU HAVE A SENSE OF THE GAME, SUÔ-SEMPAI! AND YOU'RE TALL!
YOU LOOK AFTER ME... AND EVERYBODY ON THE TEAM...
AND YOU'RE GOOD AT TEAM PLAY!! YOU REALLY ARE CUT OUT TO PLAY BASKET-BALL!!
TAWARAYA...
OH, HO!
SATSUKI-CHAN...
..... IT LOOKS LIKE EVERYONE HAS THINGS GOING ON IN THEIR LIVES...
WELL, WE ARE SECOND YEAR HIGH SCHOOL STUDENTS ...
WHAT IS IT, ERI? WHAT DO YOU HAVE GOING ON?
WELL, WELL. IF IT ISN'T THE FICKLE YOUNG LADY.
WE MEET AGAIN IN A PLACE WE NEVER EXPECTED.
DO YOU REMEMBER MY OFFER?
HAVE YOU GIVEN IT SERIOUS CONSID-ERATION?
I'LL BE EXPECTING AN ANSWER SOON.

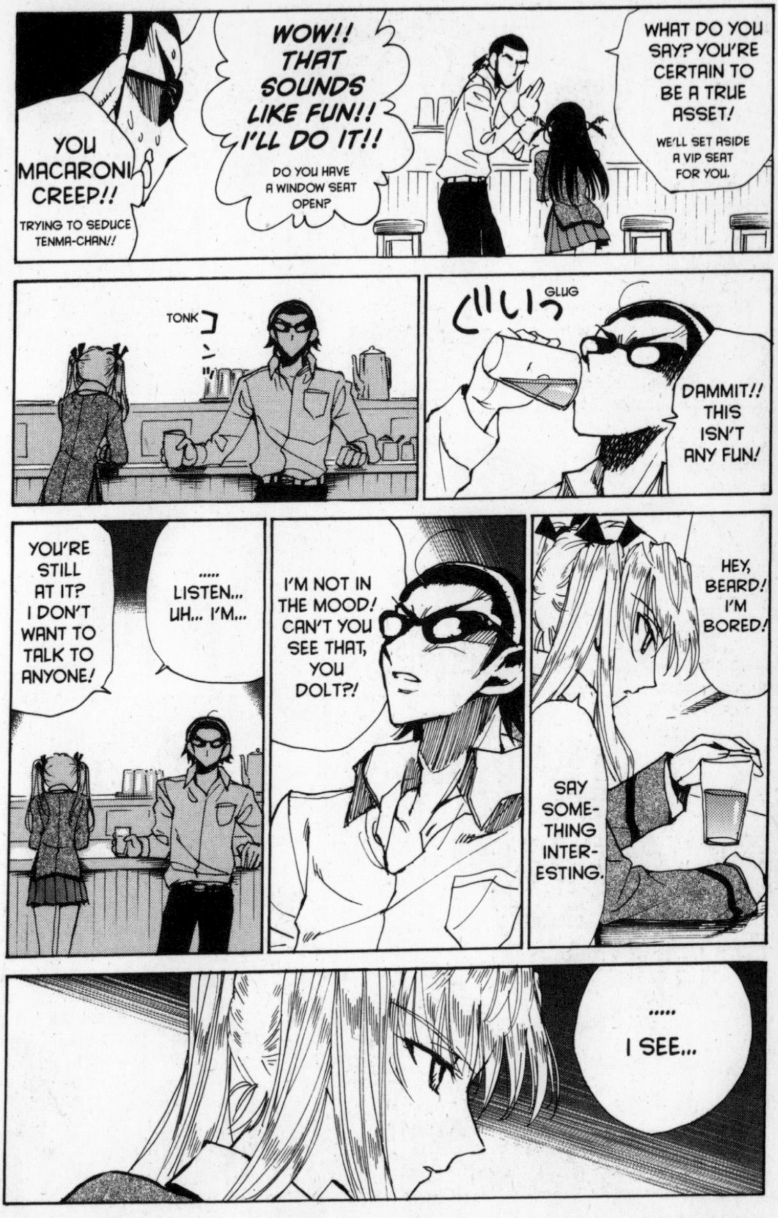
WHAT DO YOU SAY? YOU'RE CERTAIN TO BE A TRUE ASSET!
WE'LL SET ASIDE A VIP SEAT FOR YOU.
WOW!! THAT SOUNDS LIKE FUN!! I'LL DO IT!!
DO YOU HAVE A WINDOW SEAT OPEN?
YOU MACARONI CREEP!!
TRYING TO SEDUCE TENMA-CHAN!!
GLUG
DAMMIT!! THIS ISN'T ANY FUN!
TONK
HEY, BEARD! I'M BORED!
SAY SOME-THING INTER-ESTING.
I'M NOT IN THE MOOD! CAN'T YOU SEE THAT, YOU DOLT?!
..... LISTEN... UH... I'M...
YOU'RE STILL AT IT? I DON'T WANT TO TALK TO ANYONE!
..... I SEE...

Sarah Adiemus: Mei Li Restaurant's Crowd Monitor.

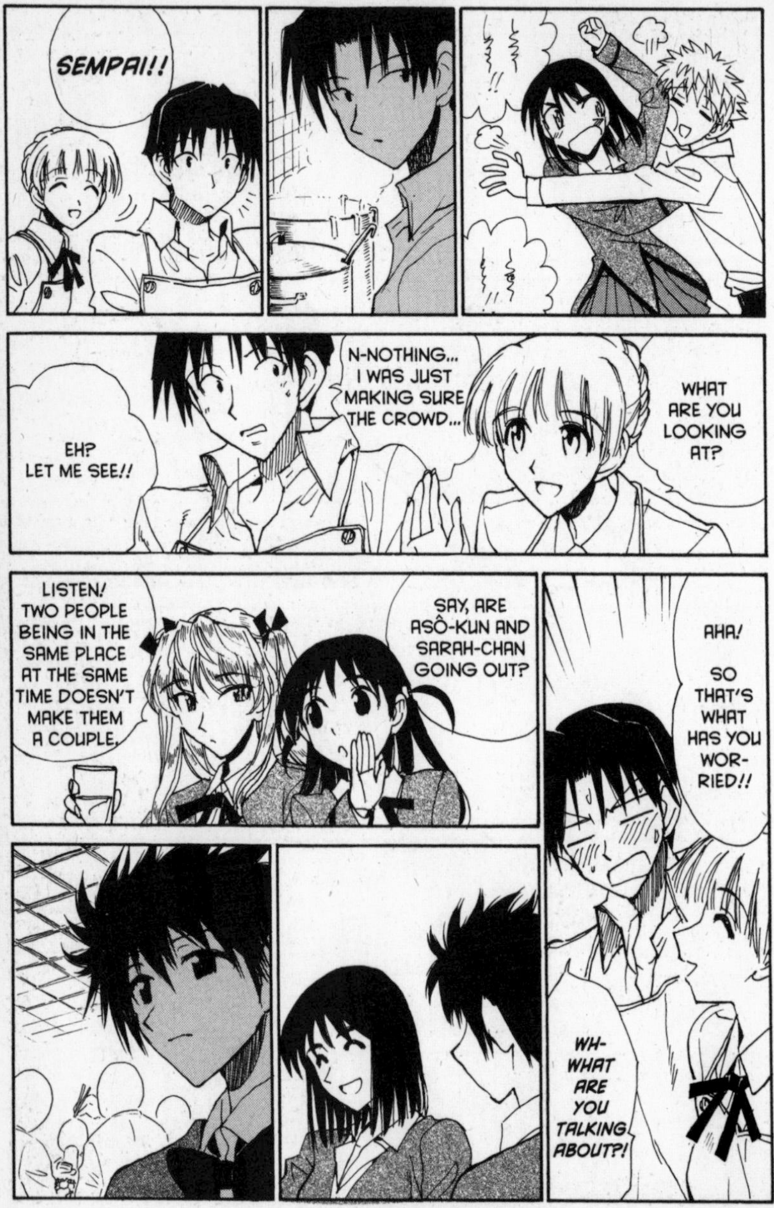
SEMPAI!!
WHAT ARE YOU LOOKING AT?
N-NOTHING... I WAS JUST MAKING SURE THE CROWD...
EH? LET ME SEE!!
AHA!
SO THAT'S WHAT HAS YOU WOR-RIED!!
WH-WHAT ARE YOU TALKING ABOUT?!
SAY, ARE ASÔ-KUN AND SARAH-CHAN GOING OUT?
LISTEN! TWO PEOPLE BEING IN THE SAME PLACE AT THE SAME TIME DOESN'T MAKE THEM A COUPLE.

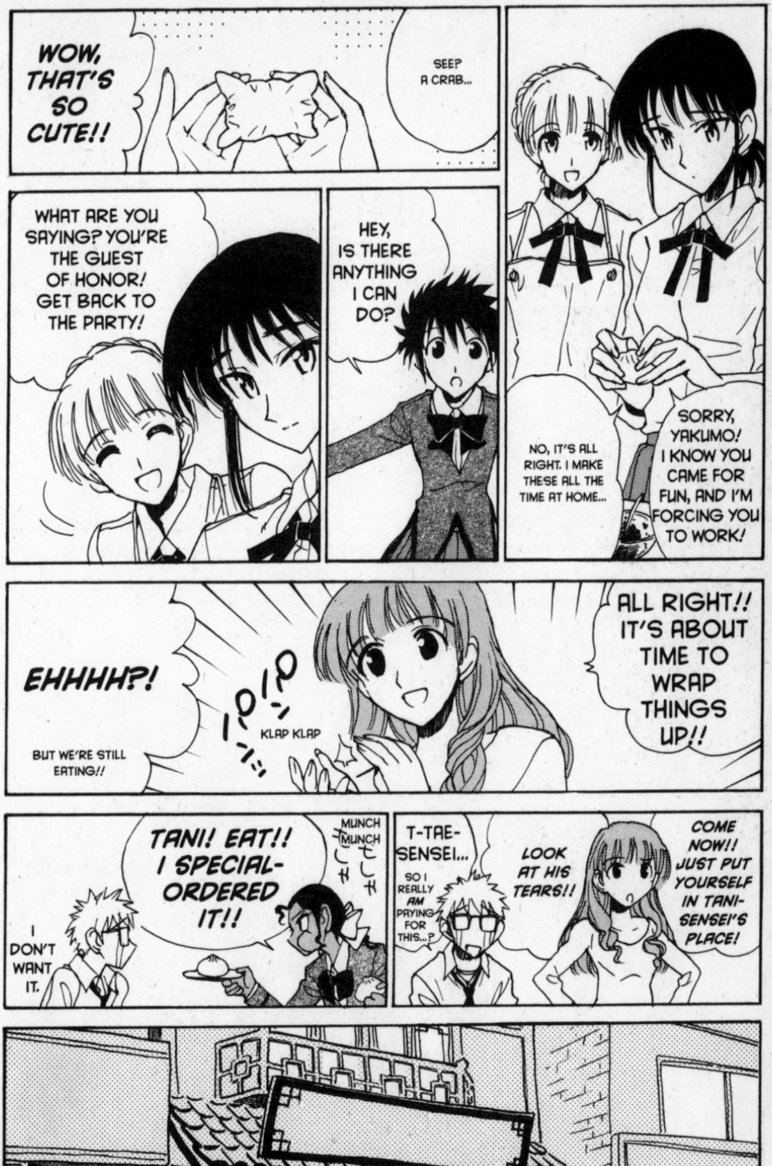
SORRY, YAKUMO! I KNOW YOU CAME FOR FUN, AND I'M FORCING YOU TO WORK!
NO, IT'S ALL RIGHT. I MAKE THESE ALL THE TIME AT HOME...
SEE? A CRAB...
WOW, THAT'S SO CUTE!!
HEY, IS THERE ANYTHING I CAN DO?
WHAT ARE YOU SAYING? YOU'RE THE GUEST OF HONOR! GET BACK TO THE PARTY!
ALL RIGHT!! IT'S ABOUT TIME TO WRAP THINGS UP!!
KLAP KLAP
EHHHH?!
BUT WE'RE STILL EATING!!
COME NOW!! JUST PUT YOURSELF IN TANI-SENSEI'S PLACE!
LOOK AT HIS TEARS!!
T-TAE-SENSEI...
SO I REALLY AM PAYING FOR THIS...?
MUNCH MUNCH
TANI! EAT!! I SPECIAL-ORDERED IT!!
I DON'T WANT IT.

Yakumo, Sara, and Satsuki Are All Classmates in 1-D. Just So You Know.

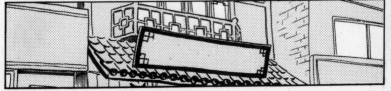

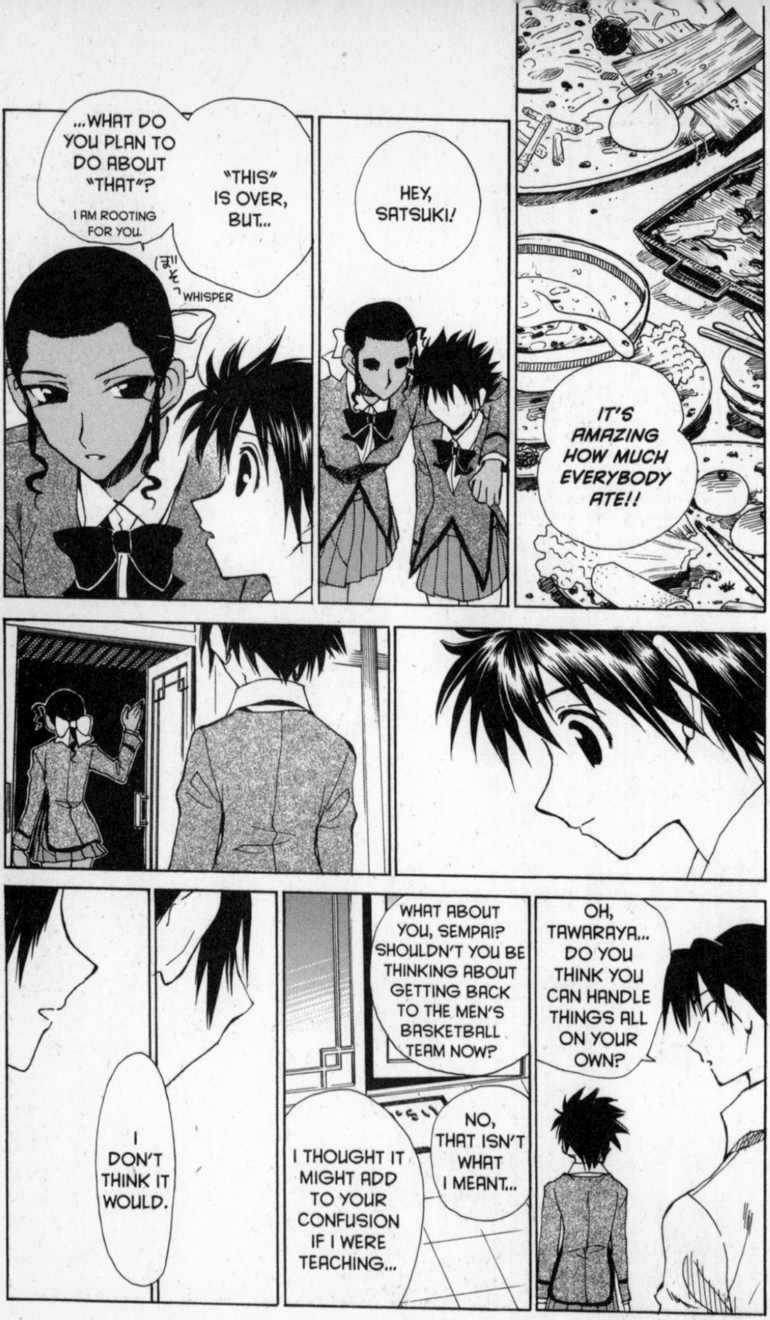
IT'S AMAZING HOW MUCH EVERYBODY ATE!!
HEY, SATSUKI!
"THIS" IS OVER, BUT...
...WHAT DO YOU PLAN TO DO ABOUT "THAT"?
I AM ROOTING FOR YOU.
WHISPER
OH, TAWARAYA... DO YOU THINK YOU CAN HANDLE THINGS ALL ON YOUR OWN?
WHAT ABOUT YOU, SEMPAI? SHOULDN'T YOU BE THINKING ABOUT GETTING BACK TO THE MEN'S BASKETBALL TEAM NOW?
NO, THAT ISN'T WHAT I MEANT...
I THOUGHT IT MIGHT ADD TO YOUR CONFUSION IF I WERE TEACHING...
I DON'T THINK IT WOULD.

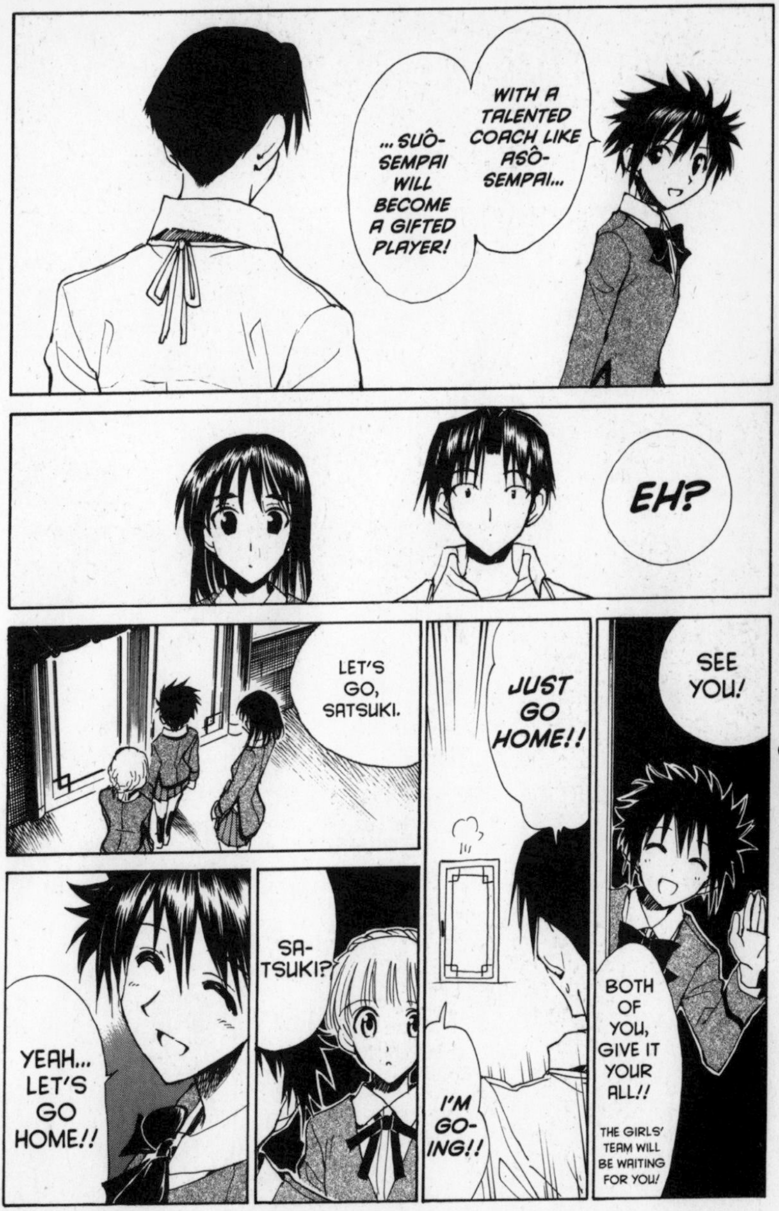
WITH A TALENTED COACH LIKE ASÔ-SEMPAI...
...SUÔ-SEMPAI WILL BECOME A GIFTED PLAYER!
EH?
SEE YOU!
BOTH OF YOU, GIVE IT YOUR ALL!!
THE GIRLS' TEAM WILL BE WAITING FOR YOU!
JUST GO HOME!!
I'M GO-ING!!
LET'S GO, SATSUKI.
SA-TSUKI?
YEAH... LET'S GO HOME!!

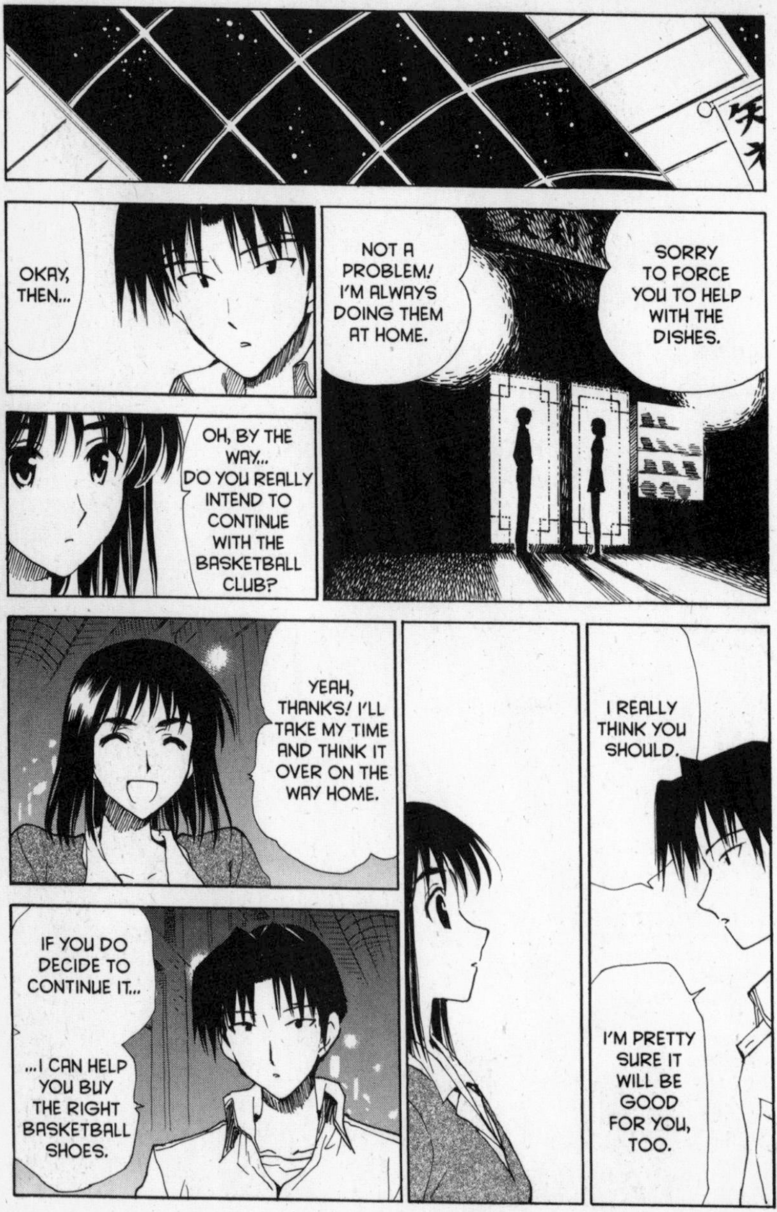
SORRY TO FORCE YOU TO HELP WITH THE DISHES.
NOT A PROBLEM! I'M ALWAYS DOING THEM AT HOME.
OKAY, THEN...
OH, BY THE WAY... DO YOU REALLY INTEND TO CONTINUE WITH THE BASKETBALL CLUB?
I REALLY THINK YOU SHOULD.
I'M PRETTY SURE IT WILL BE GOOD FOR YOU, TOO.
YEAH, THANKS! I'LL TAKE MY TIME AND THINK IT OVER ON THE WAY HOME.
IF YOU DO DECIDE TO CONTINUE IT...
...I CAN HELP YOU BUY THE RIGHT BASKETBALL SHOES.

Give It Your Best, Hanai! In All Its Meanings.

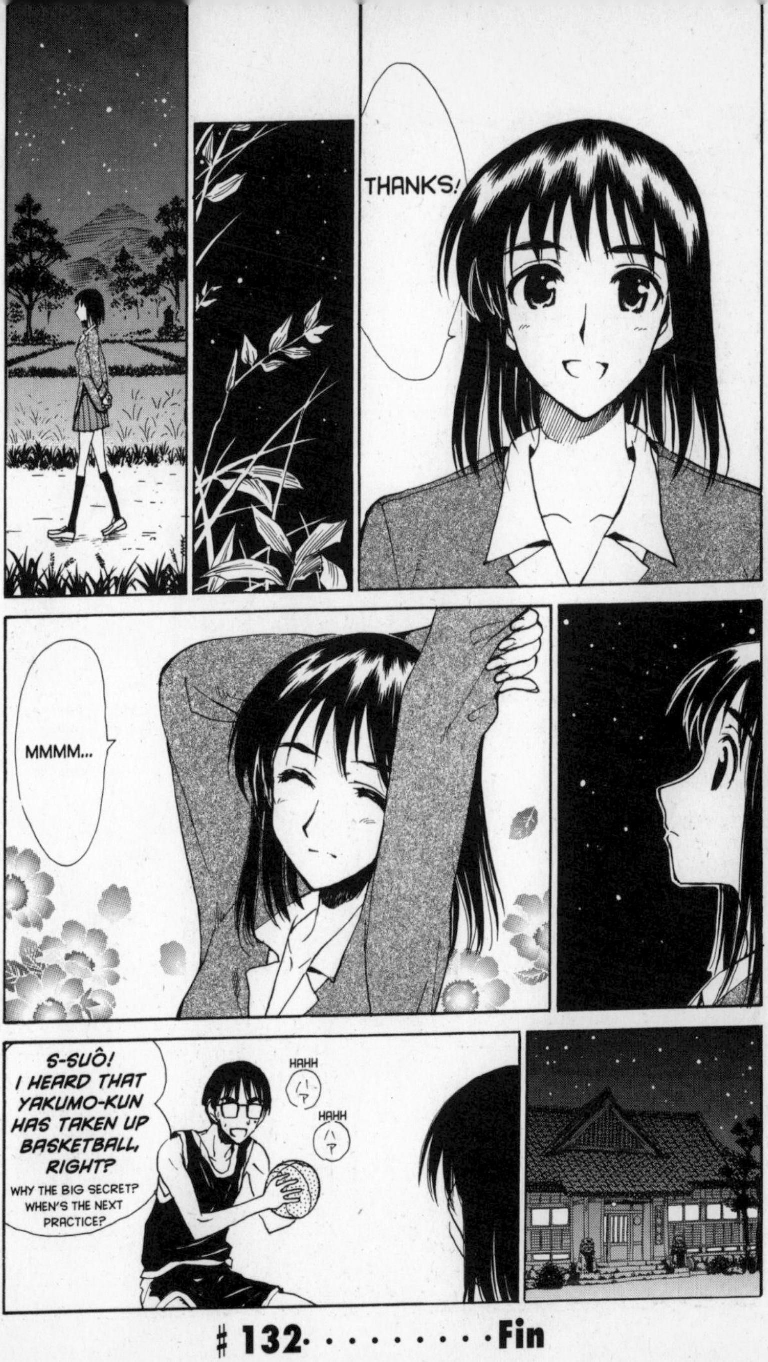
THANKS!
MMMM...
S-SUÔ! I HEARD THAT YAKUMO-KUN HAS TAKEN UP BASKETBALL, RIGHT?
WHY THE BIG SECRET? WHEN'S THE NEXT PRACTICE?
HAHH
HAHH

132· · · · · · · · ·Fin

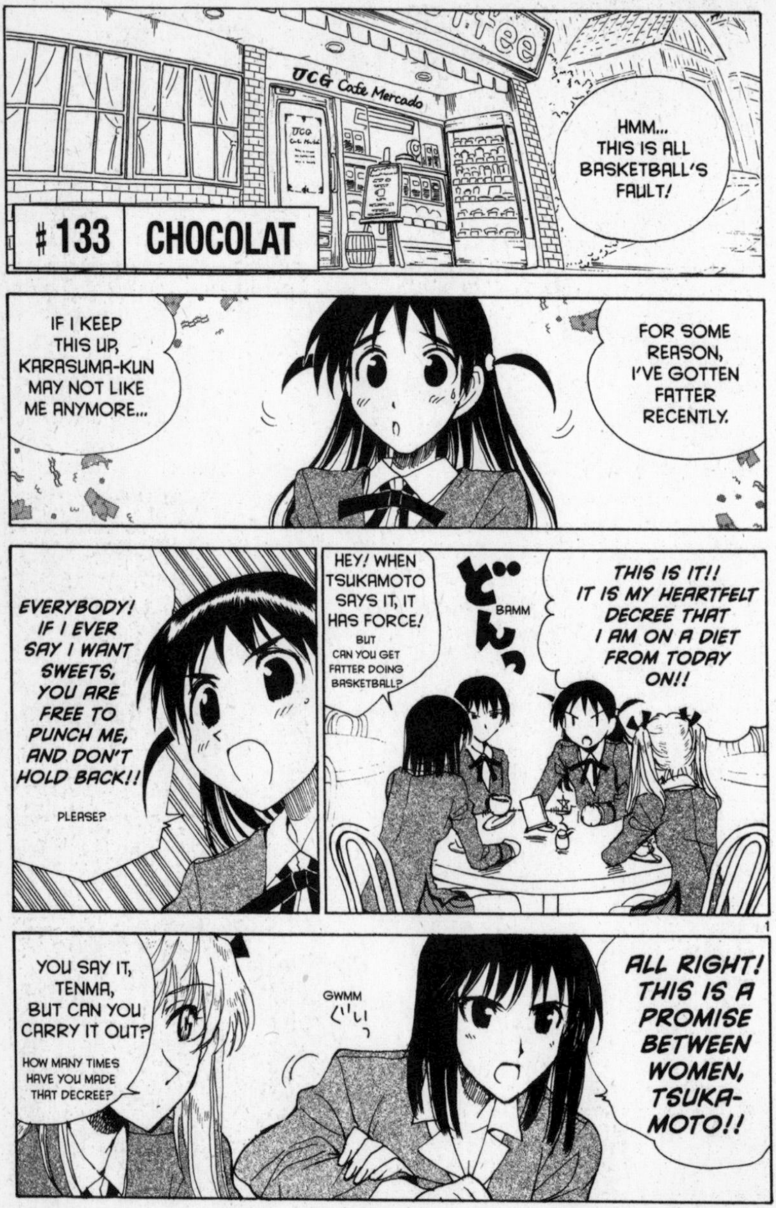

HMM... THIS IS ALL BASKETBALL'S FAULT!
#133 CHOCOLAT
UCG Cafe Mercado
FOR SOME REASON, I'VE GOTTEN FATTER RECENTLY.
IF I KEEP THIS UP, KARASUMA-KUN MAY NOT LIKE ME ANYMORE...
THIS IS IT!! IT IS MY HEARTFELT DECREE THAT I AM ON A DIET FROM TODAY ON!!
どんっ
BAMM
HEY! WHEN TSUKAMOTO SAYS IT, IT HAS FORCE!
BUT CAN YOU GET FATTER DOING BASKETBALL?
EVERYBODY! IF I EVER SAY I WANT SWEETS, YOU ARE FREE TO PUNCH ME, AND DON'T HOLD BACK!!
PLEASE?
ALL RIGHT! THIS IS A PROMISE BETWEEN WOMEN, TSUKAMOTO!!
GWMM
ぐいっ
YOU SAY IT, TENMA, BUT CAN YOU CARRY IT OUT?
HOW MANY TIMES HAVE YOU MADE THAT DECREE?

Tsukamoto Tenma: Your Decree...

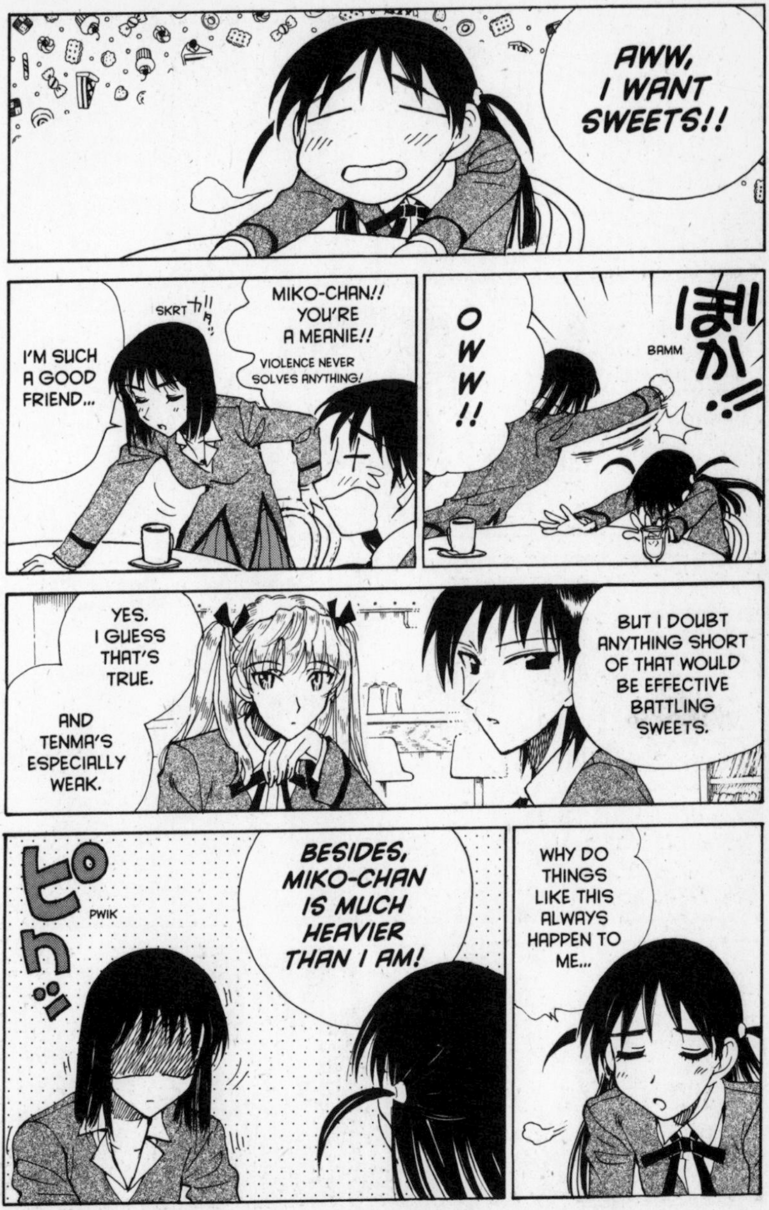

AWW, I WANT SWEETS!!
ぽか!!
BAMM
OWW!!
MIKO-CHAN!! YOU'RE A MEANIE!!
VIOLENCE NEVER SOLVES ANYTHING!
SKRT
I'M SUCH A GOOD FRIEND...
BUT I DOUBT ANYTHING SHORT OF THAT WOULD BE EFFECTIVE BATTLING SWEETS.
YES. I GUESS THAT'S TRUE.
AND TENMA'S ESPECIALLY WEAK.
WHY DO THINGS LIKE THIS ALWAYS HAPPEN TO ME...
BESIDES, MIKO-CHAN IS MUCH HEAVIER THAN I AM!
ピク
PWIK

Suô Mikoto: Armed with Logic.

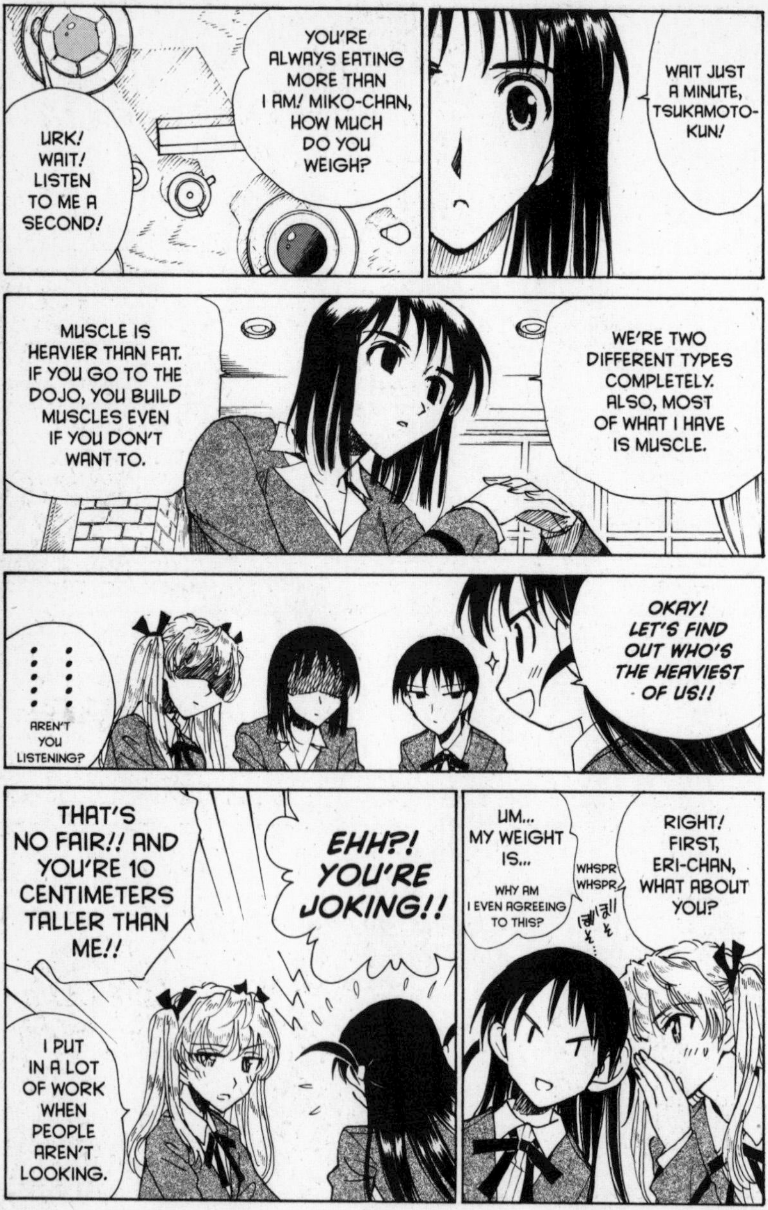
WAIT JUST A MINUTE, TSUKAMOTO-KUN!
YOU'RE ALWAYS EATING MORE THAN I AM! MIKO-CHAN, HOW MUCH DO YOU WEIGH?
URK! WAIT! LISTEN TO ME A SECOND!
WE'RE TWO DIFFERENT TYPES COMPLETELY. ALSO, MOST OF WHAT I HAVE IS MUSCLE.
MUSCLE IS HEAVIER THAN FAT. IF YOU GO TO THE DOJO, YOU BUILD MUSCLES EVEN IF YOU DON'T WANT TO.
OKAY! LET'S FIND OUT WHO'S THE HEAVIEST OF US!!
......
AREN'T YOU LISTENING?
RIGHT! FIRST, ERI-CHAN, WHAT ABOUT YOU?
UM... MY WEIGHT IS...
WHSPR WHSPR
WHY AM I EVEN AGREEING TO THIS?
EHH?! YOU'RE JOKING!!
THAT'S NO FAIR!! AND YOU'RE 10 CENTIMETERS TALLER THAN ME!!
I PUT IN A LOT OF WORK WHEN PEOPLE AREN'T LOOKING.

All Four Are the Age to Worry About Such Things.

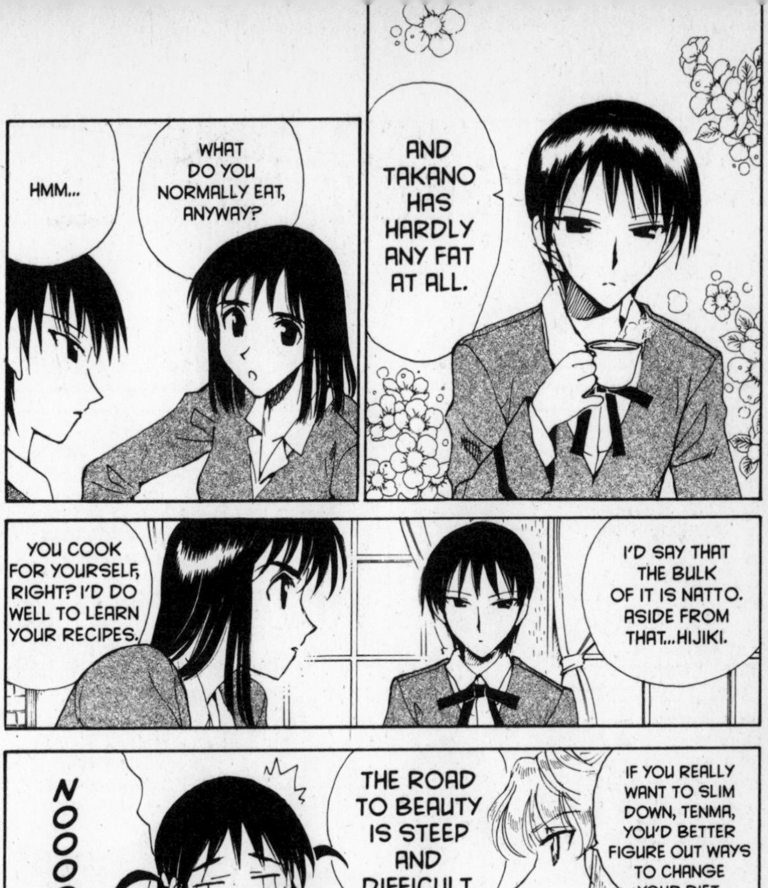
AND TAKANO HAS HARDLY ANY FAT AT ALL.
WHAT DO YOU NORMALLY EAT, ANYWAY?
HMM...
I'D SAY THAT THE BULK OF IT IS NATTO. ASIDE FROM THAT...HIJIKI.
YOU COOK FOR YOURSELF, RIGHT? I'D DO WELL TO LEARN YOUR RECIPES.
IF YOU REALLY WANT TO SLIM DOWN, TENMA, YOU'D BETTER FIGURE OUT WAYS TO CHANGE YOUR DIET.
THE ROAD TO BEAUTY IS STEEP AND DIFFICULT.
NOOOOO!!
YOU CAN'T KEEP FROM EATING, BUT YOU REALLY HAVE TO CALCULATE YOUR CALORIES.
YOU ALSO HAVE TO BALANCE YOUR DIET WITH NATURAL FOODS LIKE AKIRA EATS.
ALSO, YOU HAVE TO TAKE YOUR BODY TYPE INTO CONSIDERATION.
ONE SCIENTIFIC STUDY CLAIMS THAT IF BOTH PARENTS ARE OVERWEIGHT, THE CHILD STANDS AN 80% CHANCE OF BECOMING OBESE.
HMMM

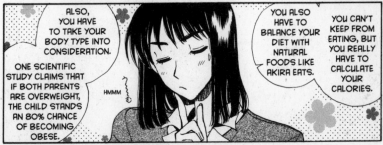

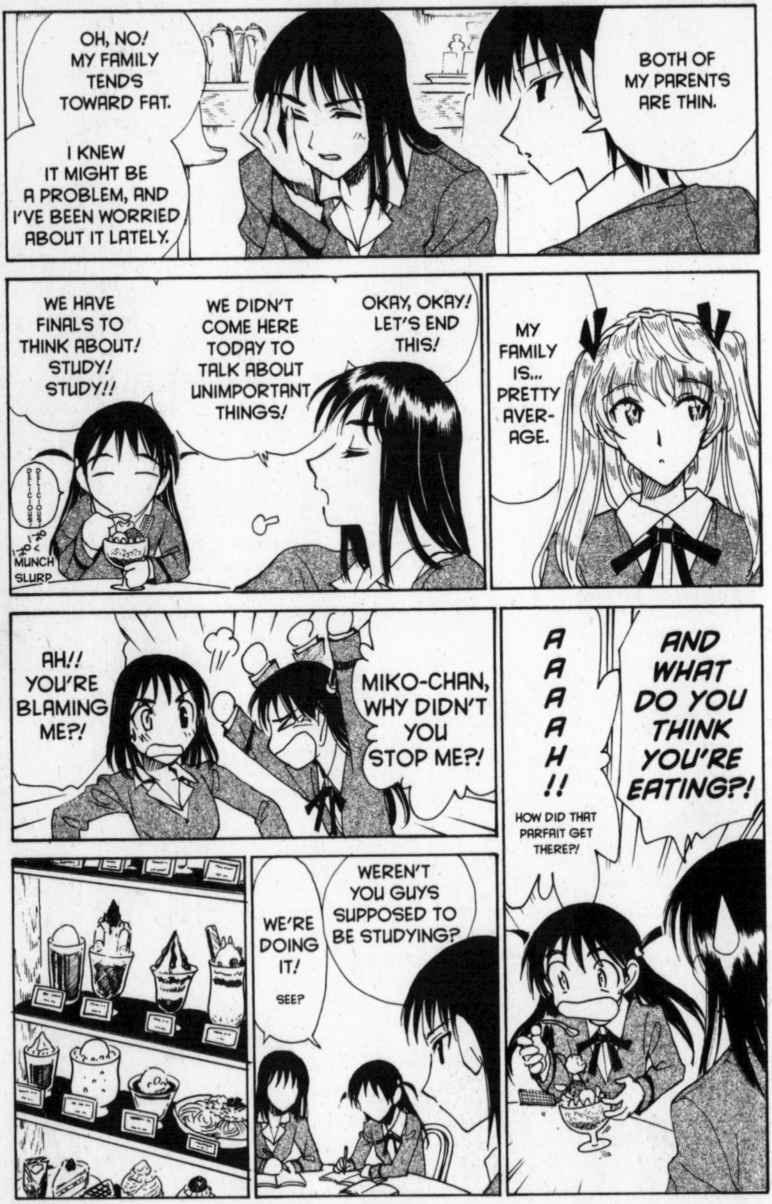
BOTH OF MY PARENTS ARE THIN.
OH, NO! MY FAMILY TENDS TOWARD FAT.
I KNEW IT MIGHT BE A PROBLEM, AND I'VE BEEN WORRIED ABOUT IT LATELY.
MY FAMILY IS... PRETTY AVERAGE.
OKAY, OKAY! LET'S END THIS!
WE DIDN'T COME HERE TODAY TO TALK ABOUT UNIMPORTANT THINGS!
WE HAVE FINALS TO THINK ABOUT! STUDY! STUDY!!
DELICIOUS! DELICIOUS!
MUNCH
SLURP
AND WHAT DO YOU THINK YOU'RE EATING?!
AAAAAH!!
HOW DID THAT PARFAIT GET THERE?!
MIKO-CHAN, WHY DIDN'T YOU STOP ME?!
AH!! YOU'RE BLAMING ME?!
WEREN'T YOU GUYS SUPPOSED TO BE STUDYING?
WE'RE DOING IT!
SEE?

Tsukamoto Tenma: Brimming Over with Ignorance.

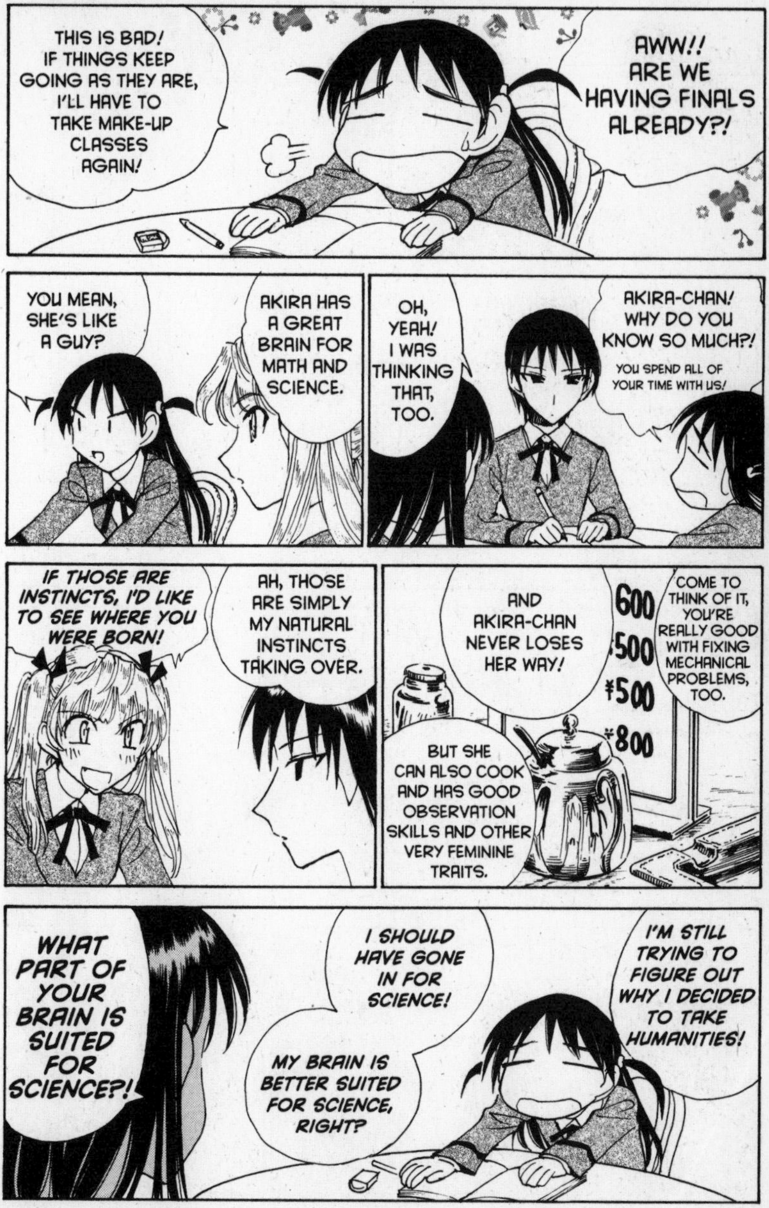
AWW!! ARE WE HAVING FINALS ALREADY?!
THIS IS BAD! IF THINGS KEEP GOING AS THEY ARE, I'LL HAVE TO TAKE MAKE-UP CLASSES AGAIN!
AKIRA-CHAN! WHY DO YOU KNOW SO MUCH?!
YOU SPEND ALL OF YOUR TIME WITH US!
OH, YEAH! I WAS THINKING THAT, TOO.
AKIRA HAS A GREAT BRAIN FOR MATH AND SCIENCE.
YOU MEAN, SHE'S LIKE A GUY?
COME TO THINK OF IT, YOU'RE REALLY GOOD WITH FIXING MECHANICAL PROBLEMS, TOO.
600
500
¥500
¥800
AND AKIRA-CHAN NEVER LOSES HER WAY!
BUT SHE CAN ALSO COOK AND HAS GOOD OBSERVATION SKILLS AND OTHER VERY FEMININE TRAITS.
AH, THOSE ARE SIMPLY MY NATURAL INSTINCTS TAKING OVER.
IF THOSE ARE INSTINCTS, I'D LIKE TO SEE WHERE YOU WERE BORN!
I'M STILL TRYING TO FIGURE OUT WHY I DECIDED TO TAKE HUMANITIES!
I SHOULD HAVE GONE IN FOR SCIENCE!
MY BRAIN IS BETTER SUITED FOR SCIENCE, RIGHT?
WHAT PART OF YOUR BRAIN IS SUITED FOR SCIENCE?!

Tsukamoto Tenma: A Brain for Cake.

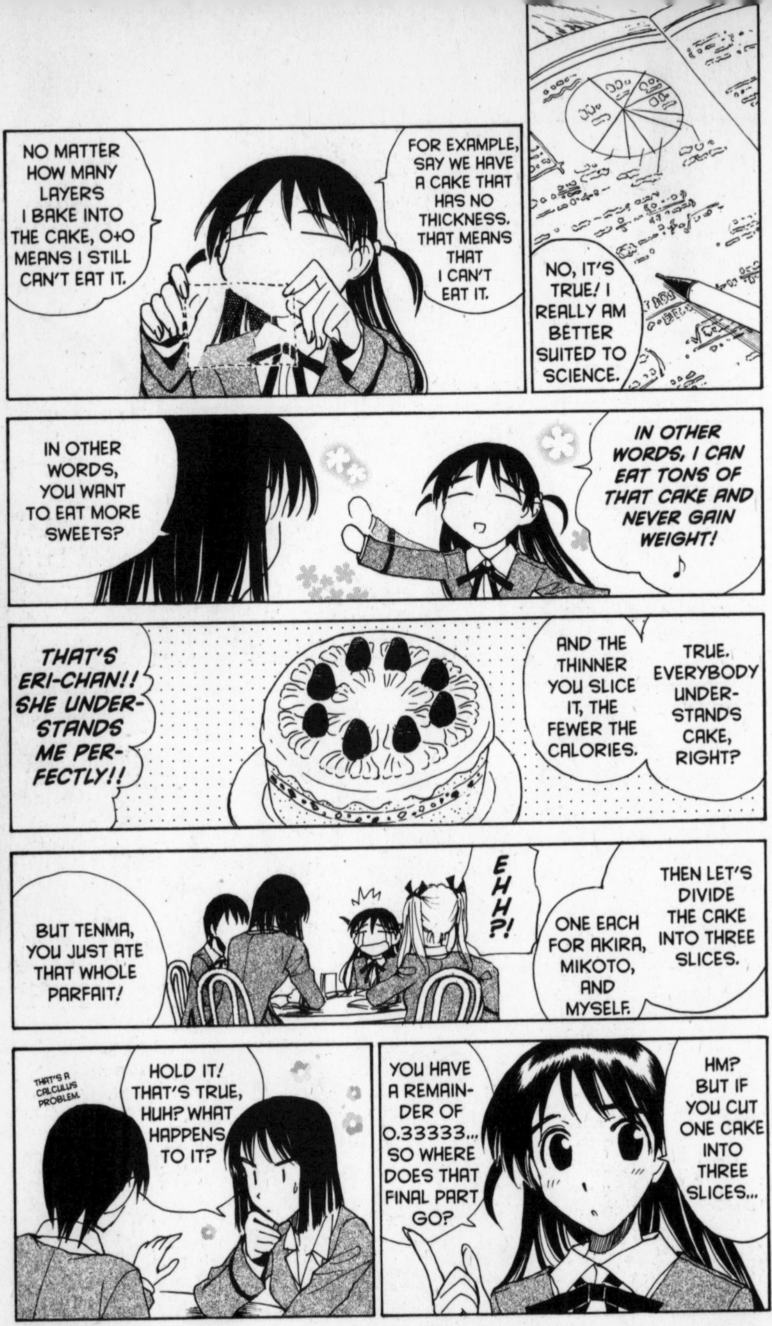
NO, IT'S TRUE! I REALLY AM BETTER SUITED TO SCIENCE.
FOR EXAMPLE, SAY WE HAVE A CAKE THAT HAS NO THICKNESS. THAT MEANS THAT I CAN'T EAT IT.
NO MATTER HOW MANY LAYERS I BAKE INTO THE CAKE, 0+0 MEANS I STILL CAN'T EAT IT.
IN OTHER WORDS, I CAN EAT TONS OF THAT CAKE AND NEVER GAIN WEIGHT! ♪
IN OTHER WORDS, YOU WANT TO EAT MORE SWEETS?
TRUE. EVERYBODY UNDER-STANDS CAKE, RIGHT?
AND THE THINNER YOU SLICE IT, THE FEWER THE CALORIES.
THAT'S ERI-CHAN!! SHE UNDER-STANDS ME PER-FECTLY!!
THEN LET'S DIVIDE THE CAKE INTO THREE SLICES.
ONE EACH FOR AKIRA, MIKOTO, AND MYSELF.
EHH?!
BUT TENMA, YOU JUST ATE THAT WHOLE PARFAIT!
HM? BUT IF YOU CUT ONE CAKE INTO THREE SLICES...
YOU HAVE A REMAIN-DER OF 0.33333... SO WHERE DOES THAT FINAL PART GO?
HOLD IT! THAT'S TRUE, HUH? WHAT HAPPENS TO IT?
THAT'S A CALCULUS PROBLEM.

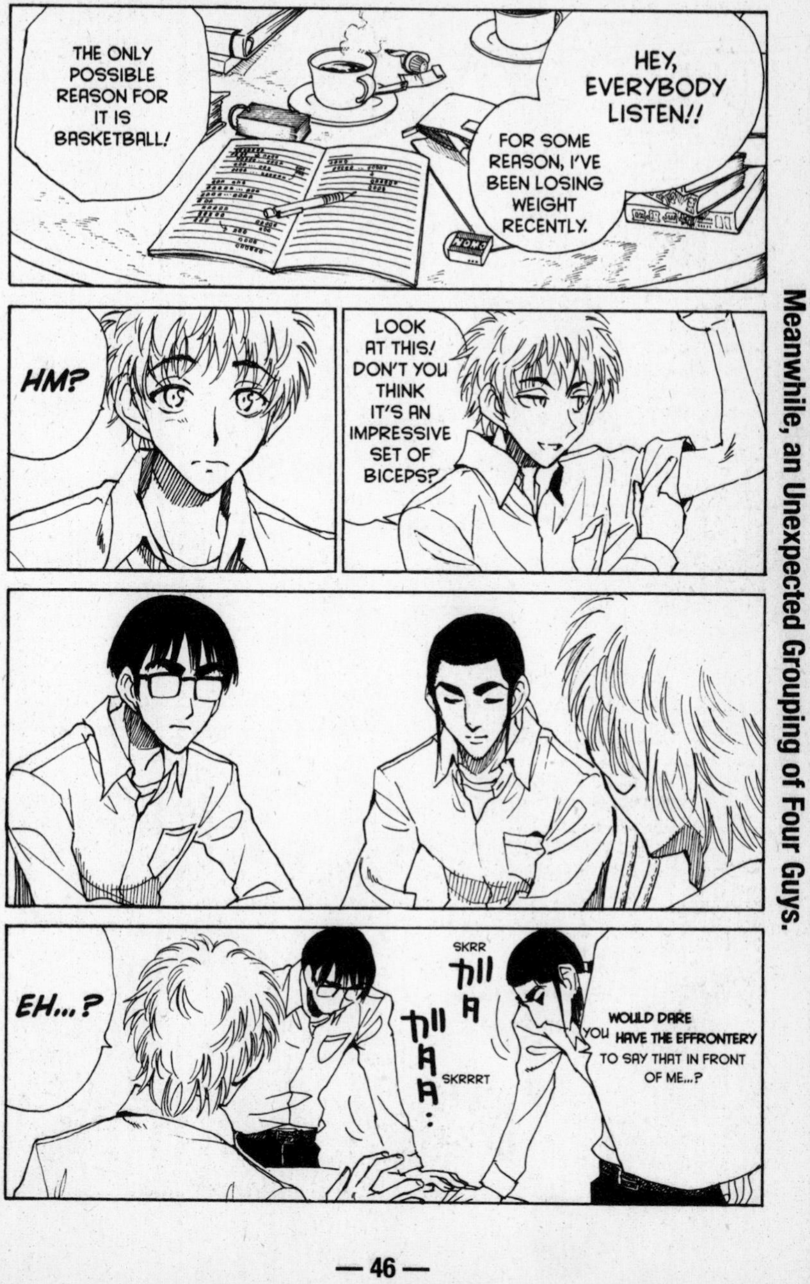
HEY, EVERYBODY LISTEN!!
FOR SOME REASON, I'VE BEEN LOSING WEIGHT RECENTLY.
THE ONLY POSSIBLE REASON FOR IT IS BASKETBALL!
LOOK AT THIS! DON'T YOU THINK IT'S AN IMPRESSIVE SET OF BICEPS?
HM?
YOU WOULD DARE HAVE THE EFFRONTERY TO SAY THAT IN FRONT OF ME...?
SKRR
SKRRRT
EH...?

Meanwhile, an Unexpected Grouping of Four Guys.

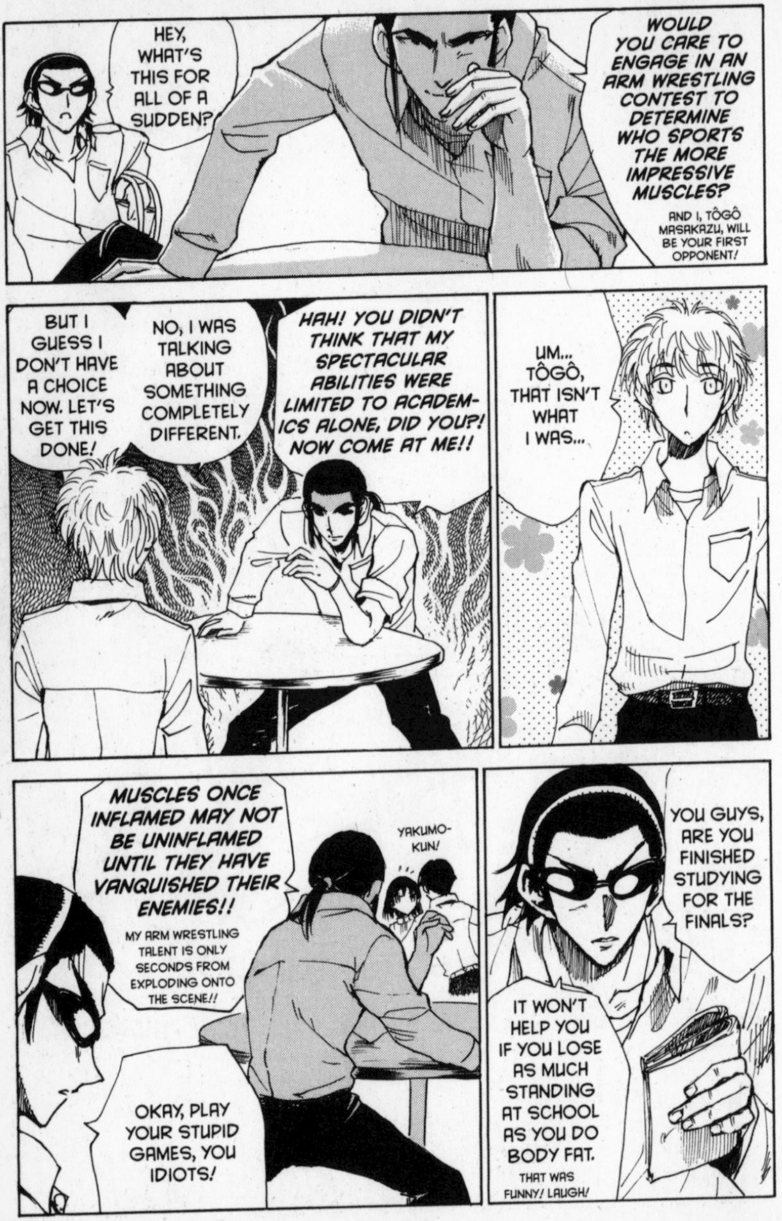
WOULD YOU CARE TO ENGAGE IN AN ARM WRESTLING CONTEST TO DETERMINE WHO SPORTS THE MORE IMPRESSIVE MUSCLES?
AND I, TÔGÔ MASAKAZU, WILL BE YOUR FIRST OPPONENT!
HEY, WHAT'S THIS FOR ALL OF A SUDDEN?
UM... TÔGÔ, THAT ISN'T WHAT I WAS...
HAH! YOU DIDN'T THINK THAT MY SPECTACULAR ABILITIES WERE LIMITED TO ACADEM-ICS ALONE, DID YOU?! NOW COME AT ME!!
NO, I WAS TALKING ABOUT SOMETHING COMPLETELY DIFFERENT.
BUT I GUESS I DON'T HAVE A CHOICE NOW. LET'S GET THIS DONE!
YOU GUYS, ARE YOU FINISHED STUDYING FOR THE FINALS?
IT WON'T HELP YOU IF YOU LOSE AS MUCH STANDING AT SCHOOL AS YOU DO BODY FAT.
THAT WAS FUNNY! LAUGH!
MUSCLES ONCE INFLAMED MAY NOT BE UNINFLAMED UNTIL THEY HAVE VANQUISHED THEIR ENEMIES!!
MY ARM WRESTLING TALENT IS ONLY SECONDS FROM EXPLODING ONTO THE SCENE!!
YAKUMO-KUN!
OKAY, PLAY YOUR STUPID GAMES, YOU IDIOTS!

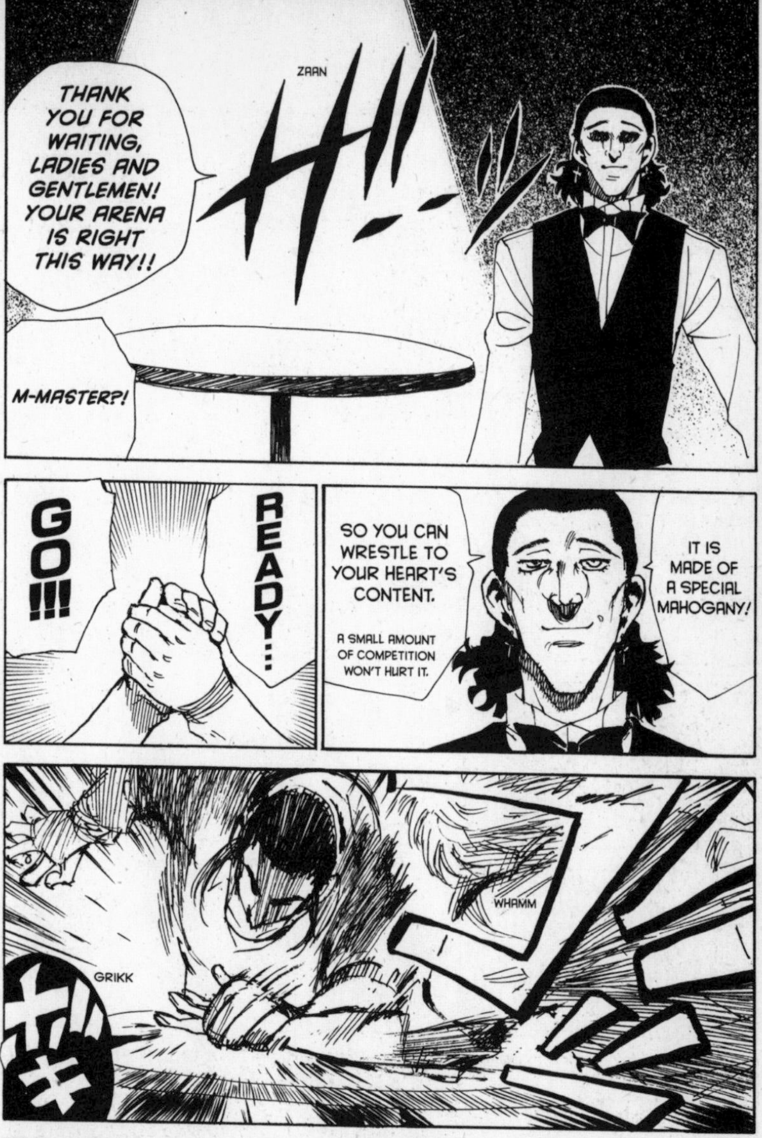
ZAAN
THANK YOU FOR WAITING, LADIES AND GENTLEMEN! YOUR ARENA IS RIGHT THIS WAY!!
M-MASTER?!
IT IS MADE OF A SPECIAL MAHOGANY!
SO YOU CAN WRESTLE TO YOUR HEART'S CONTENT.
A SMALL AMOUNT OF COMPETITION WON'T HURT IT.
READY...
GO!!!
WHAMM
GRIKK
HUSSSSH
EH...?
W-WASN'T THAT THE SOUND OF...

Mercado's Master: Zero Interest in Business.

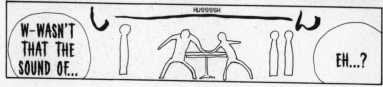

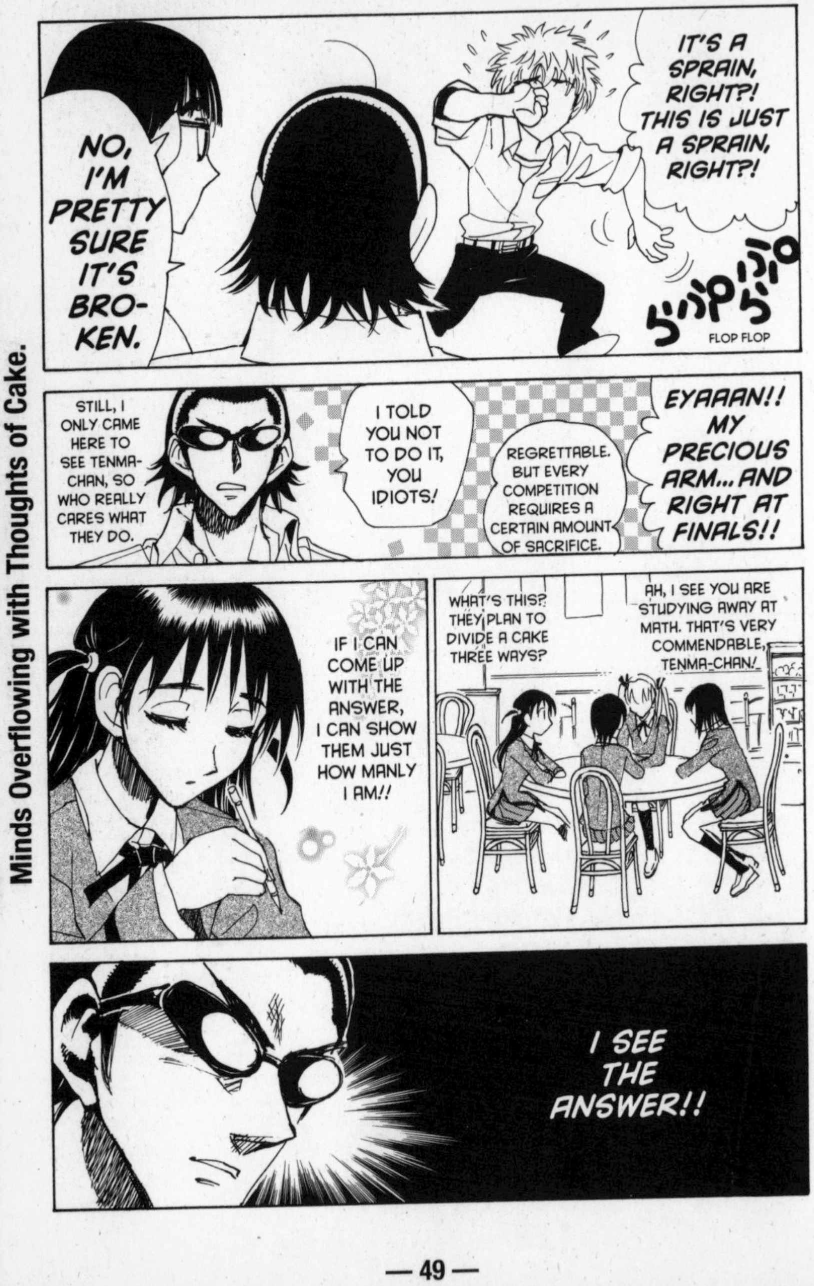
IT'S A SPRAIN, RIGHT?! THIS IS JUST A SPRAIN, RIGHT?!
FLOP FLOP
NO, I'M PRETTY SURE IT'S BRO-KEN.
EYAAAN!! MY PRECIOUS ARM... AND RIGHT AT FINALS!!
REGRETTABLE. BUT EVERY COMPETITION REQUIRES A CERTAIN AMOUNT OF SACRIFICE.
I TOLD YOU NOT TO DO IT, YOU IDIOTS!
STILL, I ONLY CAME HERE TO SEE TENMA-CHAN, SO WHO REALLY CARES WHAT THEY DO.
AH, I SEE YOU ARE STUDYING AWAY AT MATH. THAT'S VERY COMMENDABLE, TENMA-CHAN!
WHAT'S THIS? THEY PLAN TO DIVIDE A CAKE THREE WAYS?
IF I CAN COME UP WITH THE ANSWER, I CAN SHOW THEM JUST HOW MANLY I AM!!
I SEE THE ANSWER!!

Body Fat Increases, but Test Scores Decrease. Hey!! Laugh at That!!

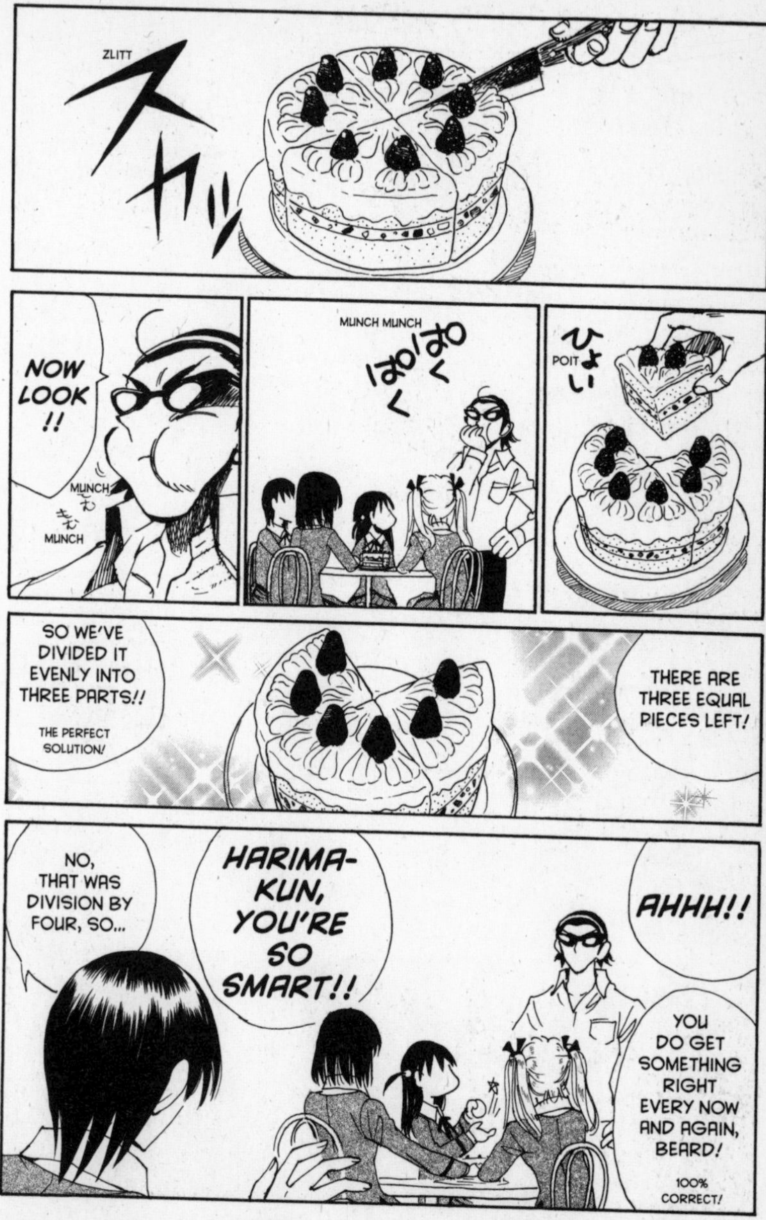
ZLITT
スカッ
POIT
ひょい
MUNCH MUNCH
ぱくぱく
NOW LOOK!!
MUNCH MUNCH
THERE ARE THREE EQUAL PIECES LEFT!
SO WE'VE DIVIDED IT EVENLY INTO THREE PARTS!!
THE PERFECT SOLUTION!
AHHH!!
YOU DO GET SOMETHING RIGHT EVERY NOW AND AGAIN, BEARD!
100% CORRECT!
HARIMA-KUN, YOU'RE SO SMART!!
NO, THAT WAS DIVISION BY FOUR, SO...

133.........Fin

#134 TOP OF THE WORLD

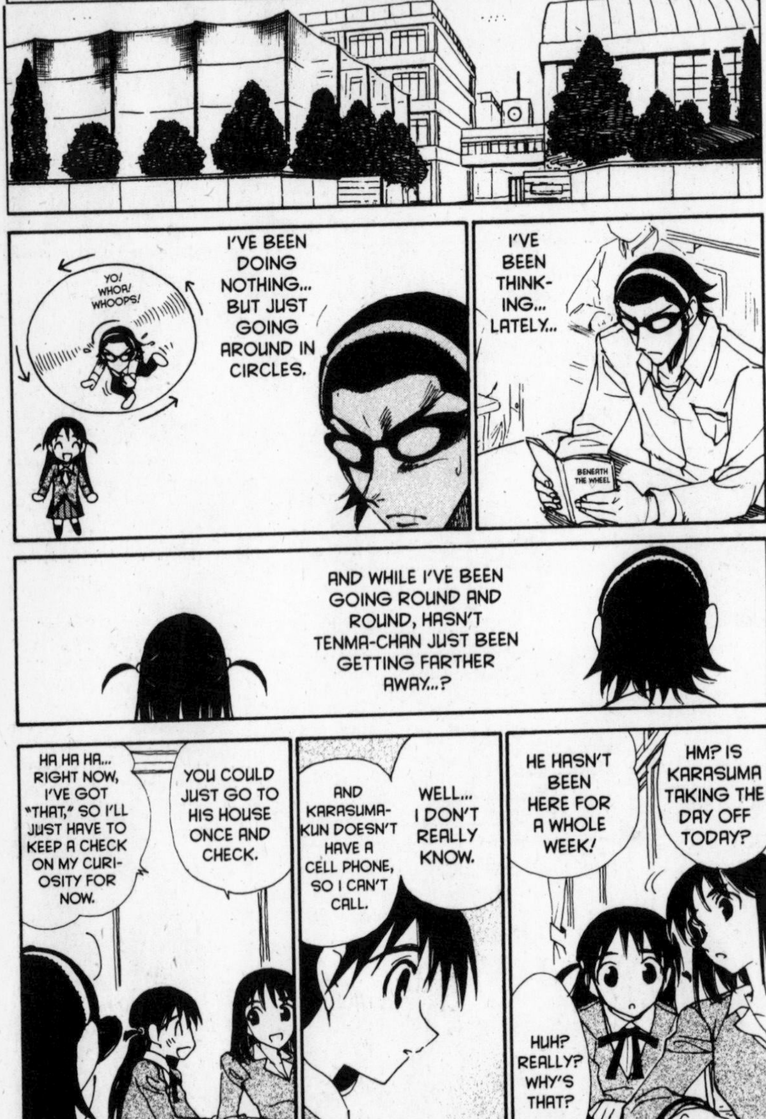
I'VE BEEN THINKING... LATELY...
BENEATH THE WHEEL
I'VE BEEN DOING NOTHING... BUT JUST GOING AROUND IN CIRCLES.
YO! WHOA! WHOOPS!
AND WHILE I'VE BEEN GOING ROUND AND ROUND, HASN'T TENMA-CHAN JUST BEEN GETTING FARTHER AWAY...?
HM? IS KARASUMA TAKING THE DAY OFF TODAY?
HE HASN'T BEEN HERE FOR A WHOLE WEEK!
HUH? REALLY? WHY'S THAT?
WELL... I DON'T REALLY KNOW.
AND KARASUMA-KUN DOESN'T HAVE A CELL PHONE, SO I CAN'T CALL.
YOU COULD JUST GO TO HIS HOUSE ONCE AND CHECK.
HA HA HA... RIGHT NOW, I'VE GOT "THAT," SO I'LL JUST HAVE TO KEEP A CHECK ON MY CURI-OSITY FOR NOW.

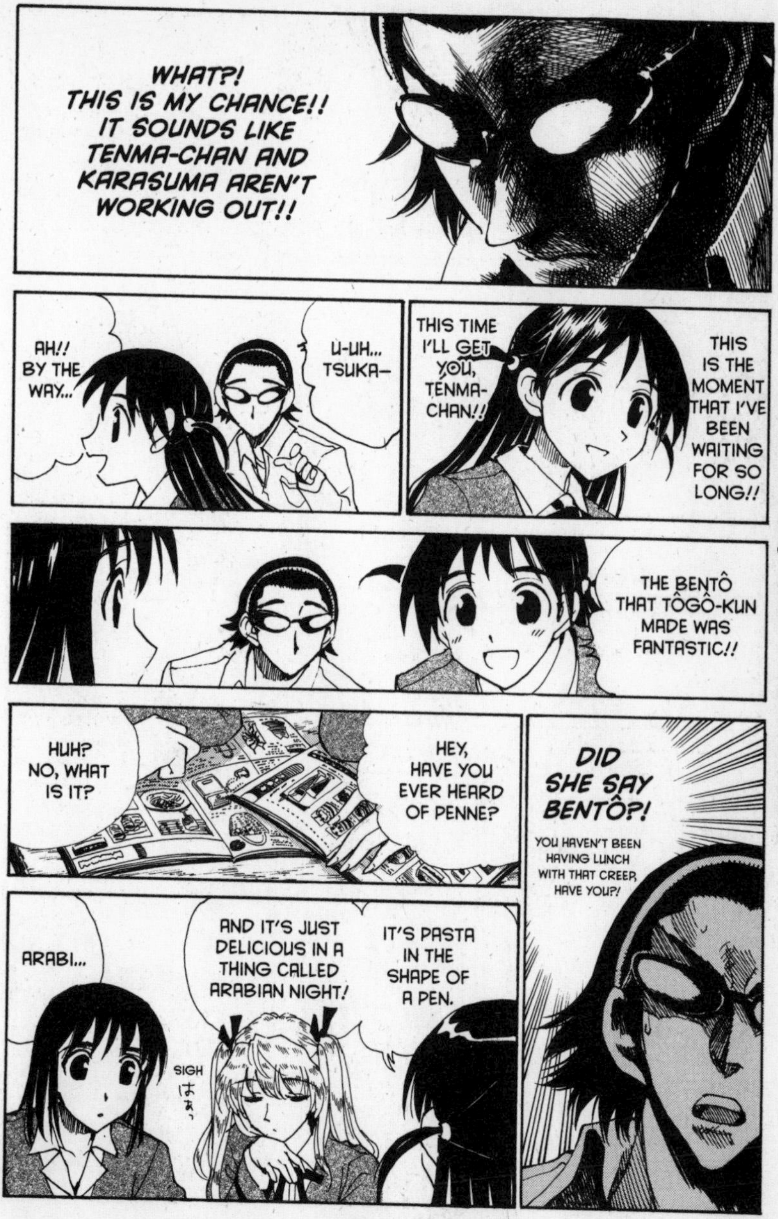
WHAT?! THIS IS MY CHANCE!! IT SOUNDS LIKE TENMA-CHAN AND KARASUMA AREN'T WORKING OUT!!
THIS IS THE MOMENT THAT I'VE BEEN WAITING FOR SO LONG!!
THIS TIME I'LL GET YOU, TENMA-CHAN!!
U-UH... TSUKA—
AH!! BY THE WAY...
THE BENTÔ THAT TÔGÔ-KUN MADE WAS FANTASTIC!!
DID SHE SAY BENTÔ?!
YOU HAVEN'T BEEN HAVING LUNCH WITH THAT CREEP, HAVE YOU?!
HEY, HAVE YOU EVER HEARD OF PENNE?
HUH? NO, WHAT IS IT?
IT'S PASTA IN THE SHAPE OF A PEN.
AND IT'S JUST DELICIOUS IN A THING CALLED ARABIAN NIGHT!
SIGH
はあっ
ARABI...

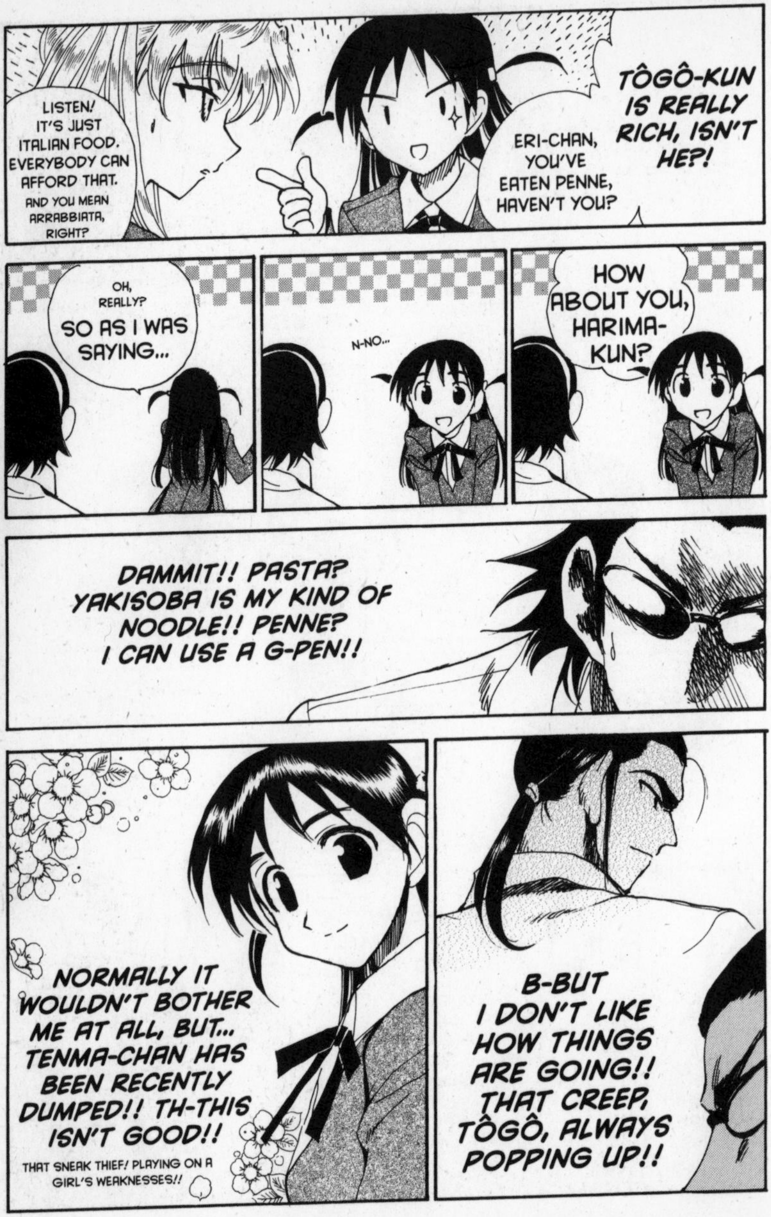
TÔGÔ-KUN IS REALLY RICH, ISN'T HE?!
ERI-CHAN, YOU'VE EATEN PENNE, HAVEN'T YOU?
LISTEN! IT'S JUST ITALIAN FOOD. EVERYBODY CAN AFFORD THAT.
AND YOU MEAN ARRABBIATA, RIGHT?
HOW ABOUT YOU, HARIMA-KUN?
N-NO...
OH, REALLY?
SO AS I WAS SAYING...
DAMMIT!! PASTA? YAKISOBA IS MY KIND OF NOODLE!! PENNE? I CAN USE A G-PEN!!
B-BUT I DON'T LIKE HOW THINGS ARE GOING!! THAT CREEP, TÔGÔ, ALWAYS POPPING UP!!
NORMALLY IT WOULDN'T BOTHER ME AT ALL, BUT... TENMA-CHAN HAS BEEN RECENTLY DUMPED!! TH-THIS ISN'T GOOD!!
THAT SNEAK THIEF! PLAYING ON A GIRL'S WEAKNESSES!!

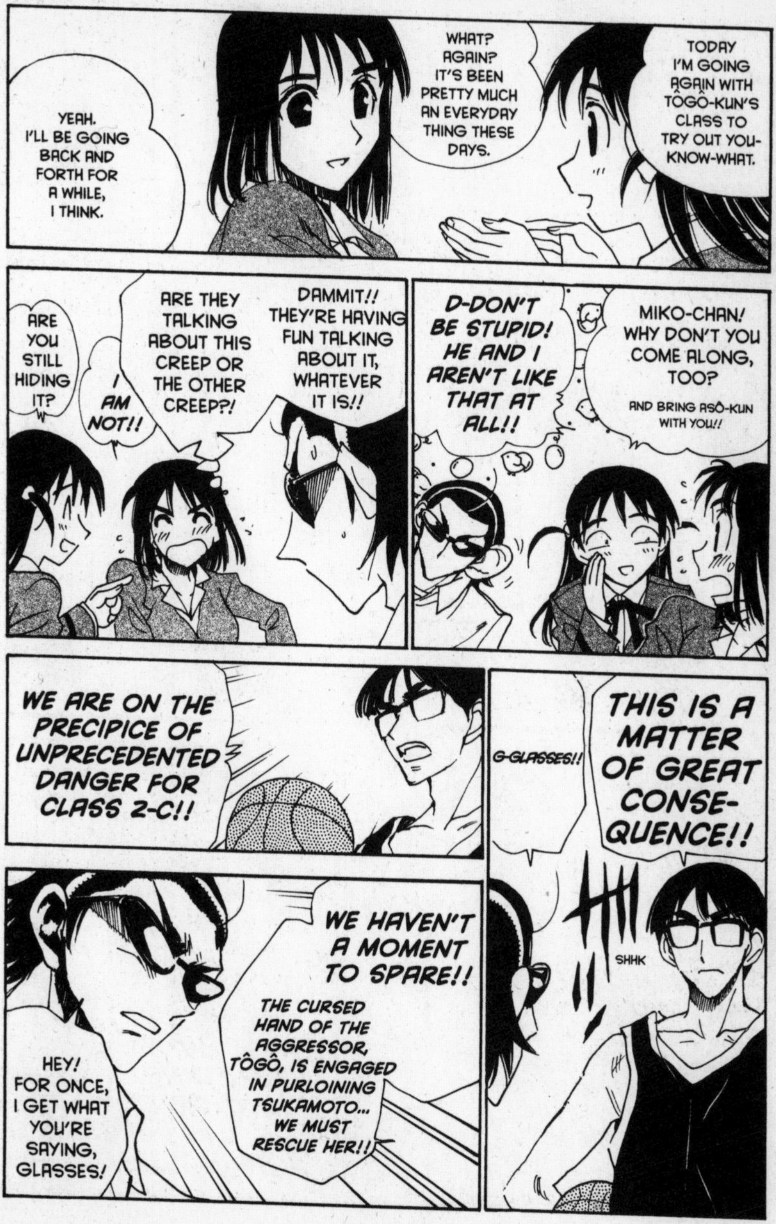
TODAY I'M GOING AGAIN WITH TÔGÔ-KUN'S CLASS TO TRY OUT YOU-KNOW-WHAT.
WHAT? AGAIN? IT'S BEEN PRETTY MUCH AN EVERYDAY THING THESE DAYS.
YEAH. I'LL BE GOING BACK AND FORTH FOR A WHILE, I THINK.
MIKO-CHAN! WHY DON'T YOU COME ALONG, TOO?
AND BRING ASÔ-KUN WITH YOU!!
D-DON'T BE STUPID! HE AND I AREN'T LIKE THAT AT ALL!!
DAMMIT!! THEY'RE HAVING FUN TALKING ABOUT IT, WHATEVER IT IS!!
ARE THEY TALKING ABOUT THIS CREEP OR THE OTHER CREEP?!
ARE YOU STILL HIDING IT?
I AM NOT!!
THIS IS A MATTER OF GREAT CONSE-QUENCE!!
G-GLASSES!!
SHHK
WE ARE ON THE PRECIPICE OF UNPRECEDENTED DANGER FOR CLASS 2-C!!
WE HAVEN'T A MOMENT TO SPARE!!
THE CURSED HAND OF THE AGGRESSOR, TÔGÔ, IS ENGAGED IN PURLOINING TSUKAMOTO... WE MUST RESCUE HER!!
HEY! FOR ONCE, I GET WHAT YOU'RE SAYING, GLASSES!

Hanai Haruki: Late to Get into the Basketball Craze.

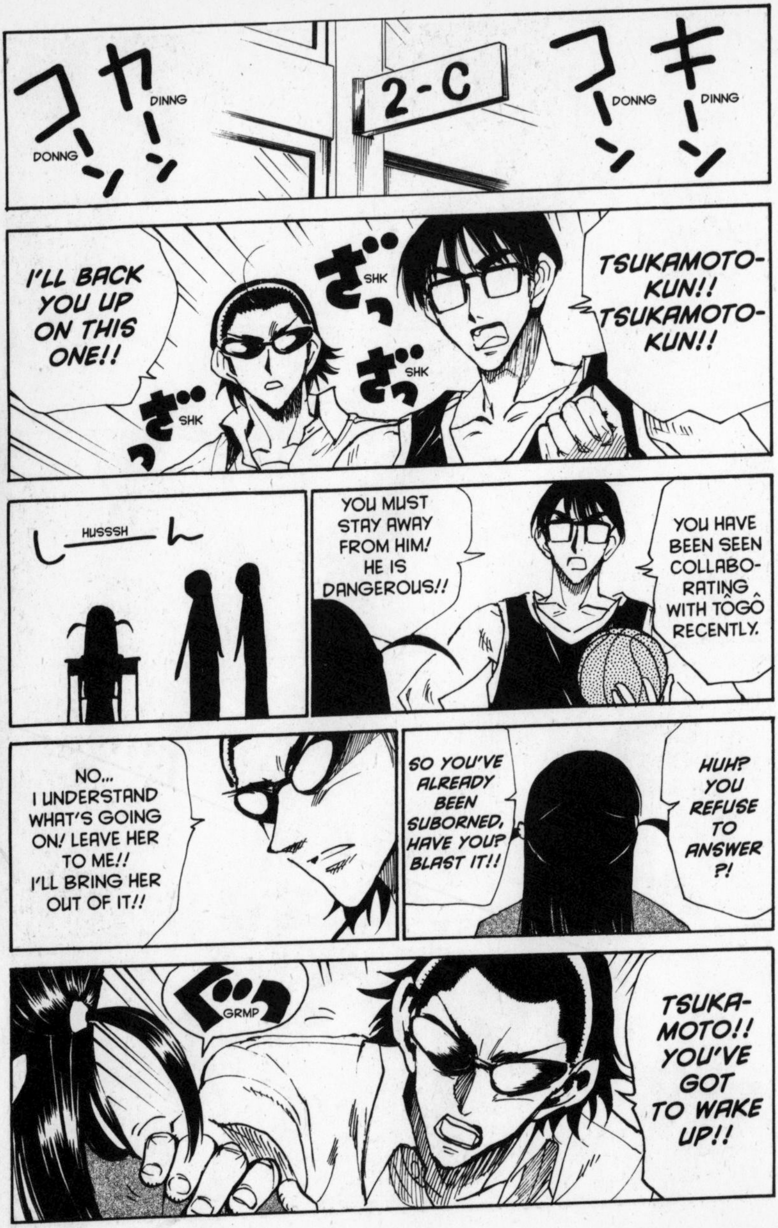
DINNG
DONNG
2-C
DINNG
DONNG
TSUKAMOTO-KUN!! TSUKAMOTO-KUN!!
SHK
SHK
I'LL BACK YOU UP ON THIS ONE!!
SHK
YOU HAVE BEEN SEEN COLLABO-RATING WITH TÔGÔ RECENTLY.
YOU MUST STAY AWAY FROM HIM! HE IS DANGEROUS!!
HUSSSH
HUH? YOU REFUSE TO ANSWER?!
SO YOU'VE ALREADY BEEN SUBORNED, HAVE YOU? BLAST IT!!
NO... I UNDERSTAND WHAT'S GOING ON! LEAVE HER TO ME!! I'LL BRING HER OUT OF IT!!
TSUKA-MOTO!! YOU'VE GOT TO WAKE UP!!
GRMP

She's Taken On a Single Distinctive Feature.

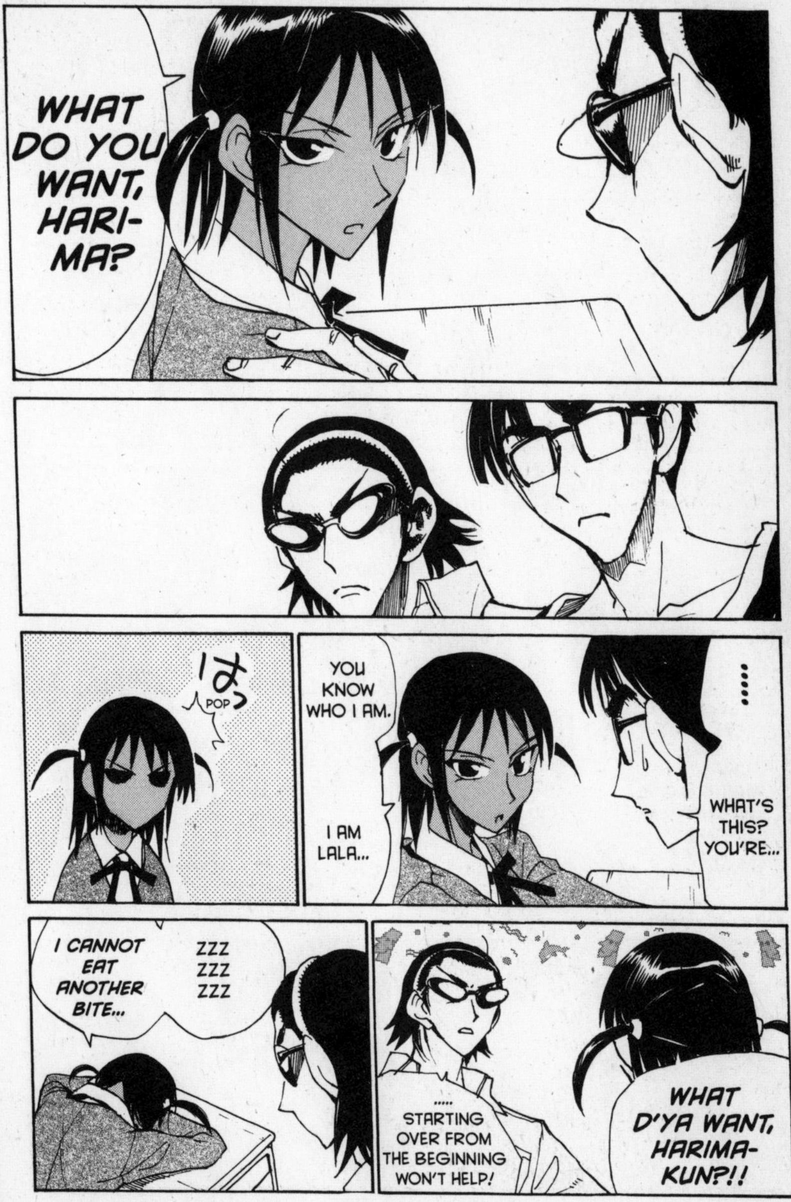
WHAT DO YOU WANT, HARIMA?
.....
WHAT'S THIS? YOU'RE...
YOU KNOW WHO I AM.
I AM LALA...
はっ
POP
WHAT D'YA WANT, HARIMA-KUN?!!
..... STARTING OVER FROM THE BEGINNING WON'T HELP!
ZZZ ZZZ ZZZ
I CANNOT EAT ANOTHER BITE...

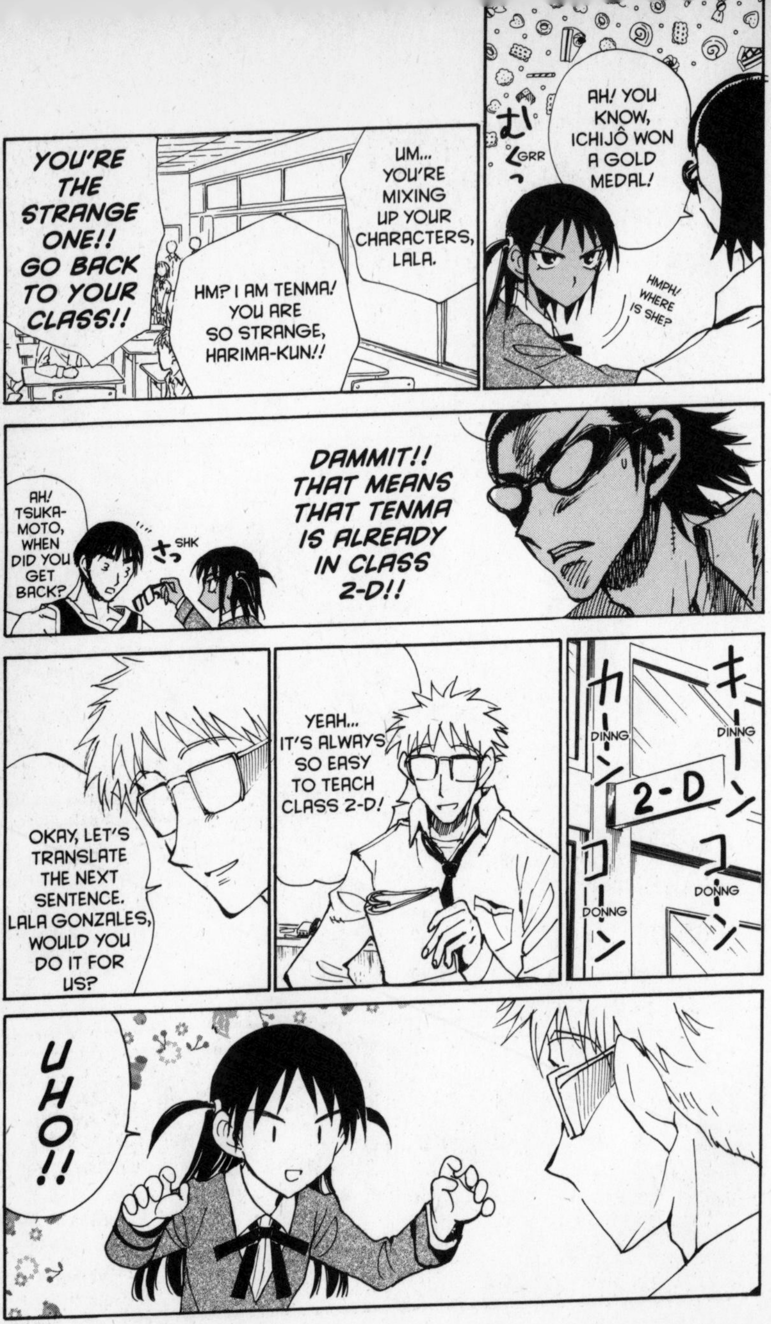
AH! YOU KNOW, ICHIJÔ WON A GOLD MEDAL!
むくっ GRR
HMPH! WHERE IS SHE?
UM... YOU'RE MIXING UP YOUR CHARACTERS, LALA.
HM? I AM TENMA! YOU ARE SO STRANGE, HARIMA-KUN!!
YOU'RE THE STRANGE ONE!! GO BACK TO YOUR CLASS!!
DAMMIT!! THAT MEANS THAT TENMA IS ALREADY IN CLASS 2-D!!
さっ SHK
AH! TSUKAMOTO, WHEN DID YOU GET BACK?
キーンコーン DINNG DONNG
カーンコーン DINNG DONNG
2-D
YEAH... IT'S ALWAYS SO EASY TO TEACH CLASS 2-D!
OKAY, LET'S TRANSLATE THE NEXT SENTENCE. LALA GONZALES, WOULD YOU DO IT FOR US?
UHO!!

Tani Hayato: No, He Isn't Just Imadori in Glasses.

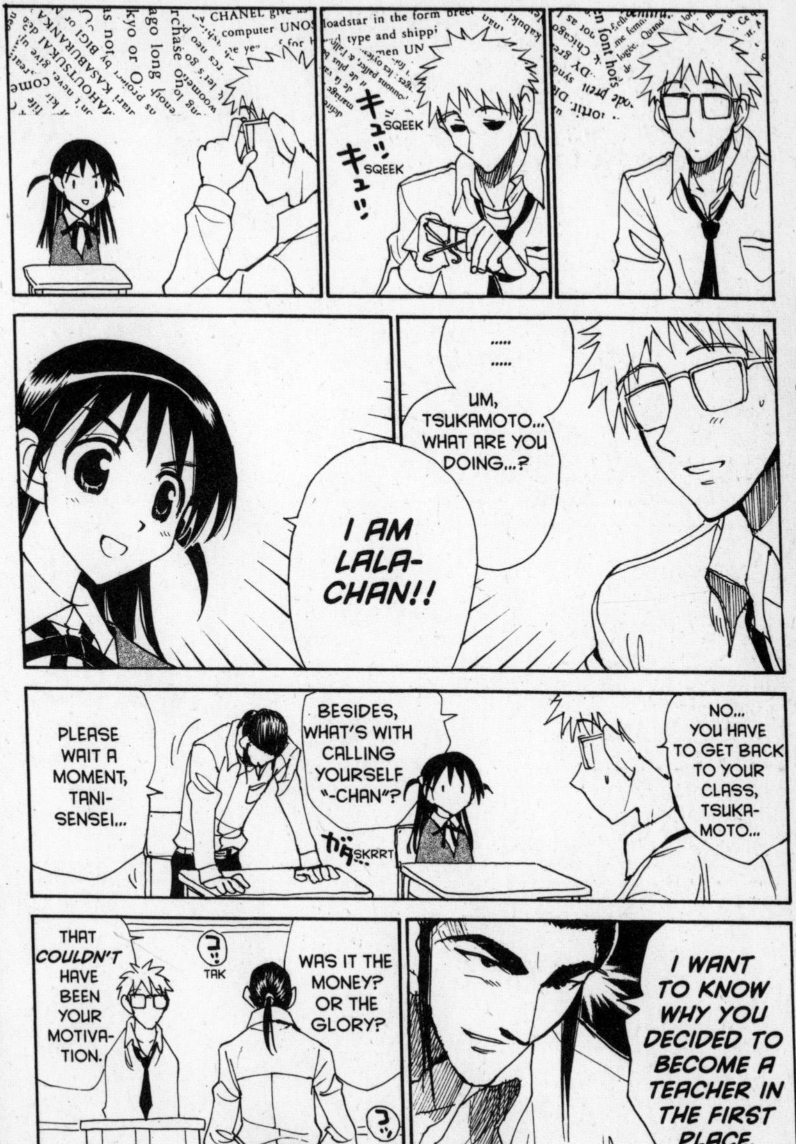
キュッ
SQEEK
キュッ
SQEEK
......
......
UM, TSUKAMOTO... WHAT ARE YOU DOING...?
I AM LALA-CHAN!!
NO... YOU HAVE TO GET BACK TO YOUR CLASS, TSUKAMOTO...
BESIDES, WHAT'S WITH CALLING YOURSELF "-CHAN"?
ガタ
SKRRT
PLEASE WAIT A MOMENT, TANI-SENSEI...
I WANT TO KNOW WHY YOU DECIDED TO BECOME A TEACHER IN THE FIRST PLACE.
WAS IT THE MONEY? OR THE GLORY?
コッ
TAK
THAT COULDN'T HAVE BEEN YOUR MOTIVATION.
コッ
TAK

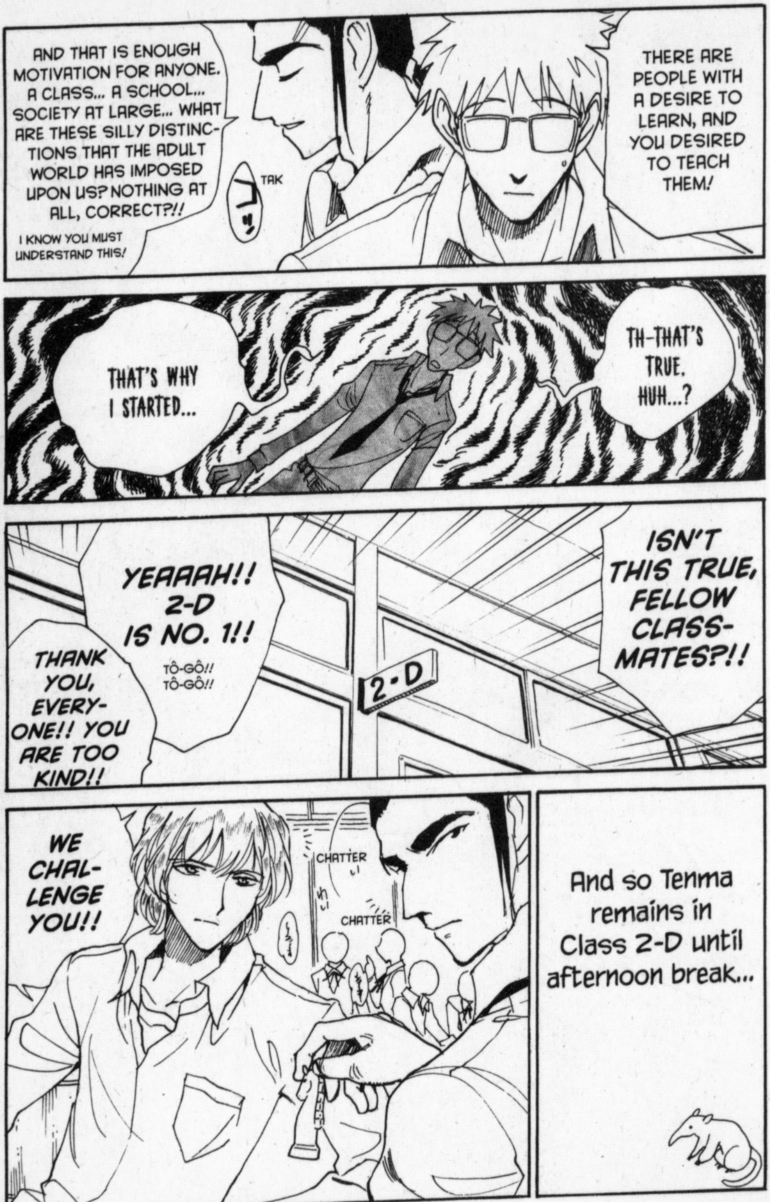
THERE ARE PEOPLE WITH A DESIRE TO LEARN, AND YOU DESIRED TO TEACH THEM!
AND THAT IS ENOUGH MOTIVATION FOR ANYONE. A CLASS... A SCHOOL... SOCIETY AT LARGE... WHAT ARE THESE SILLY DISTINCTIONS THAT THE ADULT WORLD HAS IMPOSED UPON US? NOTHING AT ALL, CORRECT?!!
TAK
I KNOW YOU MUST UNDERSTAND THIS!
TH-THAT'S TRUE. HUH...?
THAT'S WHY I STARTED...
ISN'T THIS TRUE, FELLOW CLASSMATES?!!
2-D
YEAAAH!! 2-D IS NO. 1!!
TÔ-GÔ!! TÔ-GÔ!!
THANK YOU, EVERYONE!! YOU ARE TOO KIND!!
And so Tenma remains in Class 2-D until afternoon break...
CHATTER
CHATTER
WE CHALLENGE YOU!!

Tenma Stock: Risen Sharply in Her Absence.

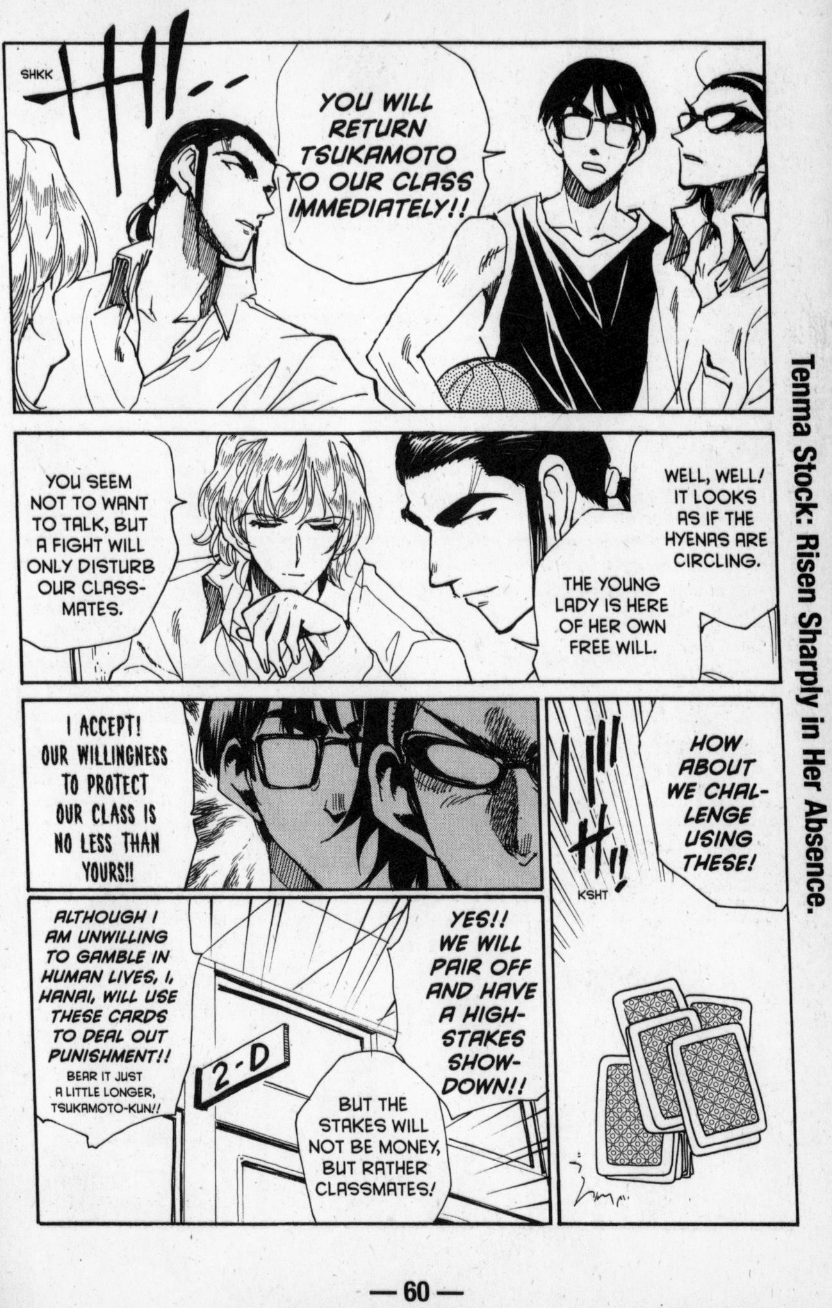
SHKK
YOU WILL RETURN TSUKAMOTO TO OUR CLASS IMMEDIATELY!!
WELL, WELL! IT LOOKS AS IF THE HYENAS ARE CIRCLING.
THE YOUNG LADY IS HERE OF HER OWN FREE WILL.
YOU SEEM NOT TO WANT TO TALK, BUT A FIGHT WILL ONLY DISTURB OUR CLASS-MATES.
HOW ABOUT WE CHAL-LENGE USING THESE!
KSHT
I ACCEPT! OUR WILLINGNESS TO PROTECT OUR CLASS IS NO LESS THAN YOURS!!
YES!! WE WILL PAIR OFF AND HAVE A HIGH-STAKES SHOW-DOWN!!
BUT THE STAKES WILL NOT BE MONEY, BUT RATHER CLASSMATES!
2-D
ALTHOUGH I AM UNWILLING TO GAMBLE IN HUMAN LIVES, I, HANAI, WILL USE THESE CARDS TO DEAL OUT PUNISHMENT!!
BEAR IT JUST A LITTLE LONGER, TSUKAMOTO-KUN!!

Never Stop Until One's Winning Streak Ends. That Is Gambling.

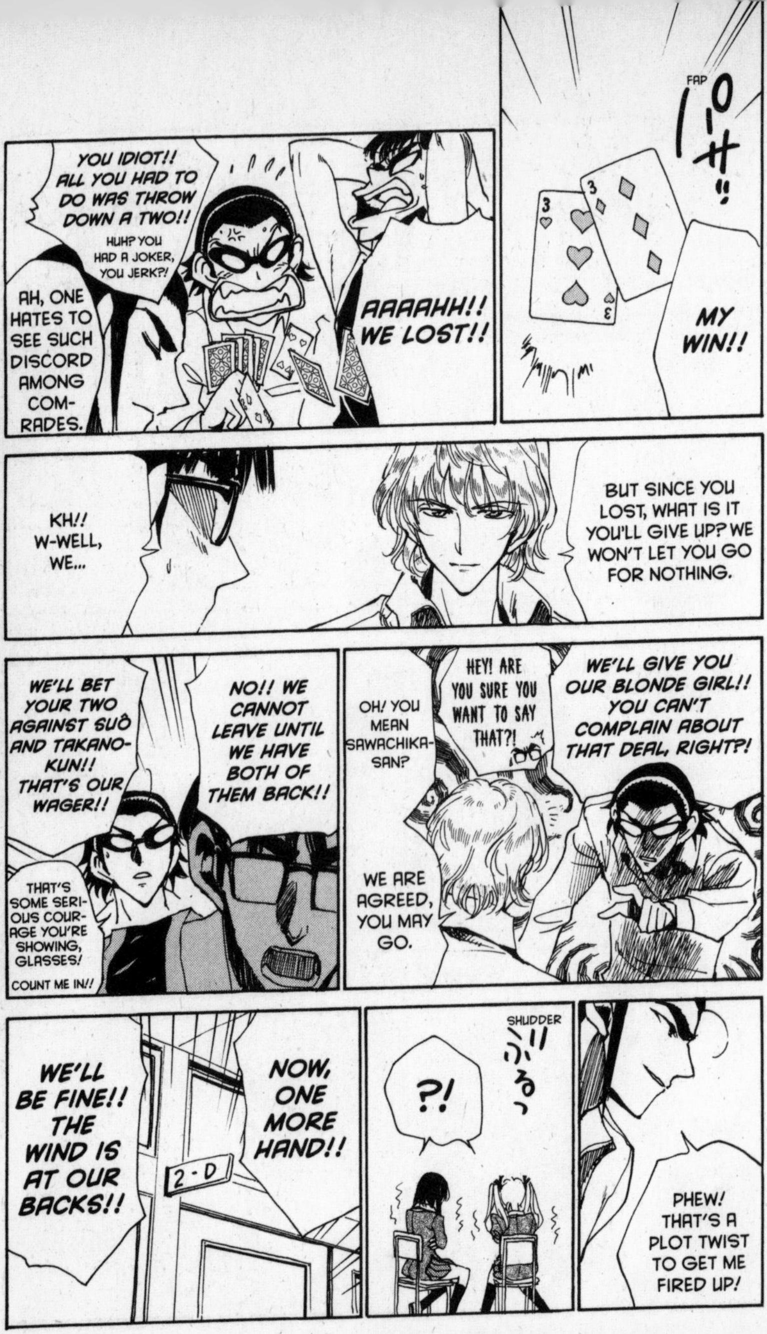
FAP
MY WIN!!
AAAAHH!! WE LOST!!
YOU IDIOT!! ALL YOU HAD TO DO WAS THROW DOWN A TWO!!
HUH? YOU HAD A JOKER, YOU JERK?!
AH, ONE HATES TO SEE SUCH DISCORD AMONG COM-RADES.
BUT SINCE YOU LOST, WHAT IS IT YOU'LL GIVE UP? WE WON'T LET YOU GO FOR NOTHING.
KH!! W-WELL, WE...
WE'LL GIVE YOU OUR BLONDE GIRL!! YOU CAN'T COMPLAIN ABOUT THAT DEAL, RIGHT?!
HEY! ARE YOU SURE YOU WANT TO SAY THAT?!
OH! YOU MEAN SAWACHIKA-SAN?
WE ARE AGREED, YOU MAY GO.
NO!! WE CANNOT LEAVE UNTIL WE HAVE BOTH OF THEM BACK!!
WE'LL BET YOUR TWO AGAINST SUÔ AND TAKANO-KUN!! THAT'S OUR WAGER!!
THAT'S SOME SERI-OUS COUR-AGE YOU'RE SHOWING, GLASSES!
COUNT ME IN!!
PHEW! THAT'S A PLOT TWIST TO GET ME FIRED UP!
SHUDDER
?!
NOW, ONE MORE HAND!!
WE'LL BE FINE!! THE WIND IS AT OUR BACKS!!
2-D

Roll Call! Hanai! Harima! .... Finished.

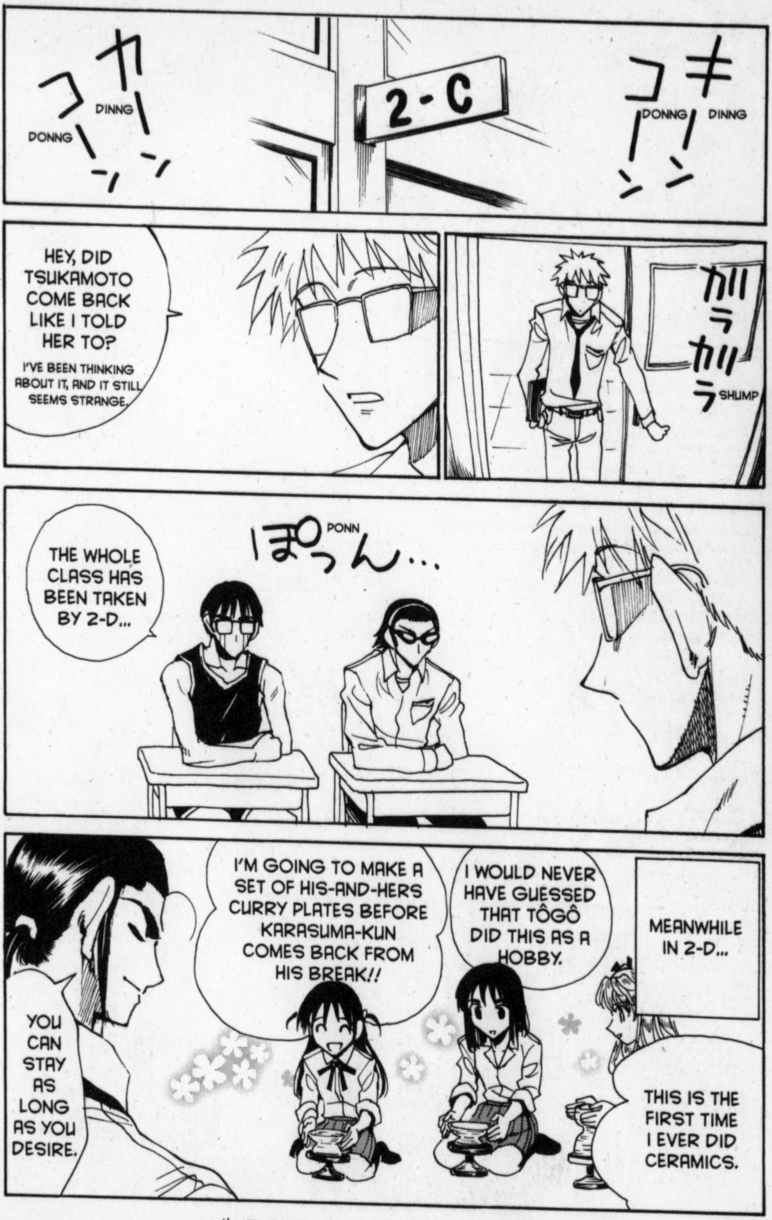
コキーン
DONNG DINNG
カコーン
DINNG DONNG
2-C
ガラガラ
SHUMP
HEY, DID TSUKAMOTO COME BACK LIKE I TOLD HER TO?
I'VE BEEN THINKING ABOUT IT, AND IT STILL SEEMS STRANGE.
ぽっん…
PONN
THE WHOLE CLASS HAS BEEN TAKEN BY 2-D...
MEANWHILE IN 2-D...
THIS IS THE FIRST TIME I EVER DID CERAMICS.
I WOULD NEVER HAVE GUESSED THAT TÔGÔ DID THIS AS A HOBBY.
I'M GOING TO MAKE A SET OF HIS-AND-HERS CURRY PLATES BEFORE KARASUMA-KUN COMES BACK FROM HIS BREAK!!
YOU CAN STAY AS LONG AS YOU DESIRE.

134. . . . . .Fin

#135 SHORT CUTS

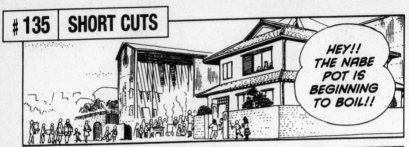

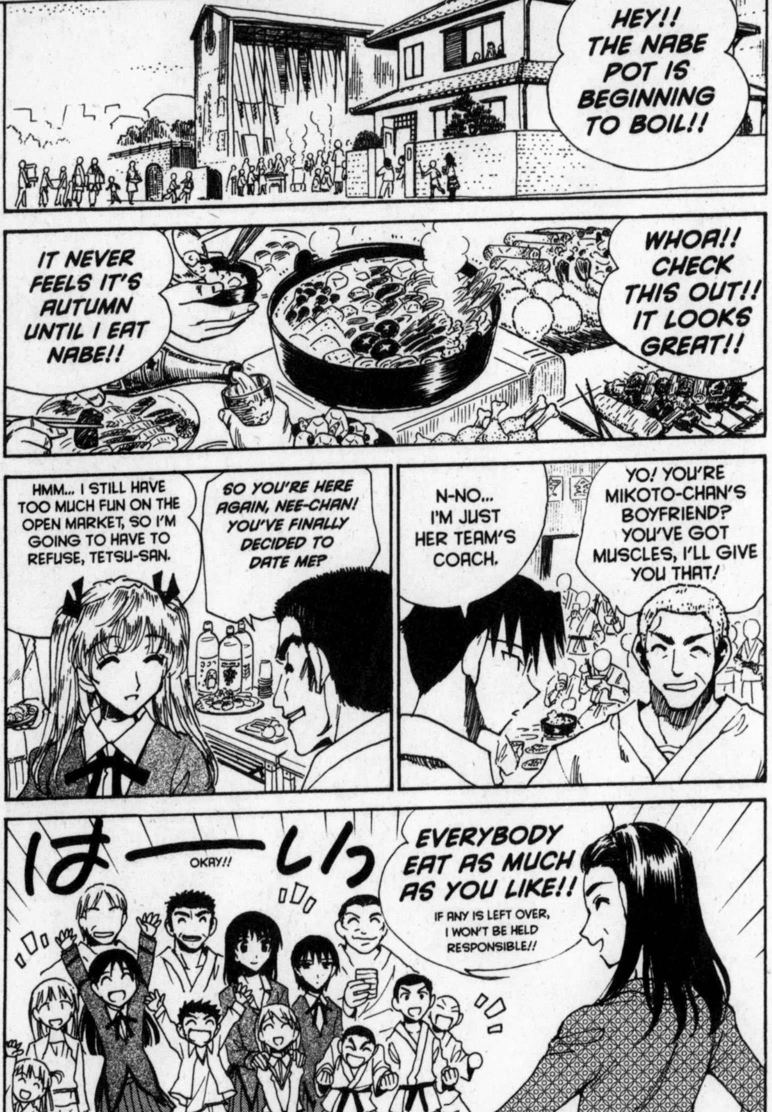
HEY!! THE NABE POT IS BEGINNING TO BOIL!!
WHOA!! CHECK THIS OUT!! IT LOOKS GREAT!!
IT NEVER FEELS IT'S AUTUMN UNTIL I EAT NABE!!
YO! YOU'RE MIKOTO-CHAN'S BOYFRIEND? YOU'VE GOT MUSCLES, I'LL GIVE YOU THAT!
N-NO... I'M JUST HER TEAM'S COACH.
SO YOU'RE HERE AGAIN, NEE-CHAN! YOU'VE FINALLY DECIDED TO DATE ME?
HMM... I STILL HAVE TOO MUCH FUN ON THE OPEN MARKET, SO I'M GOING TO HAVE TO REFUSE, TETSU-SAN.
EVERYBODY EAT AS MUCH AS YOU LIKE!!
IF ANY IS LEFT OVER, I WON'T BE HELD RESPONSIBLE!!
はーいっ
OKAY!!

Suô Building Contractor Company and Hanai's Dojo Are Having an Imonikai Party.

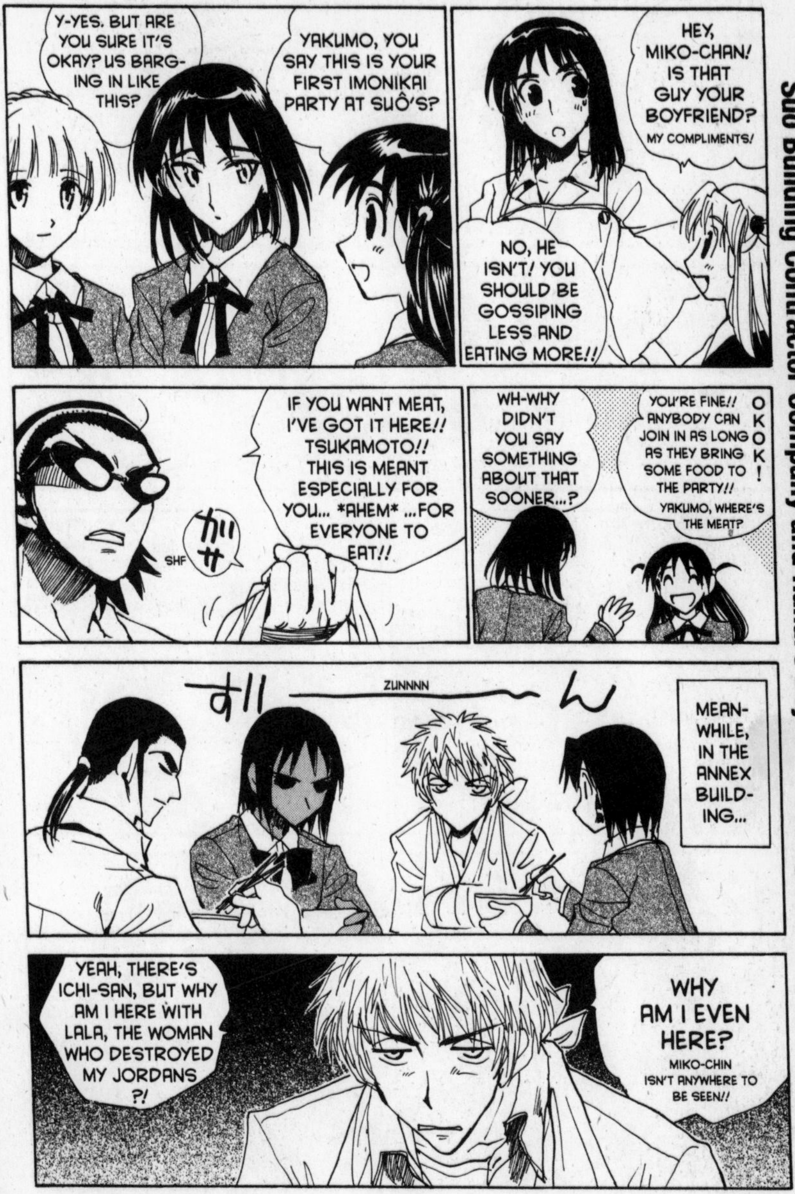
HEY, MIKO-CHAN! IS THAT GUY YOUR BOYFRIEND? MY COMPLIMENTS!
NO, HE ISN'T! YOU SHOULD BE GOSSIPING LESS AND EATING MORE!!
YAKUMO, YOU SAY THIS IS YOUR FIRST IMONIKAI PARTY AT SUÔ'S?
Y-YES. BUT ARE YOU SURE IT'S OKAY? US BARGING IN LIKE THIS?
OKOK!
YOU'RE FINE!! ANYBODY CAN JOIN IN AS LONG AS THEY BRING SOME FOOD TO THE PARTY!! YAKUMO, WHERE'S THE MEAT?
WH-WHY DIDN'T YOU SAY SOMETHING ABOUT THAT SOONER...?
IF YOU WANT MEAT, I'VE GOT IT HERE!! TSUKAMOTO!! THIS IS MEANT ESPECIALLY FOR YOU... *AHEM* ...FOR EVERYONE TO EAT!!
ガサ
SHF
MEANWHILE, IN THE ANNEX BUILDING...
ZUNNNN
WHY AM I EVEN HERE? MIKO-CHIN ISN'T ANYWHERE TO BE SEEN!!
YEAH, THERE'S ICHI-SAN, BUT WHY AM I HERE WITH LALA, THE WOMAN WHO DESTROYED MY JORDANS ?!

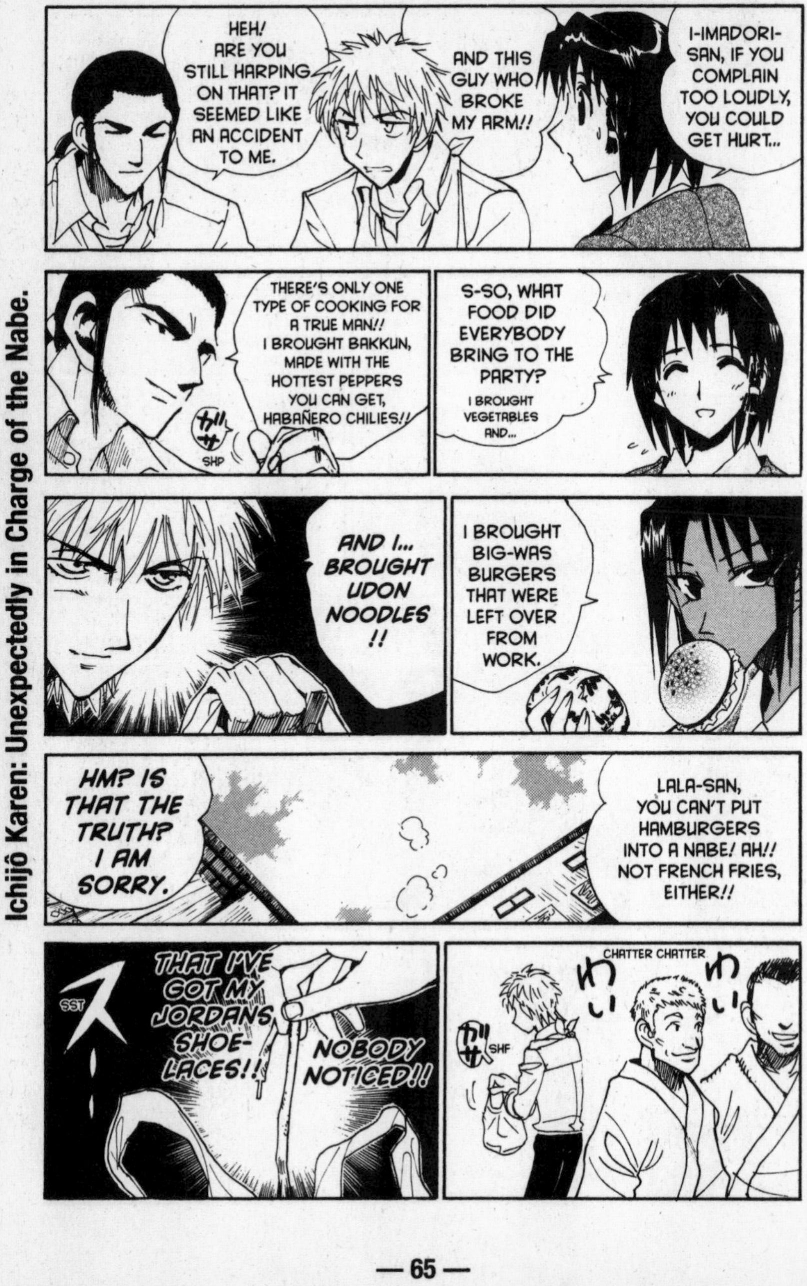
I-IMADORI-SAN, IF YOU COMPLAIN TOO LOUDLY, YOU COULD GET HURT...
AND THIS GUY WHO BROKE MY ARM!!
HEH! ARE YOU STILL HARPING ON THAT? IT SEEMED LIKE AN ACCIDENT TO ME.
S-SO, WHAT FOOD DID EVERYBODY BRING TO THE PARTY?
I BROUGHT VEGETABLES AND...
THERE'S ONLY ONE TYPE OF COOKING FOR A TRUE MAN!! I BROUGHT BAKKUN, MADE WITH THE HOTTEST PEPPERS YOU CAN GET, HABAÑERO CHILIES!!
SHP
I BROUGHT BIG-WAS BURGERS THAT WERE LEFT OVER FROM WORK.
AND I... BROUGHT UDON NOODLES !!
LALA-SAN, YOU CAN'T PUT HAMBURGERS INTO A NABE! AH!! NOT FRENCH FRIES, EITHER!!
HM? IS THAT THE TRUTH? I AM SORRY.
CHATTER CHATTER
SHF
NOBODY NOTICED!!
THAT I'VE GOT MY JORDANS SHOE-LACES!!
SST

It Tastes Like Sweat and Tears.

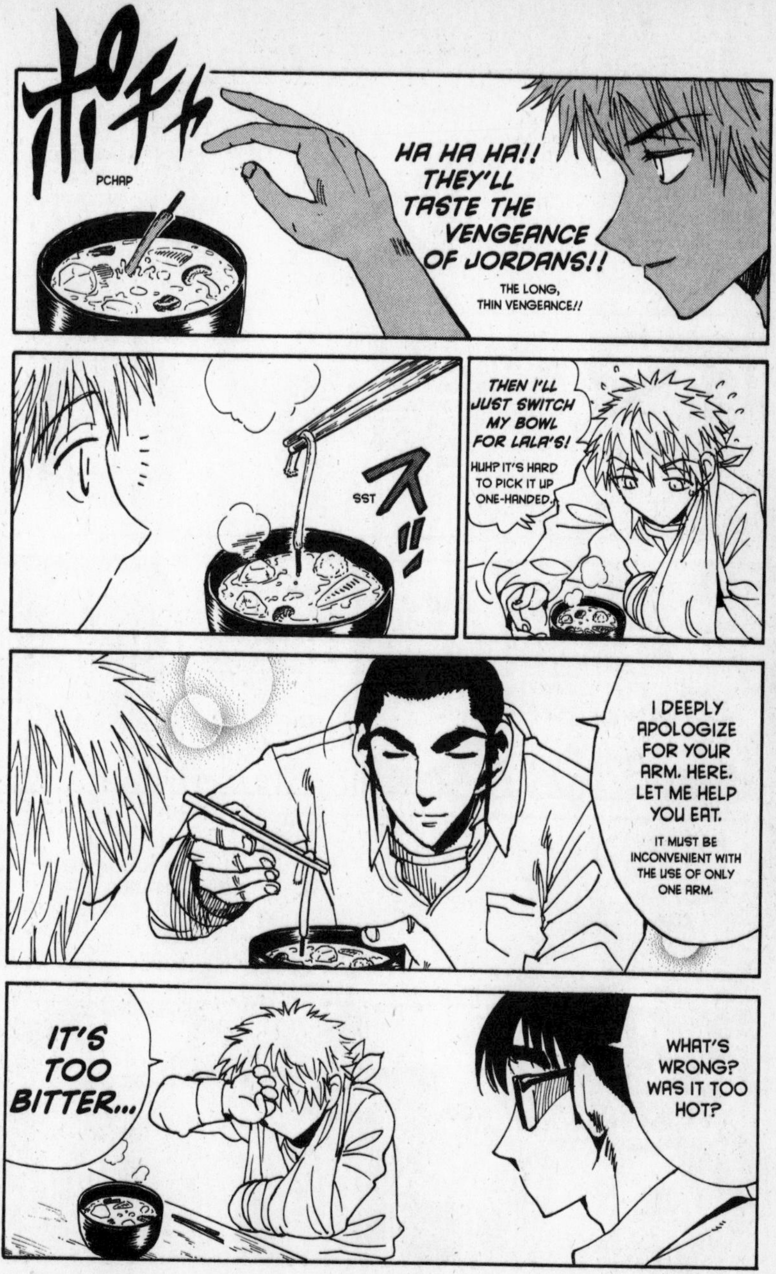
ポチャ
PCHAP
HA HA HA!! THEY'LL TASTE THE VENGEANCE OF JORDANS!!
THE LONG, THIN VENGEANCE!!
THEN I'LL JUST SWITCH MY BOWL FOR LALA'S!
HUH? IT'S HARD TO PICK IT UP ONE-HANDED.
ス
SST
I DEEPLY APOLOGIZE FOR YOUR ARM. HERE. LET ME HELP YOU EAT.
IT MUST BE INCONVENIENT WITH THE USE OF ONLY ONE ARM.
WHAT'S WRONG? WAS IT TOO HOT?
IT'S TOO BITTER...

《Grow Big and Strong!》

Napoleon Would Like to Stay Like This Forever.

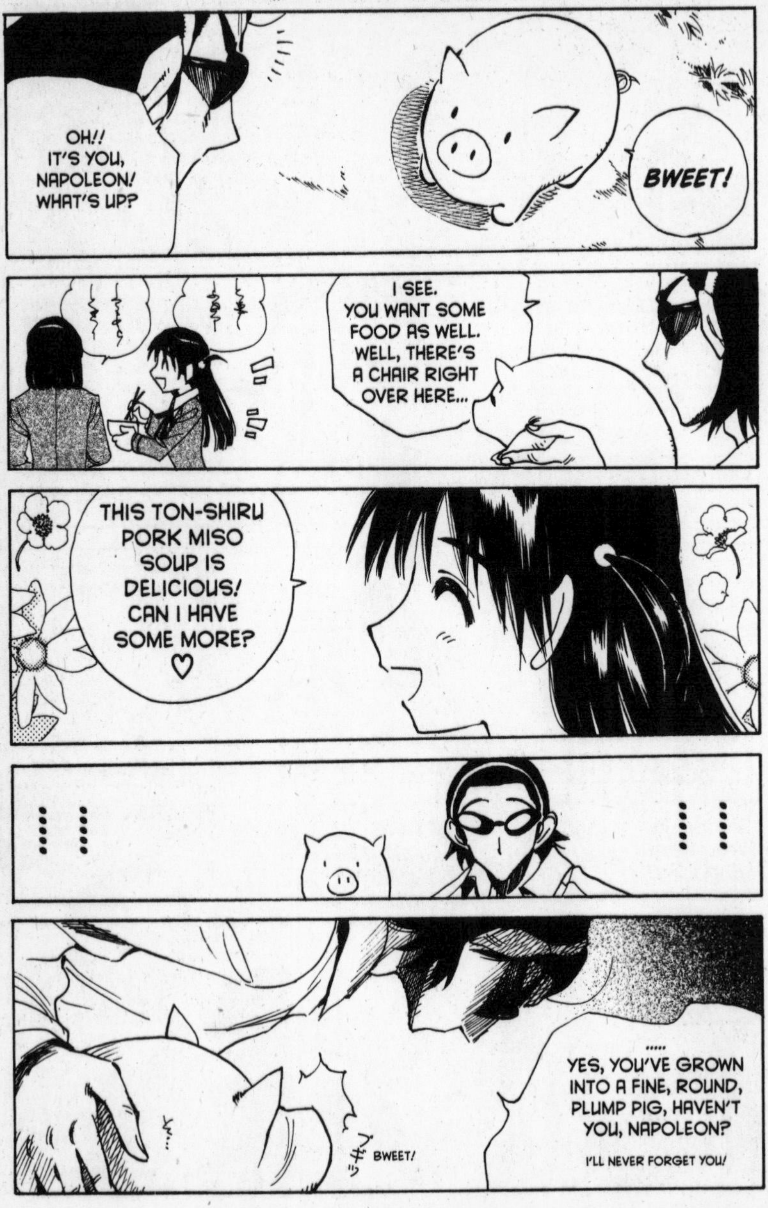
BWEET!
OH!! IT'S YOU, NAPOLEON! WHAT'S UP?
I SEE. YOU WANT SOME FOOD AS WELL. WELL, THERE'S A CHAIR RIGHT OVER HERE...
THIS TON-SHIRU PORK MISO SOUP IS DELICIOUS! CAN I HAVE SOME MORE? ♡
.....
.....
.....
.....
..... YES, YOU'VE GROWN INTO A FINE, ROUND, PLUMP PIG, HAVEN'T YOU, NAPOLEON?
I'LL NEVER FORGET YOU!
BWEET!

《Aim to Be a Ceramics Master!》

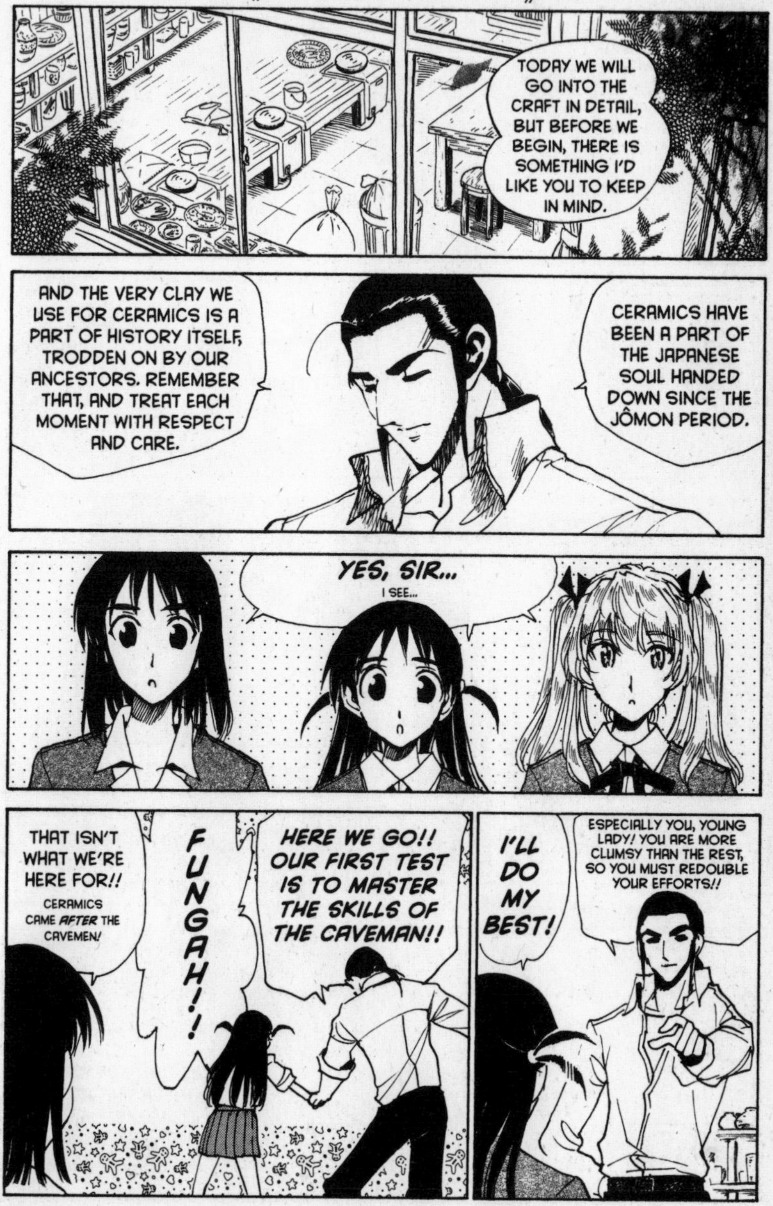
TODAY WE WILL GO INTO THE CRAFT IN DETAIL, BUT BEFORE WE BEGIN, THERE IS SOMETHING I'D LIKE YOU TO KEEP IN MIND.
CERAMICS HAVE BEEN A PART OF THE JAPANESE SOUL HANDED DOWN SINCE THE JÔMON PERIOD.
AND THE VERY CLAY WE USE FOR CERAMICS IS A PART OF HISTORY ITSELF, TRODDEN ON BY OUR ANCESTORS. REMEMBER THAT, AND TREAT EACH MOMENT WITH RESPECT AND CARE.
YES, SIR...
I SEE...
ESPECIALLY YOU, YOUNG LADY! YOU ARE MORE CLUMSY THAN THE REST, SO YOU MUST REDOUBLE YOUR EFFORTS!!
I'LL DO MY BEST!
HERE WE GO!! OUR FIRST TEST IS TO MASTER THE SKILLS OF THE CAVEMAN!!
FUNGAH!!
THAT ISN'T WHAT WE'RE HERE FOR!!
CERAMICS CAME *AFTER* THE CAVEMEN!

Tôgô Masakazu: Shows His Japanese Side.

《Aim to Be a Ceramics Master! Cont.》

Fungah! Fungah!

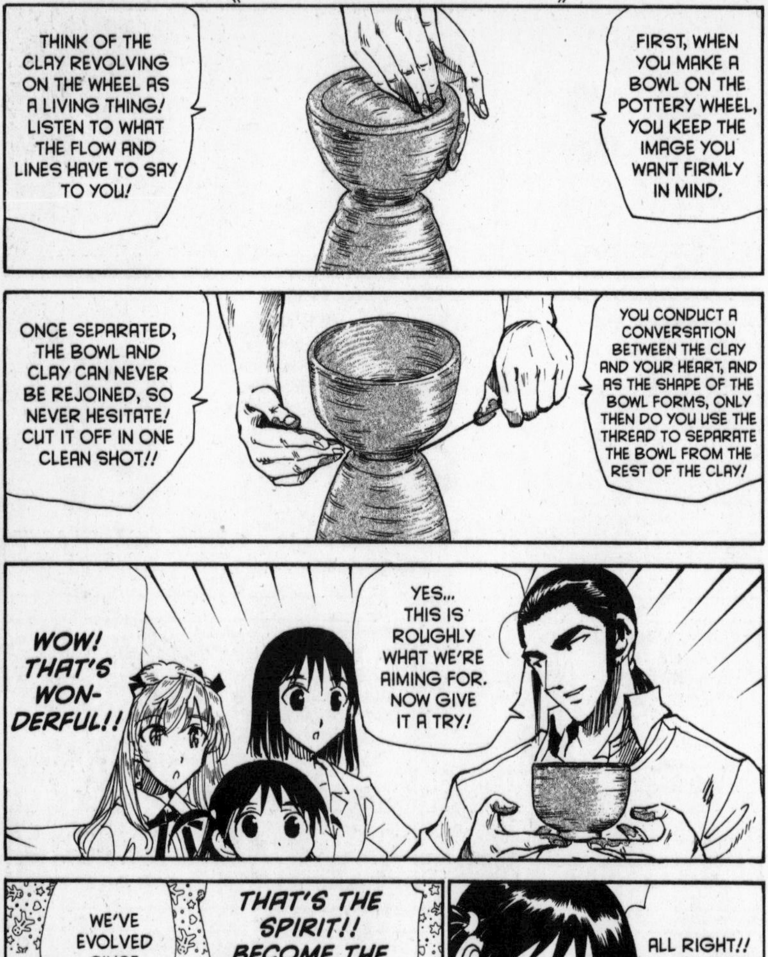
FIRST, WHEN YOU MAKE A BOWL ON THE POTTERY WHEEL, YOU KEEP THE IMAGE YOU WANT FIRMLY IN MIND.
THINK OF THE CLAY REVOLVING ON THE WHEEL AS A LIVING THING! LISTEN TO WHAT THE FLOW AND LINES HAVE TO SAY TO YOU!
YOU CONDUCT A CONVERSATION BETWEEN THE CLAY AND YOUR HEART, AND AS THE SHAPE OF THE BOWL FORMS, ONLY THEN DO YOU USE THE THREAD TO SEPARATE THE BOWL FROM THE REST OF THE CLAY!
ONCE SEPARATED, THE BOWL AND CLAY CAN NEVER BE REJOINED, SO NEVER HESITATE! CUT IT OFF IN ONE CLEAN SHOT!!
YES... THIS IS ROUGHLY WHAT WE'RE AIMING FOR. NOW GIVE IT A TRY!
WOW! THAT'S WON-DERFUL!!
ALL RIGHT!! I'LL BECOME ONE WITH THE CLAY AND FORM A CURRY BOWL OF MY OWN!!
THAT'S THE SPIRIT!! BECOME THE CAVEMAN!!
YES, SIR! COACH!!
WE'VE EVOLVED SINCE THEN!

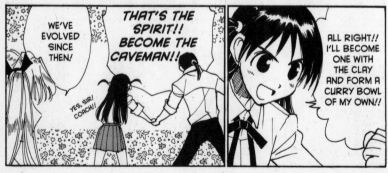

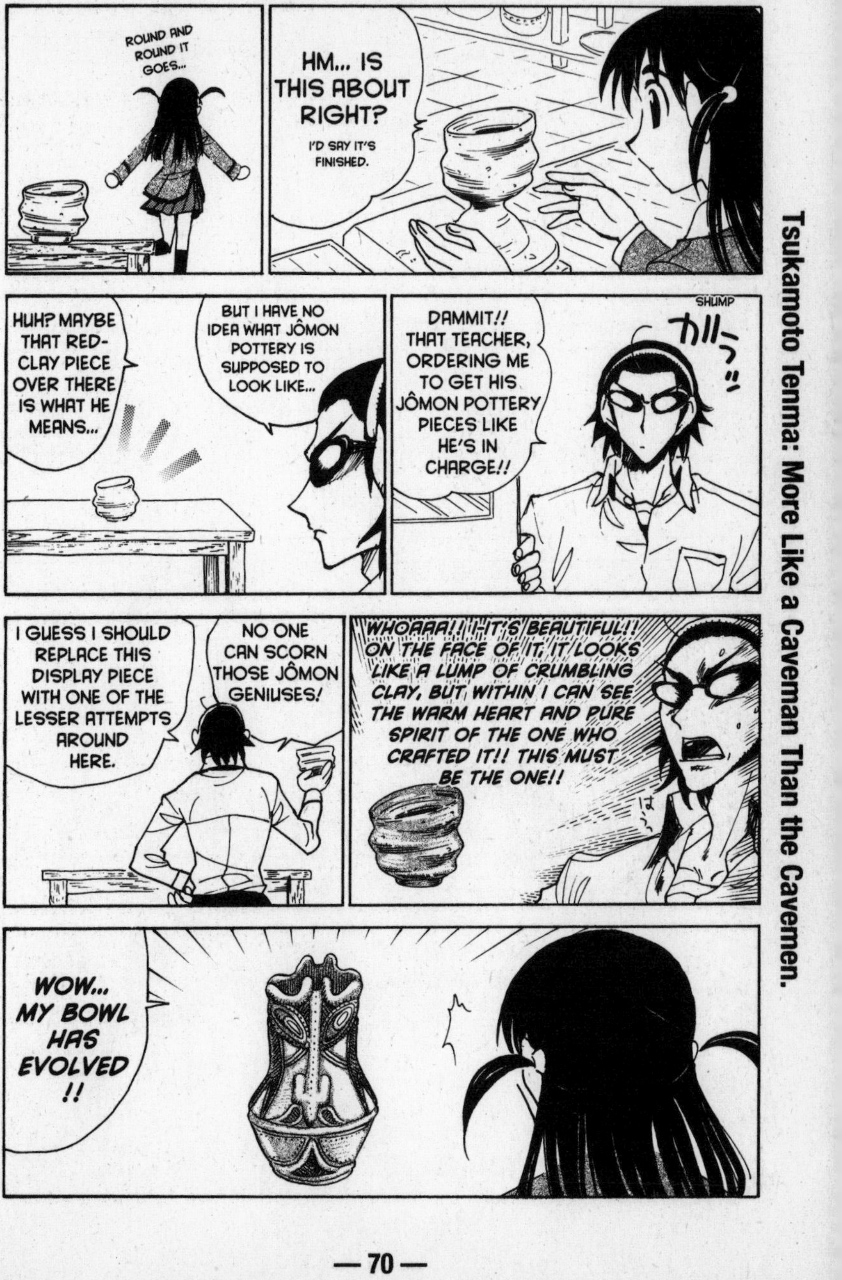
HM... IS THIS ABOUT RIGHT?
I'D SAY IT'S FINISHED.
ROUND AND ROUND IT GOES...
SHUMP
DAMMIT!! THAT TEACHER, ORDERING ME TO GET HIS JÔMON POTTERY PIECES LIKE HE'S IN CHARGE!!
BUT I HAVE NO IDEA WHAT JÔMON POTTERY IS SUPPOSED TO LOOK LIKE...
HUH? MAYBE THAT RED-CLAY PIECE OVER THERE IS WHAT HE MEANS...
WHOAAA!! I-IT'S BEAUTIFUL!! ON THE FACE OF IT, IT LOOKS LIKE A LUMP OF CRUMBLING CLAY, BUT WITHIN I CAN SEE THE WARM HEART AND PURE SPIRIT OF THE ONE WHO CRAFTED IT!! THIS MUST BE THE ONE!!
NO ONE CAN SCORN THOSE JÔMON GENIUSES!
I GUESS I SHOULD REPLACE THIS DISPLAY PIECE WITH ONE OF THE LESSER ATTEMPTS AROUND HERE.
WOW... MY BOWL HAS EVOLVED!!

Tsukamoto Tenma: More Like a Caveman Than the Cavemen.

The Correct Wording: You're Really Bad at This, Too.

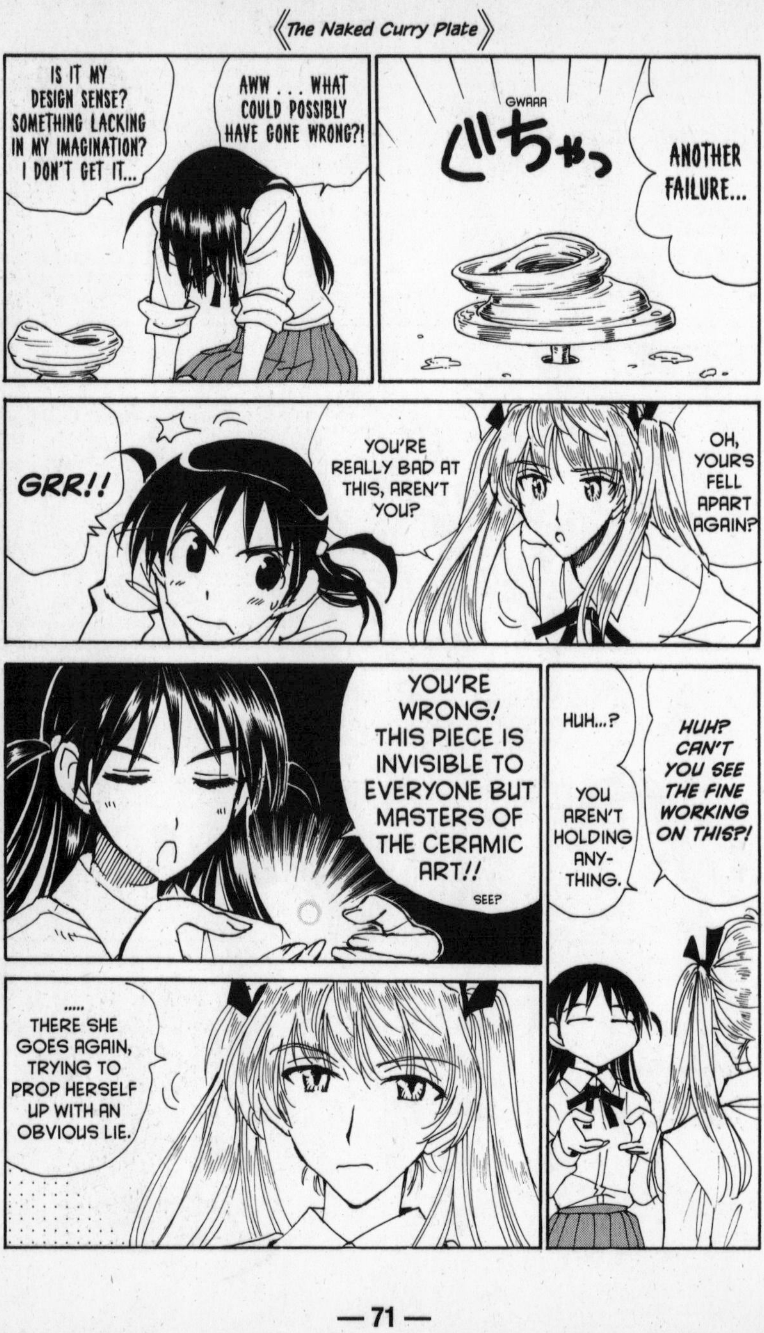
GWAAA
ぐちゃっ
ANOTHER FAILURE...
AWW . . . WHAT COULD POSSIBLY HAVE GONE WRONG?!
IS IT MY DESIGN SENSE? SOMETHING LACKING IN MY IMAGINATION? I DON'T GET IT...
OH, YOURS FELL APART AGAIN?
YOU'RE REALLY BAD AT THIS, AREN'T YOU?
GRR!!
HUH...?
YOU AREN'T HOLDING ANY-THING.
HUH? CAN'T YOU SEE THE FINE WORKING ON THIS?!
YOU'RE WRONG! THIS PIECE IS INVISIBLE TO EVERYONE BUT MASTERS OF THE CERAMIC ART!!
SEE?
..... THERE SHE GOES AGAIN, TRYING TO PROP HERSELF UP WITH AN OBVIOUS LIE.

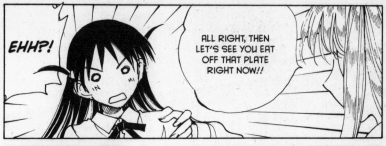

An Explosion of Imagination.

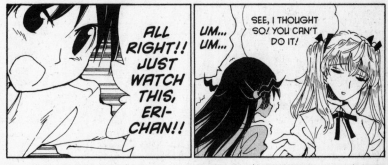

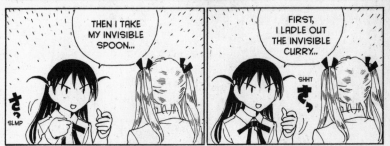

ALL RIGHT, THEN LET'S SEE YOU EAT OFF THAT PLATE RIGHT NOW!!
EHH?!
SEE, I THOUGHT SO! YOU CAN'T DO IT!
UM... UM...
ALL RIGHT!! JUST WATCH THIS, ERI-CHAN!!
FIRST, I LADLE OUT THE INVISIBLE CURRY...
さっ
SHHT
THEN I TAKE MY INVISIBLE SPOON...
さっ
SLMP
MM! THAT'S SO GOOD!!
ぱくぱく
MUNCH
MUNCH
COULD YOU GET ME A GLASS OF INVISIBLE WATER?
NO, UH... TENMA... OKAY, YOU WIN!
WHEN IS THIS GOING TO END?

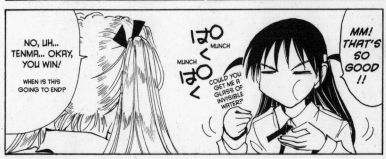

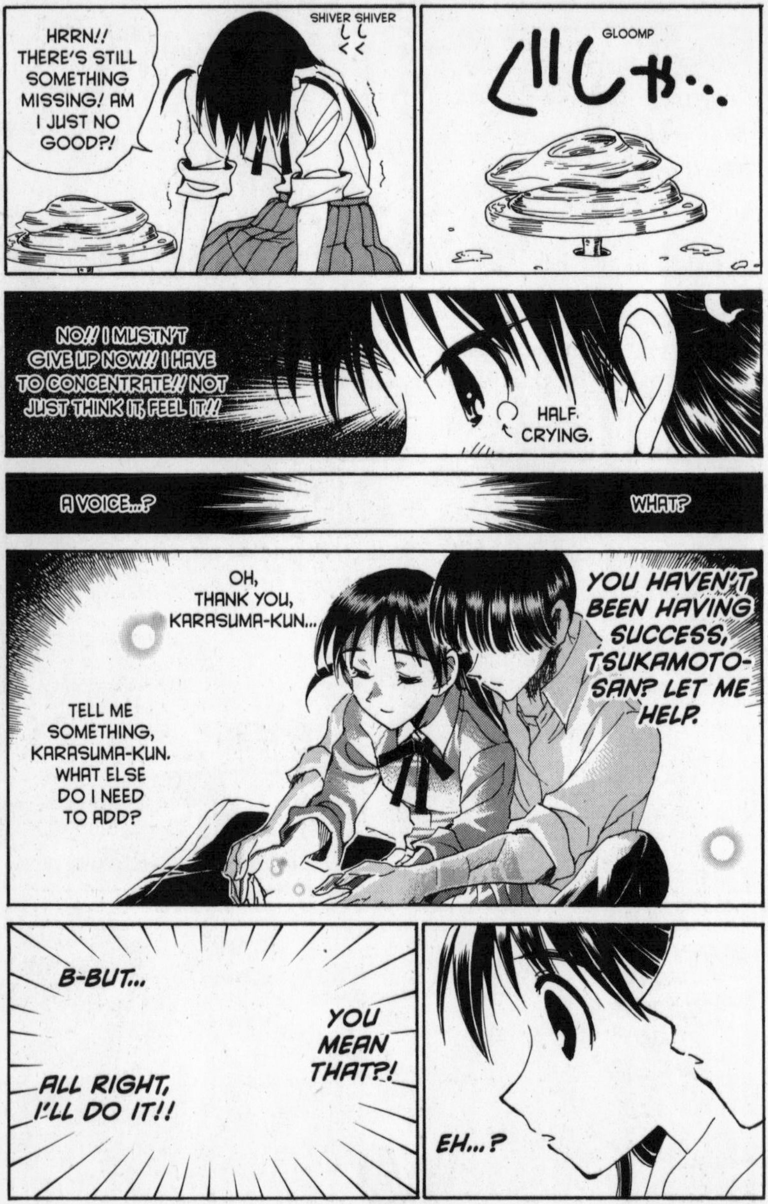
GLOOMP
ぐしゃ…
SHIVER SHIVER
HRRN!! THERE'S STILL SOMETHING MISSING! AM I JUST NO GOOD?!
NO!! I MUSTN'T GIVE UP NOW!! I HAVE TO CONCENTRATE!! NOT JUST THINK IT, FEEL IT!!
HALF CRYING.
WHAT?
A VOICE...?
YOU HAVEN'T BEEN HAVING SUCCESS, TSUKAMOTO-SAN? LET ME HELP.
OH, THANK YOU, KARASUMA-KUN...
TELL ME SOMETHING, KARASUMA-KUN. WHAT ELSE DO I NEED TO ADD?
EH...?
YOU MEAN THAT?!
B-BUT...
ALL RIGHT, I'LL DO IT!!

Karasuma Makes Things That Only True Ceramic Artists Can See…

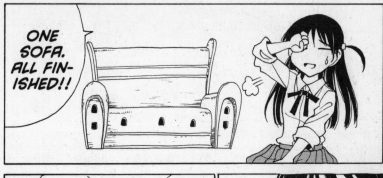

ONE SOFA. ALL FIN-ISHED!!
BUT... IS THIS WHAT I REALLY NEEDED?
....
HUH? THE NEXT THING YOU WANT IS THIS?
YEAH... YEAH... I CAN SEE HOW YOU MIGHT NEED IT.
I SHOULD HAVE EXPECTED THAT FROM YOU, KARASUMA-KUN!
YOU'RE KIDDING!! AREN'T WE GET-TING AHEAD OF OURSELVES?
BUT IF YOU SAY I SHOULD, THEN I'LL JUST HAVE TO TRY MY HARDEST!
NEE-SAN, IT'S 9 P.M. ALREADY...
カラ…
SHUMP
WE SHOULD BE GETTING HOME...
NOW, KARASUMA-KUN! SUPPER'S READY! EAT UP!

 # 135· · · · · · · · ·Fin

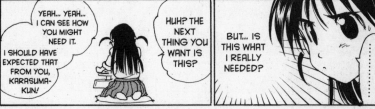

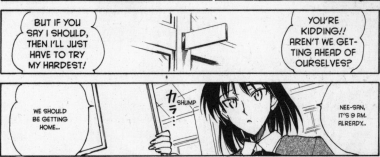

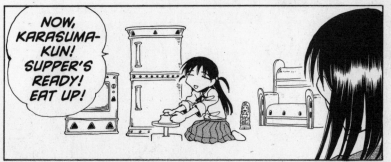

#136 THE GODS OF COOKERLY

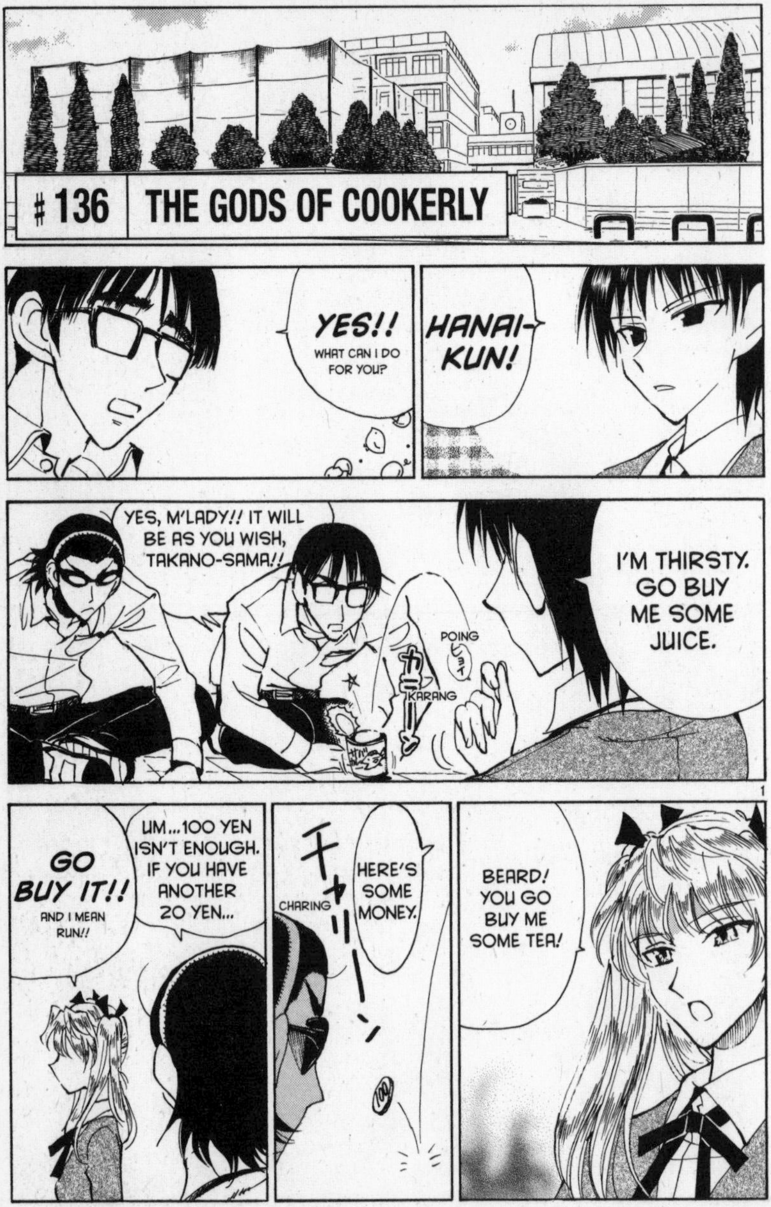
HANAI-KUN!
YES!! WHAT CAN I DO FOR YOU?
I'M THIRSTY. GO BUY ME SOME JUICE.
POING
KARANG
YES, M'LADY!! IT WILL BE AS YOU WISH, TAKANO-SAMA!!
BEARD! YOU GO BUY ME SOME TEA!
HERE'S SOME MONEY.
CHARING
UM...100 YEN ISN'T ENOUGH. IF YOU HAVE ANOTHER 20 YEN...
GO BUY IT!! AND I MEAN RUN!!

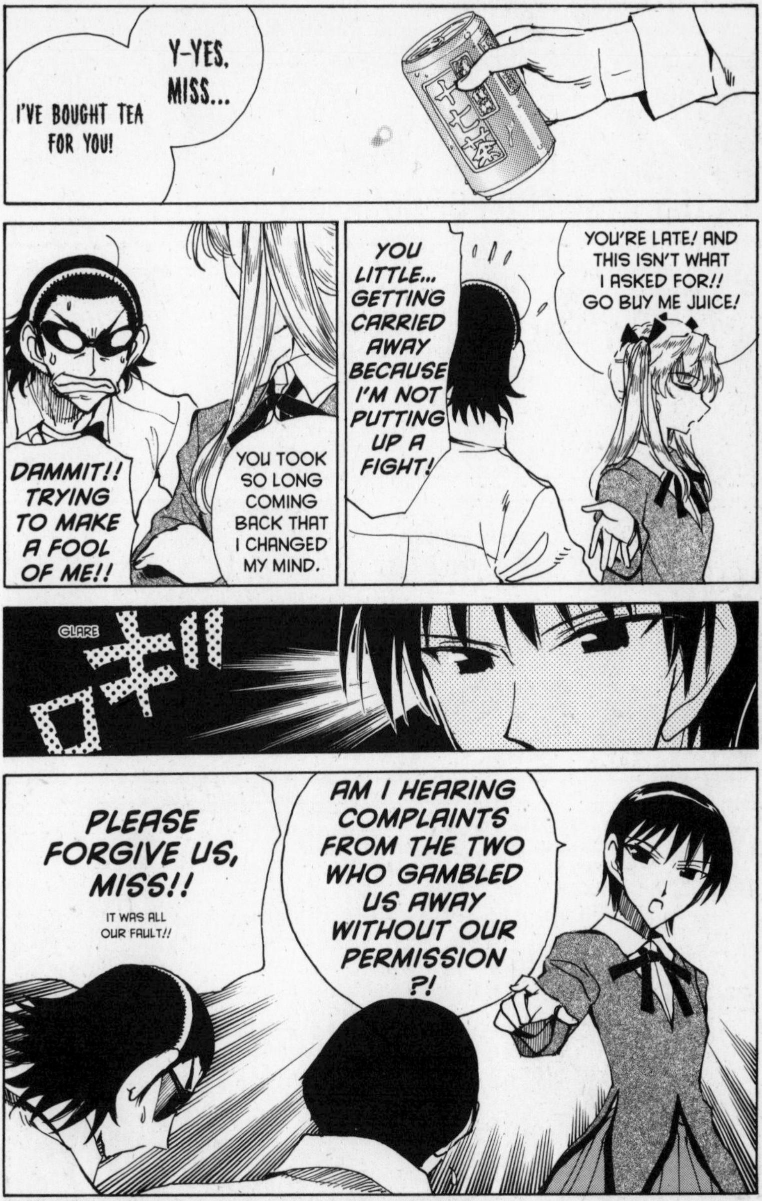
Y-YES, MISS...
I'VE BOUGHT TEA FOR YOU!
YOU'RE LATE! AND THIS ISN'T WHAT I ASKED FOR!! GO BUY ME JUICE!
YOU LITTLE... GETTING CARRIED AWAY BECAUSE I'M NOT PUTTING UP A FIGHT!
YOU TOOK SO LONG COMING BACK THAT I CHANGED MY MIND.
DAMMIT!! TRYING TO MAKE A FOOL OF ME!!
GLARE
AM I HEARING COMPLAINTS FROM THE TWO WHO GAMBLED US AWAY WITHOUT OUR PERMISSION?!
PLEASE FORGIVE US, MISS!!
IT WAS ALL OUR FAULT!!

Sister, You Are Seriously Scary.

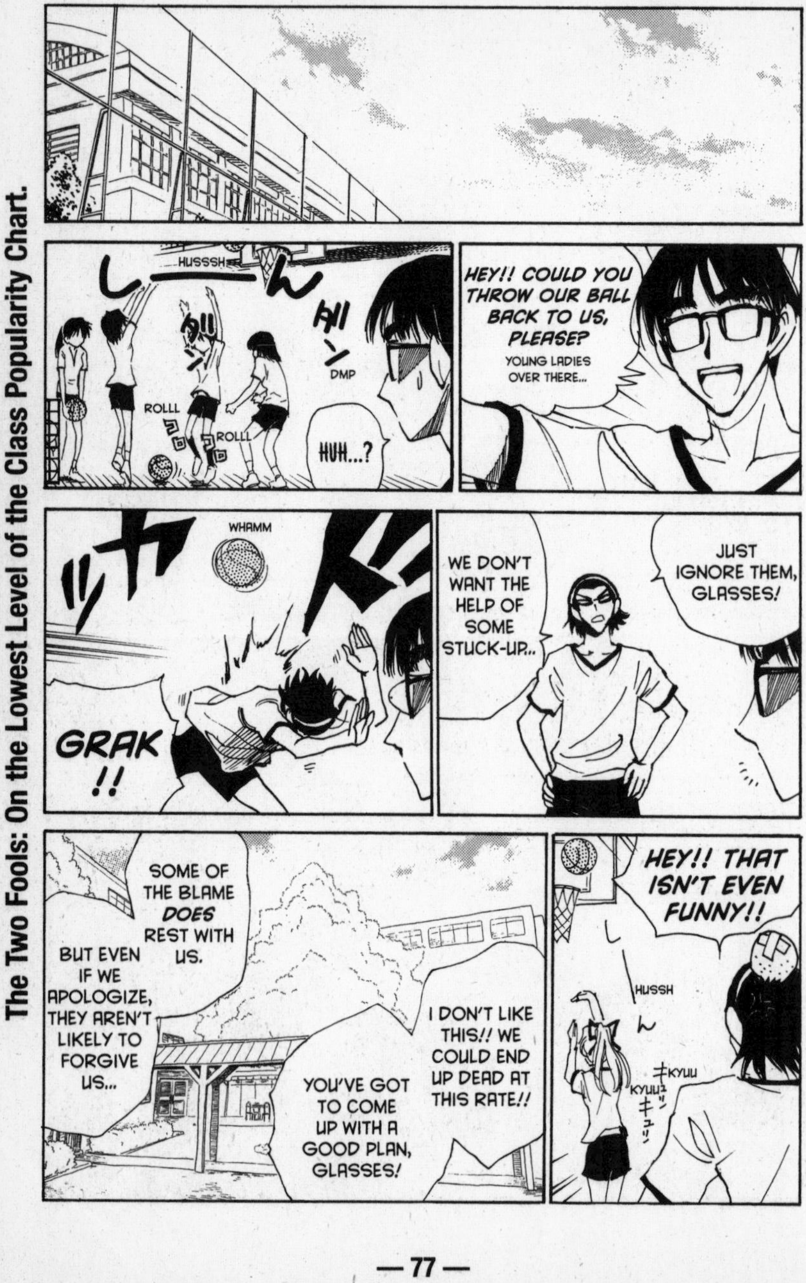
HEY!! COULD YOU THROW OUR BALL BACK TO US, PLEASE?
YOUNG LADIES OVER THERE...
HUSSSH
DMP
ROLLL
ROLLL
HUH...?
JUST IGNORE THEM, GLASSES!
WE DON'T WANT THE HELP OF SOME STUCK-UP...
WHAMM
GRAK!!
HEY!! THAT ISN'T EVEN FUNNY!!
HUSSH
KYUU
KYUU
SOME OF THE BLAME DOES REST WITH US.
BUT EVEN IF WE APOLOGIZE, THEY AREN'T LIKELY TO FORGIVE US...
I DON'T LIKE THIS!! WE COULD END UP DEAD AT THIS RATE!!
YOU'VE GOT TO COME UP WITH A GOOD PLAN, GLASSES!

Tsukamoto Tenma: Still Making Curryware for Karasuma. Just So You Know.

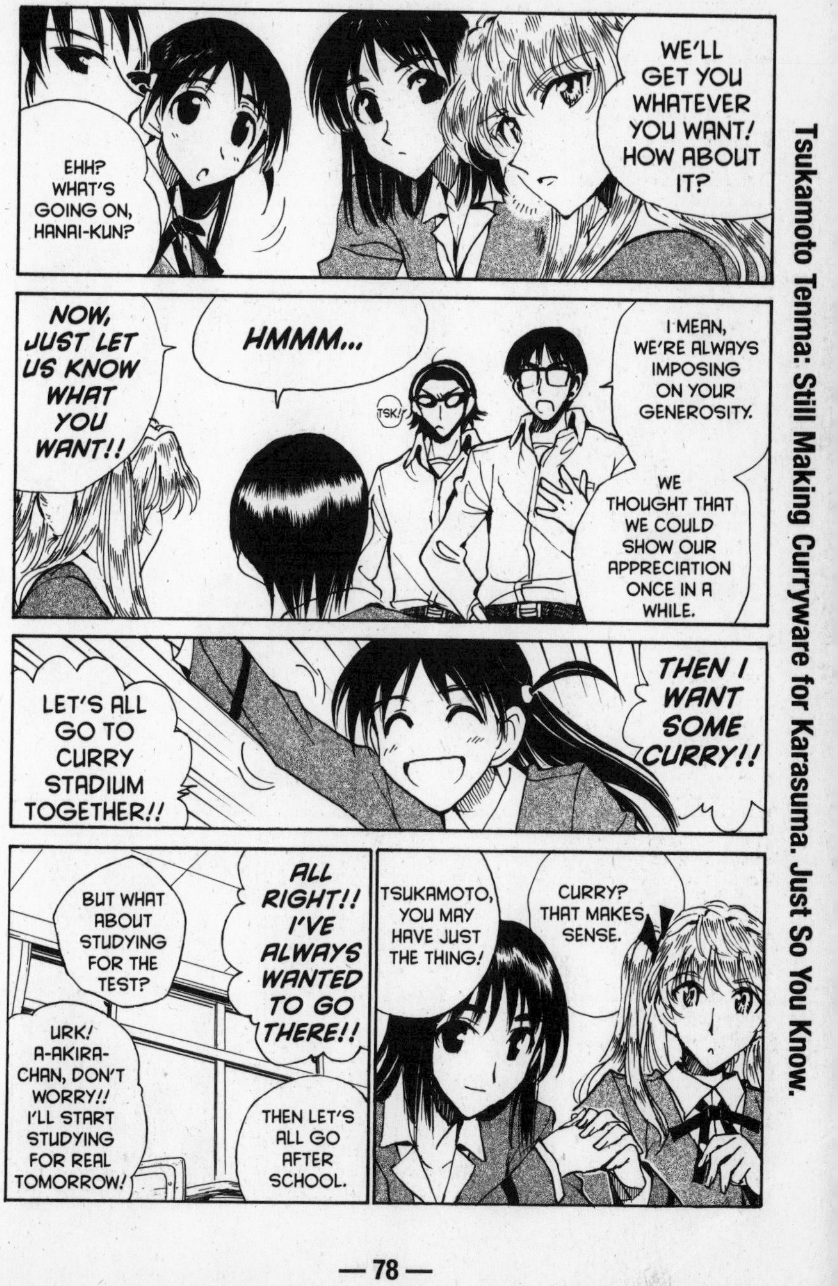
WE'LL GET YOU WHATEVER YOU WANT! HOW ABOUT IT?
EHH? WHAT'S GOING ON, HANAI-KUN?
I MEAN, WE'RE ALWAYS IMPOSING ON YOUR GENEROSITY.
WE THOUGHT THAT WE COULD SHOW OUR APPRECIATION ONCE IN A WHILE.
TSK!
HMMM...
NOW, JUST LET US KNOW WHAT YOU WANT!!
THEN I WANT SOME CURRY!!
LET'S ALL GO TO CURRY STADIUM TOGETHER!!
CURRY? THAT MAKES SENSE.
TSUKAMOTO, YOU MAY HAVE JUST THE THING!
ALL RIGHT!! I'VE ALWAYS WANTED TO GO THERE!!
BUT WHAT ABOUT STUDYING FOR THE TEST?
THEN LET'S ALL GO AFTER SCHOOL.
URK! A-AKIRA-CHAN, DON'T WORRY!! I'LL START STUDYING FOR REAL TOMORROW!

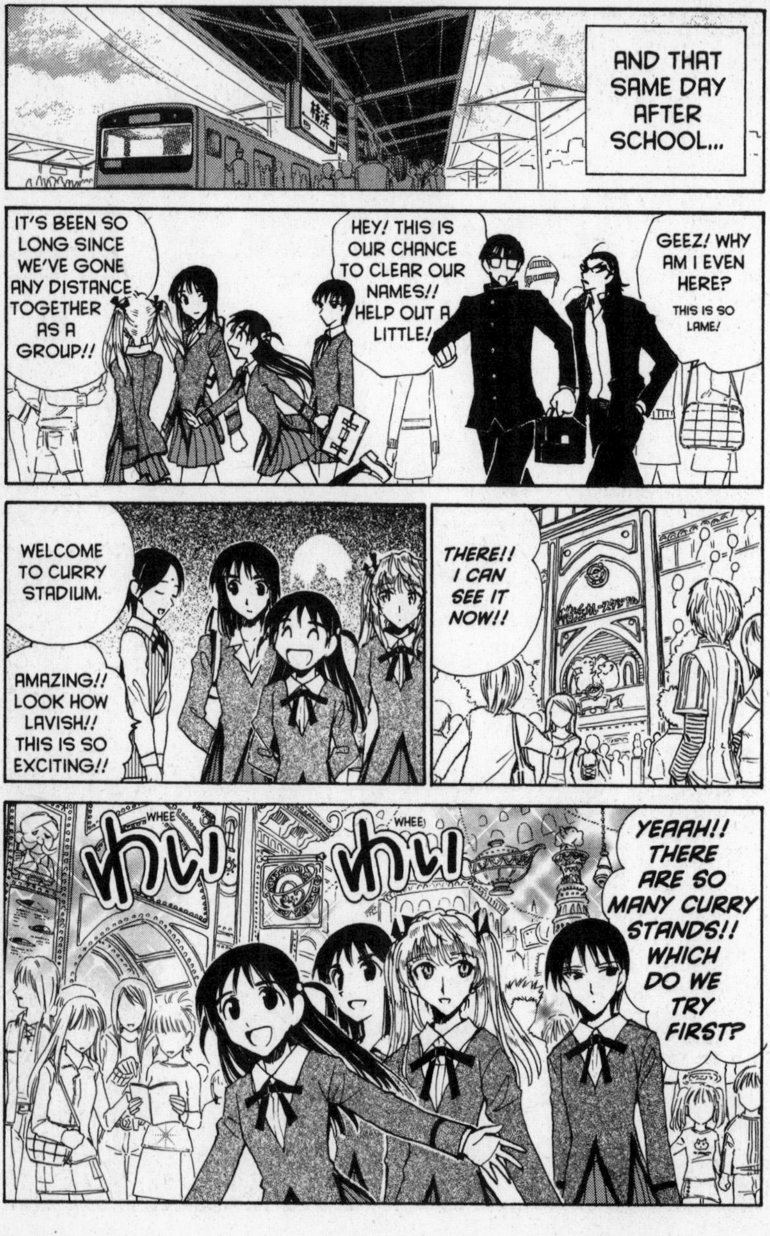
AND THAT SAME DAY AFTER SCHOOL...
GEEZ! WHY AM I EVEN HERE?
THIS IS SO LAME!
HEY! THIS IS OUR CHANCE TO CLEAR OUR NAMES!! HELP OUT A LITTLE!
IT'S BEEN SO LONG SINCE WE'VE GONE ANY DISTANCE TOGETHER AS A GROUP!!
THERE!! I CAN SEE IT NOW!!
WELCOME TO CURRY STADIUM.
AMAZING!! LOOK HOW LAVISH!! THIS IS SO EXCITING!!
YEAAH!! THERE ARE SO MANY CURRY STANDS!! WHICH DO WE TRY FIRST?
わい WHEE
わい WHEE

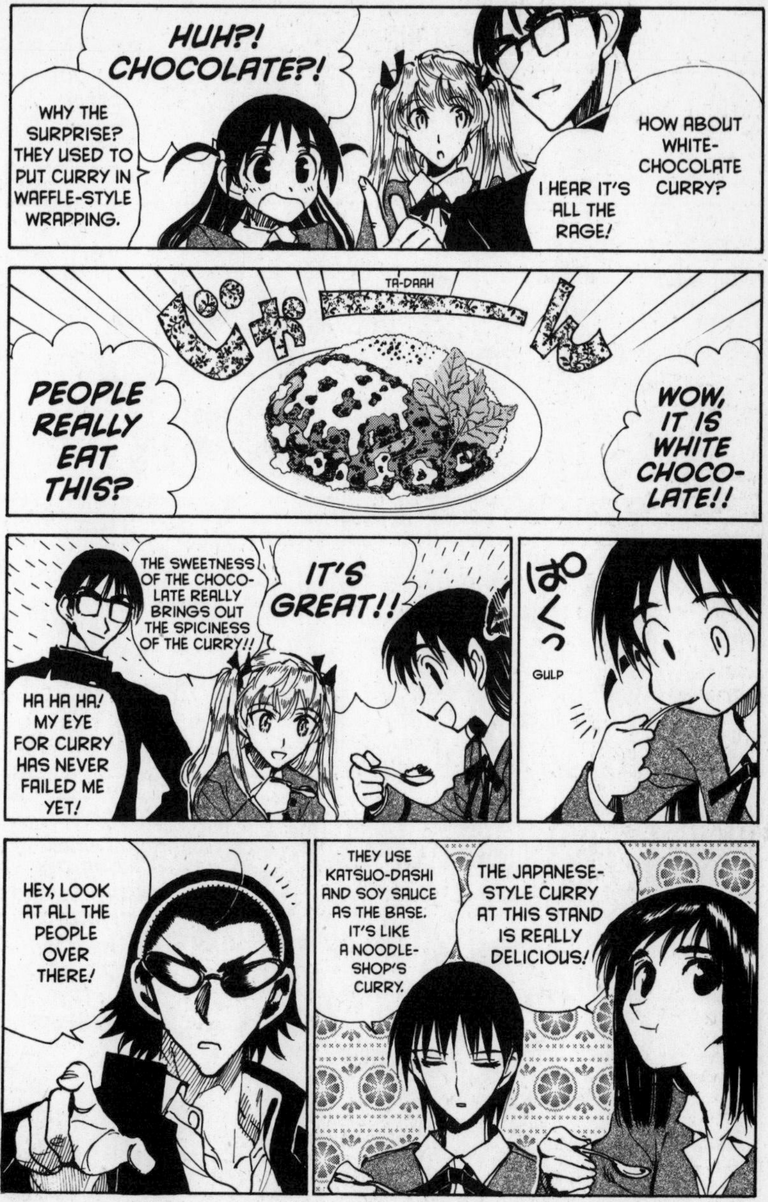
HOW ABOUT WHITE-CHOCOLATE CURRY?
I HEAR IT'S ALL THE RAGE!
HUH?! CHOCOLATE?!
WHY THE SURPRISE? THEY USED TO PUT CURRY IN WAFFLE-STYLE WRAPPING.
じゃーん
TA-DAAH
WOW, IT IS WHITE CHOCO-LATE!!
PEOPLE REALLY EAT THIS?
ぱくっ
GULP
IT'S GREAT!!
THE SWEETNESS OF THE CHOCO-LATE REALLY BRINGS OUT THE SPICINESS OF THE CURRY!!
HA HA HA! MY EYE FOR CURRY HAS NEVER FAILED ME YET!
THE JAPANESE-STYLE CURRY AT THIS STAND IS REALLY DELICIOUS!
THEY USE KATSUO-DASHI AND SOY SAUCE AS THE BASE. IT'S LIKE A NOODLE-SHOP'S CURRY.
HEY, LOOK AT ALL THE PEOPLE OVER THERE!

Hanai Haruki: Curry Professor.

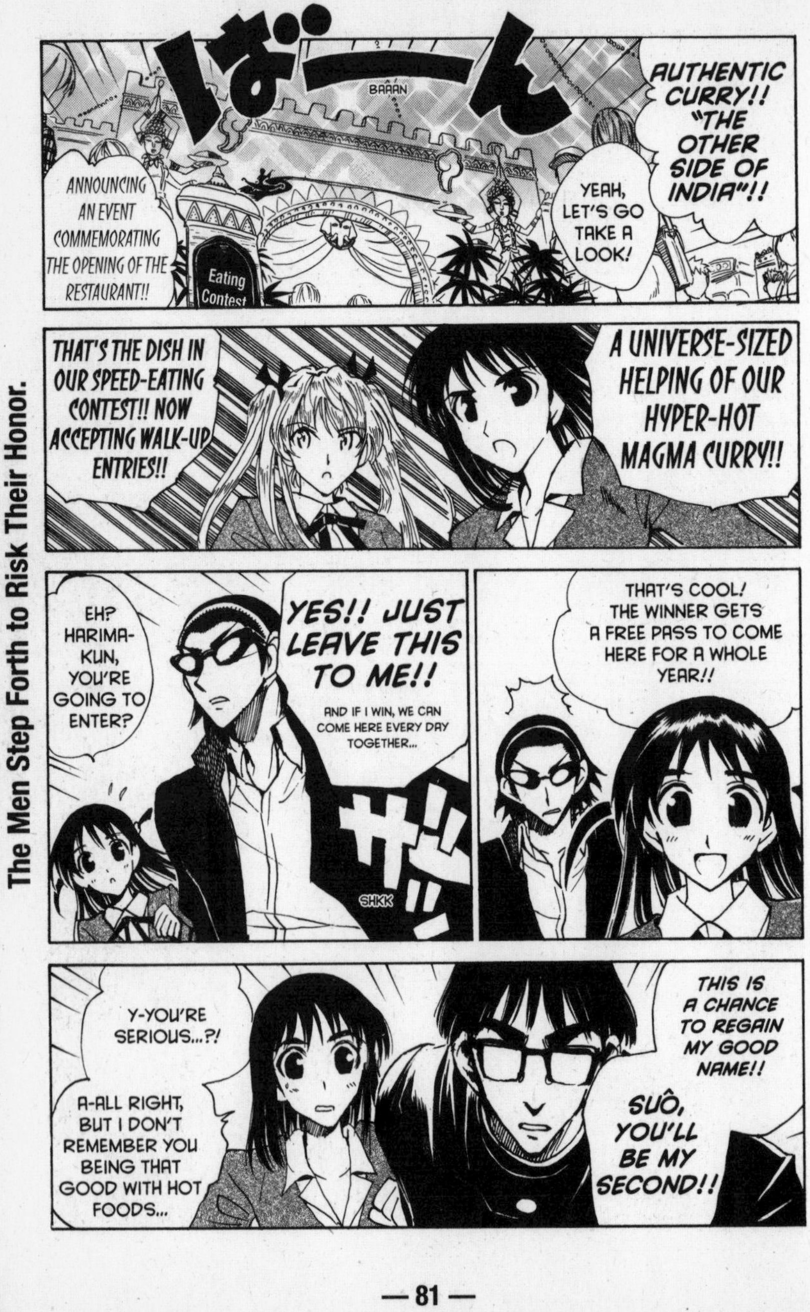
AUTHENTIC CURRY!! "THE OTHER SIDE OF INDIA"!!
YEAH, LET'S GO TAKE A LOOK!
BAAAN
ANNOUNCING AN EVENT COMMEMORATING THE OPENING OF THE RESTAURANT!!
Eating Contest
A UNIVERSE-SIZED HELPING OF OUR HYPER-HOT MAGMA CURRY!!
THAT'S THE DISH IN OUR SPEED-EATING CONTEST!! NOW ACCEPTING WALK-UP ENTRIES!!
THAT'S COOL! THE WINNER GETS A FREE PASS TO COME HERE FOR A WHOLE YEAR!!
YES!! JUST LEAVE THIS TO ME!!
AND IF I WIN, WE CAN COME HERE EVERY DAY TOGETHER...
EH? HARIMA-KUN, YOU'RE GOING TO ENTER?
SHKK
THIS IS A CHANCE TO REGAIN MY GOOD NAME!!
SUÔ, YOU'LL BE MY SECOND!!
Y-YOU'RE SERIOUS...?!
A-ALL RIGHT, BUT I DON'T REMEMBER YOU BEING THAT GOOD WITH HOT FOODS...

And So, Sister Stands In, Too.

VERY WELL. WE WILL ENTER ALSO.
GLEEM
ARE YOU SAYING THAT FOR REAL?
YOU DON'T STAND A CHANCE!! GIVE IT UP NOW!
THE RULES ARE SIMPLE. THE WINNER IS THE ONE WHO EATS THEIR BOWL OF CURRY THE FASTEST.
YOU ONLY GET ONE GLASS OF WATER TO PUT OUT THE FIRE.
Magma Curry Eating Contest
Eating
NOW, BEFORE EACH OF OUR BRAVE CURRY KNIGHTS IS A KILOGRAM-HEAVY, UNIVERSE-SIZED HELPING OF OUR HYPER-HOT MAGMA CURRY!!
READY... START!!
GOBBLE!!
GOBBLE
GOBBLE
URK...!!
AAAGGH!! THAT'S TOO HOT!!
WHOA! THAT WAS QUICK!! ONE CONTESTANT IS OUT ALREADY!!
GULP! GULP! I THINK I'M GONNA DIE!!

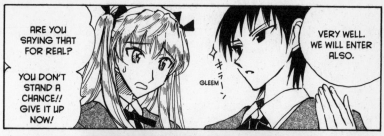

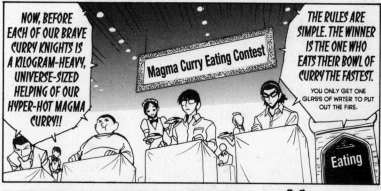

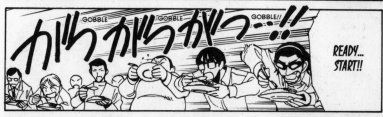

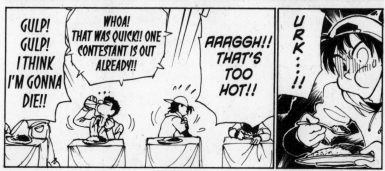

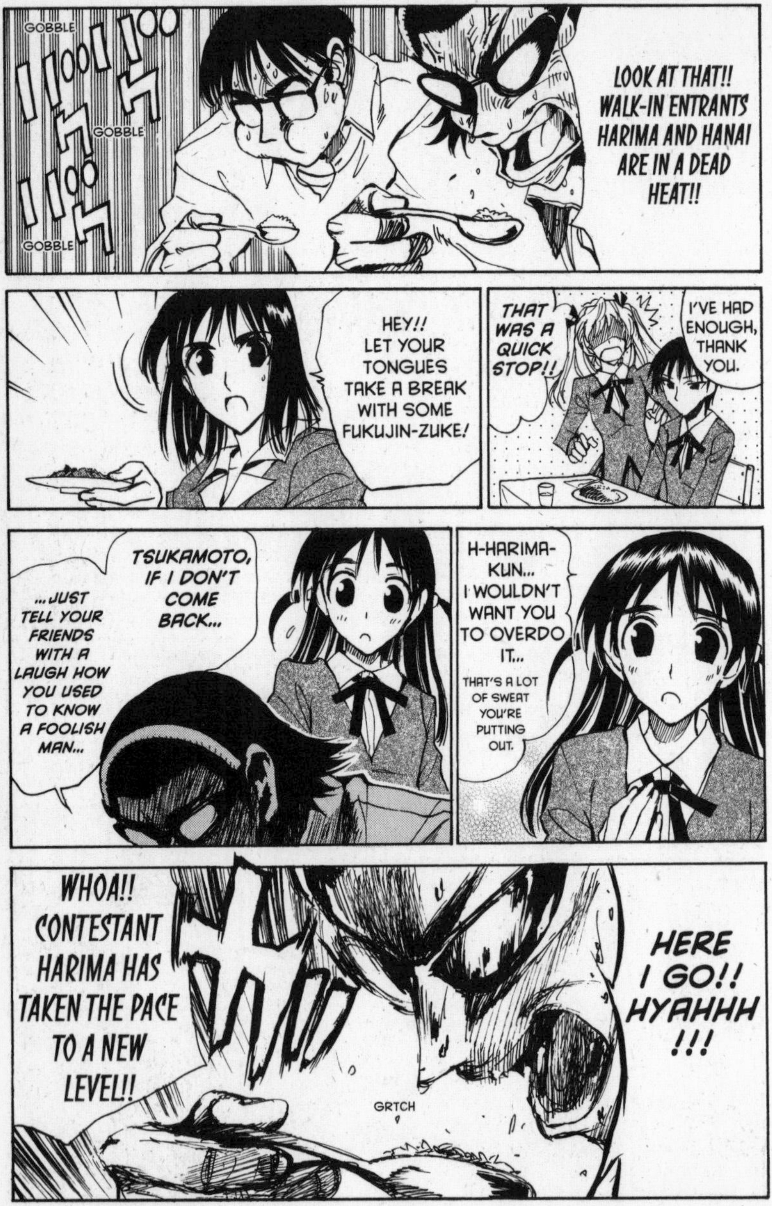
LOOK AT THAT!! WALK-IN ENTRANTS HARIMA AND HANAI ARE IN A DEAD HEAT!!
GOBBLE
GOBBLE
GOBBLE
I'VE HAD ENOUGH, THANK YOU.
THAT WAS A QUICK STOP!!
HEY!! LET YOUR TONGUES TAKE A BREAK WITH SOME FUKUJIN-ZUKE!
H-HARIMA-KUN... I WOULDN'T WANT YOU TO OVERDO IT...
THAT'S A LOT OF SWEAT YOU'RE PUTTING OUT.
TSUKAMOTO, IF I DON'T COME BACK...
...JUST TELL YOUR FRIENDS WITH A LAUGH HOW YOU USED TO KNOW A FOOLISH MAN...
HERE I GO!! HYAHHH!!!
WHOA!! CONTESTANT HARIMA HAS TAKEN THE PACE TO A NEW LEVEL!!
GRTCH

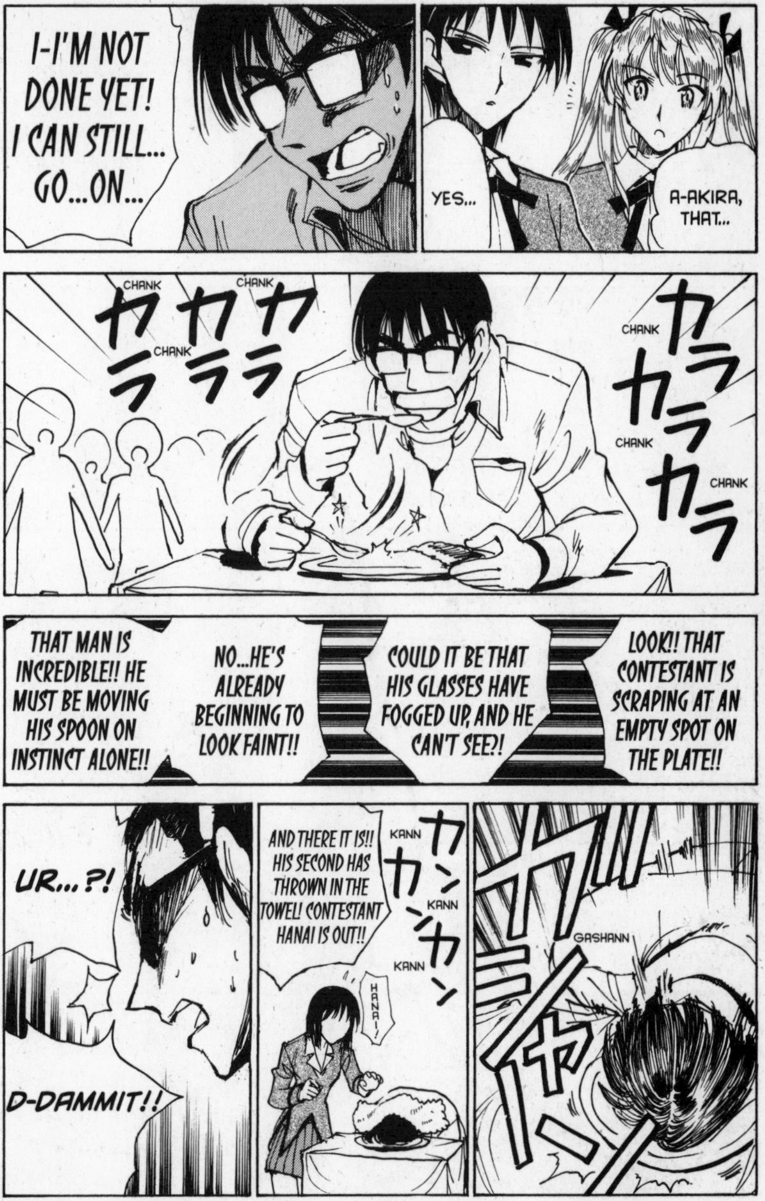
A-AKIRA, THAT...
YES...
I-I'M NOT DONE YET! I CAN STILL... GO...ON...
カラカラカラ
CHANK
CHANK
CHANK
カラ
CHANK
カラ
CHANK
カラ
CHANK
LOOK!! THAT CONTESTANT IS SCRAPING AT AN EMPTY SPOT ON THE PLATE!!
COULD IT BE THAT HIS GLASSES HAVE FOGGED UP, AND HE CAN'T SEE?!
NO...HE'S ALREADY BEGINNING TO LOOK FAINT!!
THAT MAN IS INCREDIBLE!! HE MUST BE MOVING HIS SPOON ON INSTINCT ALONE!!
ガシャーン
GASHANN
カンカンカン
KANN
KANN
KANN
AND THERE IT IS!! HIS SECOND HAS THROWN IN THE TOWEL! CONTESTANT HANAI IS OUT!!
HANAI!
UR...?!
D-DAMMIT!!

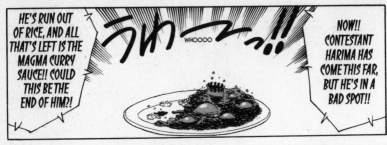

The Man Does Not Fear Death.

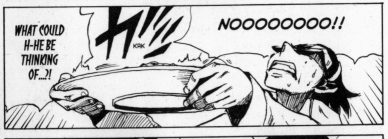

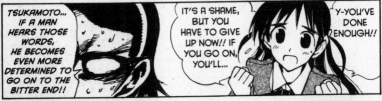

NOW!! CONTESTANT HARIMA HAS COME THIS FAR, BUT HE'S IN A BAD SPOT!!
WHOOOO
HE'S RUN OUT OF RICE, AND ALL THAT'S LEFT IS THE MAGMA CURRY SAUCE!! COULD THIS BE THE END OF HIM?!
NOOOOOOOO!!
KAK
WHAT COULD H-HE BE THINKING OF...?!
Y-YOU'VE DONE ENOUGH!!
IT'S A SHAME, BUT YOU HAVE TO GIVE UP NOW!! IF YOU GO ON, YOU'LL...
TSUKAMOTO... IF A MAN HEARS THOSE WORDS, HE BECOMES EVEN MORE DETERMINED TO GO ON TO THE BITTER END!!
GWAA
OOOOHH!! HE DOWNED IT!!
GWAAAA-GGGHHH!!
RISKING HIS VERY LIFE, HE'S DIVING INTO THE MAGMA WITH ONE BIG GULP!!
THAT DID IT! NOW, ALL I HAVE TO DO IS SWALLOW, AND...

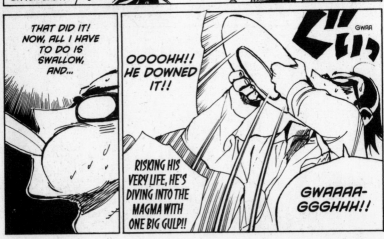

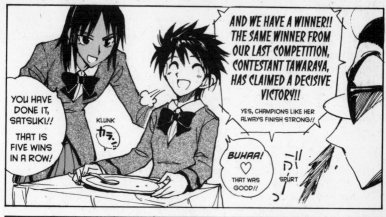

AND WE HAVE A WINNER!! THE SAME WINNER FROM OUR LAST COMPETITION, CONTESTANT TAWARAYA, HAS CLAIMED A DECISIVE VICTORY!!
YES, CHAMPIONS LIKE HER ALWAYS FINISH STRONG!!
SPURT
BUHAA! ♡ THAT WAS GOOD!!
KLUNK
YOU HAVE DONE IT, SATSUKI!!
THAT IS FIVE WINS IN A ROW!
SEMPAI! WHAT ARE YOU ALL DOING HERE?
HUMPH! IF IT ISN'T MIKO-CHIN.
U-UM... WE JUST CAME FOR THE CURRY...
THAT WAS AMAZING...
MY NOSE!! MY NOSE!!
ARE YOU ALL RIGHT, HARIMA-KUN? WE FORCED YOU TO DO ALL THAT FOR NOTHING.
N-NO!! I KNOW THAT I WAS THE REAL WINNER, BUT I LET MY KÔHAI TAKE THE PRIZE.
THAT'S AMAZING!! SO YOU'RE GOING TO WIN THE NEXT COMPETITION?!
EH? TSUKAMOTO... LET'S DO SOME OTHER KIND OF FOOD NEXT TIME...
HEY, HARIMA!! COME HELP ME CARRY HANAI!!
HE'S TOO BIG FOR ONE PERSON TO CARRY!

The Setting Sun Takes a Curry-colored Hue.

136· · · · · · · · ·Fin

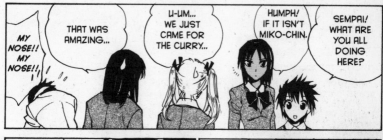

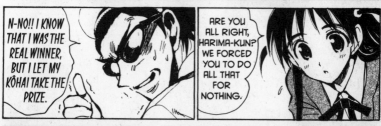

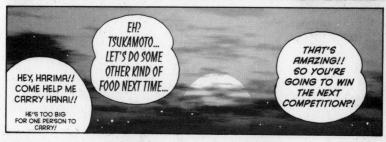

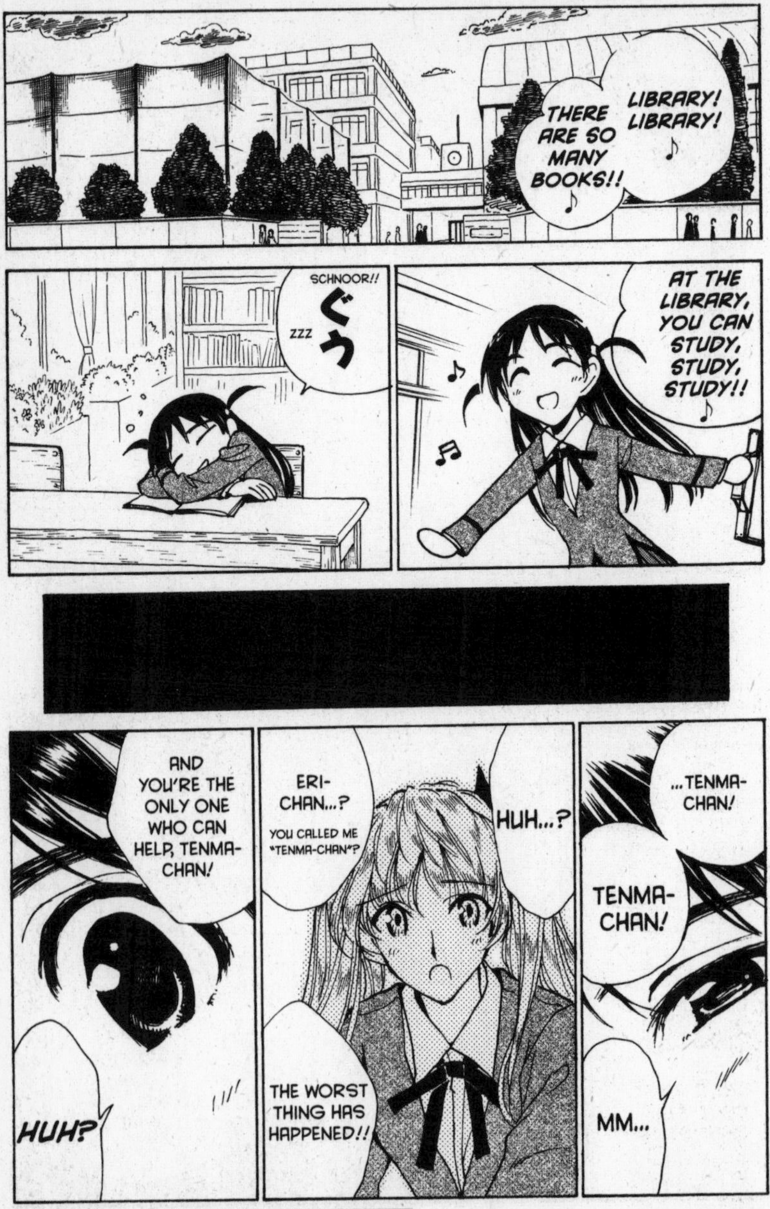
LIBRARY! LIBRARY! ♪
THERE ARE SO MANY BOOKS!! ♪
AT THE LIBRARY, YOU CAN STUDY, STUDY, STUDY!! ♪
SCHNOOR!! ぐぅ ZZZ
[redacted]
...TENMA-CHAN!
TENMA-CHAN!
MM...
HUH...?
ERI-CHAN...?
YOU CALLED ME "TENMA-CHAN"?
THE WORST THING HAS HAPPENED!!
AND YOU'RE THE ONLY ONE WHO CAN HELP, TENMA-CHAN!
HUH?

#137 IF THE SHOE FITS

For Some Reason, Tsukamoto Tenma Is Now 165 cm (5' 5").

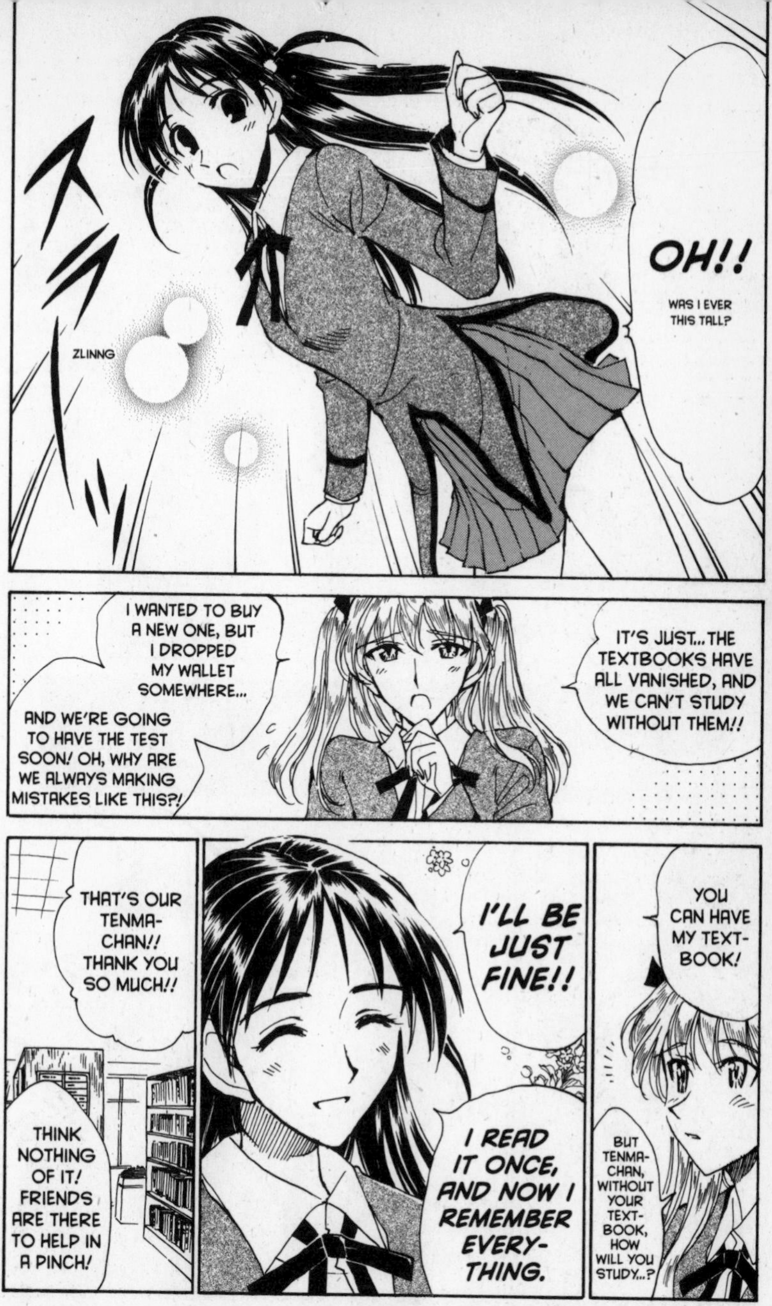
OH!!
WAS I EVER THIS TALL?
ZLINNG
IT'S JUST...THE TEXTBOOKS HAVE ALL VANISHED, AND WE CAN'T STUDY WITHOUT THEM!!
I WANTED TO BUY A NEW ONE, BUT I DROPPED MY WALLET SOMEWHERE...
AND WE'RE GOING TO HAVE THE TEST SOON! OH, WHY ARE WE ALWAYS MAKING MISTAKES LIKE THIS?!
YOU CAN HAVE MY TEXT-BOOK!
BUT TENMA-CHAN, WITHOUT YOUR TEXT-BOOK, HOW WILL YOU STUDY...?
I'LL BE JUST FINE!!
I READ IT ONCE, AND NOW I REMEMBER EVERY-THING.
THAT'S OUR TENMA-CHAN!! THANK YOU SO MUCH!!
THINK NOTHING OF IT! FRIENDS ARE THERE TO HELP IN A PINCH!

For Some Reason, Tsukamoto Tenma's IQ Is Now 165.

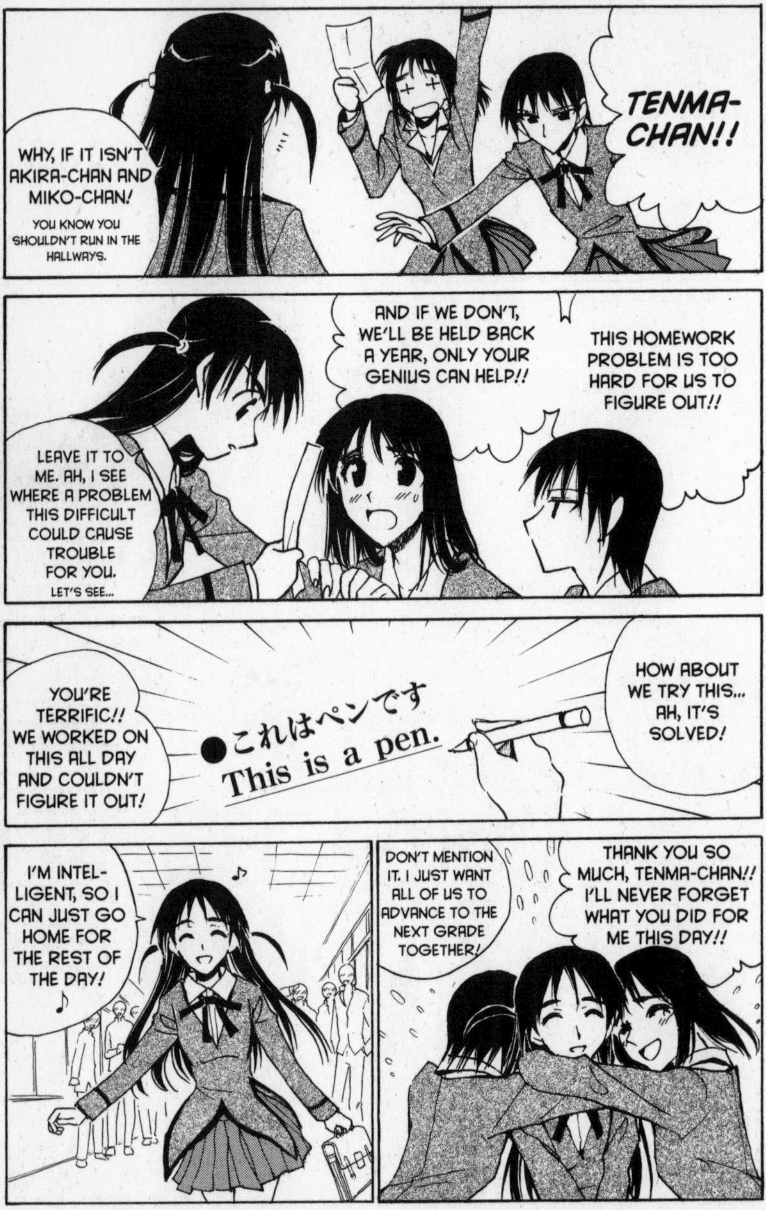
TENMA-CHAN!!
WHY, IF IT ISN'T AKIRA-CHAN AND MIKO-CHAN!
YOU KNOW YOU SHOULDN'T RUN IN THE HALLWAYS.
THIS HOMEWORK PROBLEM IS TOO HARD FOR US TO FIGURE OUT!!
AND IF WE DON'T, WE'LL BE HELD BACK A YEAR, ONLY YOUR GENIUS CAN HELP!!
LEAVE IT TO ME. AH, I SEE WHERE A PROBLEM THIS DIFFICULT COULD CAUSE TROUBLE FOR YOU.
LET'S SEE...
HOW ABOUT WE TRY THIS... AH, IT'S SOLVED!
●これはペンです
This is a pen.
YOU'RE TERRIFIC!! WE WORKED ON THIS ALL DAY AND COULDN'T FIGURE IT OUT!
THANK YOU SO MUCH, TENMA-CHAN!! I'LL NEVER FORGET WHAT YOU DID FOR ME THIS DAY!!
DON'T MENTION IT. I JUST WANT ALL OF US TO ADVANCE TO THE NEXT GRADE TOGETHER!
I'M INTEL-LIGENT, SO I CAN JUST GO HOME FOR THE REST OF THE DAY!

For Some Reason, Tsukamoto Tenma Has Turned Down 165 Talent Scouts.

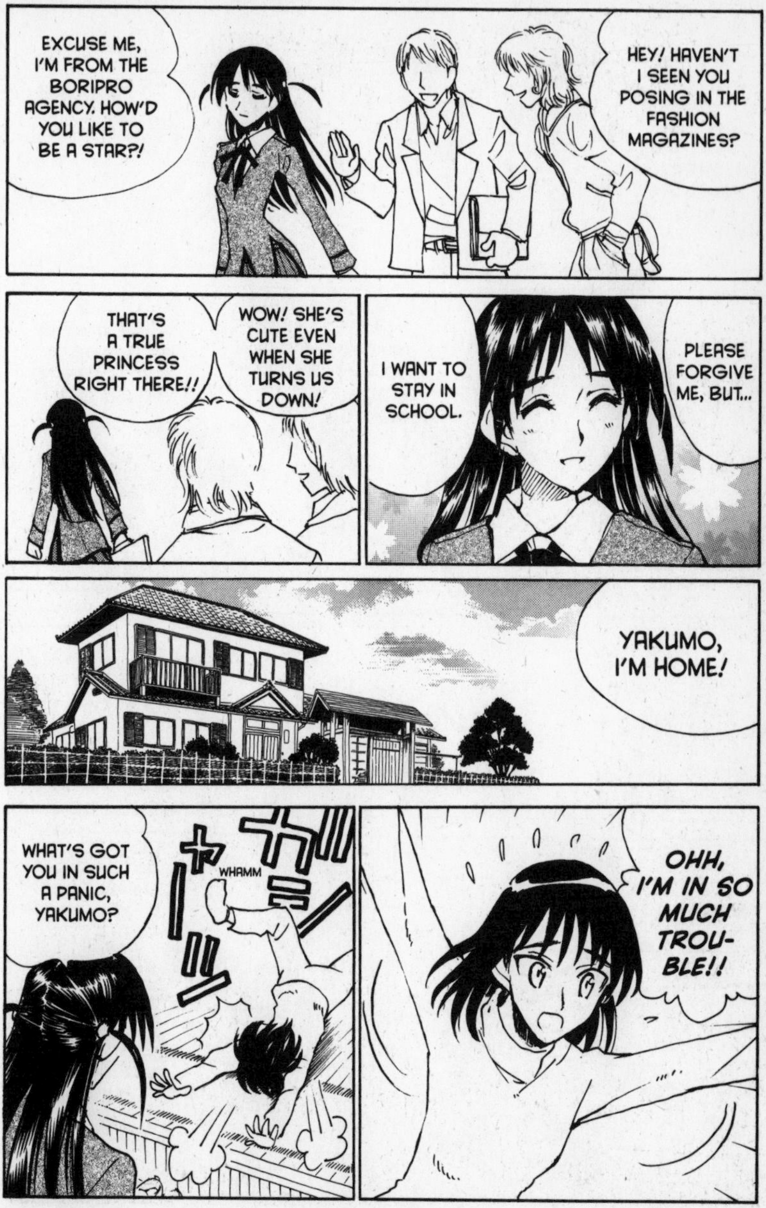
HEY! HAVEN'T I SEEN YOU POSING IN THE FASHION MAGAZINES?
EXCUSE ME, I'M FROM THE BORIPRO AGENCY. HOW'D YOU LIKE TO BE A STAR?!
PLEASE FORGIVE ME, BUT...
I WANT TO STAY IN SCHOOL.
WOW! SHE'S CUTE EVEN WHEN SHE TURNS US DOWN!
THAT'S A TRUE PRINCESS RIGHT THERE!!
YAKUMO, I'M HOME!
OHH, I'M IN SO MUCH TROU-BLE!!
WHAMM
WHAT'S GOT YOU IN SUCH A PANIC, YAKUMO?

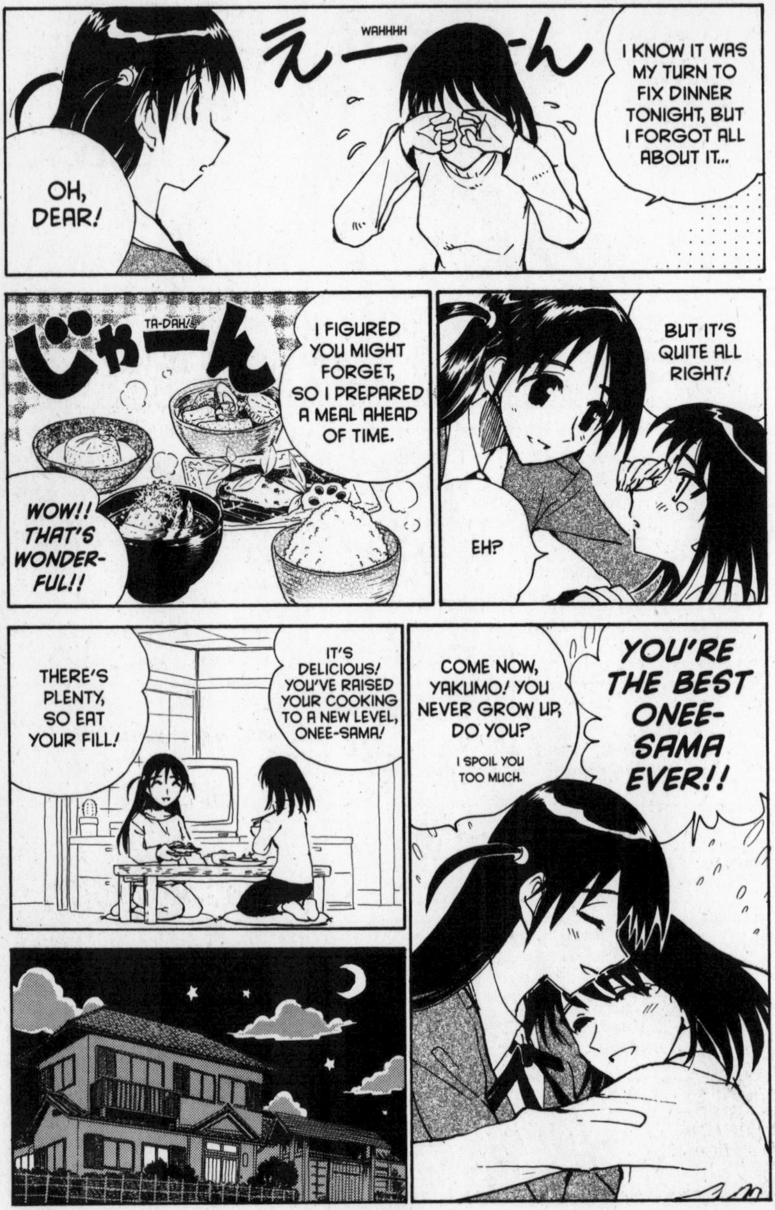
I KNOW IT WAS MY TURN TO FIX DINNER TONIGHT, BUT I FORGOT ALL ABOUT IT...
えーん
WAHHHH
OH, DEAR!
BUT IT'S QUITE ALL RIGHT!
EH?
I FIGURED YOU MIGHT FORGET, SO I PREPARED A MEAL AHEAD OF TIME.
じゃーん
TA-DAH!
WOW!! THAT'S WONDERFUL!!
YOU'RE THE BEST ONEE-SAMA EVER!!
COME NOW, YAKUMO! YOU NEVER GROW UP, DO YOU?
I SPOIL YOU TOO MUCH.
IT'S DELICIOUS! YOU'VE RAISED YOUR COOKING TO A NEW LEVEL, ONEE-SAMA!
THERE'S PLENTY, SO EAT YOUR FILL!

The Entire Town Is Enslaved by Her Charms.

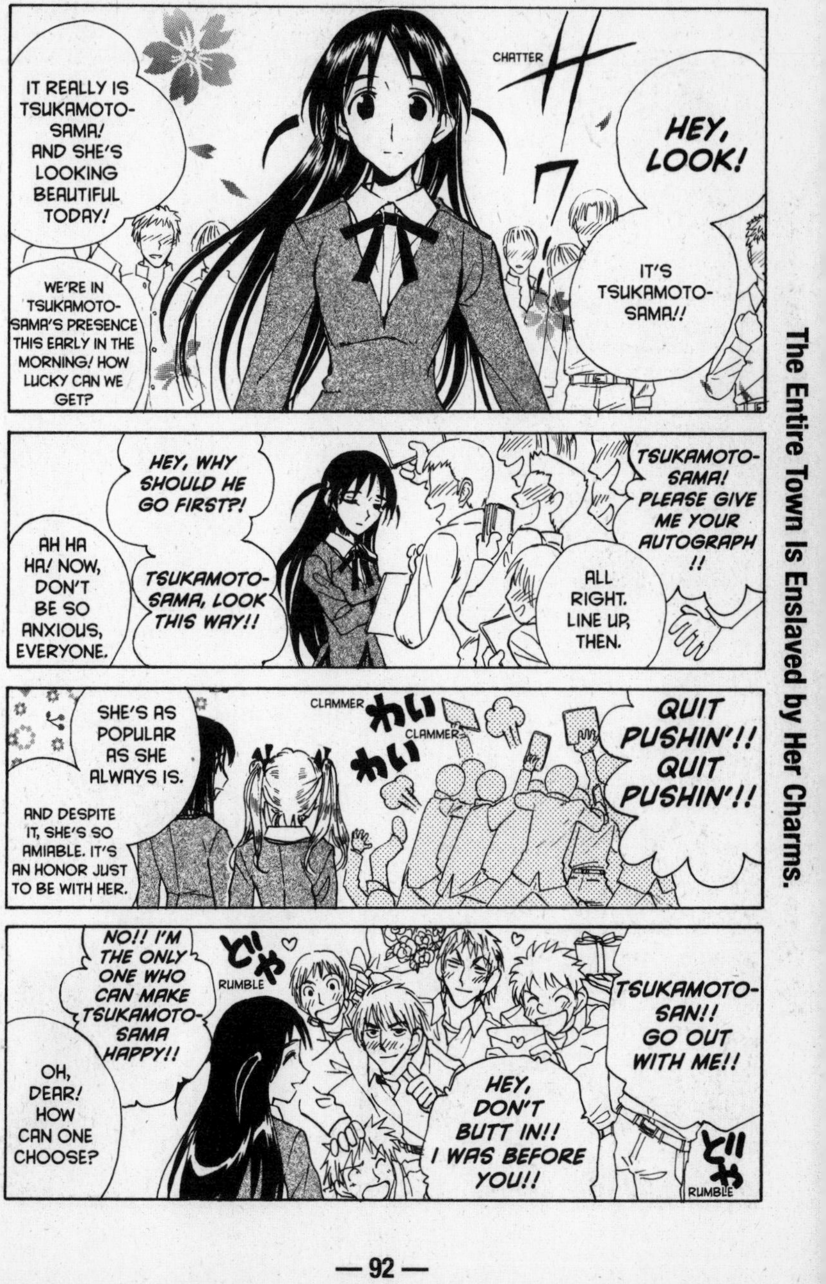
CHATTER
HEY, LOOK!
IT'S TSUKAMOTO-SAMA!!
IT REALLY IS TSUKAMOTO-SAMA! AND SHE'S LOOKING BEAUTIFUL TODAY!
WE'RE IN TSUKAMOTO-SAMA'S PRESENCE THIS EARLY IN THE MORNING! HOW LUCKY CAN WE GET?
TSUKAMOTO-SAMA! PLEASE GIVE ME YOUR AUTOGRAPH!!
ALL RIGHT. LINE UP, THEN.
HEY, WHY SHOULD HE GO FIRST?!
TSUKAMOTO-SAMA, LOOK THIS WAY!!
AH HA HA! NOW, DON'T BE SO ANXIOUS, EVERYONE.
QUIT PUSHIN'!! QUIT PUSHIN'!!
わい CLAMMER
わい CLAMMER
SHE'S AS POPULAR AS SHE ALWAYS IS.
AND DESPITE IT, SHE'S SO AMIABLE. IT'S AN HONOR JUST TO BE WITH HER.
どりゃ RUMBLE
TSUKAMOTO-SAN!! GO OUT WITH ME!!
HEY, DON'T BUTT IN!! I WAS BEFORE YOU!!
どりゃ RUMBLE
NO!! I'M THE ONLY ONE WHO CAN MAKE TSUKAMOTO-SAMA HAPPY!!
OH, DEAR! HOW CAN ONE CHOOSE?

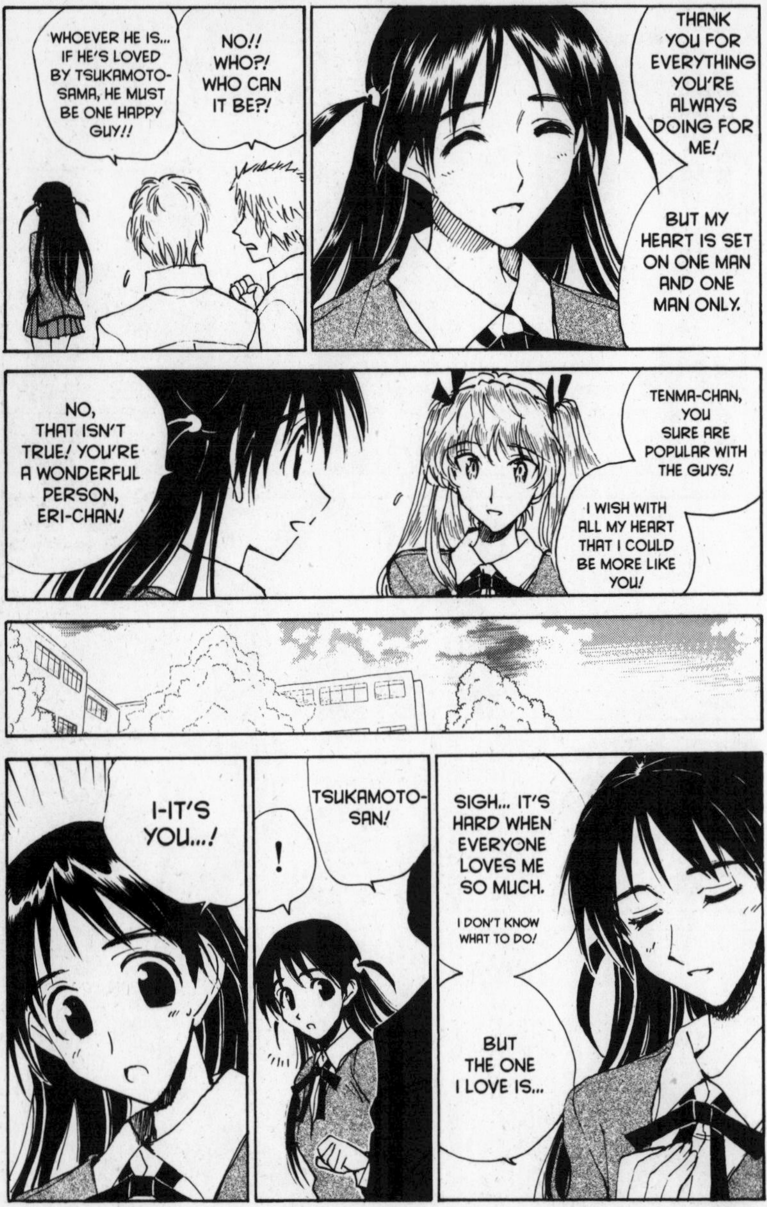
THANK YOU FOR EVERYTHING YOU'RE ALWAYS DOING FOR ME!
BUT MY HEART IS SET ON ONE MAN AND ONE MAN ONLY.
NO!! WHO?! WHO CAN IT BE?!
WHOEVER HE IS... IF HE'S LOVED BY TSUKAMOTO-SAMA, HE MUST BE ONE HAPPY GUY!!
TENMA-CHAN, YOU SURE ARE POPULAR WITH THE GUYS!
I WISH WITH ALL MY HEART THAT I COULD BE MORE LIKE YOU!
NO, THAT ISN'T TRUE! YOU'RE A WONDERFUL PERSON, ERI-CHAN!
SIGH... IT'S HARD WHEN EVERYONE LOVES ME SO MUCH.
I DON'T KNOW WHAT TO DO!
BUT THE ONE I LOVE IS...
TSUKAMOTO-SAN!
!
I-IT'S YOU...!

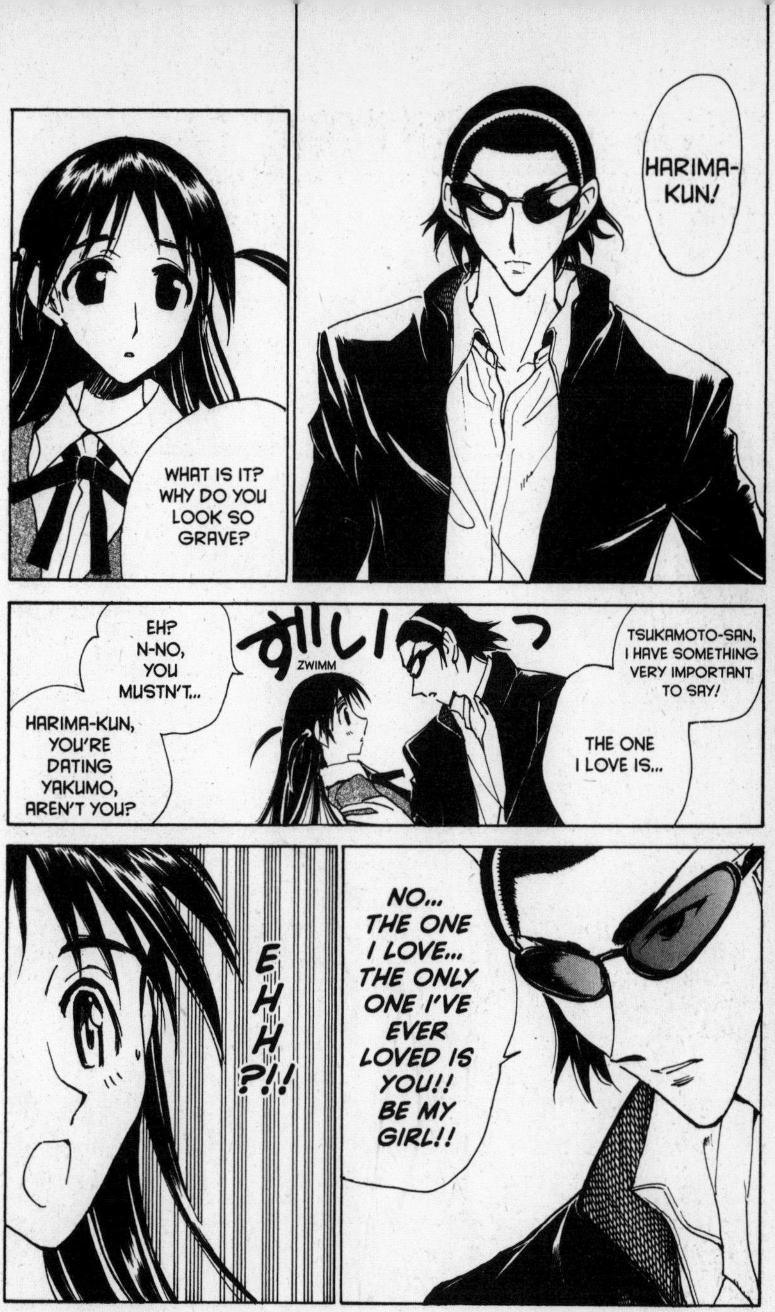
HARIMA-KUN!
WHAT IS IT? WHY DO YOU LOOK SO GRAVE?
TSUKAMOTO-SAN, I HAVE SOMETHING VERY IMPORTANT TO SAY!
THE ONE I LOVE IS...
ZWIMM
EH? N-NO, YOU MUSTN'T...
HARIMA-KUN, YOU'RE DATING YAKUMO, AREN'T YOU?
NO... THE ONE I LOVE... THE ONLY ONE I'VE EVER LOVED IS YOU!! BE MY GIRL!!
EHH?!!

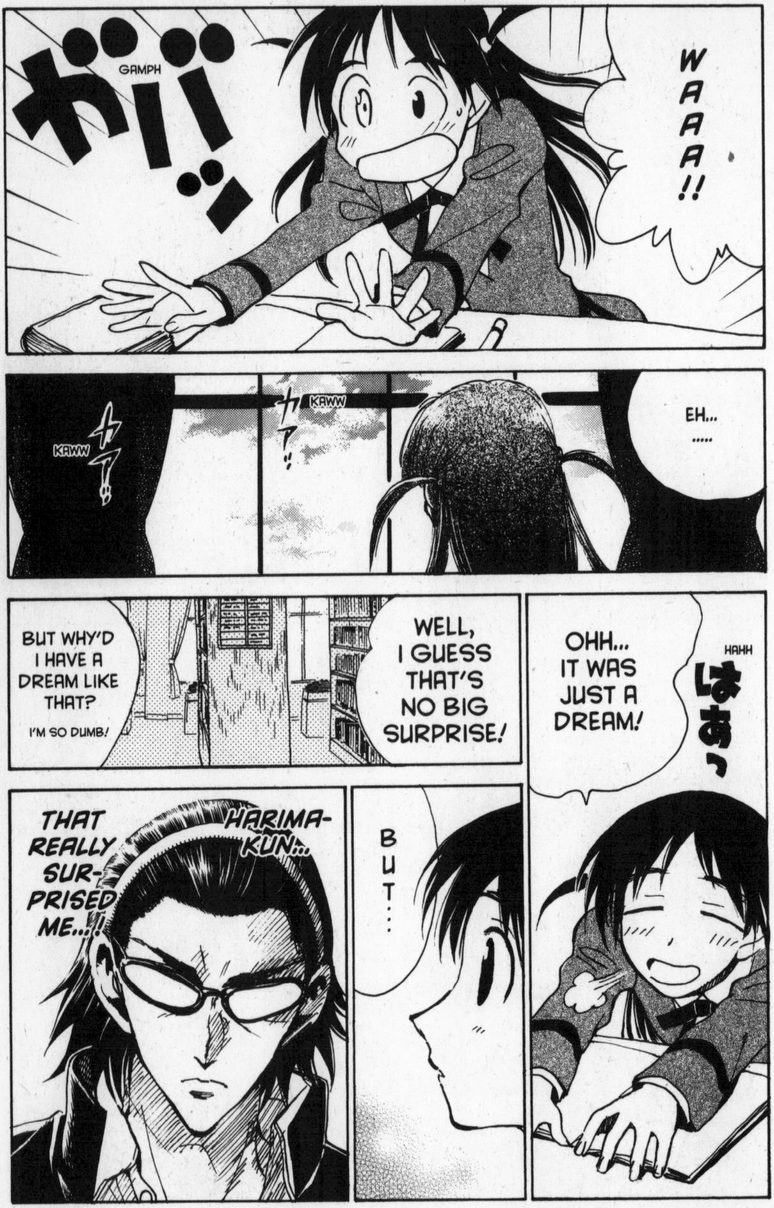
WAAAA!!
GAMPH
EH...
.....
KAWW
KAWW
HAHH
OHH... IT WAS JUST A DREAM!
WELL, I GUESS THAT'S NO BIG SURPRISE!
BUT WHY'D I HAVE A DREAM LIKE THAT?
I'M SO DUMB!
BUT...
HARIMA-KUN...
THAT REALLY SURPRISED ME...!

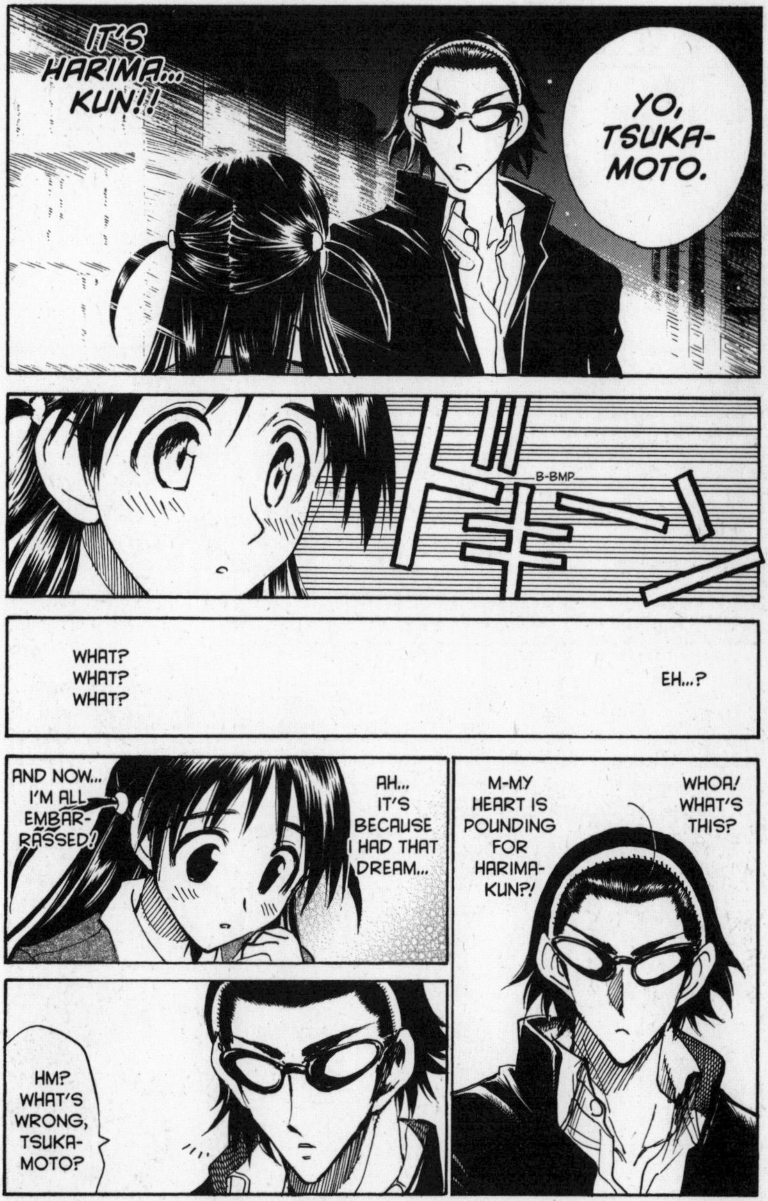
YO, TSUKA-MOTO.
IT'S HARIMA... KUN!!
B-BMP
EH...?
WHAT? WHAT? WHAT?
WHOA! WHAT'S THIS?
M-MY HEART IS POUNDING FOR HARIMA-KUN?!
AH... IT'S BECAUSE I HAD THAT DREAM...
AND NOW... I'M ALL EMBAR-RASSED!
HM? WHAT'S WRONG, TSUKA-MOTO?

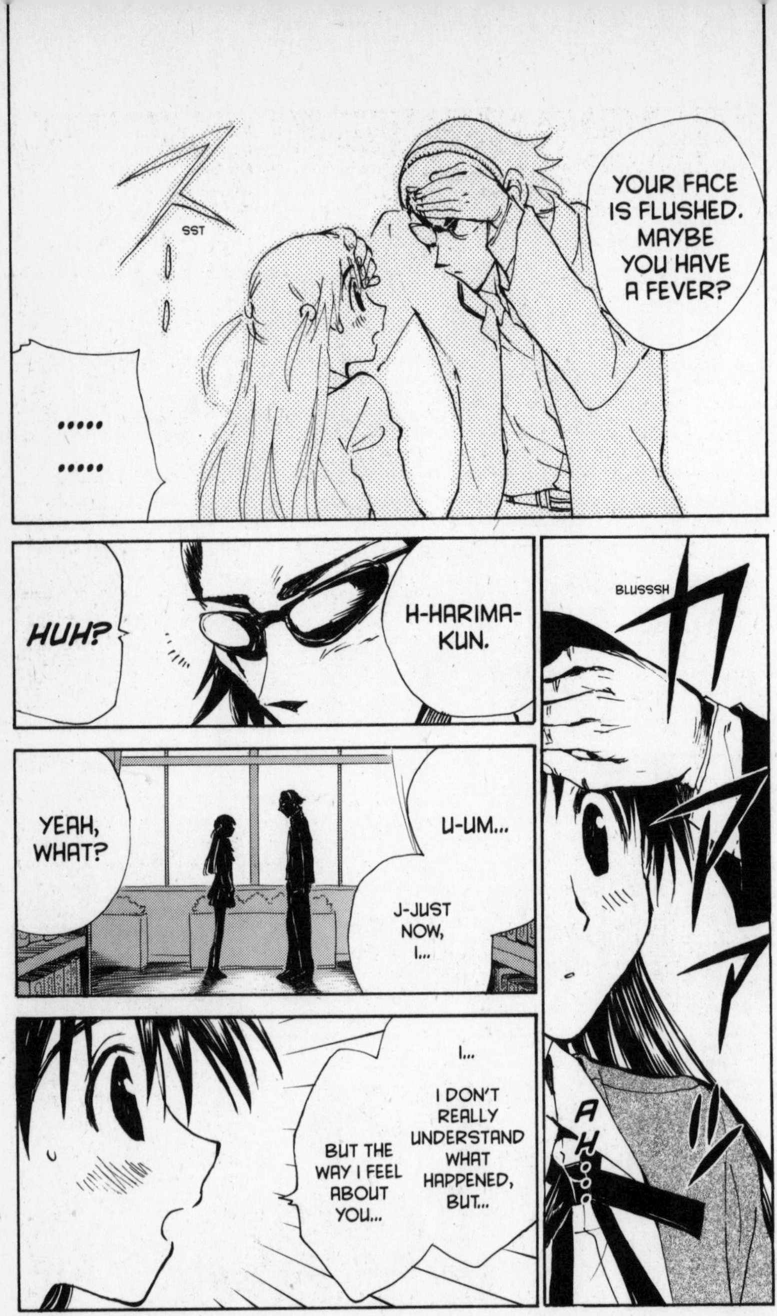
YOUR FACE IS FLUSHED. MAYBE YOU HAVE A FEVER?
SST
.....
.....
BLUSSSH
AHOOO
H-HARIMA-KUN.
HUH?
U-UM...
J-JUST NOW, I...
YEAH, WHAT?
I...
I DON'T REALLY UNDERSTAND WHAT HAPPENED, BUT...
BUT THE WAY I FEEL ABOUT YOU...

Wishing Everyone Happiness.

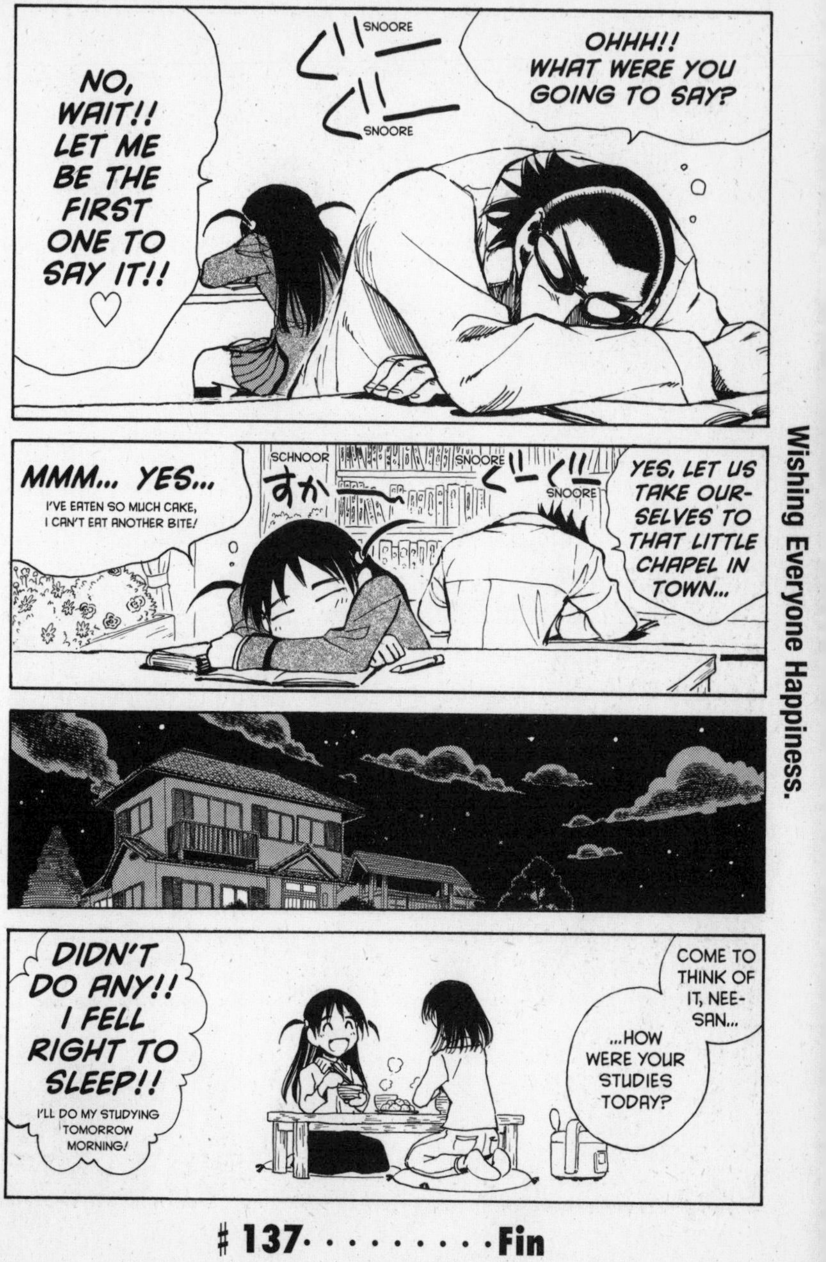
OHHH!! WHAT WERE YOU GOING TO SAY?
ぐー SNOORE
ぐー SNOORE
NO, WAIT!! LET ME BE THE FIRST ONE TO SAY IT!! ♡
YES, LET US TAKE OURSELVES TO THAT LITTLE CHAPEL IN TOWN...
ぐーぐー SNOORE SNOORE
すかー SCHNOOR
MMM... YES...
I'VE EATEN SO MUCH CAKE, I CAN'T EAT ANOTHER BITE!
COME TO THINK OF IT, NEE-SAN...
...HOW WERE YOUR STUDIES TODAY?
DIDN'T DO ANY!! I FELL RIGHT TO SLEEP!!
I'LL DO MY STUDYING TOMORROW MORNING!

 # 137· · · · · · · · ·Fin

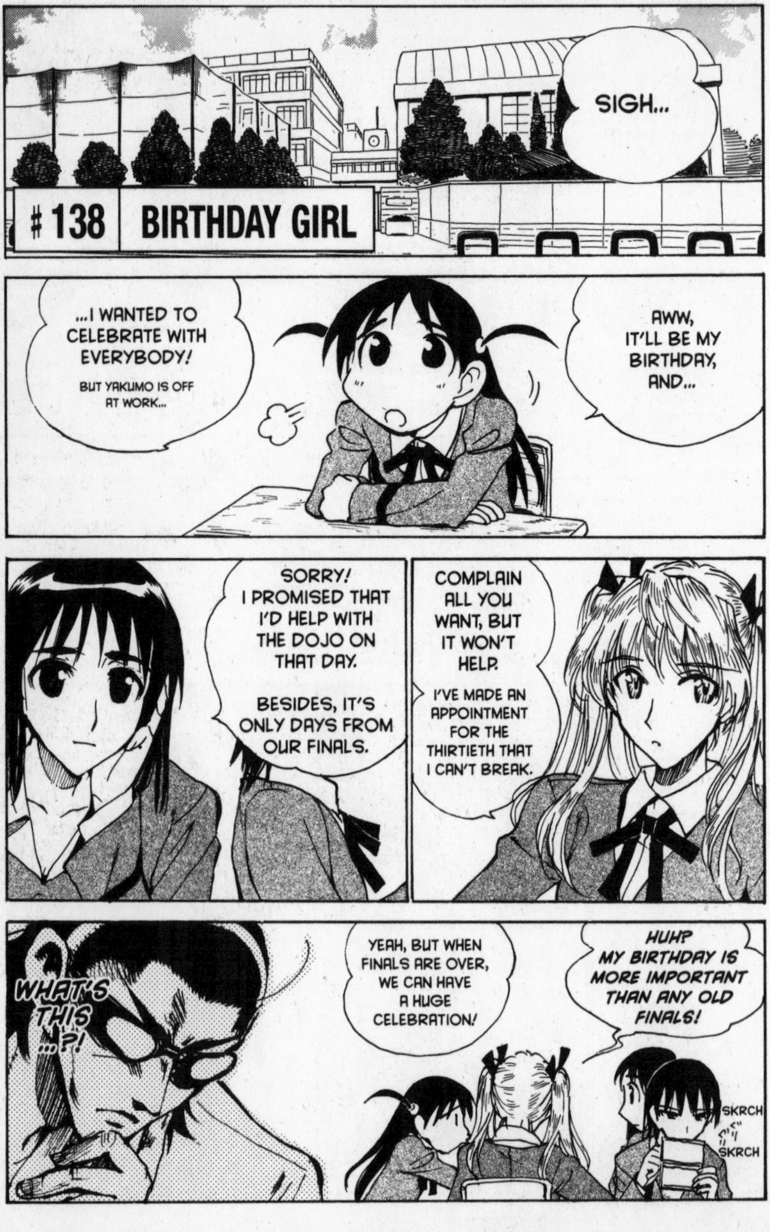

138 BIRTHDAY GIRL
SIGH...
AWW, IT'LL BE MY BIRTHDAY, AND...
...I WANTED TO CELEBRATE WITH EVERYBODY!
BUT YAKUMO IS OFF AT WORK...
COMPLAIN ALL YOU WANT, BUT IT WON'T HELP.
I'VE MADE AN APPOINTMENT FOR THE THIRTIETH THAT I CAN'T BREAK.
SORRY! I PROMISED THAT I'D HELP WITH THE DOJO ON THAT DAY.
BESIDES, IT'S ONLY DAYS FROM OUR FINALS.
HUH? MY BIRTHDAY IS MORE IMPORTANT THAN ANY OLD FINALS!
YEAH, BUT WHEN FINALS ARE OVER, WE CAN HAVE A HUGE CELEBRATION!
SKRCH
SKRCH
WHAT'S THIS ...?!

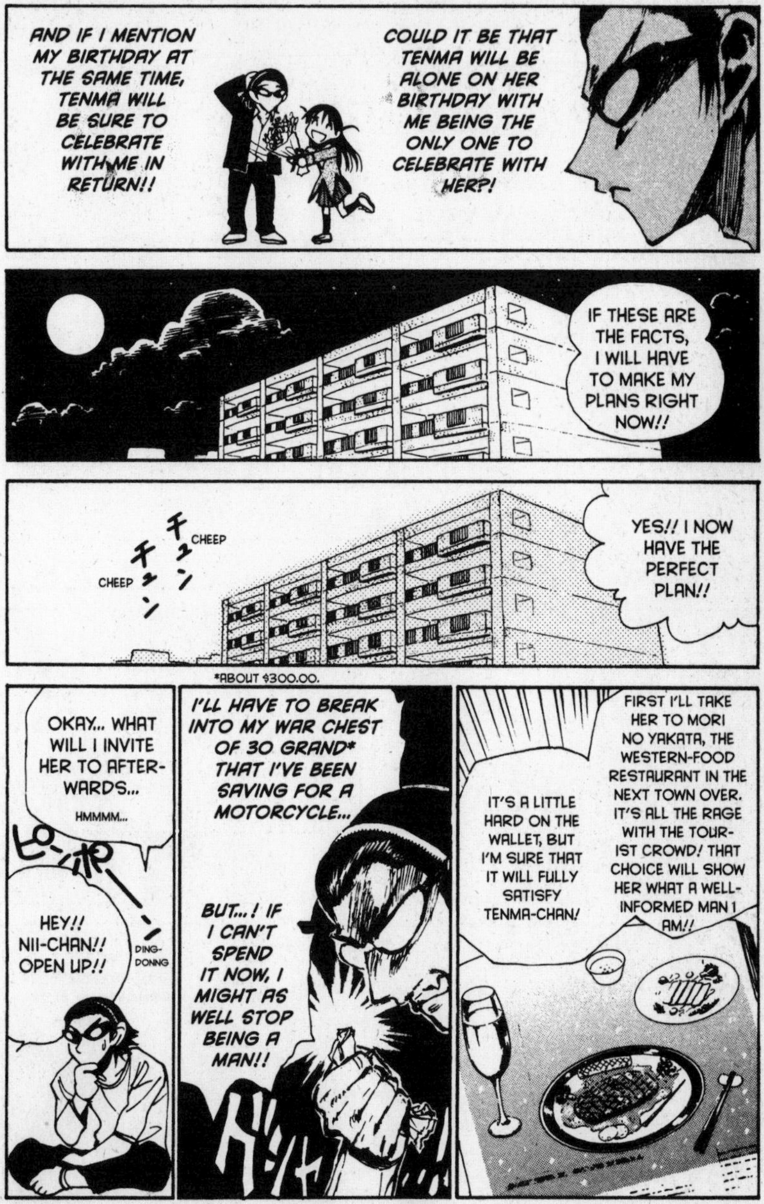
COULD IT BE THAT TENMA WILL BE ALONE ON HER BIRTHDAY WITH ME BEING THE ONLY ONE TO CELEBRATE WITH HER?!
AND IF I MENTION MY BIRTHDAY AT THE SAME TIME, TENMA WILL BE SURE TO CELEBRATE WITH ME IN RETURN!!
IF THESE ARE THE FACTS, I WILL HAVE TO MAKE MY PLANS RIGHT NOW!!
YES!! I NOW HAVE THE PERFECT PLAN!!
チュン
CHEEP
チュン
CHEEP
*ABOUT $300.00.
FIRST I'LL TAKE HER TO MORI NO YAKATA, THE WESTERN-FOOD RESTAURANT IN THE NEXT TOWN OVER. IT'S ALL THE RAGE WITH THE TOURIST CROWD! THAT CHOICE WILL SHOW HER WHAT A WELL-INFORMED MAN I AM!!
IT'S A LITTLE HARD ON THE WALLET, BUT I'M SURE THAT IT WILL FULLY SATISFY TENMA-CHAN!
I'LL HAVE TO BREAK INTO MY WAR CHEST OF 30 GRAND* THAT I'VE BEEN SAVING FOR A MOTORCYCLE...
BUT...! IF I CAN'T SPEND IT NOW, I MIGHT AS WELL STOP BEING A MAN!!
OKAY... WHAT WILL I INVITE HER TO AFTERWARDS...
HMMMM...
DING-DONNG
HEY!! NII-CHAN!! OPEN UP!!

Harima Shûji: Fifth Year of Elementary School. More Popular with the Girls Than His Nii-chan.

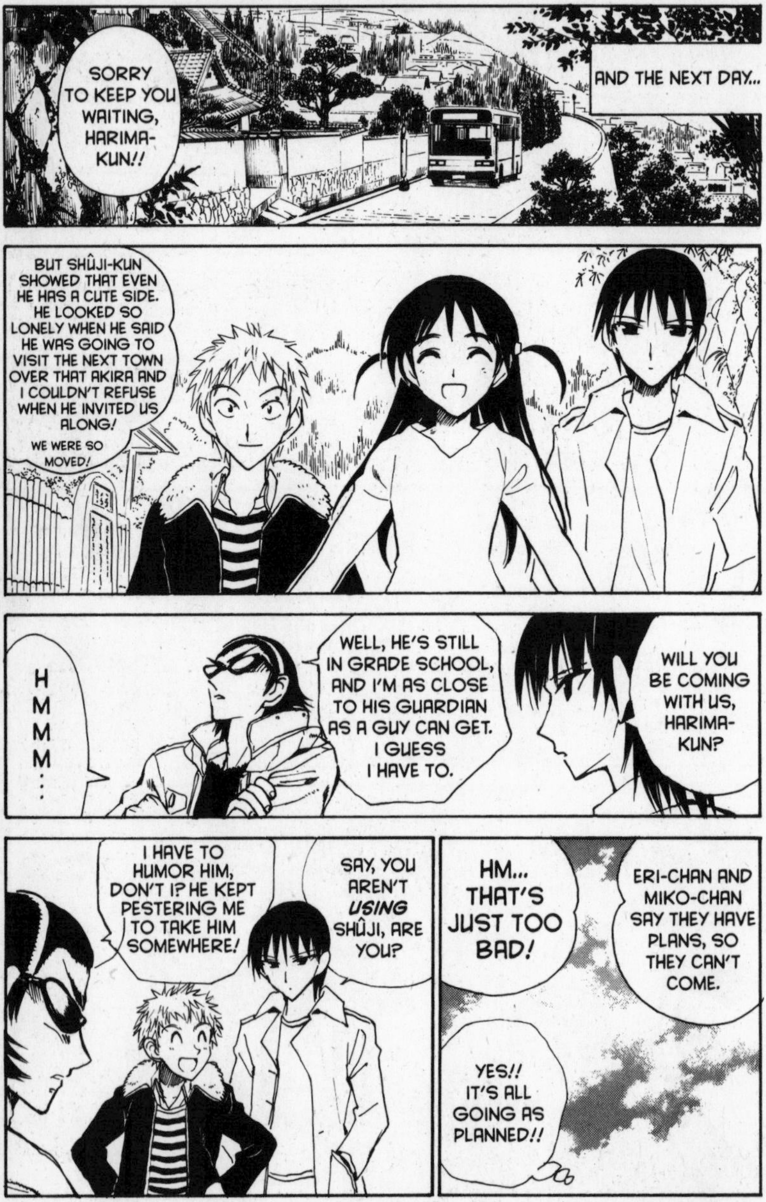
AND THE NEXT DAY...
SORRY TO KEEP YOU WAITING, HARIMA-KUN!!
BUT SHÛJI-KUN SHOWED THAT EVEN HE HAS A CUTE SIDE. HE LOOKED SO LONELY WHEN HE SAID HE WAS GOING TO VISIT THE NEXT TOWN OVER THAT AKIRA AND I COULDN'T REFUSE WHEN HE INVITED US ALONG!
WE WERE SO MOVED!
WILL YOU BE COMING WITH US, HARIMA-KUN?
WELL, HE'S STILL IN GRADE SCHOOL, AND I'M AS CLOSE TO HIS GUARDIAN AS A GUY CAN GET. I GUESS I HAVE TO.
HMMM...
ERI-CHAN AND MIKO-CHAN SAY THEY HAVE PLANS, SO THEY CAN'T COME.
HM... THAT'S JUST TOO BAD!
YES!! IT'S ALL GOING AS PLANNED!!
SAY, YOU AREN'T *USING* SHÛJI, ARE YOU?
I HAVE TO HUMOR HIM, DON'T I? HE KEPT PESTERING ME TO TAKE HIM SOMEWHERE!

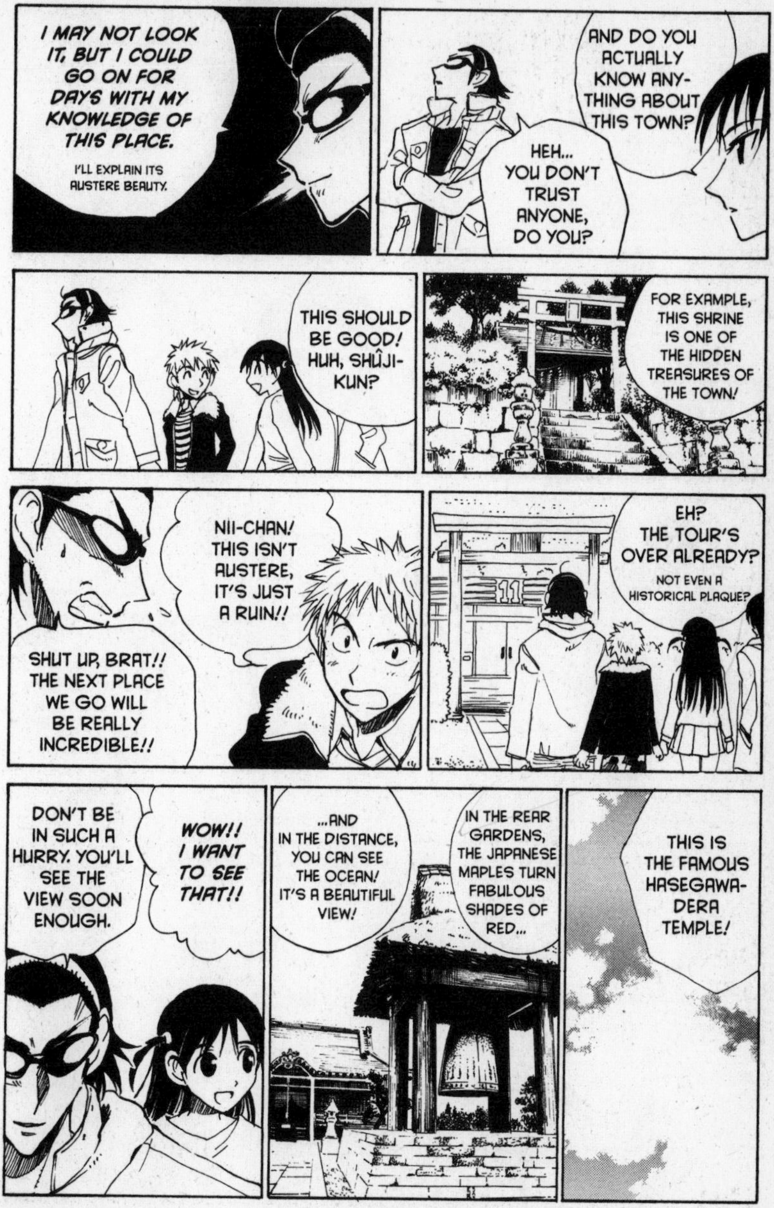
AND DO YOU ACTUALLY KNOW ANY-THING ABOUT THIS TOWN?
HEH... YOU DON'T TRUST ANYONE, DO YOU?
I MAY NOT LOOK IT, BUT I COULD GO ON FOR DAYS WITH MY KNOWLEDGE OF THIS PLACE.
I'LL EXPLAIN ITS AUSTERE BEAUTY.
FOR EXAMPLE, THIS SHRINE IS ONE OF THE HIDDEN TREASURES OF THE TOWN!
THIS SHOULD BE GOOD! HUH, SHÛJI-KUN?
EH? THE TOUR'S OVER ALREADY?
NOT EVEN A HISTORICAL PLAQUE?
NII-CHAN! THIS ISN'T AUSTERE, IT'S JUST A RUIN!!
SHUT UP, BRAT!! THE NEXT PLACE WE GO WILL BE REALLY INCREDIBLE!!
THIS IS THE FAMOUS HASEGAWA-DERA TEMPLE!
IN THE REAR GARDENS, THE JAPANESE MAPLES TURN FABULOUS SHADES OF RED...
...AND IN THE DISTANCE, YOU CAN SEE THE OCEAN! IT'S A BEAUTIFUL VIEW!
WOW!! I WANT TO SEE THAT!!
DON'T BE IN SUCH A HURRY. YOU'LL SEE THE VIEW SOON ENOUGH.

By the Way, This Was the First Location Search Trip for School Rumble.

But the Temple Was Pure Fiction.

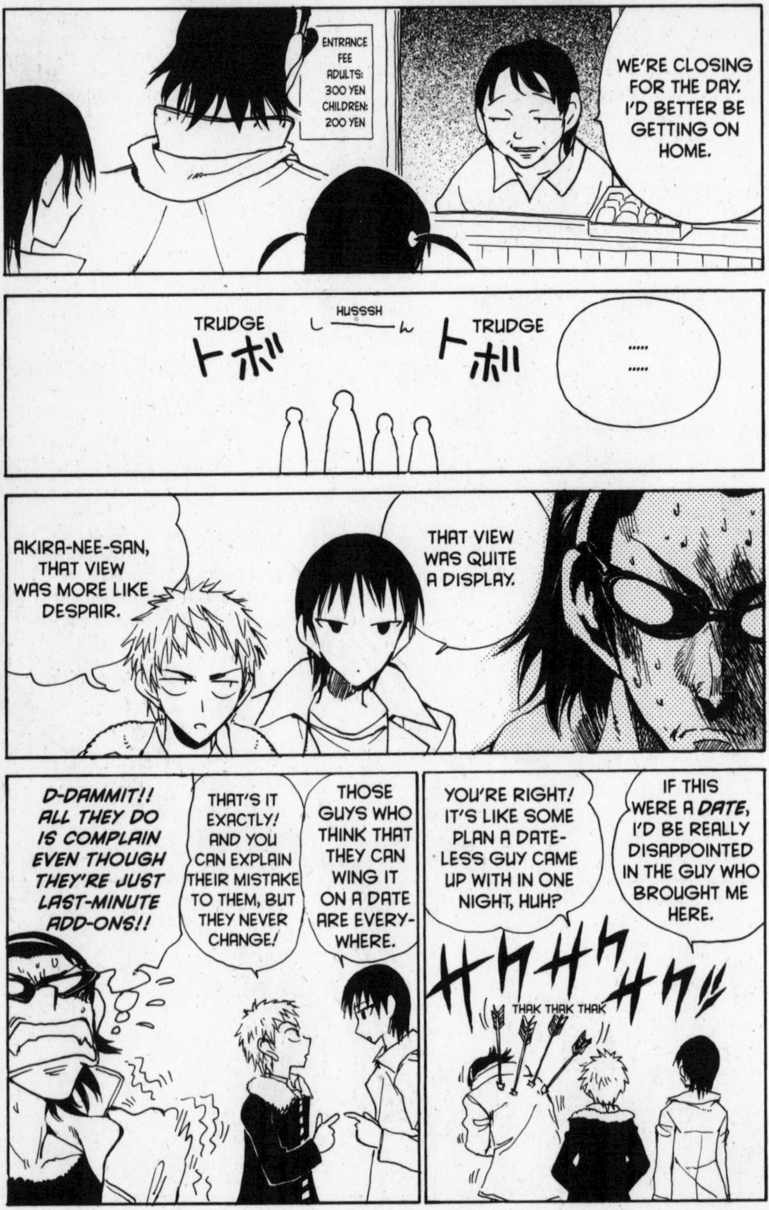

WE'RE CLOSING FOR THE DAY. I'D BETTER BE GETTING ON HOME.
ENTRANCE FEE ADULTS: 300 YEN CHILDREN: 200 YEN
…… ……
TRUDGE
トボ
HUSSSH
しーん
TRUDGE
トボ
THAT VIEW WAS QUITE A DISPLAY.
AKIRA-NEE-SAN, THAT VIEW WAS MORE LIKE DESPAIR.
IF THIS WERE A *DATE*, I'D BE REALLY DISAPPOINTED IN THE GUY WHO BROUGHT ME HERE.
YOU'RE RIGHT! IT'S LIKE SOME PLAN A DATE-LESS GUY CAME UP WITH IN ONE NIGHT, HUH?
サクサクサク!!
THAK THAK THAK
THOSE GUYS WHO THINK THAT THEY CAN WING IT ON A DATE ARE EVERY-WHERE.
THAT'S IT EXACTLY! AND YOU CAN EXPLAIN THEIR MISTAKE TO THEM, BUT THEY NEVER CHANGE!
D-DAMMIT!! ALL THEY DO IS COMPLAIN EVEN THOUGH THEY'RE JUST LAST-MINUTE ADD-ONS!!

Her Kindness Leads to Pain.

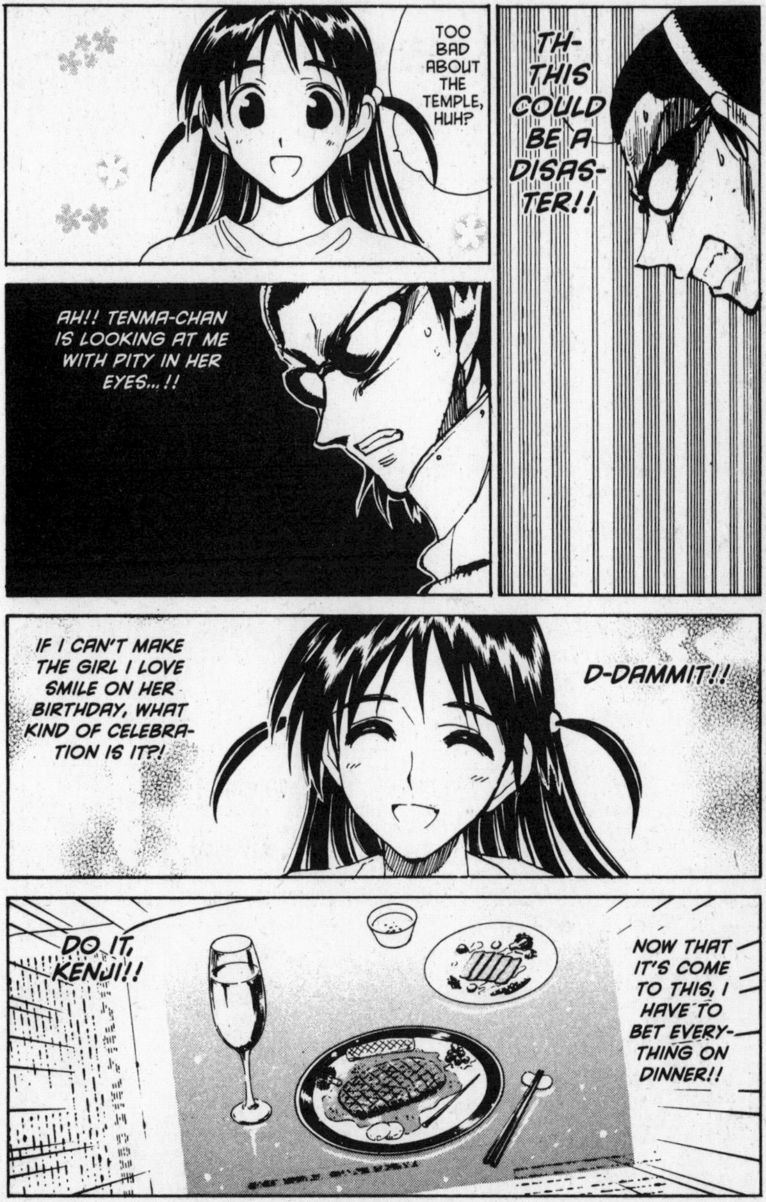

TH- THIS COULD BE A DISASTER!!
TOO BAD ABOUT THE TEMPLE, HUH?
AH!! TENMA-CHAN IS LOOKING AT ME WITH PITY IN HER EYES...!!
D-DAMMIT!!
IF I CAN'T MAKE THE GIRL I LOVE SMILE ON HER BIRTHDAY, WHAT KIND OF CELEBRATION IS IT?!
NOW THAT IT'S COME TO THIS, I HAVE TO BET EVERYTHING ON DINNER!!
DO IT, KENJI!!

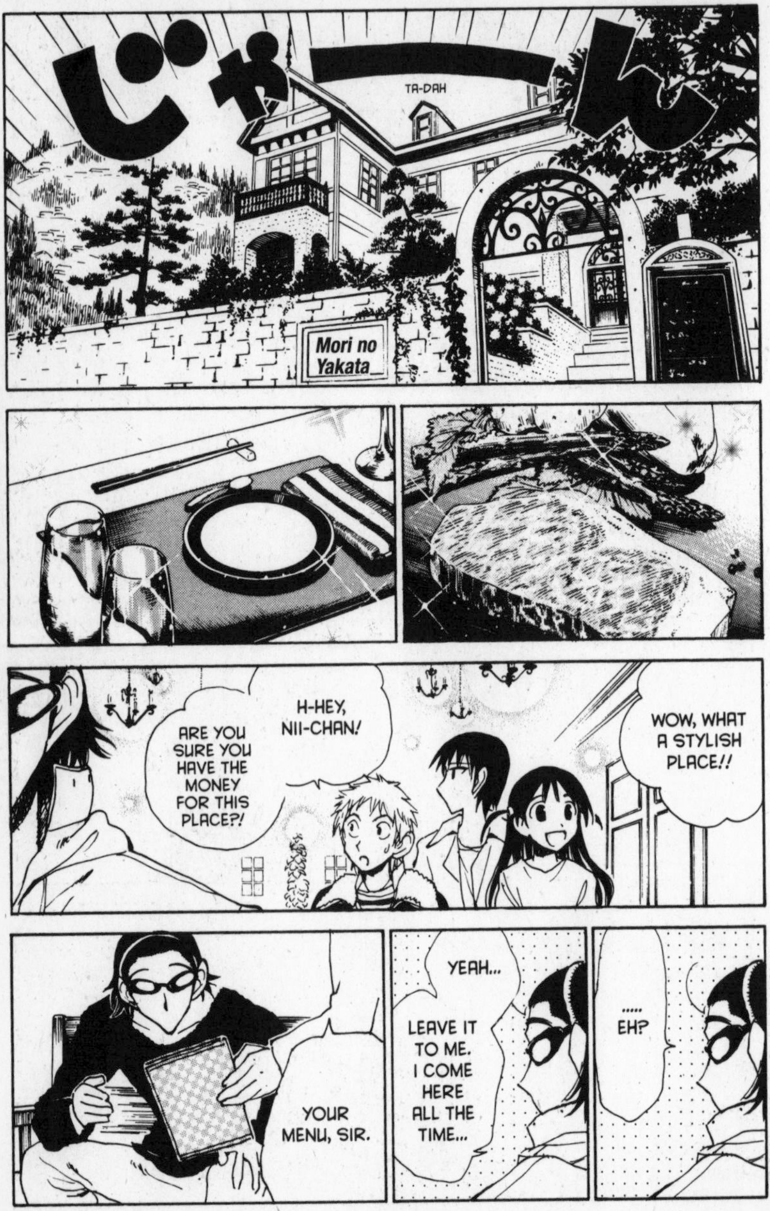
TA-DAH
Mori no Yakata
WOW, WHAT A STYLISH PLACE!!
H-HEY, NII-CHAN!
ARE YOU SURE YOU HAVE THE MONEY FOR THIS PLACE?!
...... EH?
YEAH...
LEAVE IT TO ME. I COME HERE ALL THE TIME...
YOUR MENU, SIR.

This Restaurant Is Fiction, Too.

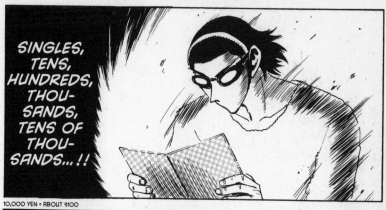

SINGLES, TENS, HUNDREDS, THOUSANDS, TENS OF THOUSANDS...!!

10,000 YEN = ABOUT $100

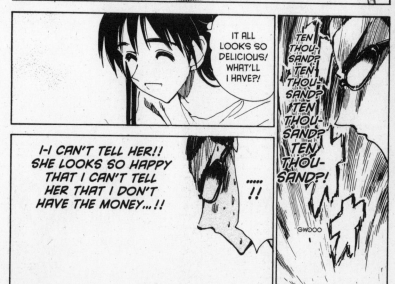

<MAIN COURSES>

JAPANESE BEEF HIDÉ-STYLE STEAK FILET (100G)	25,000 YEN
HINAIJI-DORI HERBAL FRY	16,000 YEN
SATSUMA BLACK-FUR PORK PICCATA	14,000 YEN
BROILED SANRIKU SEA BASS WITH SHIMEJI MUSHROOMS	10,000 YEN
HIMI YELLOWTAIL SAUTÉ SERVED AS THE CHEF WISHES	8000 YEN
	8000 YEN
	6000 YEN

IT ALL LOOKS SO DELICIOUS! WHAT'LL I HAVE?!

TEN THOU-SAND? TEN THOU-SAND? TEN THOU-SAND? TEN THOU-SAND?!

I-I CAN'T TELL HER!! SHE LOOKS SO HAPPY THAT I CAN'T TELL HER THAT I DON'T HAVE THE MONEY...!!

····· !!

GWOOO

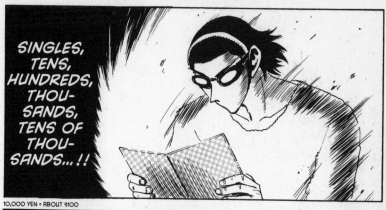

He Only Tastes His Own Tears...

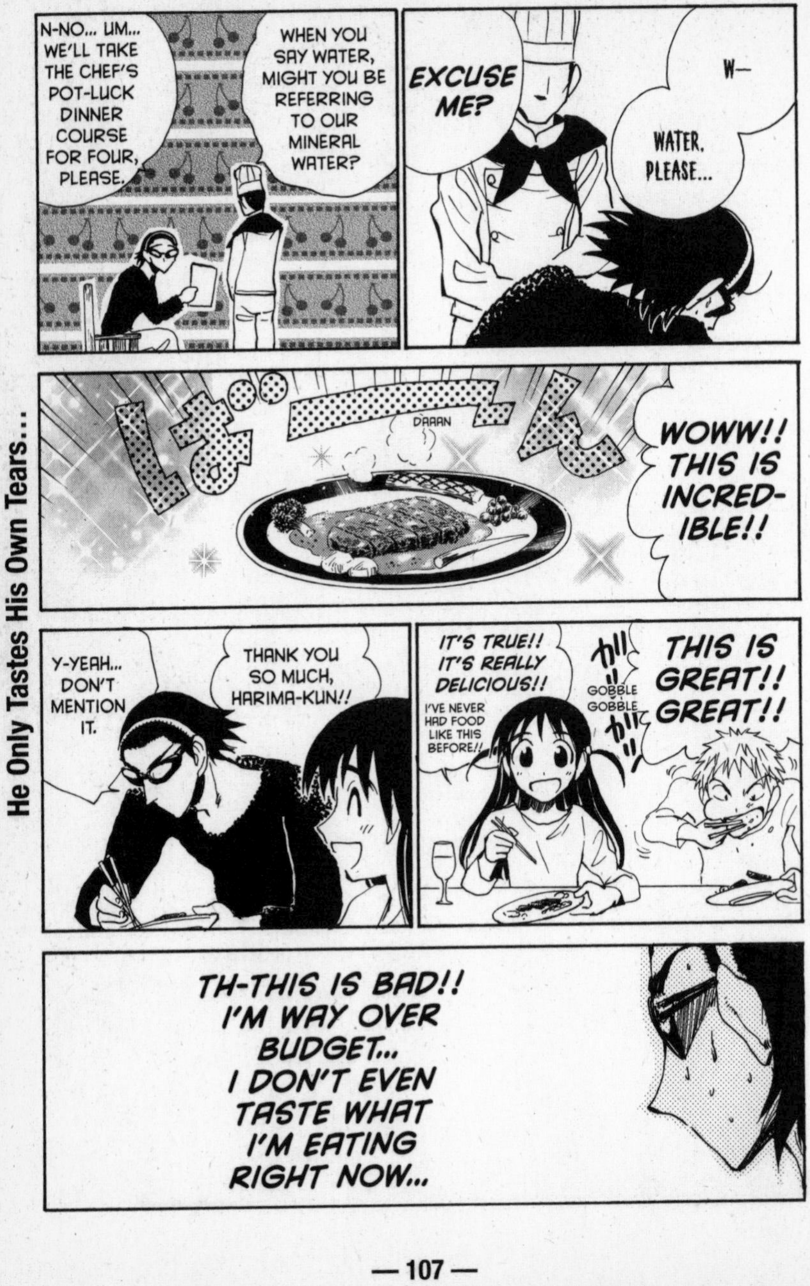
W—
WATER, PLEASE...
EXCUSE ME?
WHEN YOU SAY WATER, MIGHT YOU BE REFERRING TO OUR MINERAL WATER?
N-NO... UM... WE'LL TAKE THE CHEF'S POT-LUCK DINNER COURSE FOR FOUR, PLEASE.
WOWW!! THIS IS INCRED-IBLE!!
DAAAN
THIS IS GREAT!! GREAT!!
GOBBLE GOBBLE
IT'S TRUE!! IT'S REALLY DELICIOUS!!
I'VE NEVER HAD FOOD LIKE THIS BEFORE!!
THANK YOU SO MUCH, HARIMA-KUN!!
Y-YEAH... DON'T MENTION IT.
TH-THIS IS BAD!! I'M WAY OVER BUDGET... I DON'T EVEN TASTE WHAT I'M EATING RIGHT NOW...

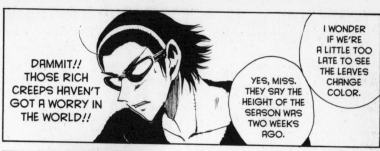

I WONDER IF WE'RE A LITTLE TOO LATE TO SEE THE LEAVES CHANGE COLOR.
YES, MISS. THEY SAY THE HEIGHT OF THE SEASON WAS TWO WEEKS AGO.
DAMMIT!! THOSE RICH CREEPS HAVEN'T GOT A WORRY IN THE WORLD!!
YOU SAY YOU TAKE CARDS?
YES, OF COURSE WE DO, MISS.
Y-YOU MEAN I CAN USE A CARD?!
I-I'VE GOT MY COMMUTER PASS CARD AND MY SCHOOL ID CARD...
N-NO!! I'M SURE THEY MEAN SOME DIFFERENT CARD...
SIR... IT IS ABOUT TIME THAT THE CHECK WAS PAID...
THERE IT IS!!
WH-WHAT'LL I DO?!
I-I GUESS THE ONLY THING TO DO NOW IS PRETEND THAT I'M RICH AND PUT ONE OVER ON THEM!!

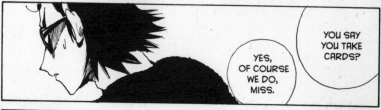

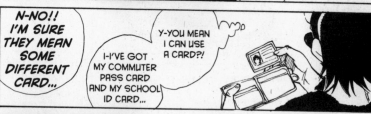

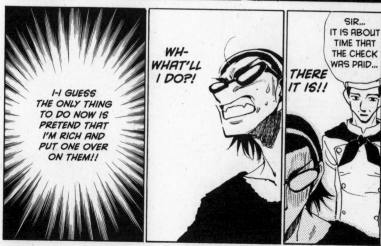

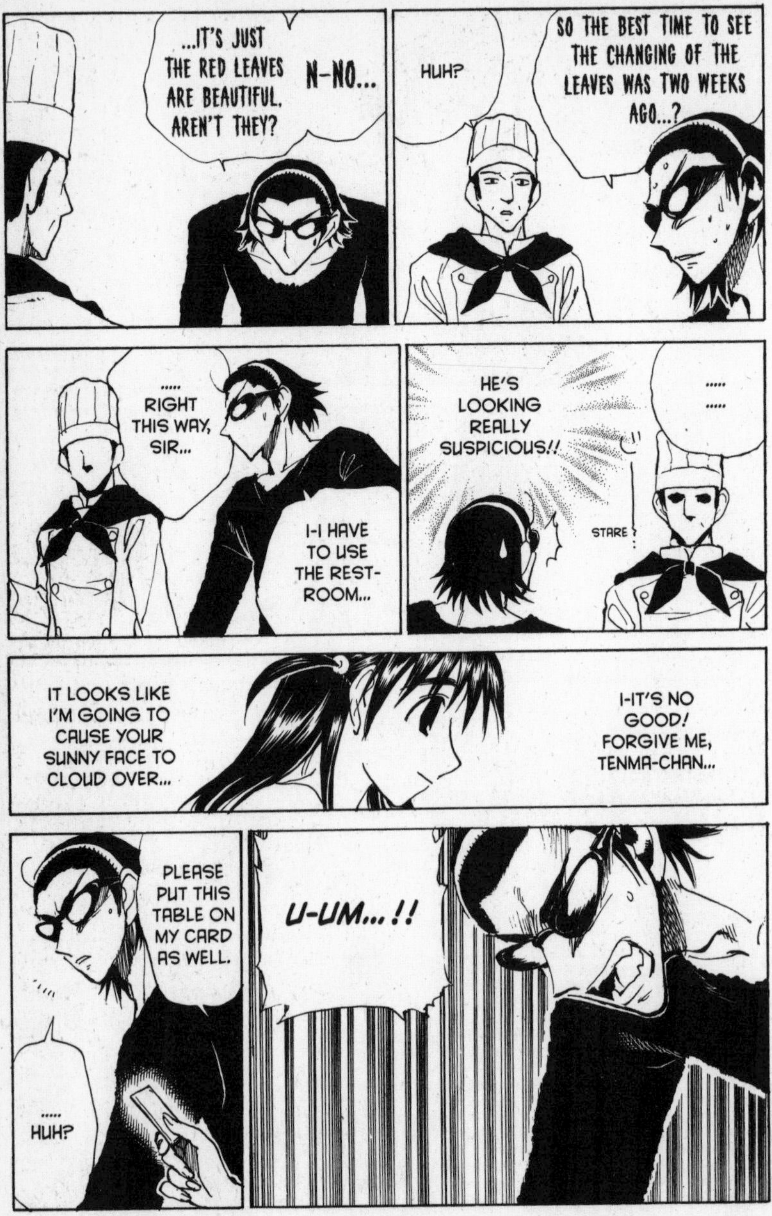
SO THE BEST TIME TO SEE THE CHANGING OF THE LEAVES WAS TWO WEEKS AGO...?
HUH?
N-NO...
...IT'S JUST THE RED LEAVES ARE BEAUTIFUL, AREN'T THEY?
....
HE'S LOOKING REALLY SUSPICIOUS!!
STARE
..... RIGHT THIS WAY, SIR...
I-I HAVE TO USE THE REST-ROOM...
I-IT'S NO GOOD! FORGIVE ME, TENMA-CHAN...
IT LOOKS LIKE I'M GOING TO CAUSE YOUR SUNNY FACE TO CLOUD OVER...
U-UM...!!
PLEASE PUT THIS TABLE ON MY CARD AS WELL.
..... HUH?

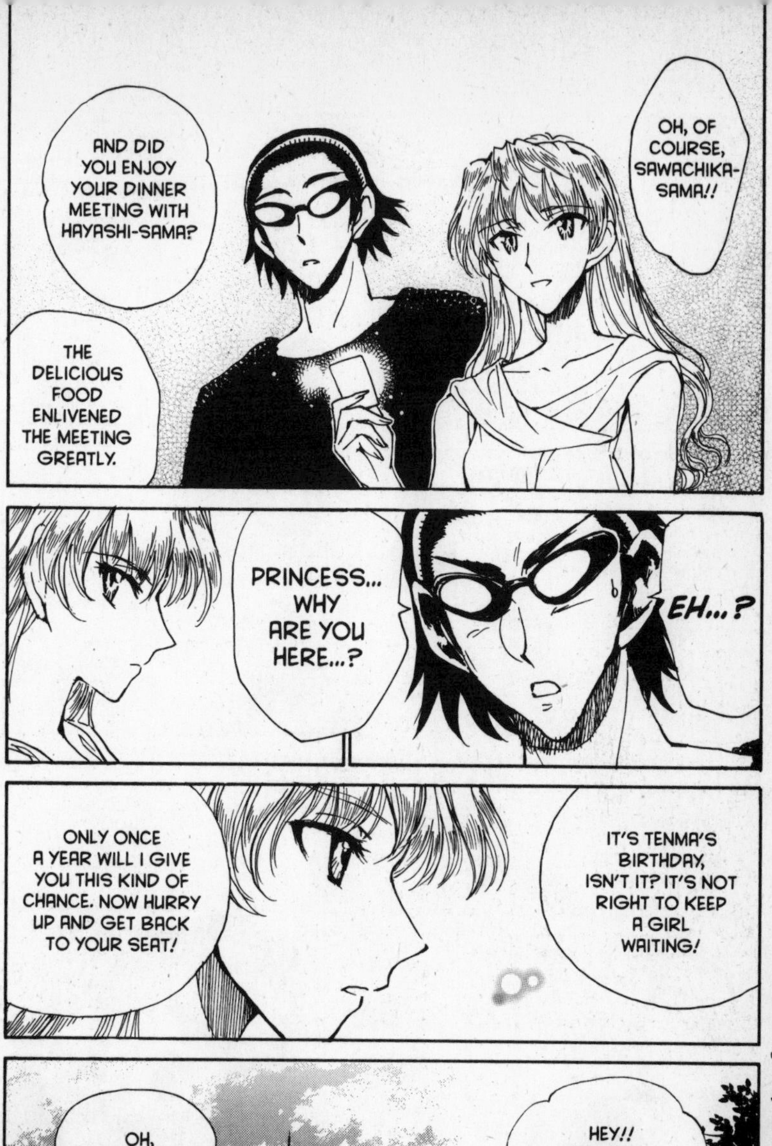
OH, OF COURSE, SAWACHIKA-SAMA!!
AND DID YOU ENJOY YOUR DINNER MEETING WITH HAYASHI-SAMA?
THE DELICIOUS FOOD ENLIVENED THE MEETING GREATLY.
EH...?
PRINCESS... WHY ARE YOU HERE...?
IT'S TENMA'S BIRTHDAY, ISN'T IT? IT'S NOT RIGHT TO KEEP A GIRL WAITING!
ONLY ONCE A YEAR WILL I GIVE YOU THIS KIND OF CHANCE. NOW HURRY UP AND GET BACK TO YOUR SEAT!
HEY!! ERI-CHAN, YOU'RE HERE, TOO?!
COME HAVE DESSERT WITH US!!
OH, TENMA! WHAT A COINCIDENCE! MAYBE I'LL JOIN YOU FOR JUST A BIT!

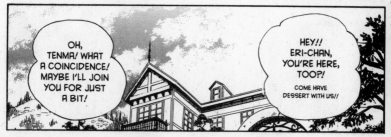

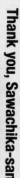

Thank you, Sawachika-san.

138· · · · · · · · ·Fin

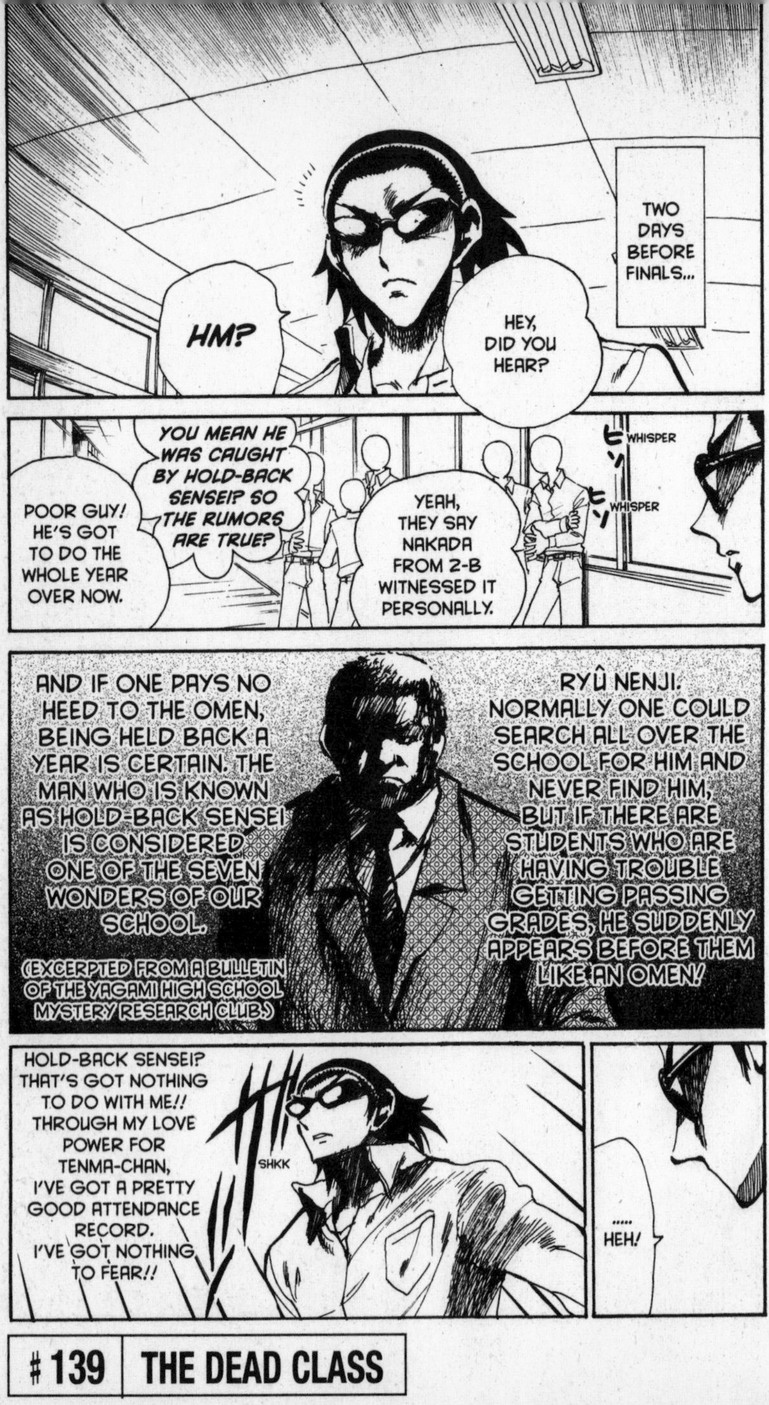
TWO DAYS BEFORE FINALS...
HEY, DID YOU HEAR?
HM?
WHISPER
WHISPER
YEAH, THEY SAY NAKADA FROM 2-B WITNESSED IT PERSONALLY.
YOU MEAN HE WAS CAUGHT BY HOLD-BACK SENSEI? SO THE RUMORS ARE TRUE?
POOR GUY! HE'S GOT TO DO THE WHOLE YEAR OVER NOW.
RYÛ NENJI. NORMALLY ONE COULD SEARCH ALL OVER THE SCHOOL FOR HIM AND NEVER FIND HIM, BUT IF THERE ARE STUDENTS WHO ARE HAVING TROUBLE GETTING PASSING GRADES, HE SUDDENLY APPEARS BEFORE THEM LIKE AN OMEN!
AND IF ONE PAYS NO HEED TO THE OMEN, BEING HELD BACK A YEAR IS CERTAIN. THE MAN WHO IS KNOWN AS HOLD-BACK SENSEI IS CONSIDERED ONE OF THE SEVEN WONDERS OF OUR SCHOOL.
(EXCERPTED FROM A BULLETIN OF THE YAGAMI HIGH SCHOOL MYSTERY RESEARCH CLUB.)
...... HEH!
HOLD-BACK SENSEI? THAT'S GOT NOTHING TO DO WITH ME!! THROUGH MY LOVE POWER FOR TENMA-CHAN, I'VE GOT A PRETTY GOOD ATTENDANCE RECORD. I'VE GOT NOTHING TO FEAR!!
SHKK

#139 THE DEAD CLASS

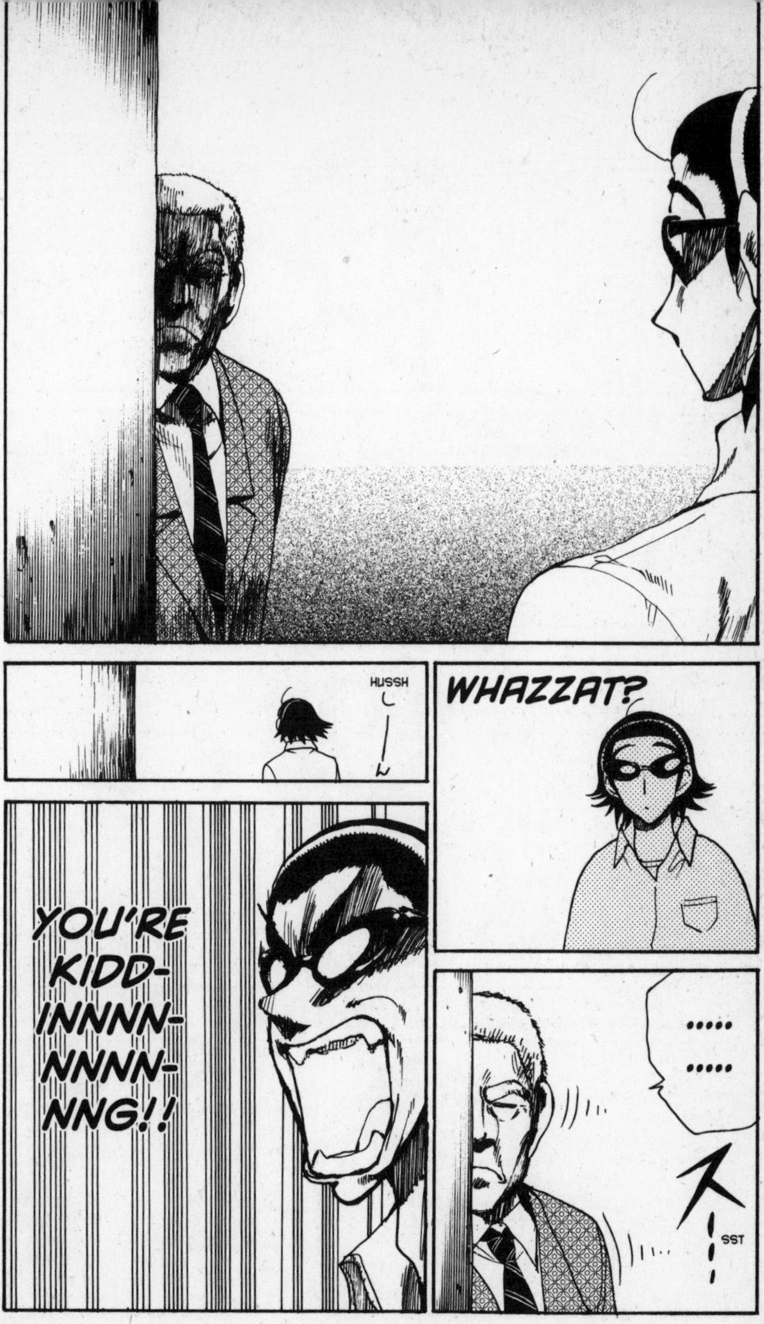
WHAZZAT?
HUSSH
YOU'RE KIDD-INNNN-NNNN-NNG!!
.....
.....
SST

You May Not Realize It, but This Is a Fated Second Meeting for Harima. (See Volume 1)

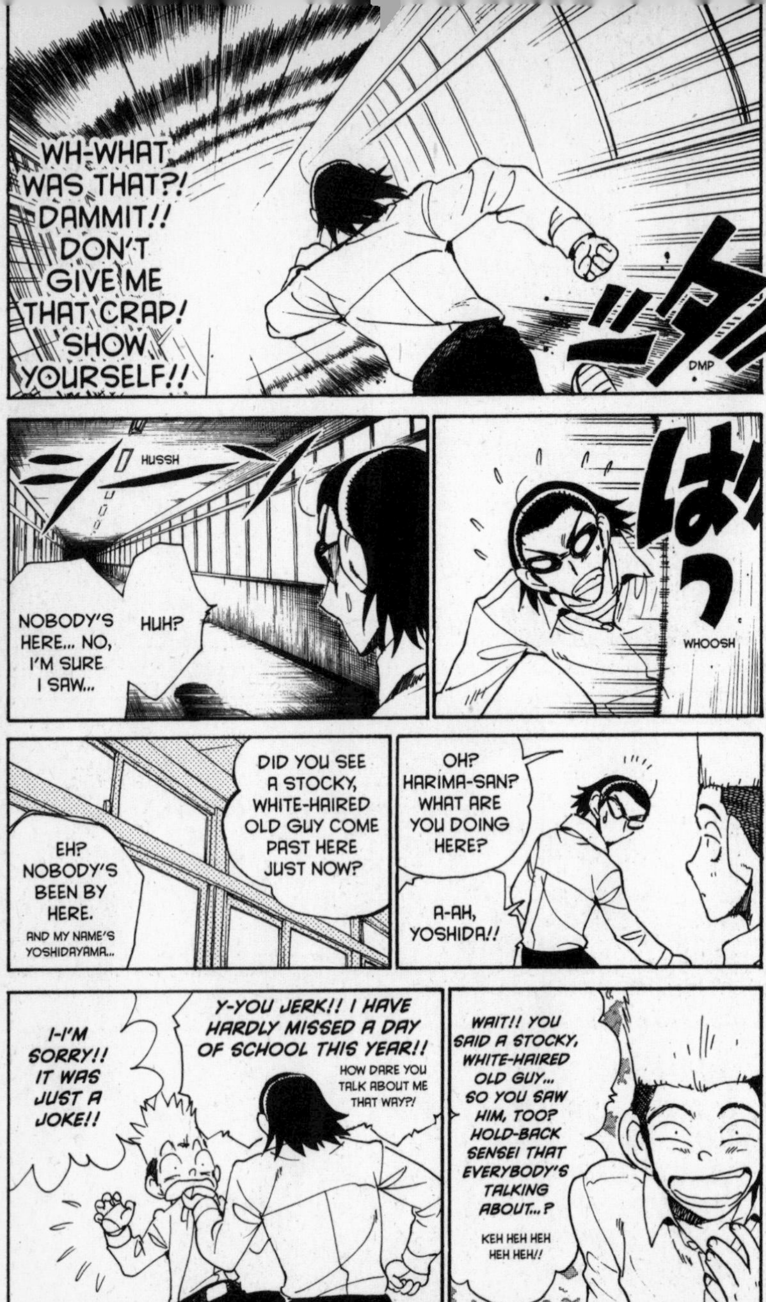
WH-WHAT WAS THAT?! DAMMIT!! DON'T GIVE ME THAT CRAP! SHOW YOURSELF!!
DMP
はっ
WHOOSH
HUSSH
HUH?
NOBODY'S HERE... NO, I'M SURE I SAW...
OH? HARIMA-SAN? WHAT ARE YOU DOING HERE?
A-AH, YOSHIDA!!
DID YOU SEE A STOCKY, WHITE-HAIRED OLD GUY COME PAST HERE JUST NOW?
EH? NOBODY'S BEEN BY HERE.
AND MY NAME'S YOSHIDAYAMA...
WAIT!! YOU SAID A STOCKY, WHITE-HAIRED OLD GUY... SO YOU SAW HIM, TOO? HOLD-BACK SENSEI THAT EVERYBODY'S TALKING ABOUT...?
KEH HEH HEH HEH HEH!!
Y-YOU JERK!! I HAVE HARDLY MISSED A DAY OF SCHOOL THIS YEAR!!
HOW DARE YOU TALK ABOUT ME THAT WAY?!
I-I'M SORRY!! IT WAS JUST A JOKE!!

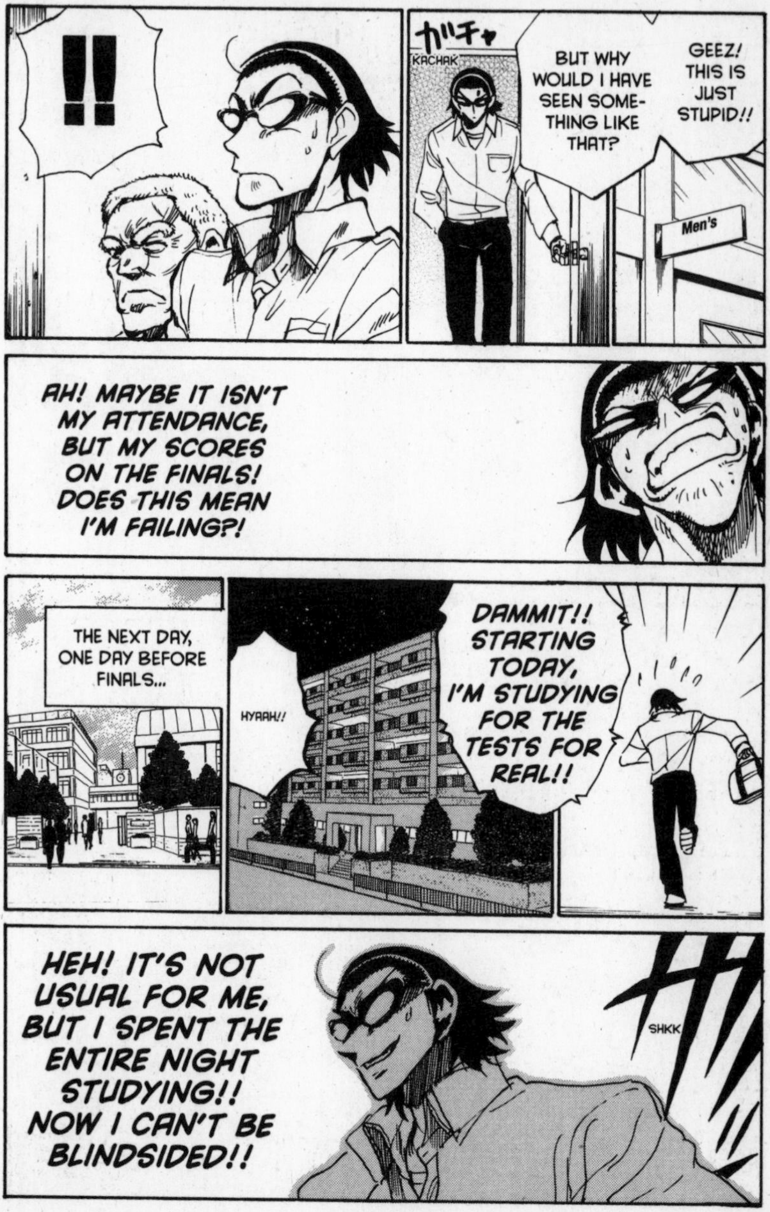
GEEZ! THIS IS JUST STUPID!!
BUT WHY WOULD I HAVE SEEN SOME-THING LIKE THAT?
ガチャ
KACHAK
Men's
!!
AH! MAYBE IT ISN'T MY ATTENDANCE, BUT MY SCORES ON THE FINALS! DOES THIS MEAN I'M FAILING?!
DAMMIT!! STARTING TODAY, I'M STUDYING FOR THE TESTS FOR REAL!!
HYAAH!!
THE NEXT DAY, ONE DAY BEFORE FINALS...
SHKK
HEH! IT'S NOT USUAL FOR ME, BUT I SPENT THE ENTIRE NIGHT STUDYING!! NOW I CAN'T BE BLINDSIDED!!

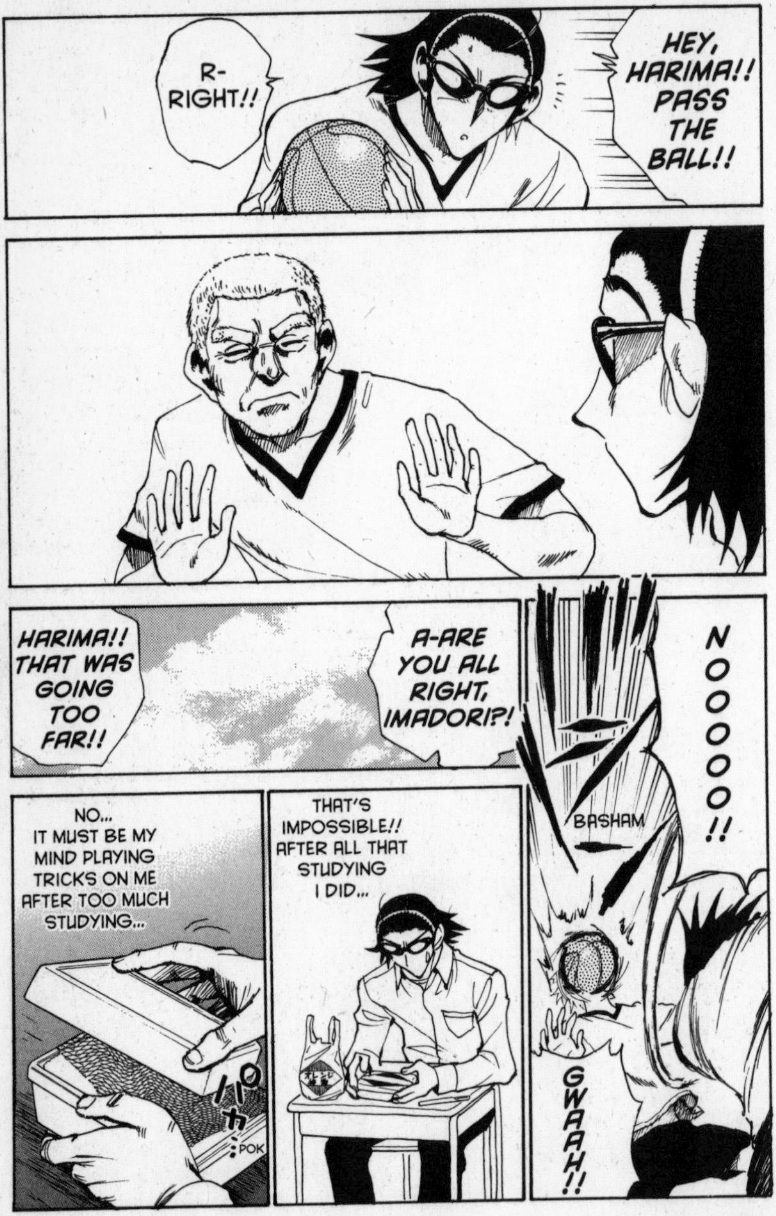
HEY, HARIMA!! PASS THE BALL!!
R-RIGHT!!
NOOOOOO!!
BASHAM
GWAAH!!
A-ARE YOU ALL RIGHT, IMADORI?!
HARIMA!! THAT WAS GOING TOO FAR!!
THAT'S IMPOSSIBLE!! AFTER ALL THAT STUDYING I DID...
NO... IT MUST BE MY MIND PLAYING TRICKS ON ME AFTER TOO MUCH STUDYING...
POK

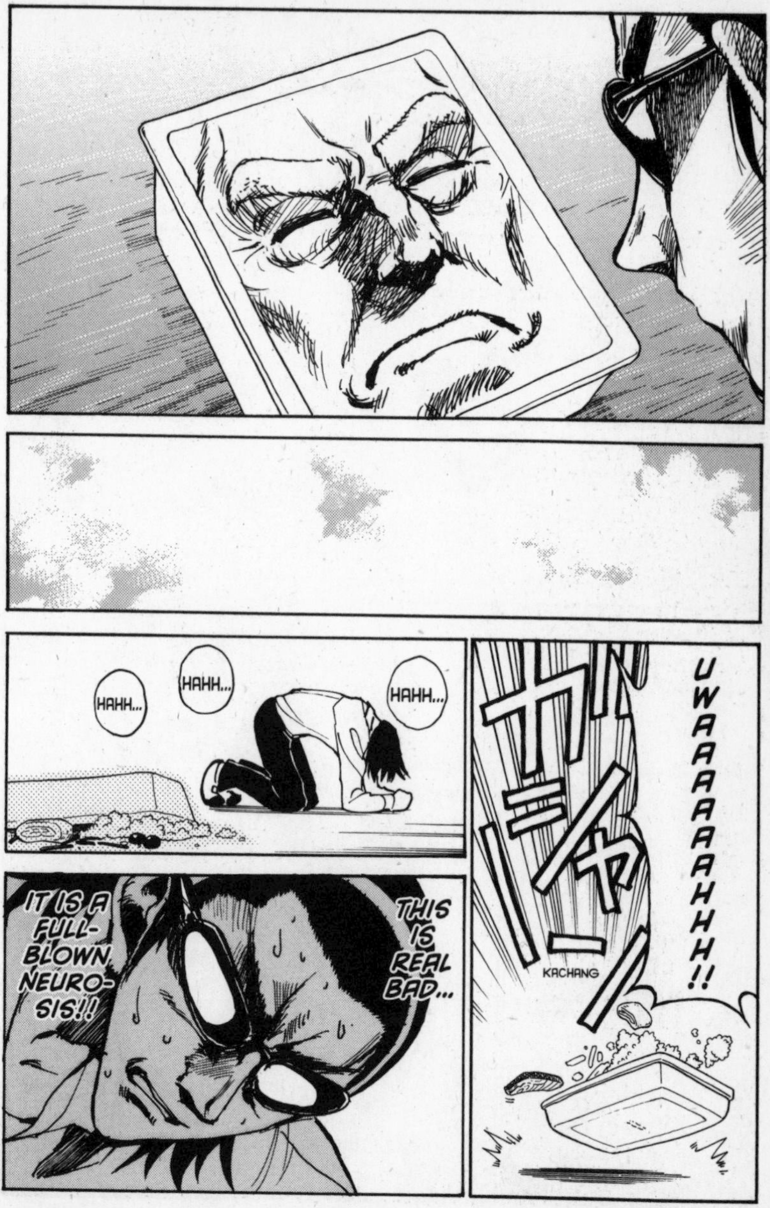
UWAAAAAAHHH!!
KACHANG
HAHH...
HAHH...
HAHH...
THIS IS REAL BAD...
IT IS A FULL-BLOWN NEURO-SIS!!

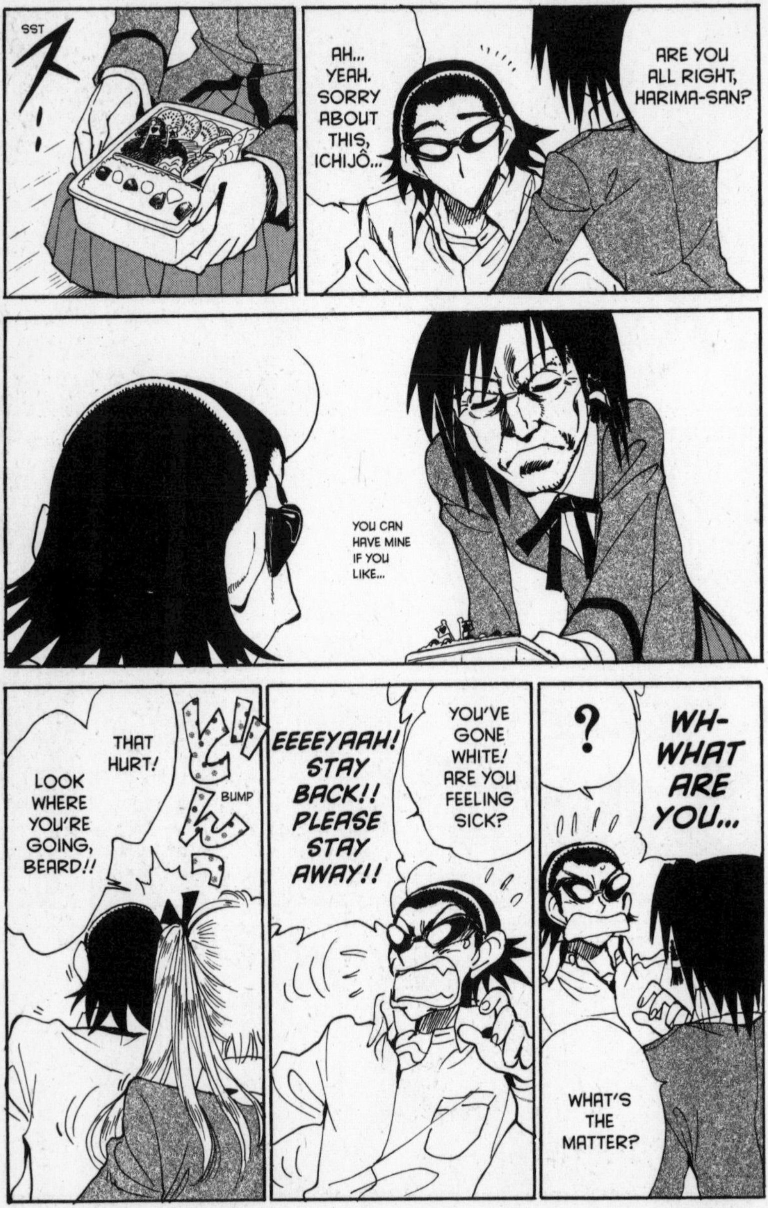
ARE YOU ALL RIGHT, HARIMA-SAN?
AH... YEAH. SORRY ABOUT THIS, ICHIJÔ...
SST
YOU CAN HAVE MINE IF YOU LIKE...
WH-WHAT ARE YOU...
?
WHAT'S THE MATTER?
YOU'VE GONE WHITE! ARE YOU FEELING SICK?
EEEEYAAH! STAY BACK!! PLEASE STAY AWAY!!
BUMP
THAT HURT!
LOOK WHERE YOU'RE GOING, BEARD!!

Takano Akira: Not Quite Changed Yet.

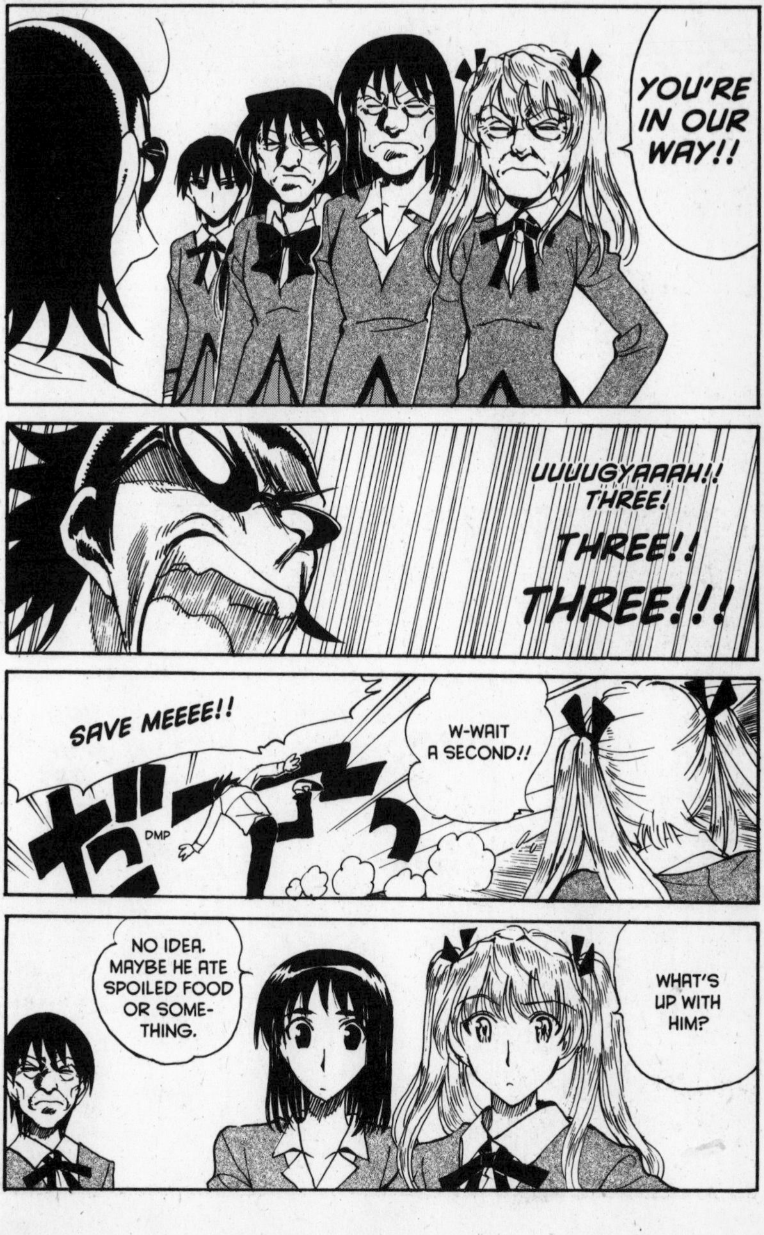
YOU'RE IN OUR WAY!!
UUUUGYAAAH!! THREE!
THREE!!
THREE!!!
W-WAIT A SECOND!!
SAVE MEEEE!!
DMP
WHAT'S UP WITH HIM?
NO IDEA. MAYBE HE ATE SPOILED FOOD OR SOME-THING.

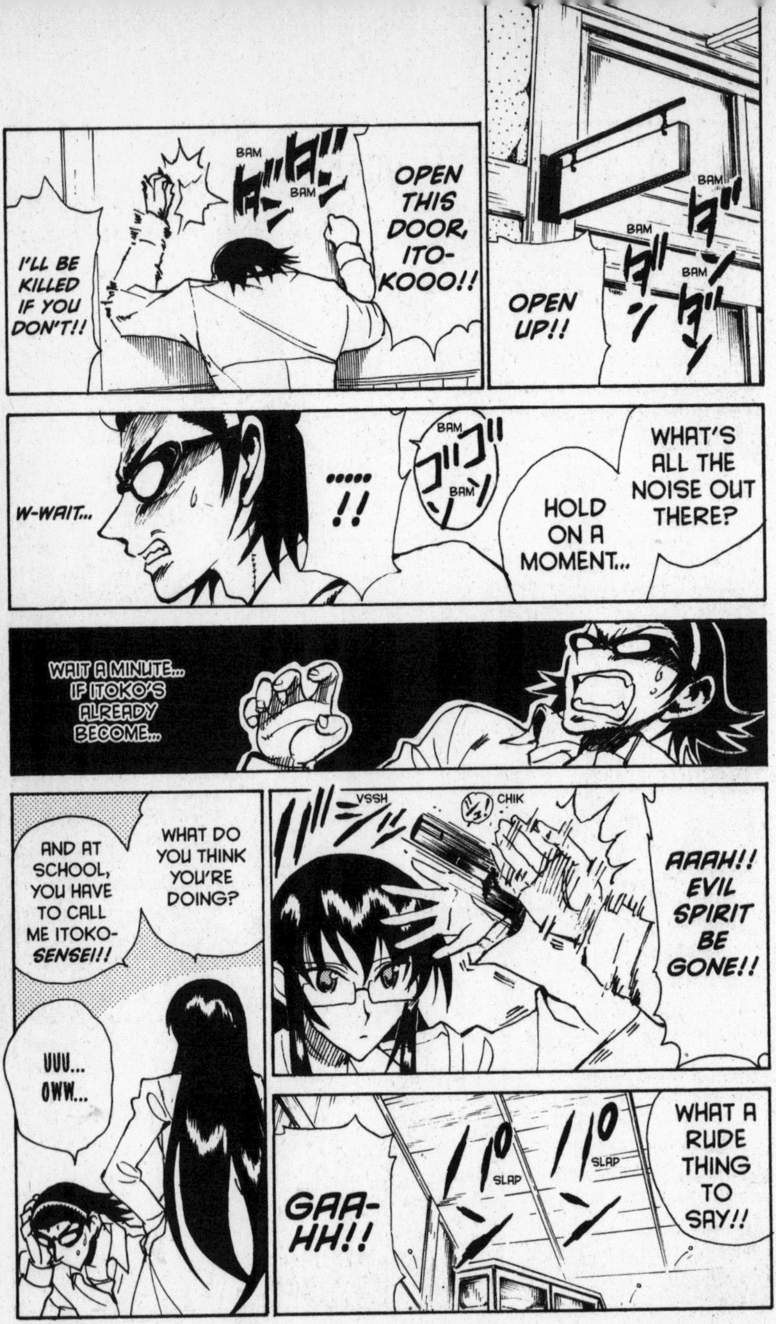
OPEN UP!!
BAM
BAM
BAM
BAM
BAM
OPEN THIS DOOR, ITO-KOOO!!
I'LL BE KILLED IF YOU DON'T!!
WHAT'S ALL THE NOISE OUT THERE?
HOLD ON A MOMENT...
BAM
BAM
......!!
W-WAIT...
WAIT A MINUTE... IF ITOKO'S ALREADY BECOME...
AAAH!! EVIL SPIRIT BE GONE!!
CHIK
VSSH
WHAT A RUDE THING TO SAY!!
SLAP
SLAP
GAA-HH!!
WHAT DO YOU THINK YOU'RE DOING?
AND AT SCHOOL, YOU HAVE TO CALL ME ITOKO-SENSEI!!
UUU... OWW...

Osakabe Itoko: Harima's Cousin. Physics Teacher.

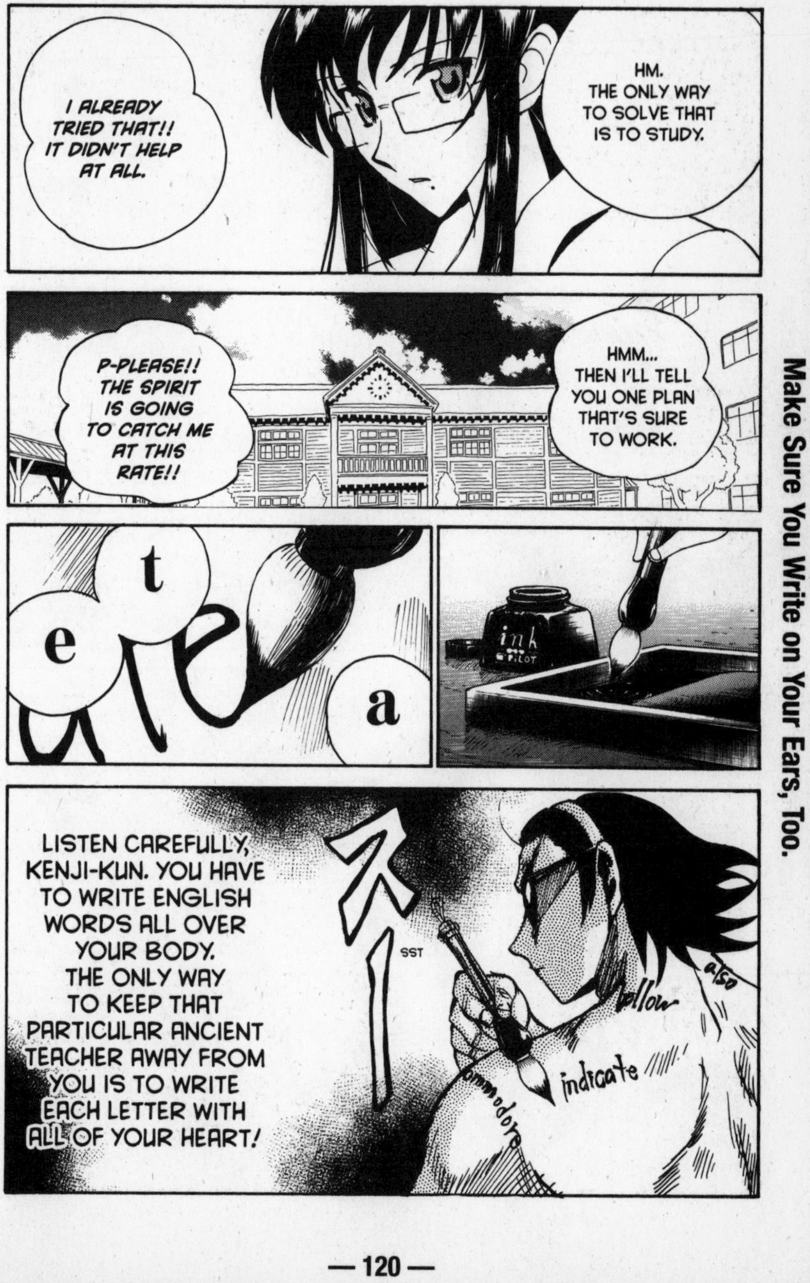
HM. THE ONLY WAY TO SOLVE THAT IS TO STUDY.
I ALREADY TRIED THAT!! IT DIDN'T HELP AT ALL.
HMM... THEN I'LL TELL YOU ONE PLAN THAT'S SURE TO WORK.
P-PLEASE!! THE SPIRIT IS GOING TO CATCH ME AT THIS RATE!!
ink
PILOT
t
e
a
LISTEN CAREFULLY, KENJI-KUN. YOU HAVE TO WRITE ENGLISH WORDS ALL OVER YOUR BODY. THE ONLY WAY TO KEEP THAT PARTICULAR ANCIENT TEACHER AWAY FROM YOU IS TO WRITE EACH LETTER WITH ALL OF YOUR HEART!
SST
also
indicate

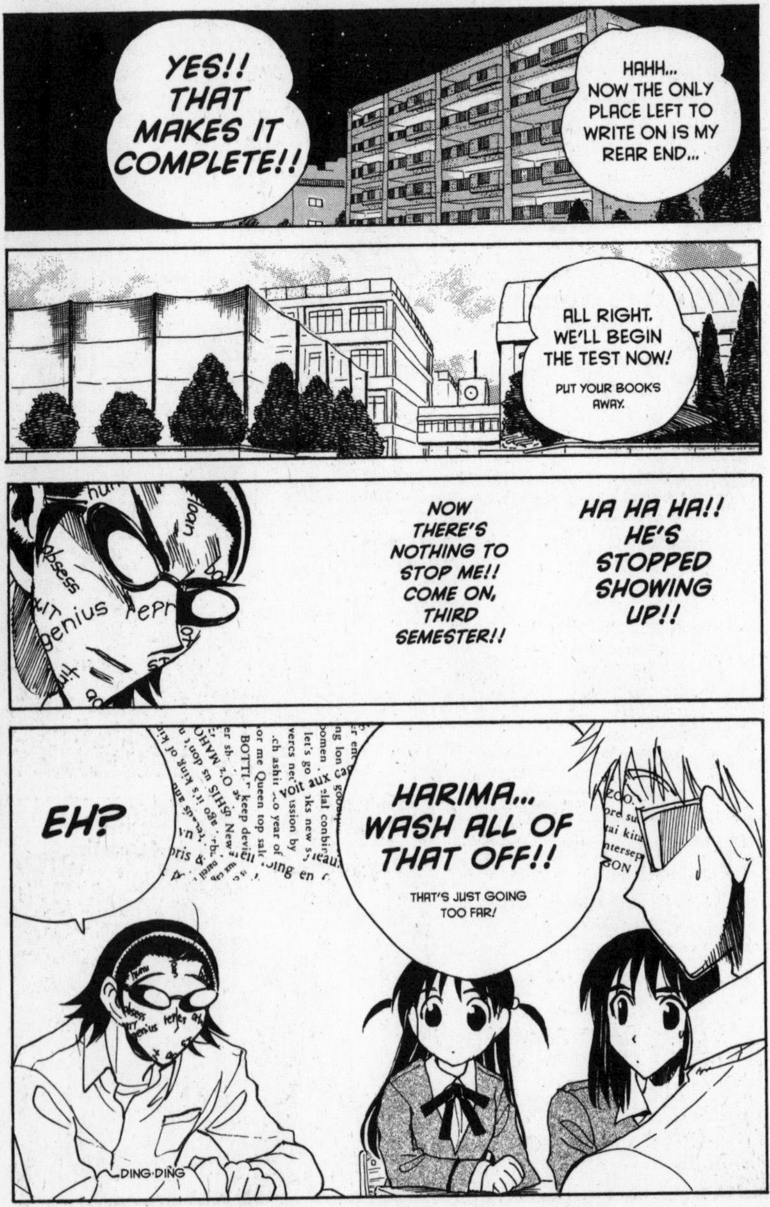
HAHH... NOW THE ONLY PLACE LEFT TO WRITE ON IS MY REAR END...
YES!! THAT MAKES IT COMPLETE!!
ALL RIGHT. WE'LL BEGIN THE TEST NOW!
PUT YOUR BOOKS AWAY.
HA HA HA!! HE'S STOPPED SHOWING UP!!
NOW THERE'S NOTHING TO STOP ME!! COME ON, THIRD SEMESTER!!
HARIMA... WASH ALL OF THAT OFF!!
THAT'S JUST GOING TOO FAR!
EH?
DING DING

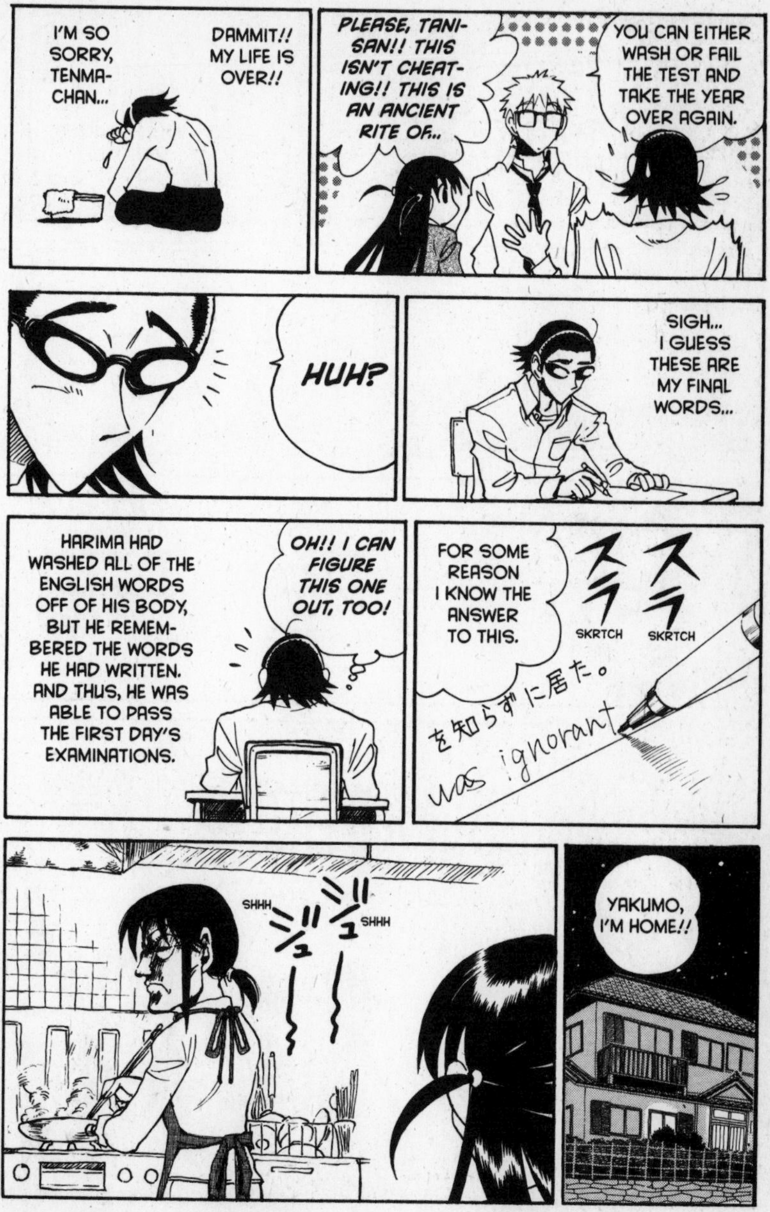
YOU CAN EITHER WASH OR FAIL THE TEST AND TAKE THE YEAR OVER AGAIN.
PLEASE, TANI-SAN!! THIS ISN'T CHEATING!! THIS IS AN ANCIENT RITE OF...
DAMMIT!! MY LIFE IS OVER!!
I'M SO SORRY, TENMA-CHAN...
SIGH... I GUESS THESE ARE MY FINAL WORDS...
HUH?
FOR SOME REASON I KNOW THE ANSWER TO THIS.
スラ
SKRTCH
スラ
SKRTCH
を知らずに居た。
was ignorant
OH!! I CAN FIGURE THIS ONE OUT, TOO!
HARIMA HAD WASHED ALL OF THE ENGLISH WORDS OFF OF HIS BODY, BUT HE REMEMBERED THE WORDS HE HAD WRITTEN. AND THUS, HE WAS ABLE TO PASS THE FIRST DAY'S EXAMINATIONS.
YAKUMO, I'M HOME!!
シュ
SHHH
シュ
SHHH

Are There Any Dumb People Present?

 # 139 . . . . Fin

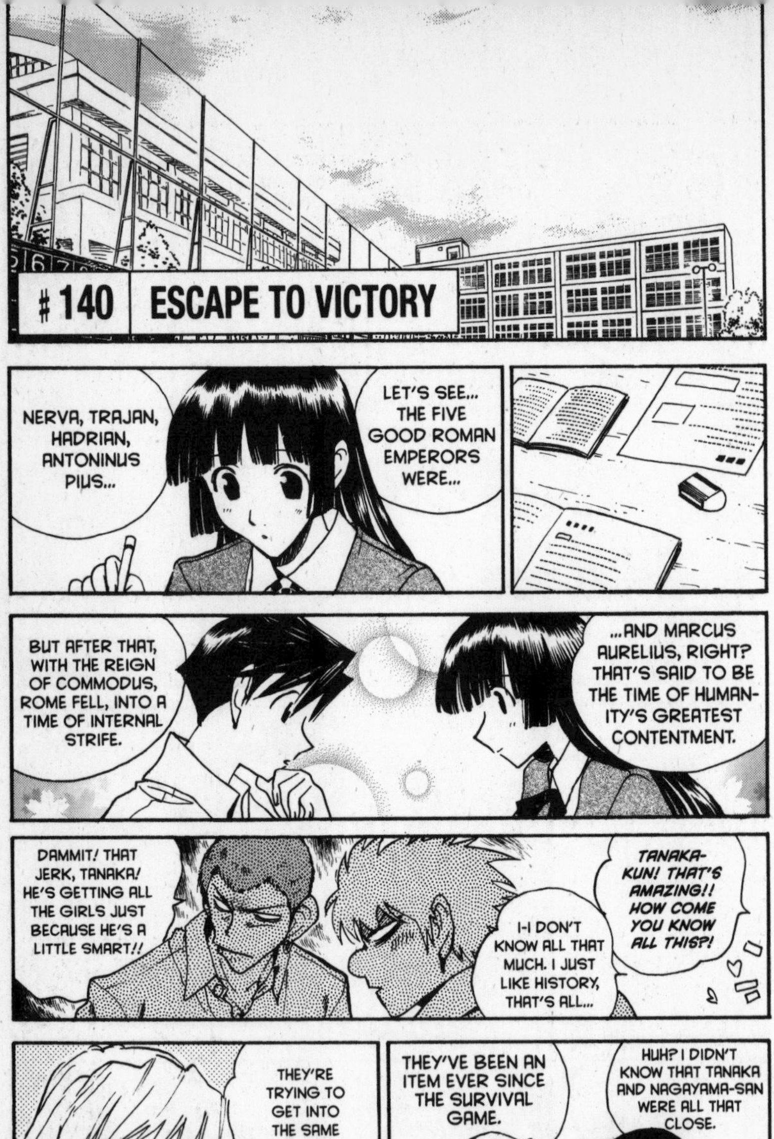

140 ESCAPE TO VICTORY
LET'S SEE... THE FIVE GOOD ROMAN EMPERORS WERE...
NERVA, TRAJAN, HADRIAN, ANTONINUS PIUS...
...AND MARCUS AURELIUS, RIGHT? THAT'S SAID TO BE THE TIME OF HUMANITY'S GREATEST CONTENTMENT.
BUT AFTER THAT, WITH THE REIGN OF COMMODUS, ROME FELL, INTO A TIME OF INTERNAL STRIFE.
TANAKA-KUN! THAT'S AMAZING!! HOW COME YOU KNOW ALL THIS?!
I-I DON'T KNOW ALL THAT MUCH. I JUST LIKE HISTORY, THAT'S ALL...
DAMMIT! THAT JERK, TANAKA! HE'S GETTING ALL THE GIRLS JUST BECAUSE HE'S A LITTLE SMART!!
HUH? I DIDN'T KNOW THAT TANAKA AND NAGAYAMA-SAN WERE ALL THAT CLOSE.
THEY'VE BEEN AN ITEM EVER SINCE THE SURVIVAL GAME.
THEY'RE TRYING TO GET INTO THE SAME COLLEGE.
DO YOUR BEST WITH YOUR STUDIES, TOO, SHIGEO!
SO YOU CAN GET INTO THE SAME COLLEGE I'M GOING TO!

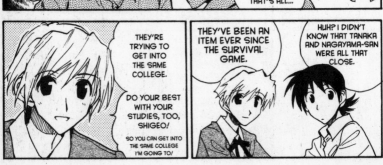

Harima: Spends Each Day Haunted by the Shadow of Hold-Back Sensei.

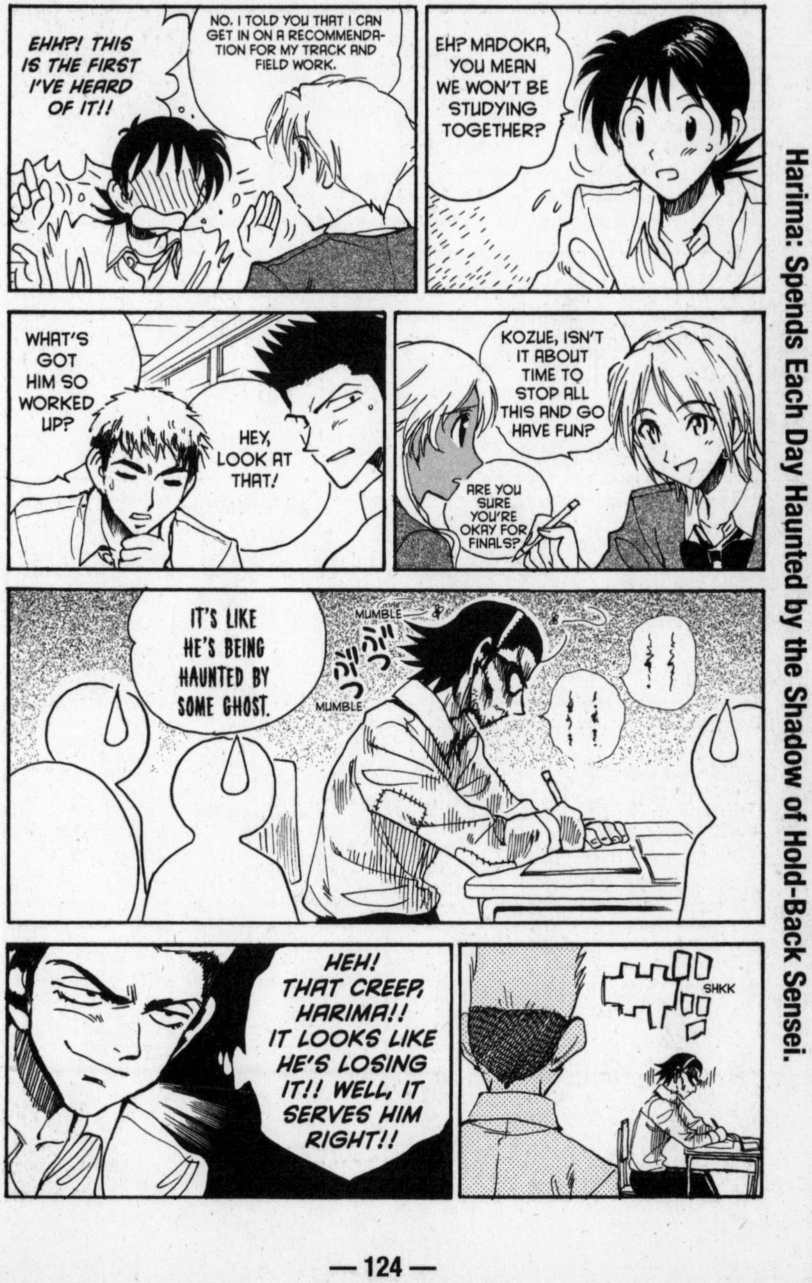
EH? MADOKA, YOU MEAN WE WON'T BE STUDYING TOGETHER?
NO. I TOLD YOU THAT I CAN GET IN ON A RECOMMENDATION FOR MY TRACK AND FIELD WORK.
EHH?! THIS IS THE FIRST I'VE HEARD OF IT!!
KOZUE, ISN'T IT ABOUT TIME TO STOP ALL THIS AND GO HAVE FUN?
ARE YOU SURE YOU'RE OKAY FOR FINALS?
HEY, LOOK AT THAT!
WHAT'S GOT HIM SO WORKED UP?
MUMBLE
MUMBLE
IT'S LIKE HE'S BEING HAUNTED BY SOME GHOST.
SHKK
HEH! THAT CREEP, HARIMA!! IT LOOKS LIKE HE'S LOSING IT!! WELL, IT SERVES HIM RIGHT!!

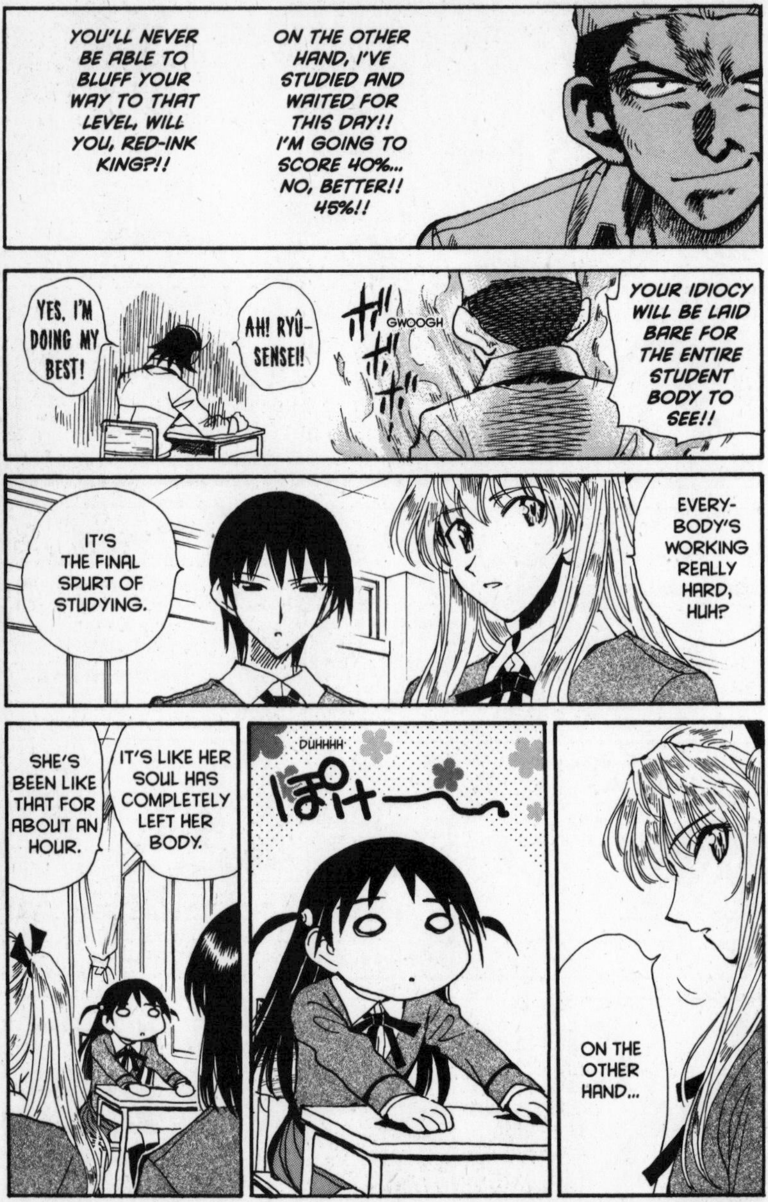
ON THE OTHER HAND, I'VE STUDIED AND WAITED FOR THIS DAY!! I'M GOING TO SCORE 40%... NO, BETTER!! 45%!!
YOU'LL NEVER BE ABLE TO BLUFF YOUR WAY TO THAT LEVEL, WILL YOU, RED-INK KING?!!
YOUR IDIOCY WILL BE LAID BARE FOR THE ENTIRE STUDENT BODY TO SEE!!
GWOOGH
AH! RYÛ-SENSEI!!
YES, I'M DOING MY BEST!
EVERY-BODY'S WORKING REALLY HARD, HUH?
IT'S THE FINAL SPURT OF STUDYING.
ON THE OTHER HAND...
DUHHHH
ぽけ～～
IT'S LIKE HER SOUL HAS COMPLETELY LEFT HER BODY.
SHE'S BEEN LIKE THAT FOR ABOUT AN HOUR.

Yoshidayama Jirô: An Extremely Small Man's Pride.

If She's Held Back a Year, She'll Be in the Same Year as Yakumo.

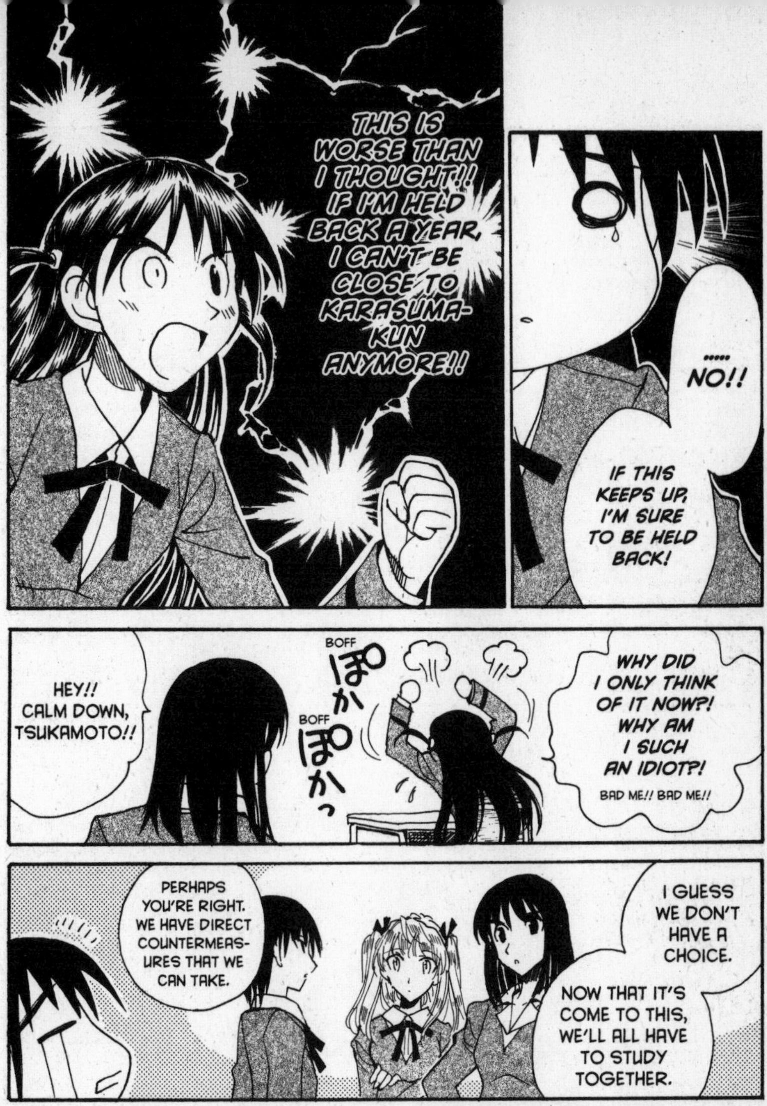

...... NO!!
IF THIS KEEPS UP, I'M SURE TO BE HELD BACK!
THIS IS WORSE THAN I THOUGHT!! IF I'M HELD BACK A YEAR, I CAN'T BE CLOSE TO KARASUMA-KUN ANYMORE!!
WHY DID I ONLY THINK OF IT NOW?! WHY AM I SUCH AN IDIOT?!
BAD ME!! BAD ME!!
BOFF ぽか
BOFF ぽかっ
HEY!! CALM DOWN, TSUKAMOTO!!
I GUESS WE DON'T HAVE A CHOICE.
NOW THAT IT'S COME TO THIS, WE'LL ALL HAVE TO STUDY TOGETHER.
PERHAPS YOU'RE RIGHT. WE HAVE DIRECT COUNTERMEASURES THAT WE CAN TAKE.
TH-THANK YOU, EVERYBODY!!
HEY, DON'T CRY! LET'S GET EVERYBODY TO THE NEXT GRADE TOGETHER, HUH?

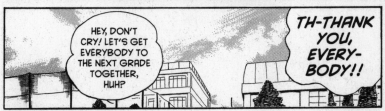

Tsukamoto Tenma: A Close Miss, in a Way.

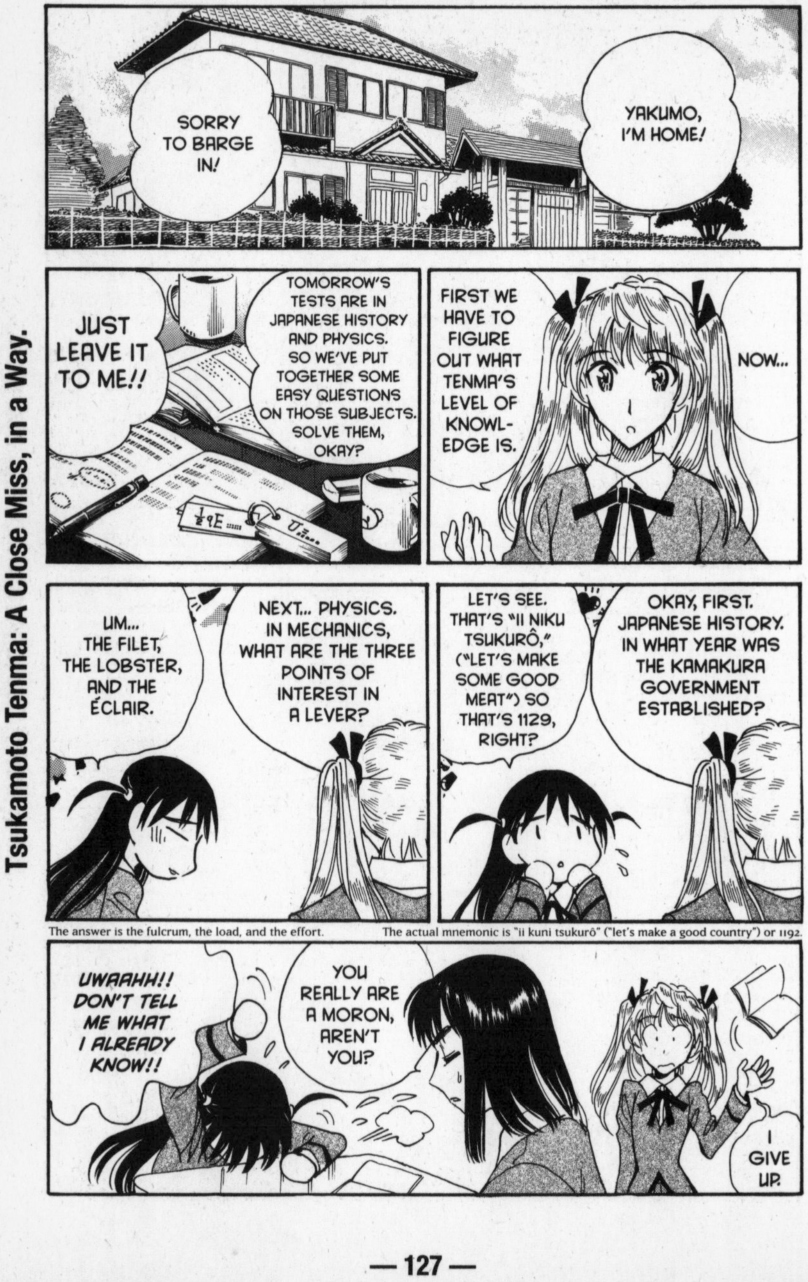
YAKUMO, I'M HOME!
SORRY TO BARGE IN!
NOW...
FIRST WE HAVE TO FIGURE OUT WHAT TENMA'S LEVEL OF KNOWL-EDGE IS.
TOMORROW'S TESTS ARE IN JAPANESE HISTORY AND PHYSICS. SO WE'VE PUT TOGETHER SOME EASY QUESTIONS ON THOSE SUBJECTS. SOLVE THEM, OKAY?
JUST LEAVE IT TO ME!!
OKAY, FIRST. JAPANESE HISTORY. IN WHAT YEAR WAS THE KAMAKURA GOVERNMENT ESTABLISHED?
LET'S SEE. THAT'S "II NIKU TSUKURÔ," ("LET'S MAKE SOME GOOD MEAT") SO THAT'S 1129, RIGHT?
NEXT... PHYSICS. IN MECHANICS, WHAT ARE THE THREE POINTS OF INTEREST IN A LEVER?
UM... THE FILET, THE LOBSTER, AND THE ÉCLAIR.
I GIVE UP.
YOU REALLY ARE A MORON, AREN'T YOU?
UWAAHH!! DON'T TELL ME WHAT I ALREADY KNOW!!

The actual mnemonic is "ii kuni tsukurô" ("let's make a good country") or 1192.

The answer is the fulcrum, the load, and the effort.

She Certainly Has Been Doing...Something.

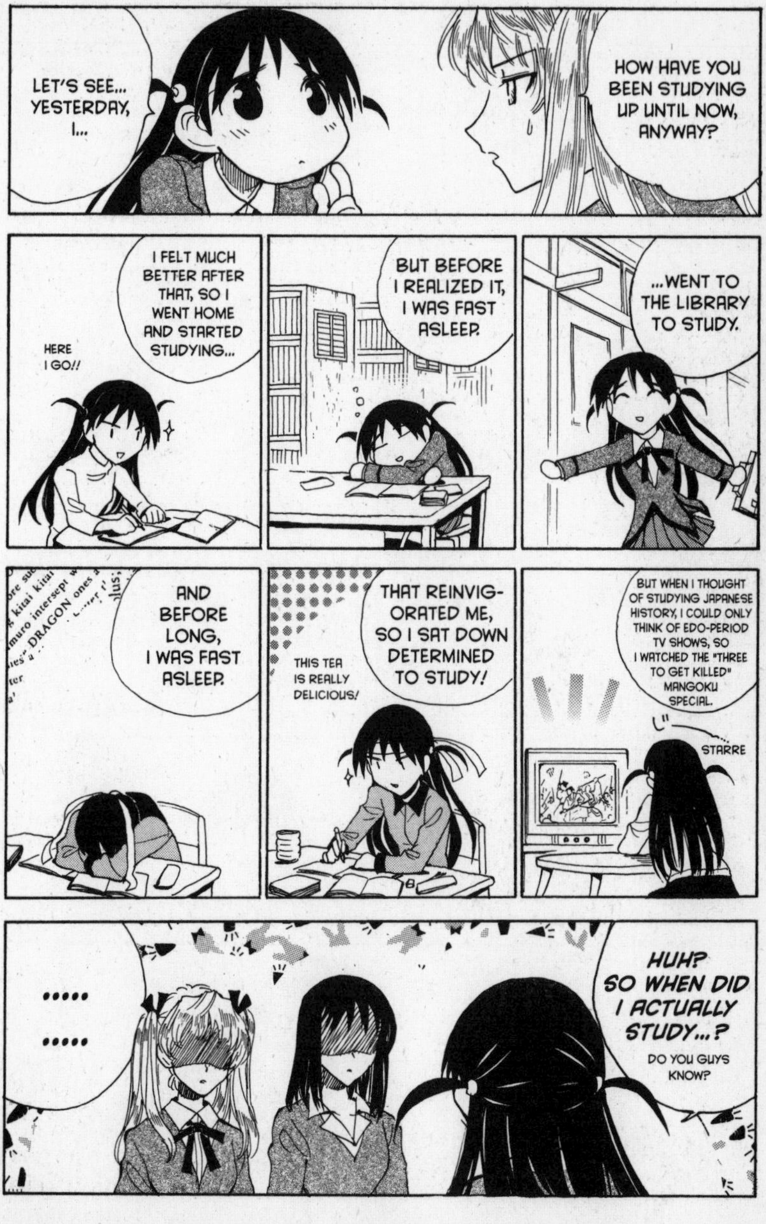
HOW HAVE YOU BEEN STUDYING UP UNTIL NOW, ANYWAY?
LET'S SEE... YESTERDAY, I...
...WENT TO THE LIBRARY TO STUDY.
BUT BEFORE I REALIZED IT, I WAS FAST ASLEEP.
I FELT MUCH BETTER AFTER THAT, SO I WENT HOME AND STARTED STUDYING...
HERE I GO!!
BUT WHEN I THOUGHT OF STUDYING JAPANESE HISTORY, I COULD ONLY THINK OF EDO-PERIOD TV SHOWS, SO I WATCHED THE "THREE TO GET KILLED" MANGOKU SPECIAL.
STARRE
THAT REINVIG-ORATED ME, SO I SAT DOWN DETERMINED TO STUDY!
THIS TEA IS REALLY DELICIOUS!
AND BEFORE LONG, I WAS FAST ASLEEP.
HUH? SO WHEN DID I ACTUALLY STUDY...?
DO YOU GUYS KNOW?
.....
.....

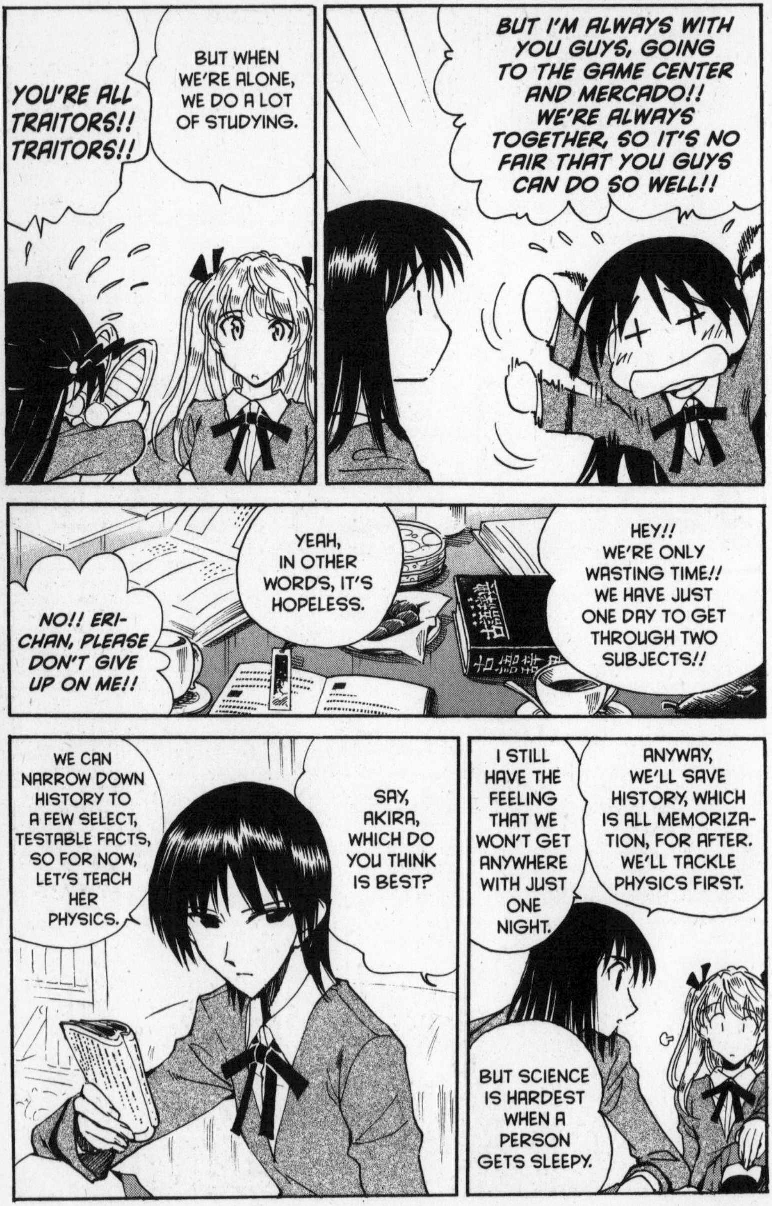
BUT I'M ALWAYS WITH YOU GUYS, GOING TO THE GAME CENTER AND MERCADO!! WE'RE ALWAYS TOGETHER, SO IT'S NO FAIR THAT YOU GUYS CAN DO SO WELL!!
BUT WHEN WE'RE ALONE, WE DO A LOT OF STUDYING.
YOU'RE ALL TRAITORS!! TRAITORS!!
HEY!! WE'RE ONLY WASTING TIME!! WE HAVE JUST ONE DAY TO GET THROUGH TWO SUBJECTS!!
YEAH, IN OTHER WORDS, IT'S HOPELESS.
NO!! ERI-CHAN, PLEASE DON'T GIVE UP ON ME!!
ANYWAY, WE'LL SAVE HISTORY, WHICH IS ALL MEMORIZATION, FOR AFTER. WE'LL TACKLE PHYSICS FIRST.
I STILL HAVE THE FEELING THAT WE WON'T GET ANYWHERE WITH JUST ONE NIGHT.
BUT SCIENCE IS HARDEST WHEN A PERSON GETS SLEEPY.
SAY, AKIRA, WHICH DO YOU THINK IS BEST?
WE CAN NARROW DOWN HISTORY TO A FEW SELECT, TESTABLE FACTS, SO FOR NOW, LET'S TEACH HER PHYSICS.

Tsukamoto Tenma: Fuller Than Full.

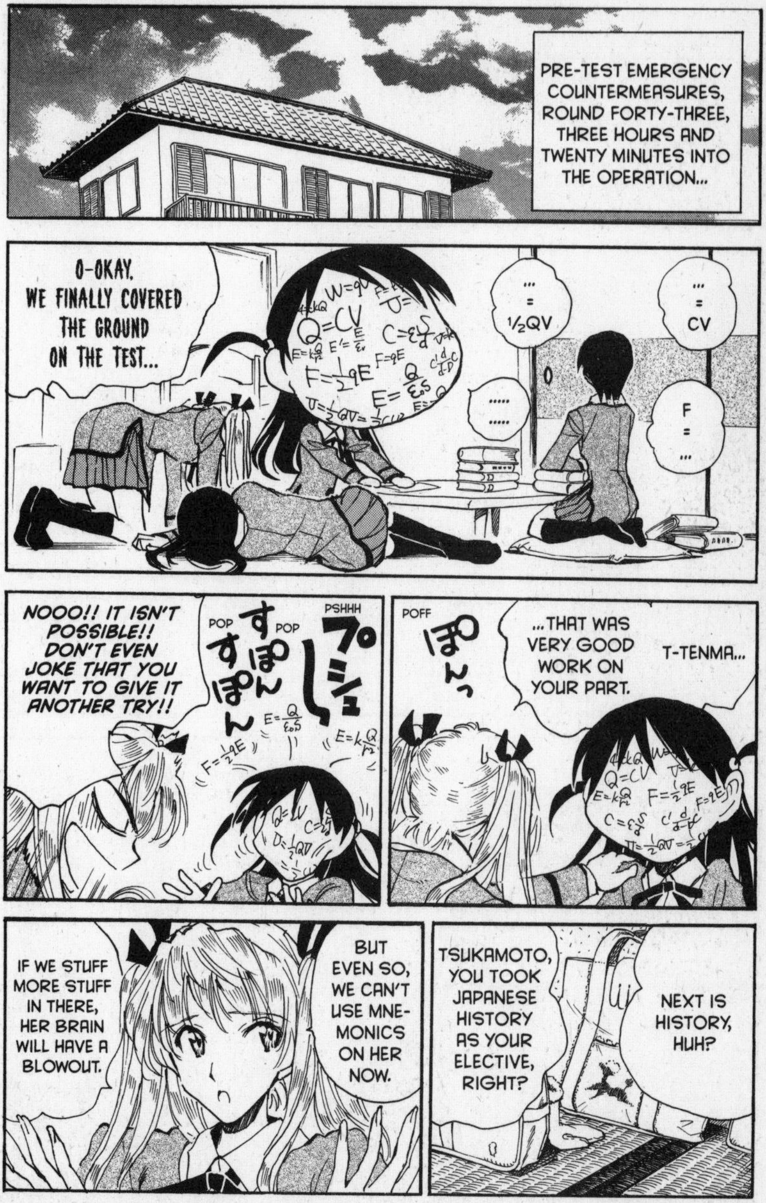
PRE-TEST EMERGENCY COUNTERMEASURES, ROUND FORTY-THREE, THREE HOURS AND TWENTY MINUTES INTO THE OPERATION...
... = CV
F = ...
... = ½QV
....
O-OKAY. WE FINALLY COVERED THE GROUND ON THE TEST...
T-TENMA...
...THAT WAS VERY GOOD WORK ON YOUR PART.
POFF
ぽんっ
PSHHH
プシュしー
POP
すぽん
POP
すぽん
NOOO!! IT ISN'T POSSIBLE!! DON'T EVEN JOKE THAT YOU WANT TO GIVE IT ANOTHER TRY!!
NEXT IS HISTORY, HUH?
TSUKAMOTO, YOU TOOK JAPANESE HISTORY AS YOUR ELECTIVE, RIGHT?
BUT EVEN SO, WE CAN'T USE MNE-MONICS ON HER NOW.
IF WE STUFF MORE STUFF IN THERE, HER BRAIN WILL HAVE A BLOWOUT.

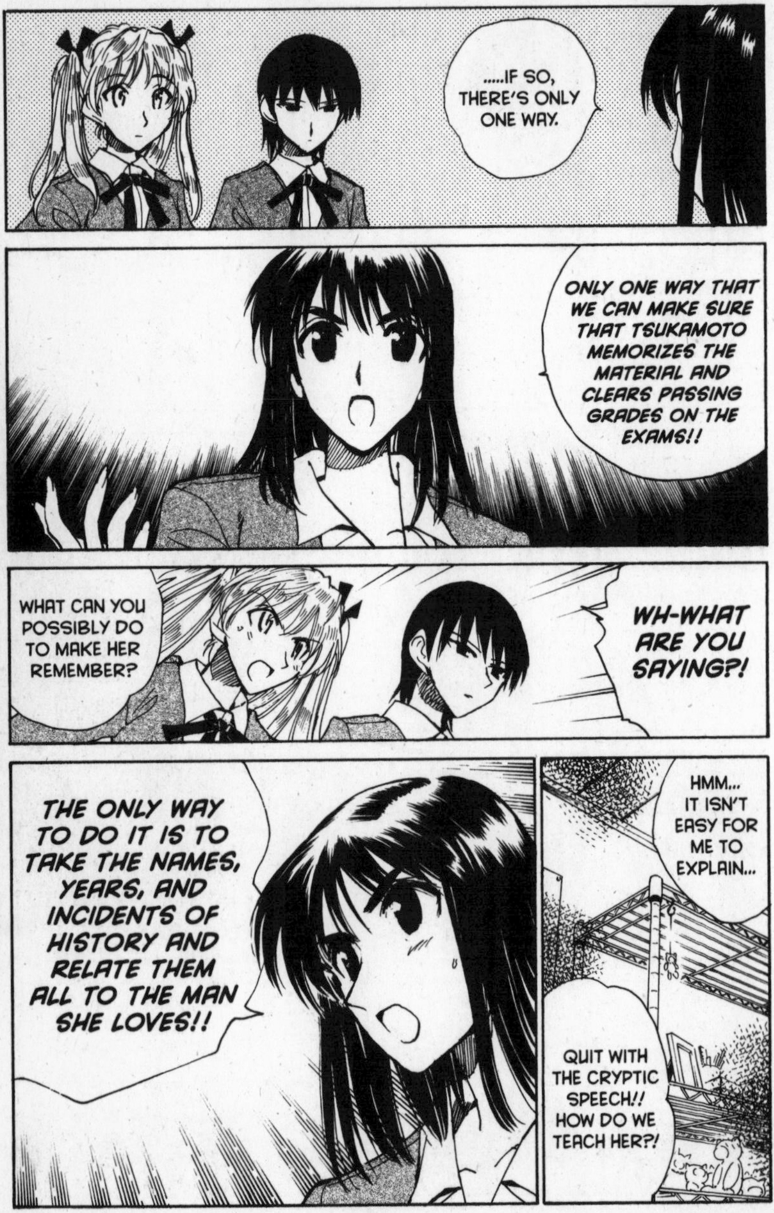
.....IF SO, THERE'S ONLY ONE WAY.
ONLY ONE WAY THAT WE CAN MAKE SURE THAT TSUKAMOTO MEMORIZES THE MATERIAL AND CLEARS PASSING GRADES ON THE EXAMS!!
WH-WHAT ARE YOU SAYING?!
WHAT CAN YOU POSSIBLY DO TO MAKE HER REMEMBER?
HMM... IT ISN'T EASY FOR ME TO EXPLAIN...
QUIT WITH THE CRYPTIC SPEECH!! HOW DO WE TEACH HER?!
THE ONLY WAY TO DO IT IS TO TAKE THE NAMES, YEARS, AND INCIDENTS OF HISTORY AND RELATE THEM ALL TO THE MAN SHE LOVES!!

Caution: Does Not Work for Everyone.

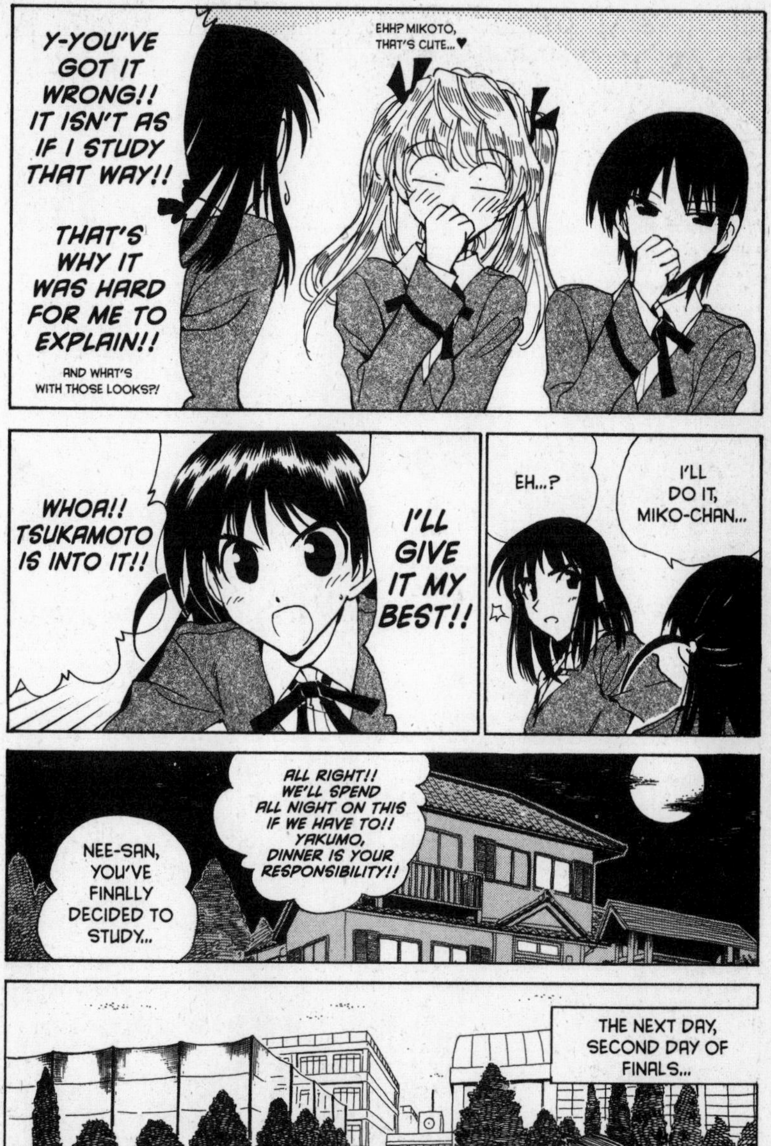
EHH? MIKOTO, THAT'S CUTE...♥
Y-YOU'VE GOT IT WRONG!! IT ISN'T AS IF I STUDY THAT WAY!!
THAT'S WHY IT WAS HARD FOR ME TO EXPLAIN!!
AND WHAT'S WITH THOSE LOOKS?!
I'LL DO IT, MIKO-CHAN...
EH...?
I'LL GIVE IT MY BEST!!
WHOA!! TSUKAMOTO IS INTO IT!!
ALL RIGHT!! WE'LL SPEND ALL NIGHT ON THIS IF WE HAVE TO!! YAKUMO, DINNER IS YOUR RESPONSIBILITY!!
NEE-SAN, YOU'VE FINALLY DECIDED TO STUDY...
THE NEXT DAY, SECOND DAY OF FINALS...

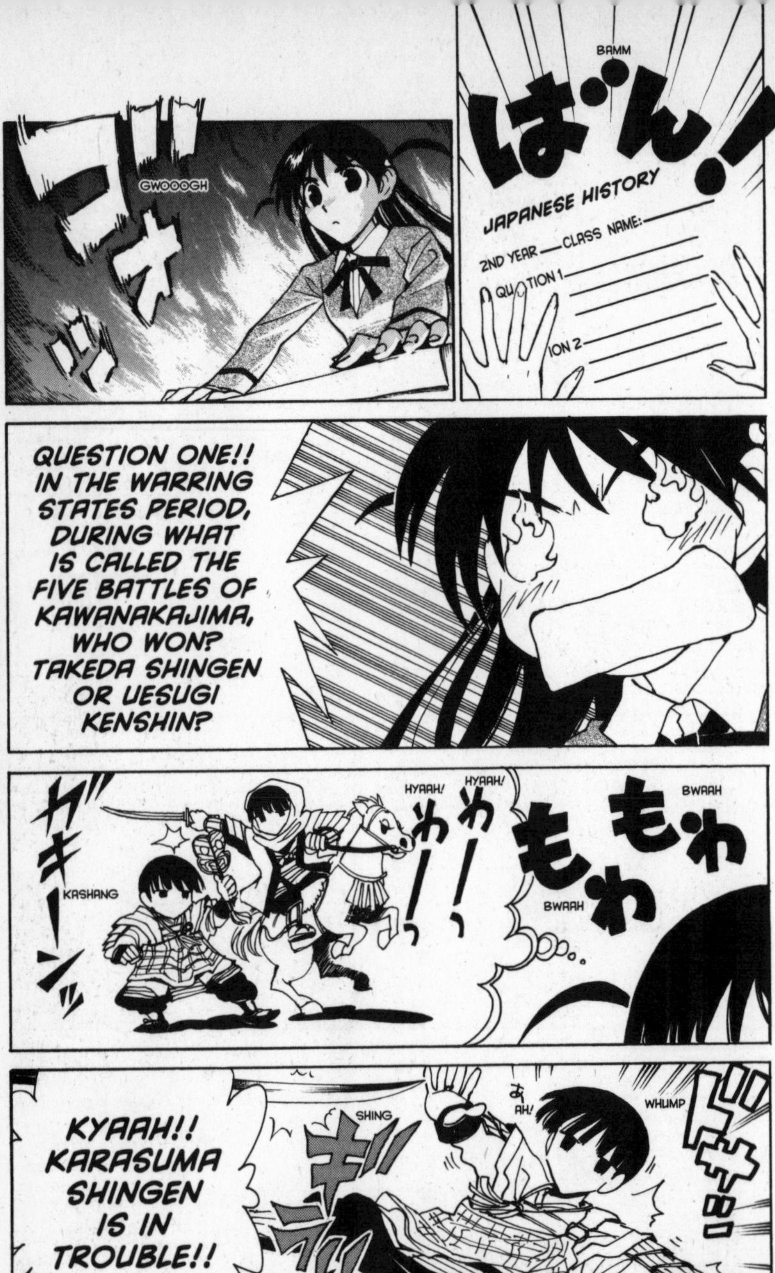
BAMM
ばん!
JAPANESE HISTORY
2ND YEAR — CLASS NAME:
QU TION 1
ION 2
GWOOOGH
QUESTION ONE!! IN THE WARRING STATES PERIOD, DURING WHAT IS CALLED THE FIVE BATTLES OF KAWANAKAJIMA, WHO WON? TAKEDA SHINGEN OR UESUGI KENSHIN?
BWAAH
BWAAH
HYAAH!
HYAAH!
KASHANG
WHUMP
AH!
SHING
KYAAH!! KARASUMA SHINGEN IS IN TROUBLE!!

Yoshidayama, Behind You! Behind You!

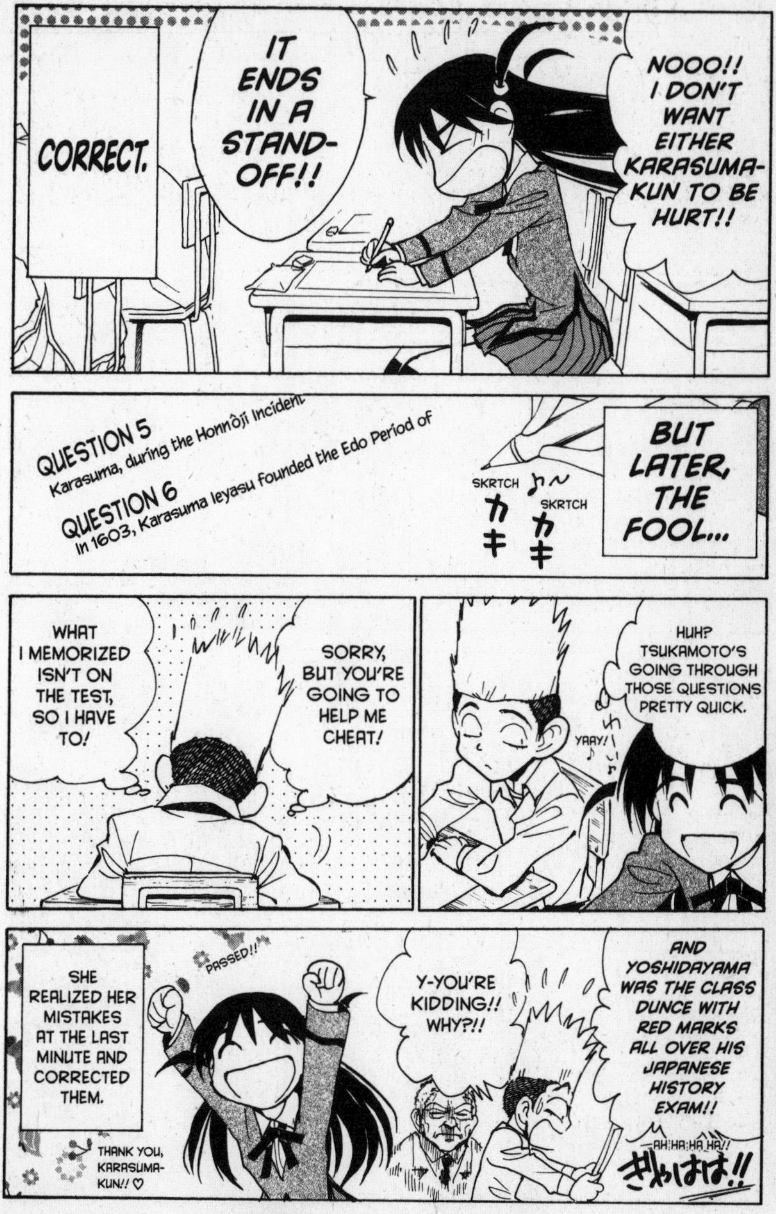
NOOO!! I DON'T WANT EITHER KARASUMA-KUN TO BE HURT!!
IT ENDS IN A STAND-OFF!!
CORRECT.
BUT LATER, THE FOOL...
SKRTCH
SKRTCH
QUESTION 5
Karasuma, during the Honnôji Incident
QUESTION 6
In 1603, Karasuma Ieyasu founded the Edo Period of
HUH? TSUKAMOTO'S GOING THROUGH THOSE QUESTIONS PRETTY QUICK.
YAAY!
SORRY, BUT YOU'RE GOING TO HELP ME CHEAT!
WHAT I MEMORIZED ISN'T ON THE TEST, SO I HAVE TO!
AND YOSHIDAYAMA WAS THE CLASS DUNCE WITH RED MARKS ALL OVER HIS JAPANESE HISTORY EXAM!!
AH HA HA HA!!
Y-YOU'RE KIDDING!! WHY?!!
PASSED!!
SHE REALIZED HER MISTAKES AT THE LAST MINUTE AND CORRECTED THEM.
THANK YOU, KARASUMA-KUN!! ♡

140 . . . . Fin

♭30 ASSAULT ON A QUEEN

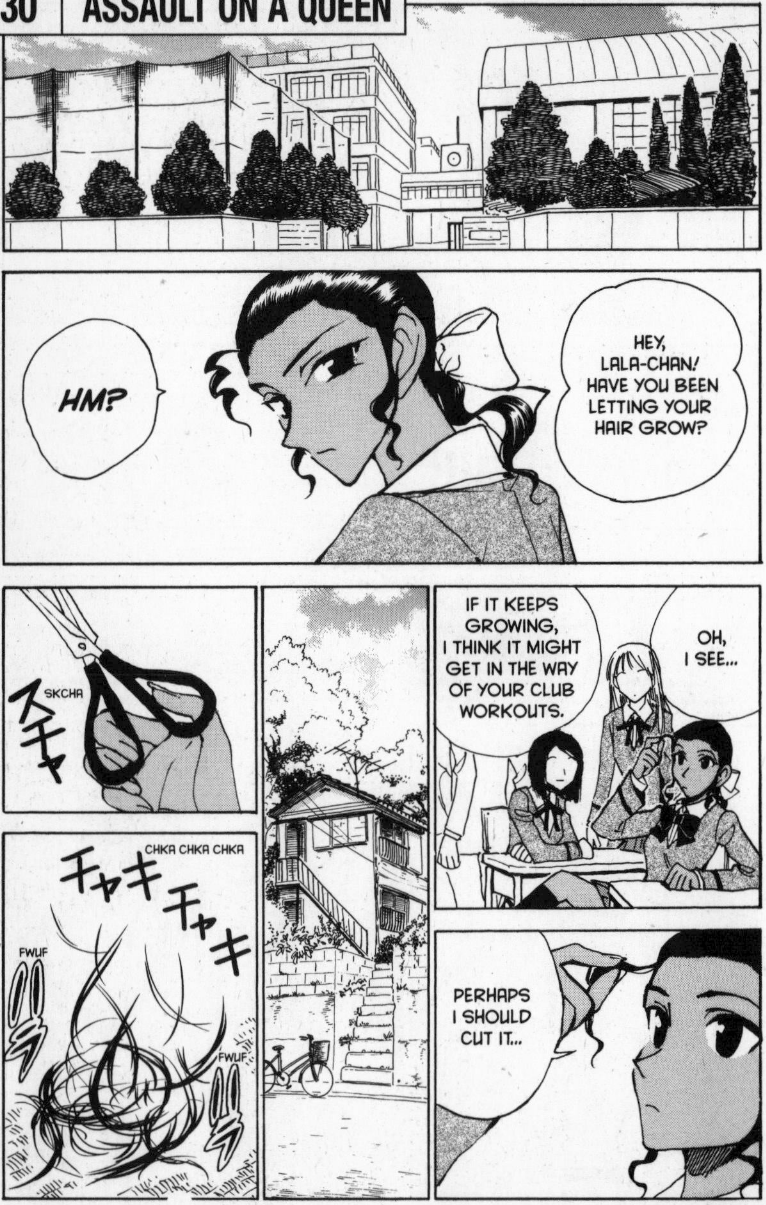
HEY, LALA-CHAN! HAVE YOU BEEN LETTING YOUR HAIR GROW?
HM?
OH, I SEE...
IF IT KEEPS GROWING, I THINK IT MIGHT GET IN THE WAY OF YOUR CLUB WORKOUTS.
PERHAPS I SHOULD CUT IT...
スチャ
SKCHA
チャキ チャキ
CHKA CHKA CHKA
FWUF
FWUF

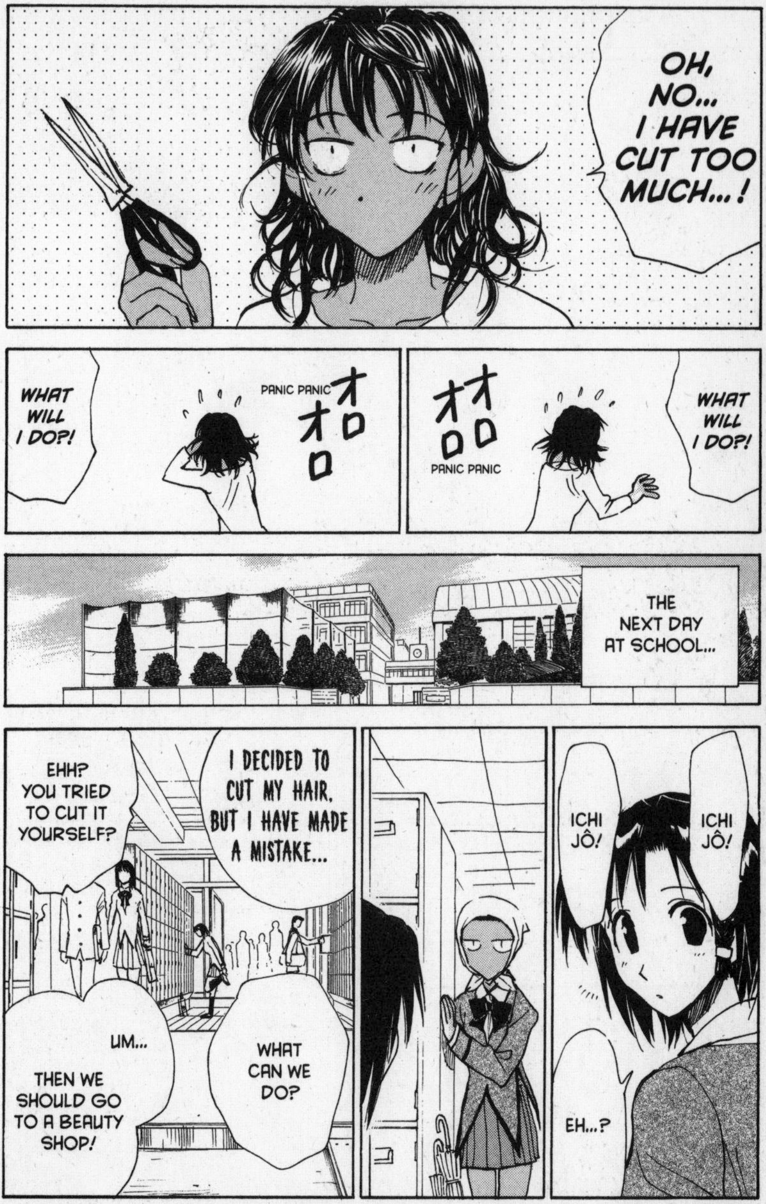

OH, NO... I HAVE CUT TOO MUCH...!
WHAT WILL I DO?!
PANIC PANIC
WHAT WILL I DO?!
PANIC PANIC
THE NEXT DAY AT SCHOOL...
ICHI JÔ!
ICHI JÔ!
EH...?
I DECIDED TO CUT MY HAIR, BUT I HAVE MADE A MISTAKE...
EHH? YOU TRIED TO CUT IT YOURSELF?
WHAT CAN WE DO?
UM...
THEN WE SHOULD GO TO A BEAUTY SHOP!

Lala: First Beauty Shop Experience.

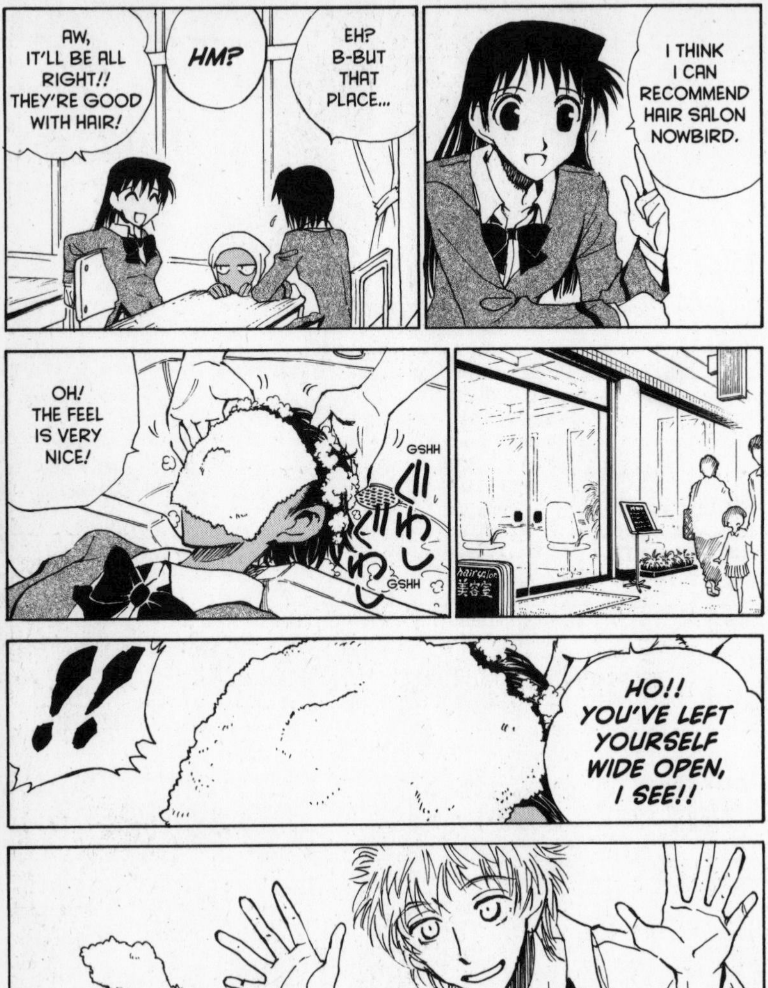
I THINK I CAN RECOMMEND HAIR SALON NOWBIRD.
EH? B-BUT THAT PLACE...
HM?
AW, IT'LL BE ALL RIGHT!! THEY'RE GOOD WITH HAIR!
美容室
GSHH
GSHH
OH! THE FEEL IS VERY NICE!
HO!! YOU'VE LEFT YOURSELF WIDE OPEN, I SEE!!
!!
YO!

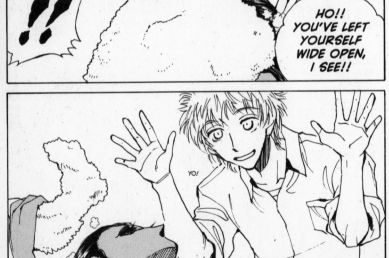

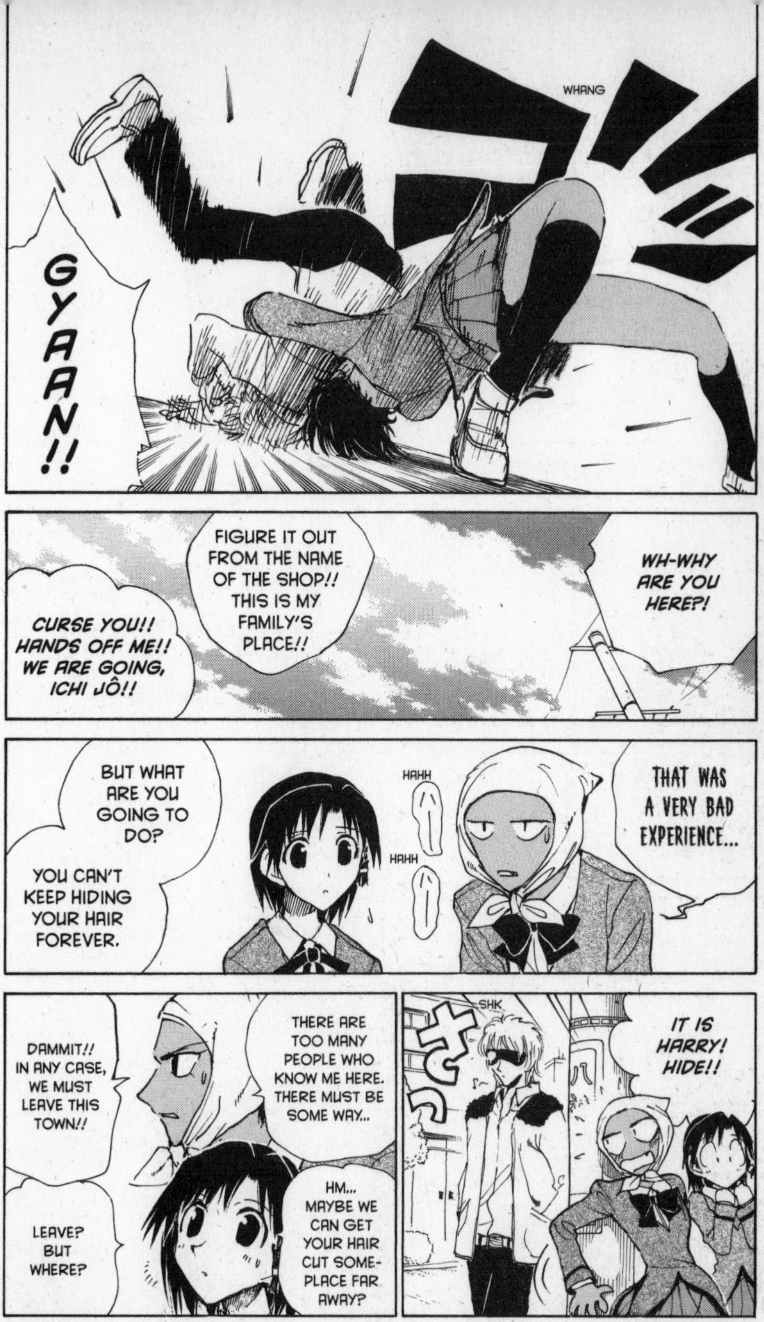
WHANG
GYAAAN!!
WH-WHY ARE YOU HERE?!
FIGURE IT OUT FROM THE NAME OF THE SHOP!! THIS IS MY FAMILY'S PLACE!!
CURSE YOU!! HANDS OFF ME!! WE ARE GOING, ICHI JÔ!!
THAT WAS A VERY BAD EXPERIENCE...
HAHH
HAHH
BUT WHAT ARE YOU GOING TO DO?
YOU CAN'T KEEP HIDING YOUR HAIR FOREVER.
IT IS HARRY! HIDE!!
SHK
THERE ARE TOO MANY PEOPLE WHO KNOW ME HERE. THERE MUST BE SOME WAY...
DAMMIT!! IN ANY CASE, WE MUST LEAVE THIS TOWN!!
HM... MAYBE WE CAN GET YOUR HAIR CUT SOME-PLACE FAR AWAY?
LEAVE? BUT WHERE?

Imadori Kyôsuke: Family Owns a Beauty Salon.

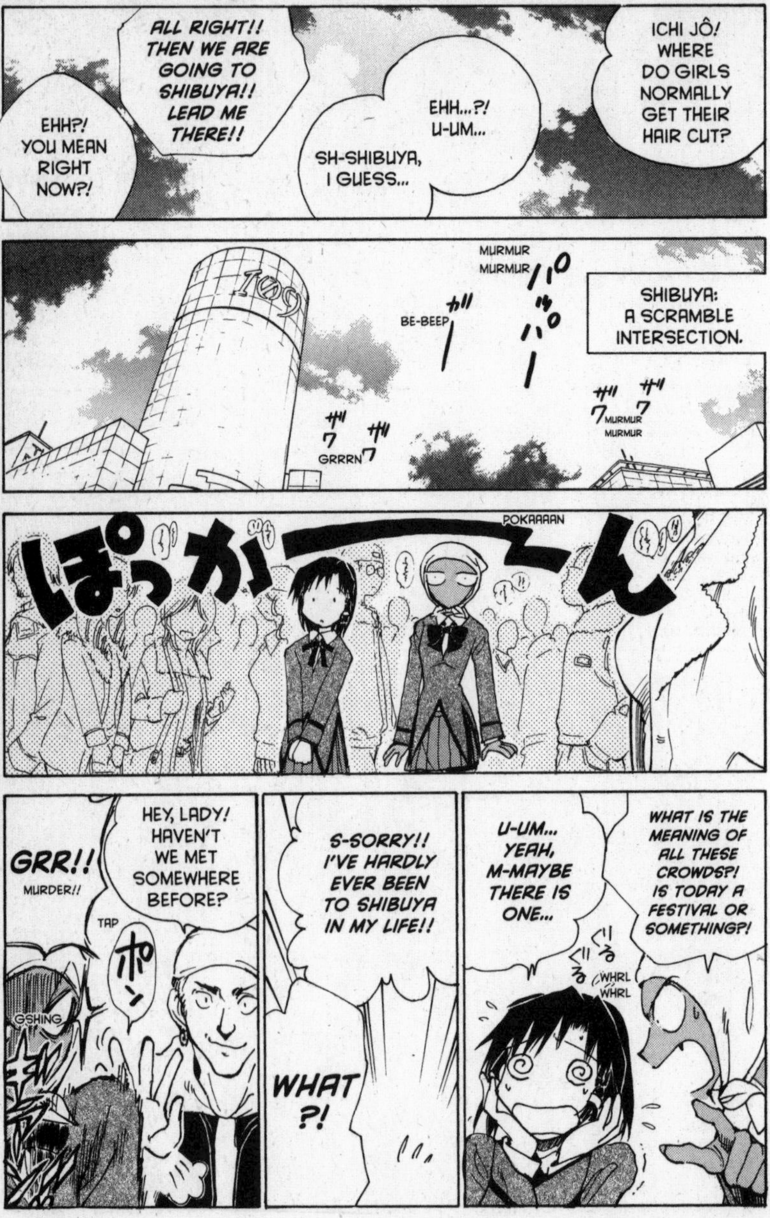
ICHI JÔ! WHERE DO GIRLS NORMALLY GET THEIR HAIR CUT?
EHH...?! U-UM...
SH-SHIBUYA, I GUESS...
ALL RIGHT!! THEN WE ARE GOING TO SHIBUYA!! LEAD ME THERE!!
EHH?! YOU MEAN RIGHT NOW?!
SHIBUYA: A SCRAMBLE INTERSECTION.
MURMUR MURMUR
MURMUR MURMUR
BE-BEEP
GRRRN
ぽっかーーん
POKAAAAN
WHAT IS THE MEANING OF ALL THESE CROWDS?! IS TODAY A FESTIVAL OR SOMETHING?!
U-UM... YEAH, M-MAYBE THERE IS ONE...
WHRL WHRL
S-SORRY!! I'VE HARDLY EVER BEEN TO SHIBUYA IN MY LIFE!!
WHAT ?!
HEY, LADY! HAVEN'T WE MET SOMEWHERE BEFORE?
ポン
TAP
GRR!!
MURDER!!
GSHING

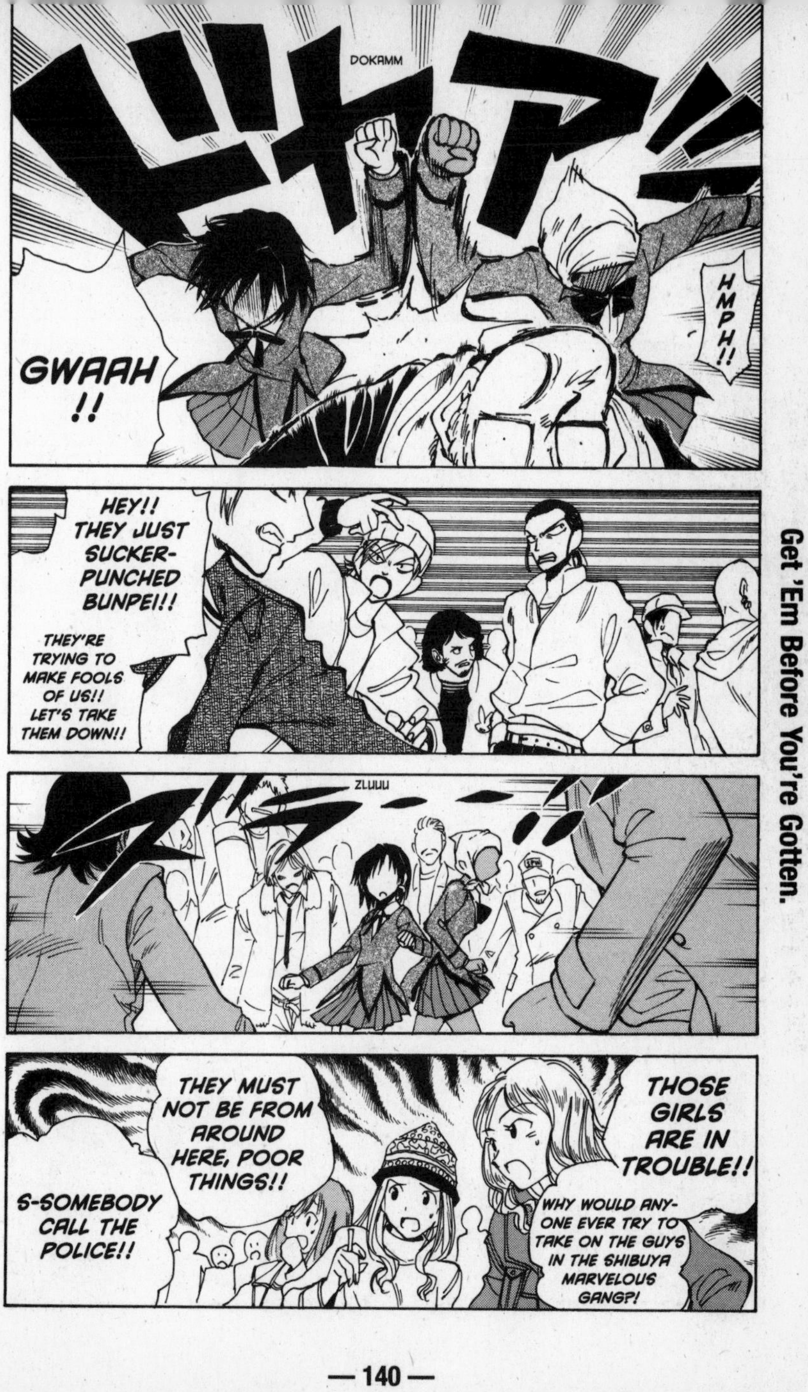
DOKAMM
HMPH!!
GWAAH!!
HEY!! THEY JUST SUCKER-PUNCHED BUNPEI!!
THEY'RE TRYING TO MAKE FOOLS OF US!! LET'S TAKE THEM DOWN!!
ZLUUU
THOSE GIRLS ARE IN TROUBLE!!
WHY WOULD ANYONE EVER TRY TO TAKE ON THE GUYS IN THE SHIBUYA MARVELOUS GANG?!
THEY MUST NOT BE FROM AROUND HERE, POOR THINGS!!
S-SOMEBODY CALL THE POLICE!!

Warrior Worth 1000 Men x 2 = Power Times 20 Million.

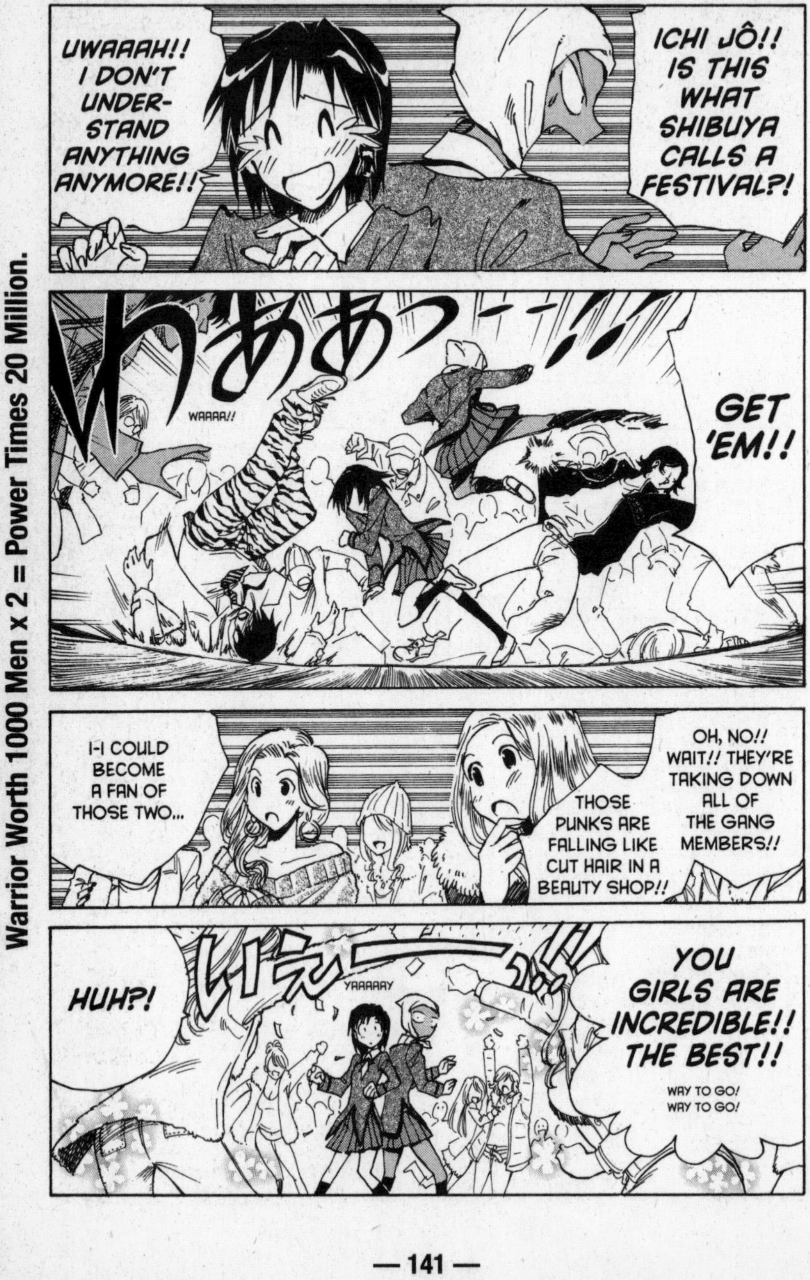
ICHI JÔ!! IS THIS WHAT SHIBUYA CALLS A FESTIVAL?!
UWAAAH!! I DON'T UNDER-STAND ANYTHING ANYMORE!!
わあああっーーー!!
GET 'EM!!
WAAAA!!
OH, NO!! WAIT!! THEY'RE TAKING DOWN ALL OF THE GANG MEMBERS!!
THOSE PUNKS ARE FALLING LIKE CUT HAIR IN A BEAUTY SHOP!!
I-I COULD BECOME A FAN OF THOSE TWO...
YOU GIRLS ARE INCREDIBLE!! THE BEST!!
WAY TO GO! WAY TO GO!
いえーーーっ!!
YAAAAAY
HUH?!

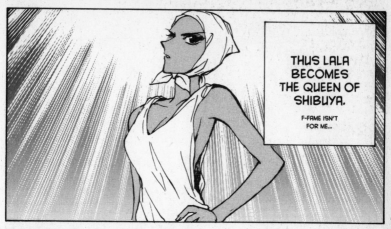

THUS LALA BECOMES THE QUEEN OF SHIBUYA.
F-FAME ISN'T FOR ME...
LA-LA!! LA-LA!!
LA-LA!! LA-LA!!
"GIRLS BE LALA" BECOMES A CATCHPHRASE AMONG ALL OF THE HIGH SCHOOL-AGED GIRLS IN THE AREA AROUND SHIBUYA, AND THE COVERED-HEAD "LALA LOOK" BECOMES ALL THE RAGE.
BUSINESSES START TAKING NOTICE OF WOMEN WHO ARE BOTH BEAUTIFUL AND STRONG.
Lala
AND IN ONLY A WEEK, SHE IS FOUND ON ADVERTISING FOR LINES OF COSMETICS AND APPAREL.
THEY SAY THEY WANT ME TO RELEASE A SINGLE!!
THE TITLE IS, "MY BOYFRIEND IS MASKMAN"!
YOU'RE KIDDING!!
BUT THE CD IS A DUD, AND LALA SOON RETURNS TO SCHOOL.
GOOD THING, TOO, HUH?

♭30· · · · · · · · · Fin

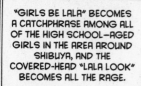

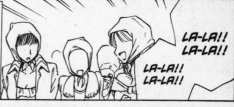

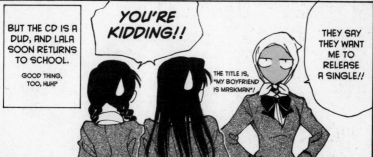

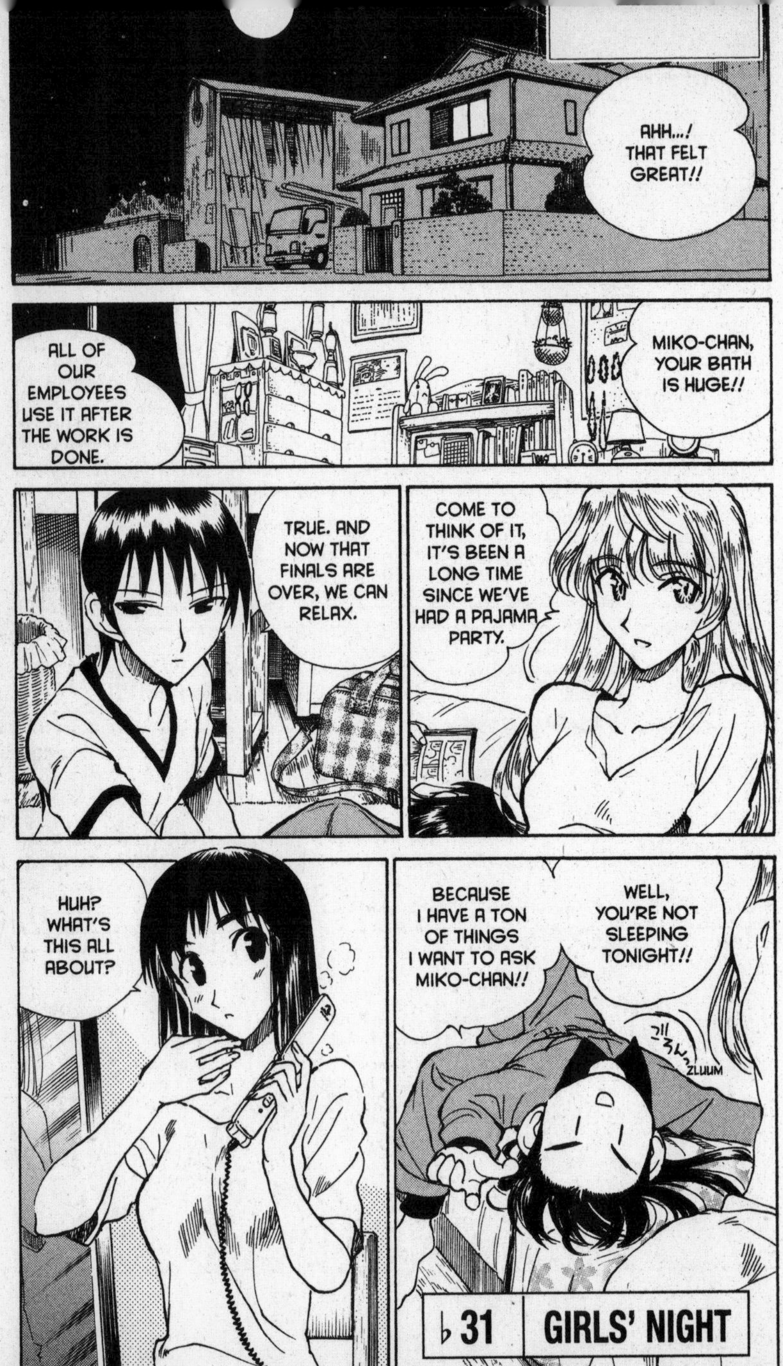
AHH...! THAT FELT GREAT!!
MIKO-CHAN, YOUR BATH IS HUGE!!
ALL OF OUR EMPLOYEES USE IT AFTER THE WORK IS DONE.
COME TO THINK OF IT, IT'S BEEN A LONG TIME SINCE WE'VE HAD A PAJAMA PARTY.
TRUE. AND NOW THAT FINALS ARE OVER, WE CAN RELAX.
WELL, YOU'RE NOT SLEEPING TONIGHT!!
BECAUSE I HAVE A TON OF THINGS I WANT TO ASK MIKO-CHAN!!
ZLUUM
♭ 31 GIRLS' NIGHT
HUH? WHAT'S THIS ALL ABOUT?

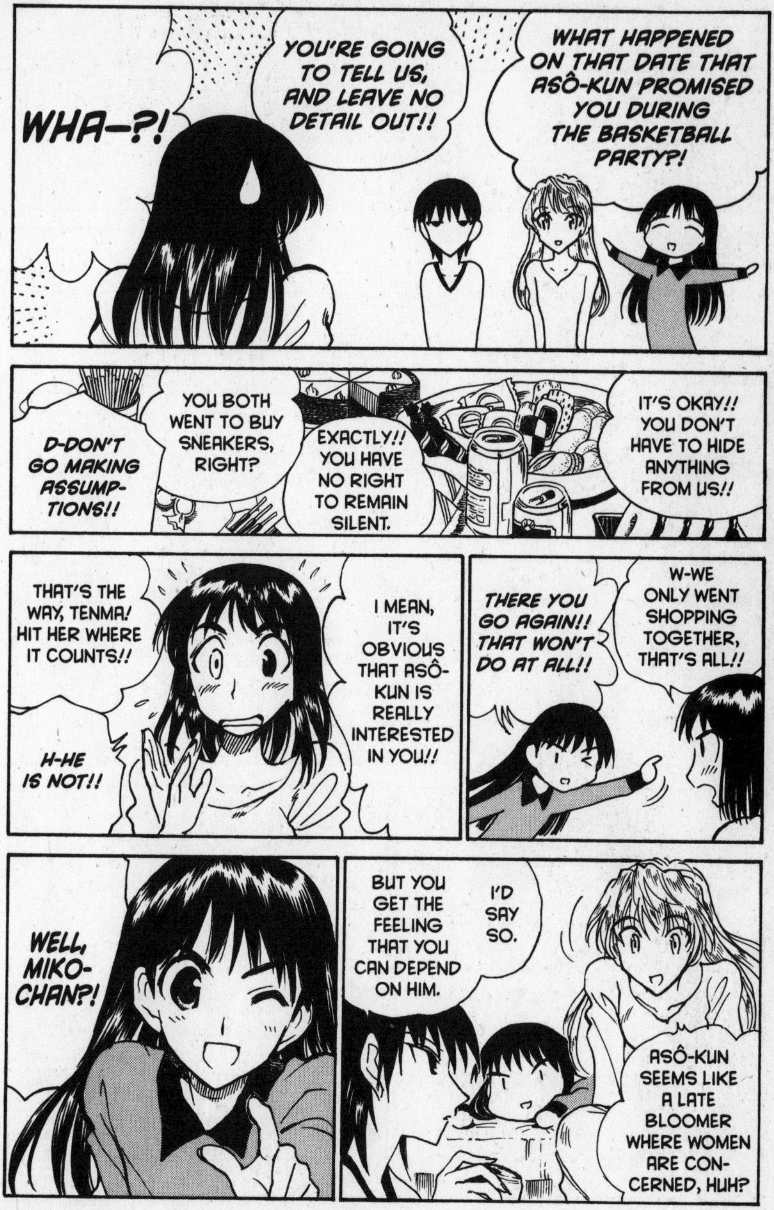
WHAT HAPPENED ON THAT DATE THAT ASÔ-KUN PROMISED YOU DURING THE BASKETBALL PARTY?!
YOU'RE GOING TO TELL US, AND LEAVE NO DETAIL OUT!!
WHA-?!
IT'S OKAY!! YOU DON'T HAVE TO HIDE ANYTHING FROM US!!
EXACTLY!! YOU HAVE NO RIGHT TO REMAIN SILENT.
YOU BOTH WENT TO BUY SNEAKERS, RIGHT?
D-DON'T GO MAKING ASSUMP-TIONS!!
W-WE ONLY WENT SHOPPING TOGETHER, THAT'S ALL!!
THERE YOU GO AGAIN!! THAT WON'T DO AT ALL!!
I MEAN, IT'S OBVIOUS THAT ASÔ-KUN IS REALLY INTERESTED IN YOU!!
THAT'S THE WAY, TENMA! HIT HER WHERE IT COUNTS!!
H-HE IS NOT!!
I'D SAY SO.
BUT YOU GET THE FEELING THAT YOU CAN DEPEND ON HIM.
ASÔ-KUN SEEMS LIKE A LATE BLOOMER WHERE WOMEN ARE CON-CERNED, HUH?
WELL, MIKO-CHAN?!

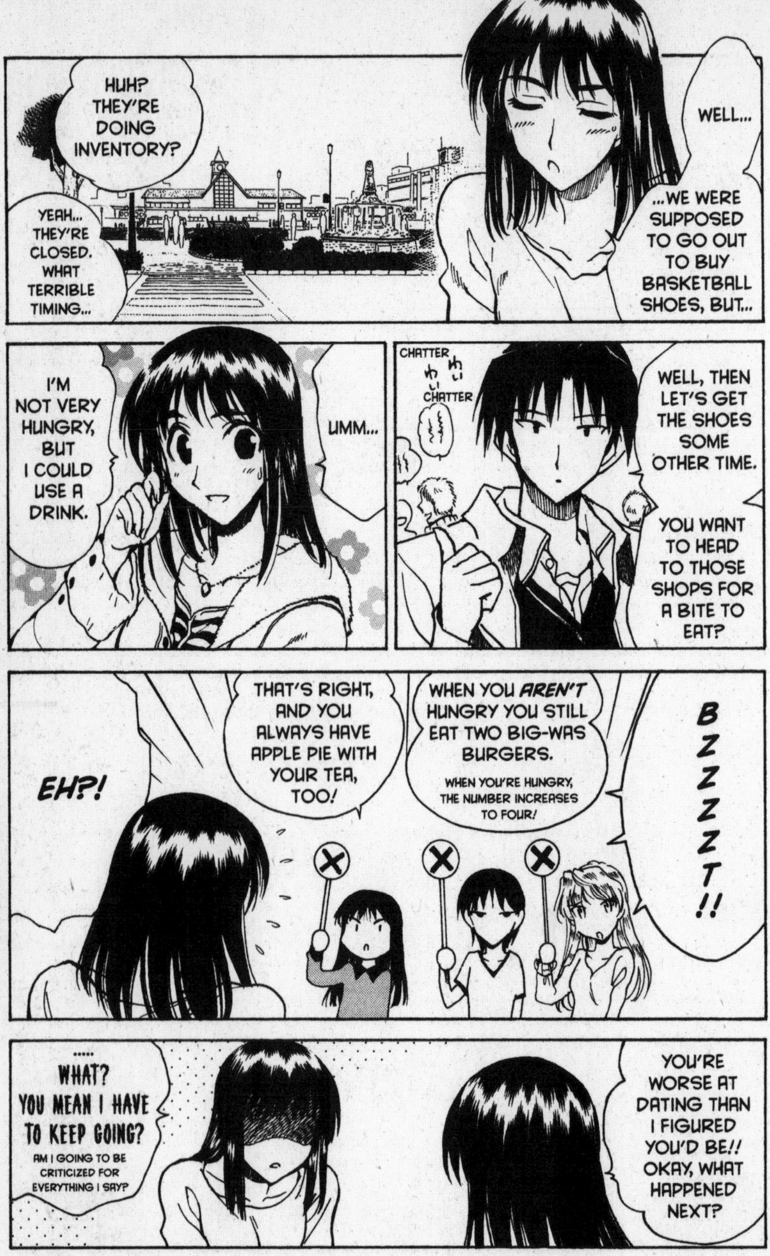
WELL...
...WE WERE SUPPOSED TO GO OUT TO BUY BASKETBALL SHOES, BUT...
HUH? THEY'RE DOING INVENTORY?
YEAH... THEY'RE CLOSED. WHAT TERRIBLE TIMING...
CHATTER
CHATTER
WELL, THEN LET'S GET THE SHOES SOME OTHER TIME.
YOU WANT TO HEAD TO THOSE SHOPS FOR A BITE TO EAT?
UMM...
I'M NOT VERY HUNGRY, BUT I COULD USE A DRINK.
BZZZZZT!!
WHEN YOU *AREN'T* HUNGRY YOU STILL EAT TWO BIG-WAS BURGERS.
WHEN YOU'RE HUNGRY, THE NUMBER INCREASES TO FOUR!
THAT'S RIGHT, AND YOU ALWAYS HAVE APPLE PIE WITH YOUR TEA, TOO!
EH?!
YOU'RE WORSE AT DATING THAN I FIGURED YOU'D BE!! OKAY, WHAT HAPPENED NEXT?
...... WHAT? YOU MEAN I HAVE TO KEEP GOING?
AM I GOING TO BE CRITICIZED FOR EVERYTHING I SAY?

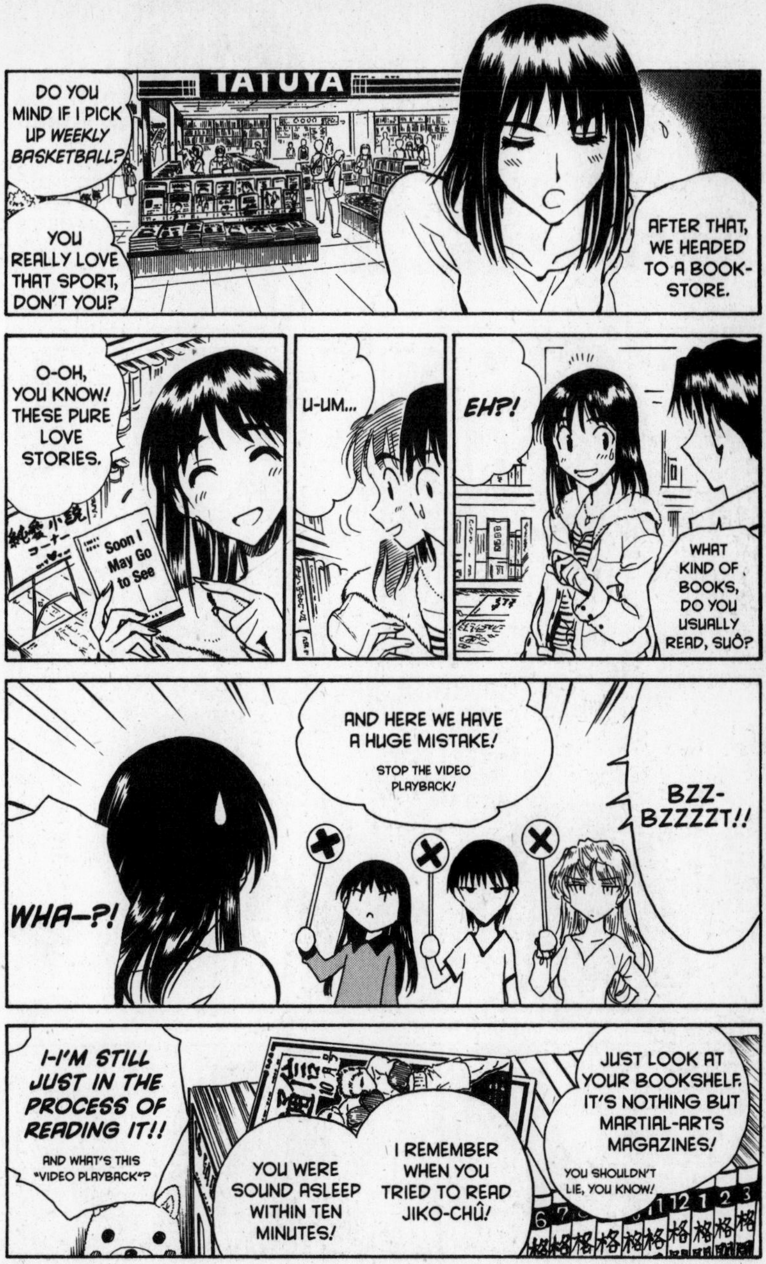
AFTER THAT, WE HEADED TO A BOOK-STORE.
TATUYA
DO YOU MIND IF I PICK UP WEEKLY BASKETBALL?
YOU REALLY LOVE THAT SPORT, DON'T YOU?
WHAT KIND OF BOOKS, DO YOU USUALLY READ, SUÔ?
EH?!
U-UM...
O-OH, YOU KNOW! THESE PURE LOVE STORIES.
純愛小説コーナー
Soon I May Go to See
BZZ-BZZZZT!!
AND HERE WE HAVE A HUGE MISTAKE!
STOP THE VIDEO PLAYBACK!
WHA-?!
JUST LOOK AT YOUR BOOKSHELF. IT'S NOTHING BUT MARTIAL-ARTS MAGAZINES!
YOU SHOULDN'T LIE, YOU KNOW!
I REMEMBER WHEN YOU TRIED TO READ JIKO-CHÛ!
YOU WERE SOUND ASLEEP WITHIN TEN MINUTES!
I-I'M STILL JUST IN THE PROCESS OF READING IT!!
AND WHAT'S THIS "VIDEO PLAYBACK"?

Suô Mikoto: At Least Shows Evidence of Hard Work.

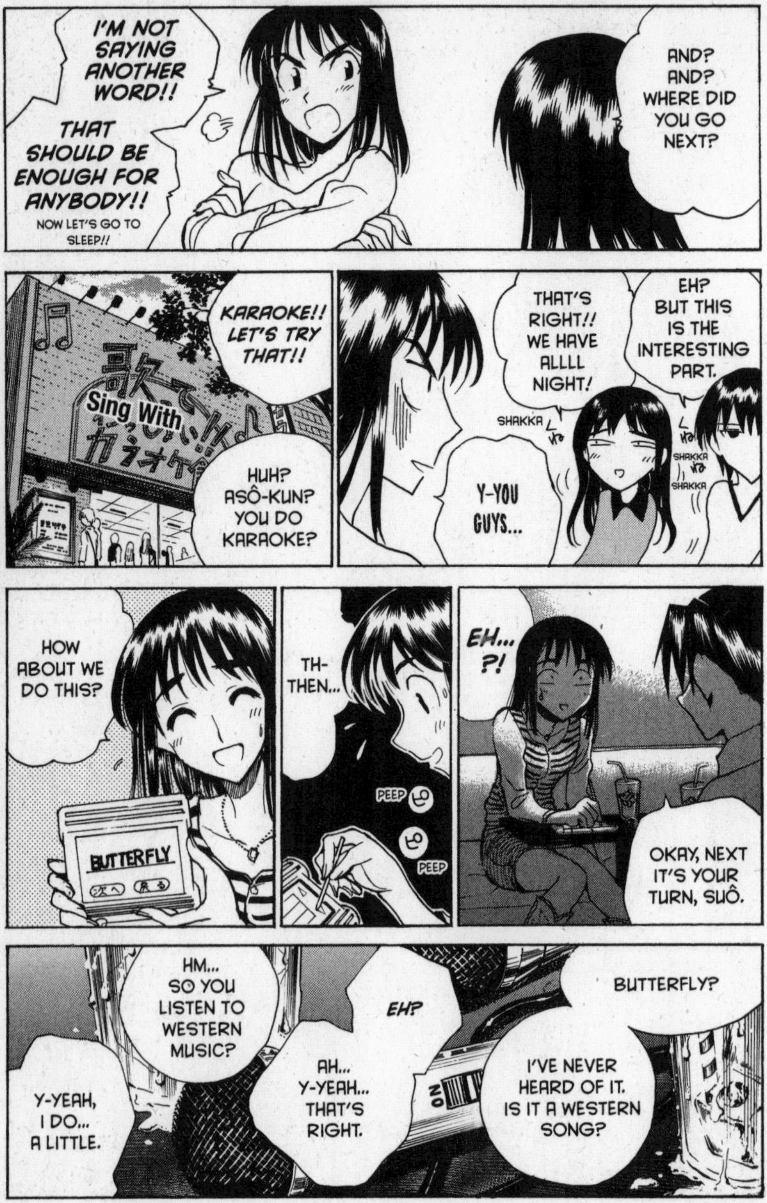
AND? AND? WHERE DID YOU GO NEXT?
I'M NOT SAYING ANOTHER WORD!!
THAT SHOULD BE ENOUGH FOR ANYBODY!!
NOW LET'S GO TO SLEEP!!
EH? BUT THIS IS THE INTERESTING PART.
THAT'S RIGHT!! WE HAVE ALLLL NIGHT!
SHAKKA
SHAKKA
SHAKKA
Y-YOU GUYS...
KARAOKE!! LET'S TRY THAT!!
Sing With
HUH? ASÔ-KUN? YOU DO KARAOKE?
EH... ?!
OKAY, NEXT IT'S YOUR TURN, SUÔ.
TH-THEN...
PEEP
PEEP
HOW ABOUT WE DO THIS?
BUTTERFLY
BUTTERFLY?
I'VE NEVER HEARD OF IT. IS IT A WESTERN SONG?
EH?
AH... Y-YEAH... THAT'S RIGHT.
HM... SO YOU LISTEN TO WESTERN MUSIC?
Y-YEAH, I DO... A LITTLE.

Should Have Known.

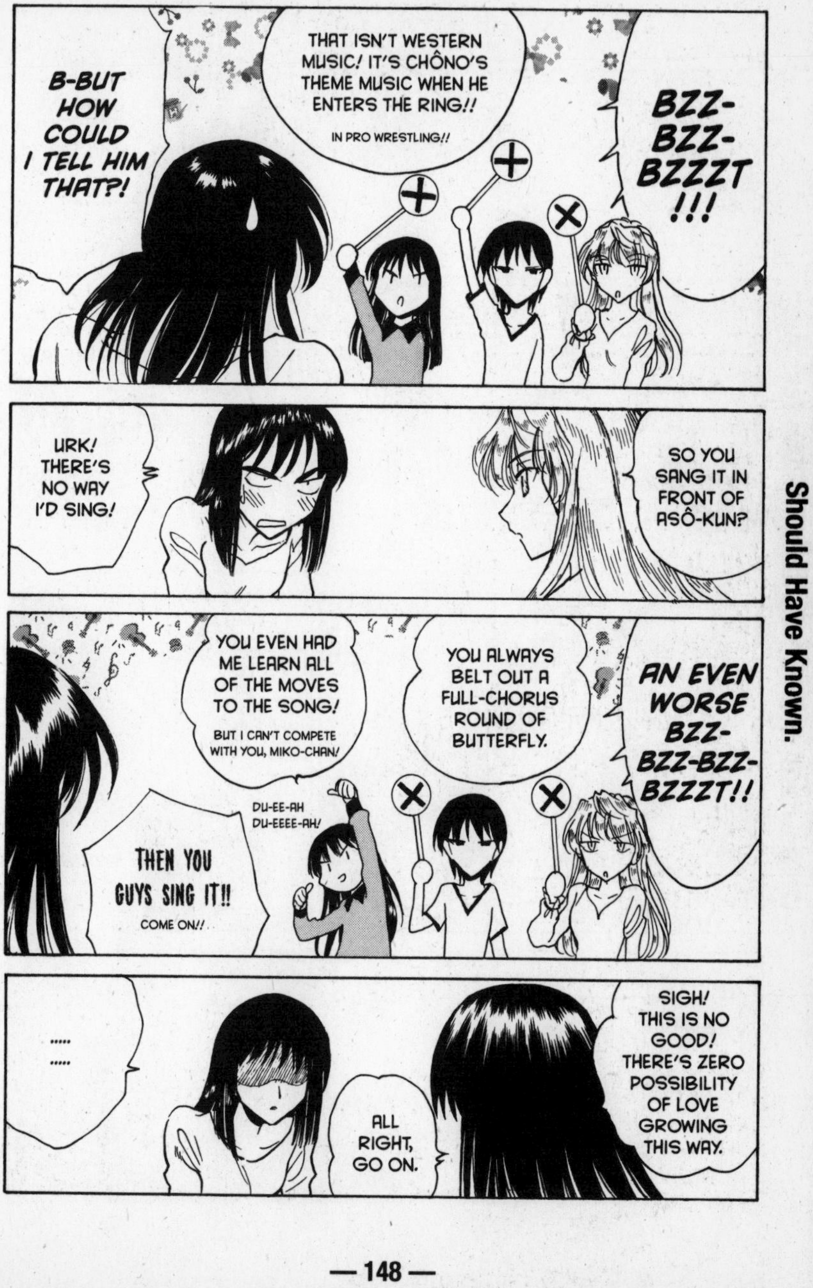
BZZ-BZZ-BZZZT!!!
THAT ISN'T WESTERN MUSIC! IT'S CHÔNO'S THEME MUSIC WHEN HE ENTERS THE RING!!
IN PRO WRESTLING!!
B-BUT HOW COULD I TELL HIM THAT?!
SO YOU SANG IT IN FRONT OF ASÔ-KUN?
URK! THERE'S NO WAY I'D SING!
AN EVEN WORSE BZZ-BZZ-BZZ-BZZZT!!
YOU ALWAYS BELT OUT A FULL-CHORUS ROUND OF BUTTERFLY.
YOU EVEN HAD ME LEARN ALL OF THE MOVES TO THE SONG!
BUT I CAN'T COMPETE WITH YOU, MIKO-CHAN!
DU-EE-AH DU-EEEE-AH!
THEN YOU GUYS SING IT!!
COME ON!!
SIGH! THIS IS NO GOOD! THERE'S ZERO POSSIBILITY OF LOVE GROWING THIS WAY.
ALL RIGHT, GO ON.
....

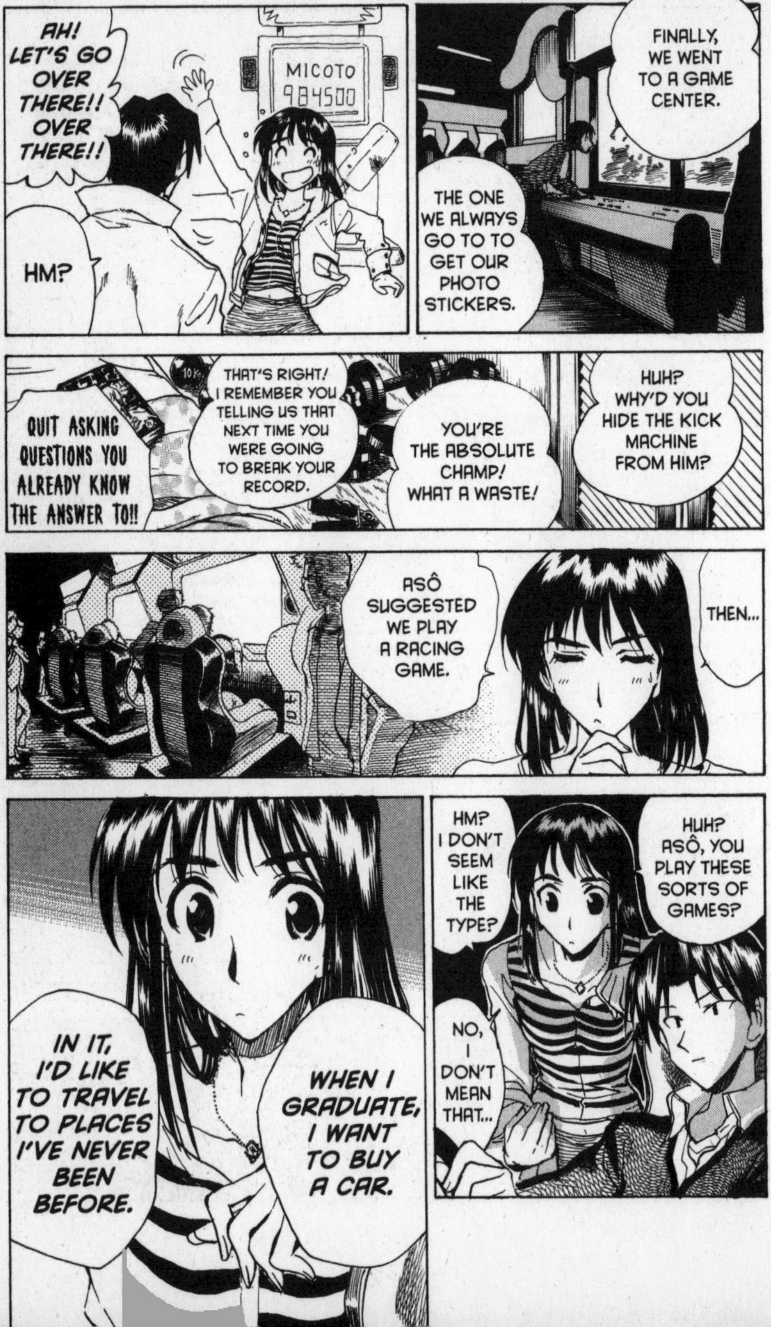
FINALLY, WE WENT TO A GAME CENTER.
THE ONE WE ALWAYS GO TO TO GET OUR PHOTO STICKERS.
MICOTO
984500
AH! LET'S GO OVER THERE!! OVER THERE!!
HM?
HUH? WHY'D YOU HIDE THE KICK MACHINE FROM HIM?
YOU'RE THE ABSOLUTE CHAMP! WHAT A WASTE!
THAT'S RIGHT! I REMEMBER YOU TELLING US THAT NEXT TIME YOU WERE GOING TO BREAK YOUR RECORD.
QUIT ASKING QUESTIONS YOU ALREADY KNOW THE ANSWER TO!!
THEN...
ASÔ SUGGESTED WE PLAY A RACING GAME.
HUH? ASÔ, YOU PLAY THESE SORTS OF GAMES?
HM? I DON'T SEEM LIKE THE TYPE?
NO, I DON'T MEAN THAT...
WHEN I GRADUATE, I WANT TO BUY A CAR.
IN IT, I'D LIKE TO TRAVEL TO PLACES I'VE NEVER BEEN BEFORE.

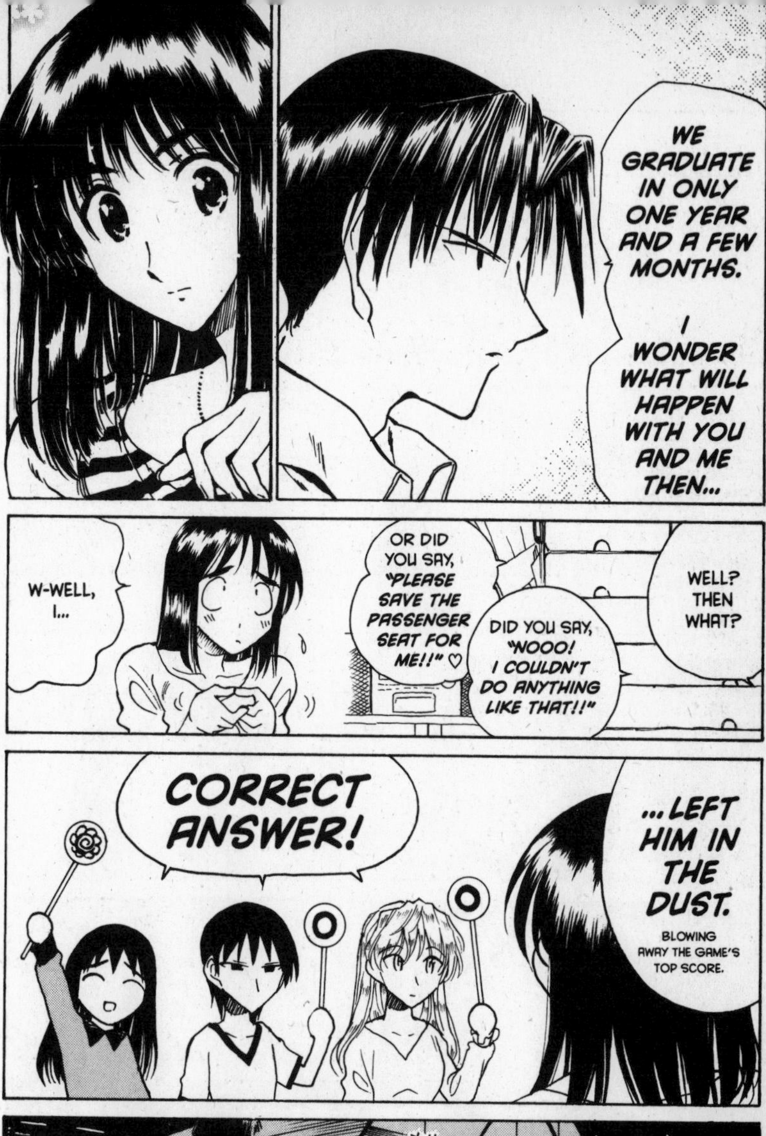

WE GRADUATE IN ONLY ONE YEAR AND A FEW MONTHS.
I WONDER WHAT WILL HAPPEN WITH YOU AND ME THEN...
WELL? THEN WHAT?
DID YOU SAY, "NOOO! I COULDN'T DO ANYTHING LIKE THAT!!"
OR DID YOU SAY, "PLEASE SAVE THE PASSENGER SEAT FOR ME!!" ♡
W-WELL, I...
...LEFT HIM IN THE DUST.
BLOWING AWAY THE GAME'S TOP SCORE.
CORRECT ANSWER!
......
......
GRRRN
SIR... WE'RE CLOSING.

That's Big Sister Mikoto.

♭31· · · · · · · ·Fin

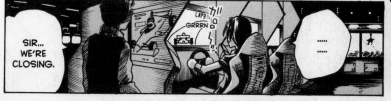

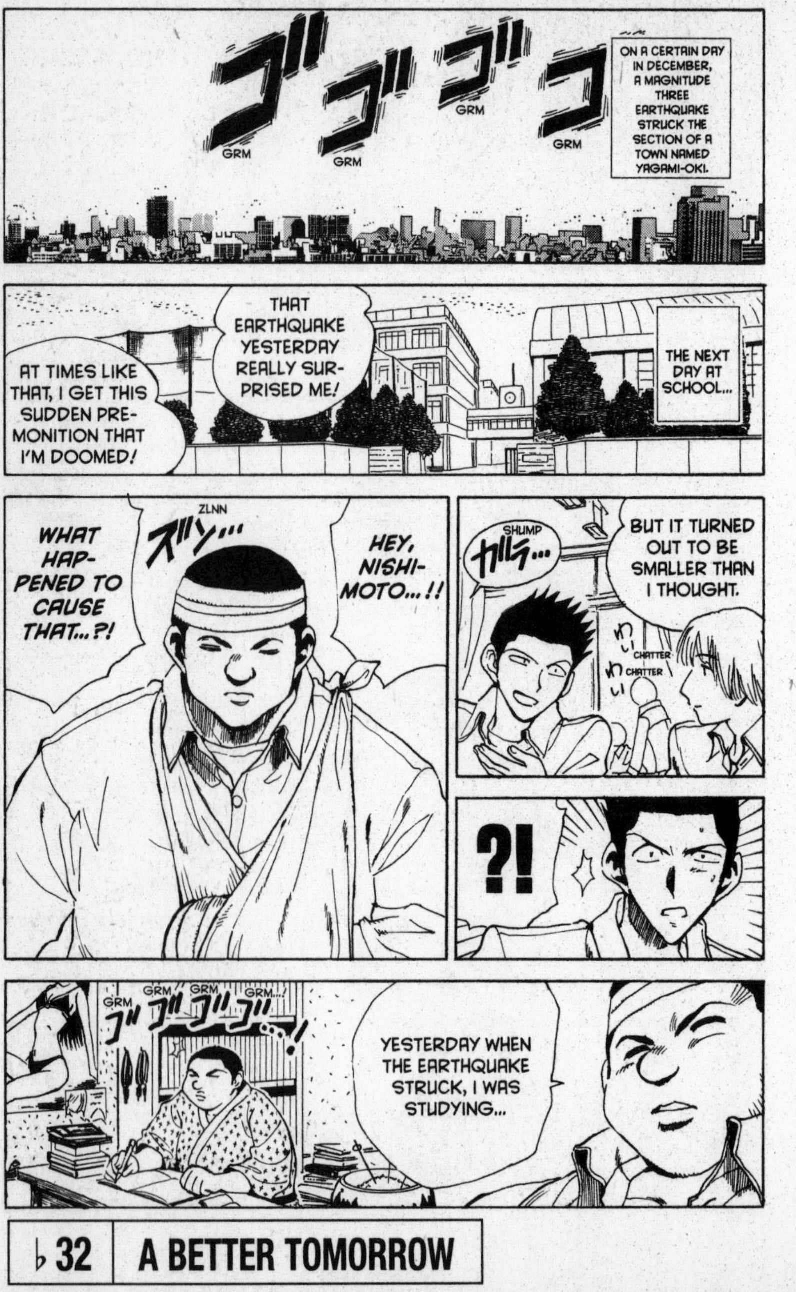
ON A CERTAIN DAY IN DECEMBER, A MAGNITUDE THREE EARTHQUAKE STRUCK THE SECTION OF A TOWN NAMED YAGAMI-OKI.
GRM
GRM
GRM
GRM
THE NEXT DAY AT SCHOOL...
THAT EARTHQUAKE YESTERDAY REALLY SURPRISED ME!
AT TIMES LIKE THAT, I GET THIS SUDDEN PREMONITION THAT I'M DOOMED!
BUT IT TURNED OUT TO BE SMALLER THAN I THOUGHT.
SHUMP
CHATTER
CHATTER
?!
HEY, NISHIMOTO...!!
ZLNN
WHAT HAPPENED TO CAUSE THAT...?!
YESTERDAY WHEN THE EARTHQUAKE STRUCK, I WAS STUDYING...
GRM...!
GRM
GRM
GRM

♭32 A BETTER TOMORROW

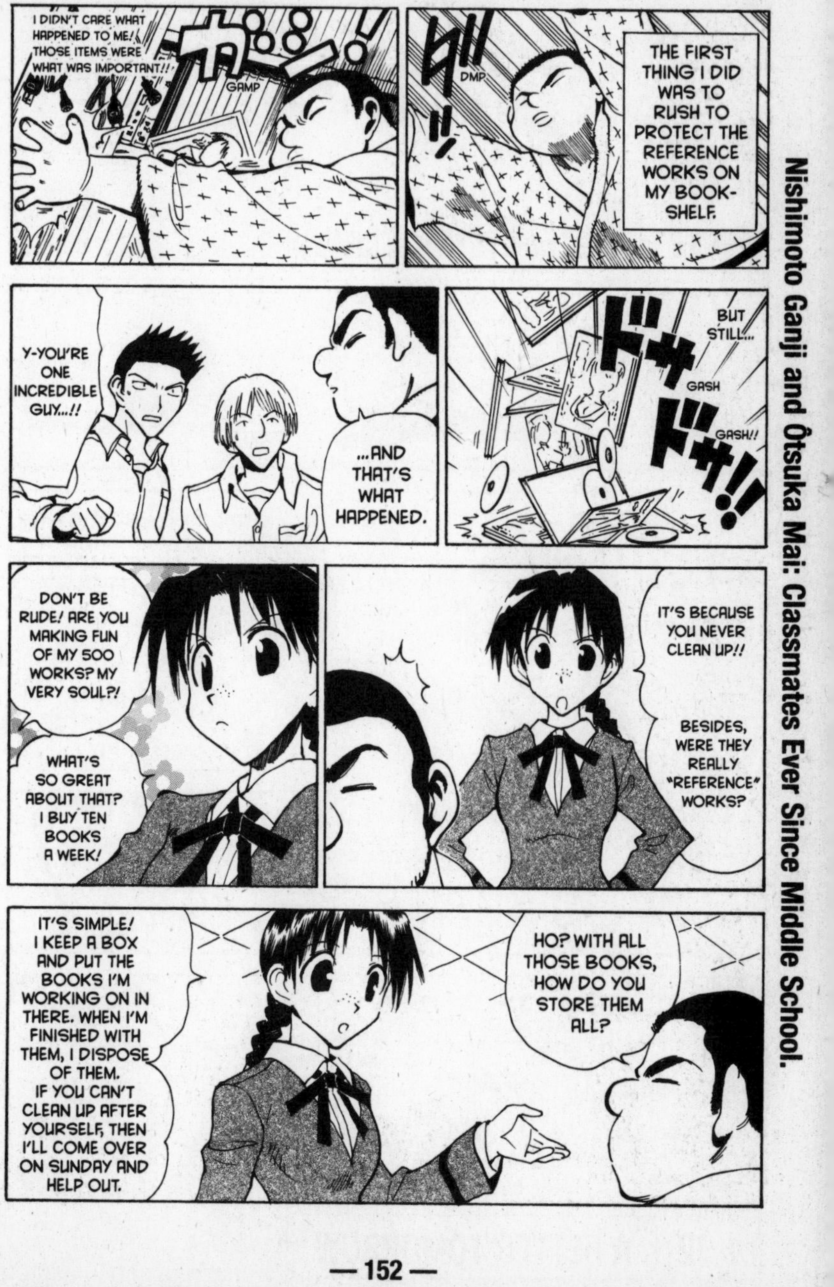
DMP
THE FIRST THING I DID WAS TO RUSH TO PROTECT THE REFERENCE WORKS ON MY BOOK-SHELF.
I DIDN'T CARE WHAT HAPPENED TO ME! THOSE ITEMS WERE WHAT WAS IMPORTANT!!
GAMP
BUT STILL...
GASH
GASH!!
...AND THAT'S WHAT HAPPENED.
Y-YOU'RE ONE INCREDIBLE GUY...!!
IT'S BECAUSE YOU NEVER CLEAN UP!!
BESIDES, WERE THEY REALLY "REFERENCE" WORKS?
DON'T BE RUDE! ARE YOU MAKING FUN OF MY 500 WORKS? MY VERY SOUL?!
WHAT'S SO GREAT ABOUT THAT? I BUY TEN BOOKS A WEEK!
HO? WITH ALL THOSE BOOKS, HOW DO YOU STORE THEM ALL?
IT'S SIMPLE! I KEEP A BOX AND PUT THE BOOKS I'M WORKING ON IN THERE. WHEN I'M FINISHED WITH THEM, I DISPOSE OF THEM. IF YOU CAN'T CLEAN UP AFTER YOURSELF, THEN I'LL COME OVER ON SUNDAY AND HELP OUT.

Nishimoto Ganji and Ôtsuka Mai: Classmates Ever Since Middle School.

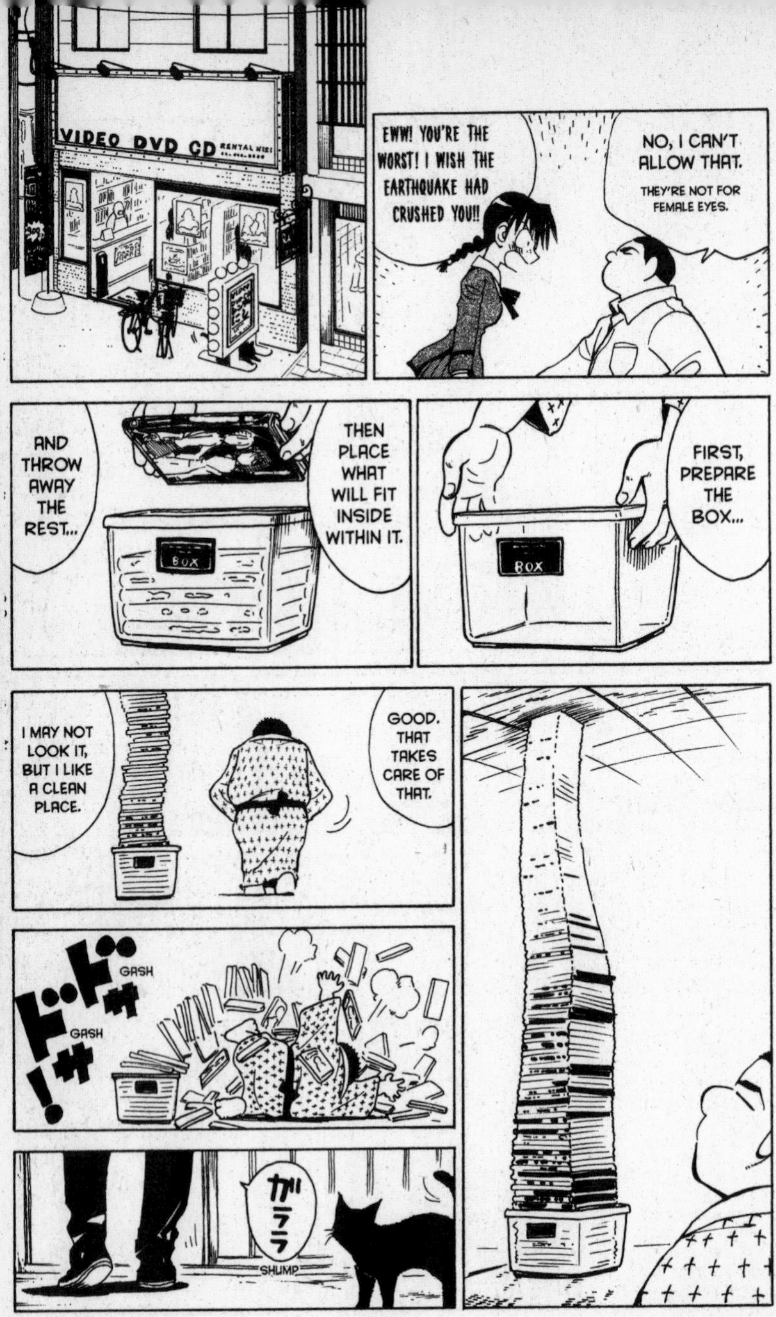
NO, I CAN'T ALLOW THAT.
THEY'RE NOT FOR FEMALE EYES.
EWW! YOU'RE THE WORST! I WISH THE EARTHQUAKE HAD CRUSHED YOU!!
VIDEO DVD CD RENTAL
FIRST, PREPARE THE BOX...
BOX
THEN PLACE WHAT WILL FIT INSIDE WITHIN IT.
AND THROW AWAY THE REST...
BOX
GOOD. THAT TAKES CARE OF THAT.
I MAY NOT LOOK IT, BUT I LIKE A CLEAN PLACE.
ドサ GASH
ドサ! GASH
ガララ
SHUMP

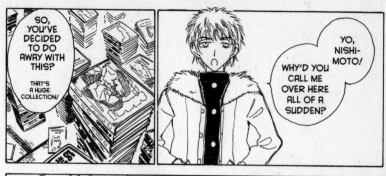

Nishimoto Battalion: Emergency Summons.

YO, NISHIMOTO!
WHY'D YOU CALL ME OVER HERE ALL OF A SUDDEN?
SO, YOU'VE DECIDED TO DO AWAY WITH THIS?
THAT'S A HUGE COLLECTION!
BUT I'VE GOT A DATE TONIGHT, AND...
YOU SEE... I DON'T NEED THIS STUFF.
THIS IS FROM 1984! BEFORE I WAS BORN!
YOU UNDERESTIMATE ME, SERGEANT IMADORI!!
KSHNK
JUST LOOK AT THIS!!
WHAT? YEAH, I KNEW IT'D BE BORING.
DON'T BE SO HASTY!
HASTE MAKES WASTE!
THIS POINT HERE.
OH ...
OHHHH!!
I HAVE TO ADMIT THAT THIS...
THE BRILLIANCE OF THIS MOMENT IS WHY I COULD NOT THROW IT AWAY.

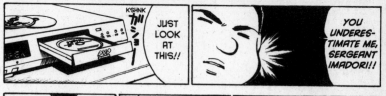

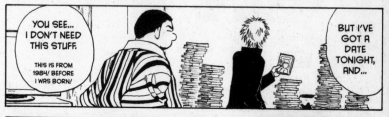

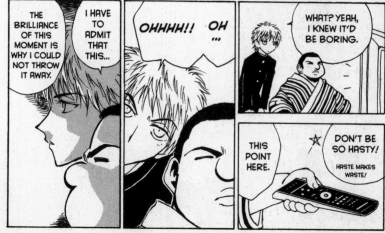

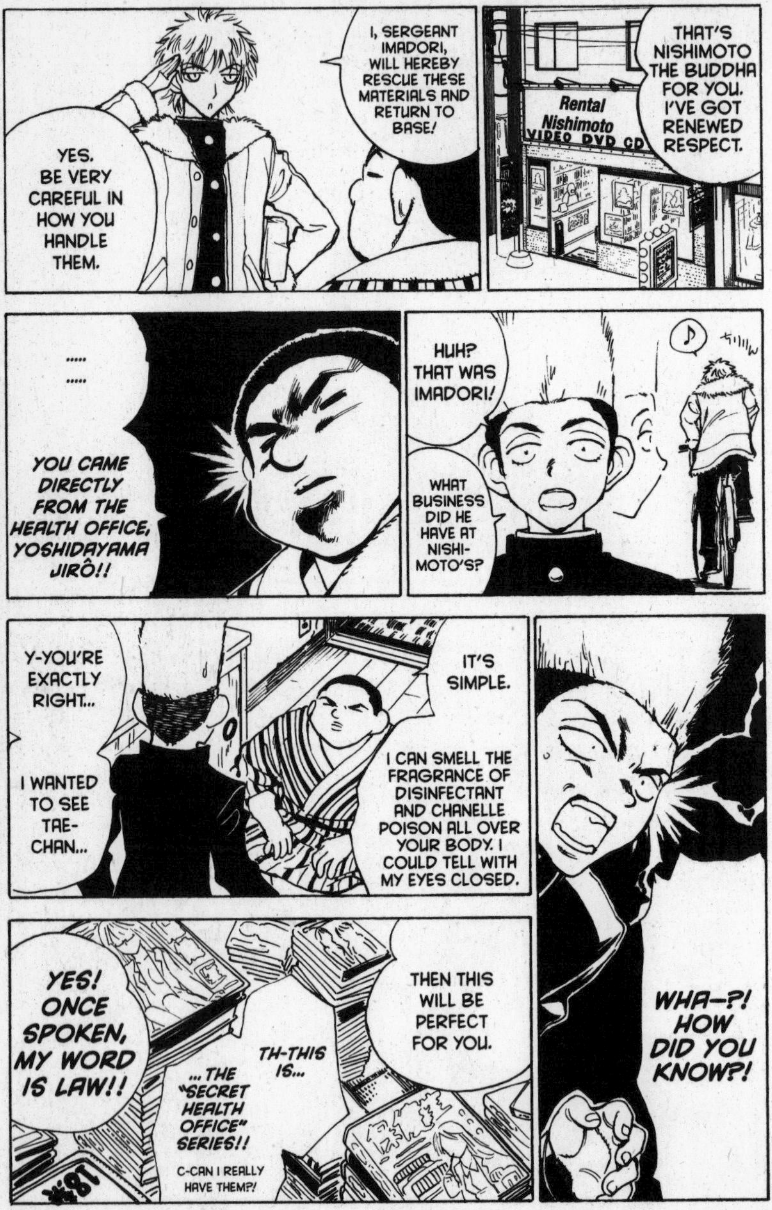
Rental Nishimoto
VIDEO DVD CD
THAT'S NISHIMOTO THE BUDDHA FOR YOU. I'VE GOT RENEWED RESPECT.
I, SERGEANT IMADORI, WILL HEREBY RESCUE THESE MATERIALS AND RETURN TO BASE!
YES. BE VERY CAREFUL IN HOW YOU HANDLE THEM.
♪
HUH? THAT WAS IMADORI!
WHAT BUSINESS DID HE HAVE AT NISHIMOTO'S?
.....
.....
YOU CAME DIRECTLY FROM THE HEALTH OFFICE, YOSHIDAYAMA JIRÔ!!
WHA—?! HOW DID YOU KNOW?!
IT'S SIMPLE.
I CAN SMELL THE FRAGRANCE OF DISINFECTANT AND CHANELLE POISON ALL OVER YOUR BODY. I COULD TELL WITH MY EYES CLOSED.
Y-YOU'RE EXACTLY RIGHT...
I WANTED TO SEE TAE-CHAN...
THEN THIS WILL BE PERFECT FOR YOU.
TH-THIS IS...
...THE "SECRET HEALTH OFFICE" SERIES!!
C-CAN I REALLY HAVE THEM?!
YES! ONCE SPOKEN, MY WORD IS LAW!!
#81

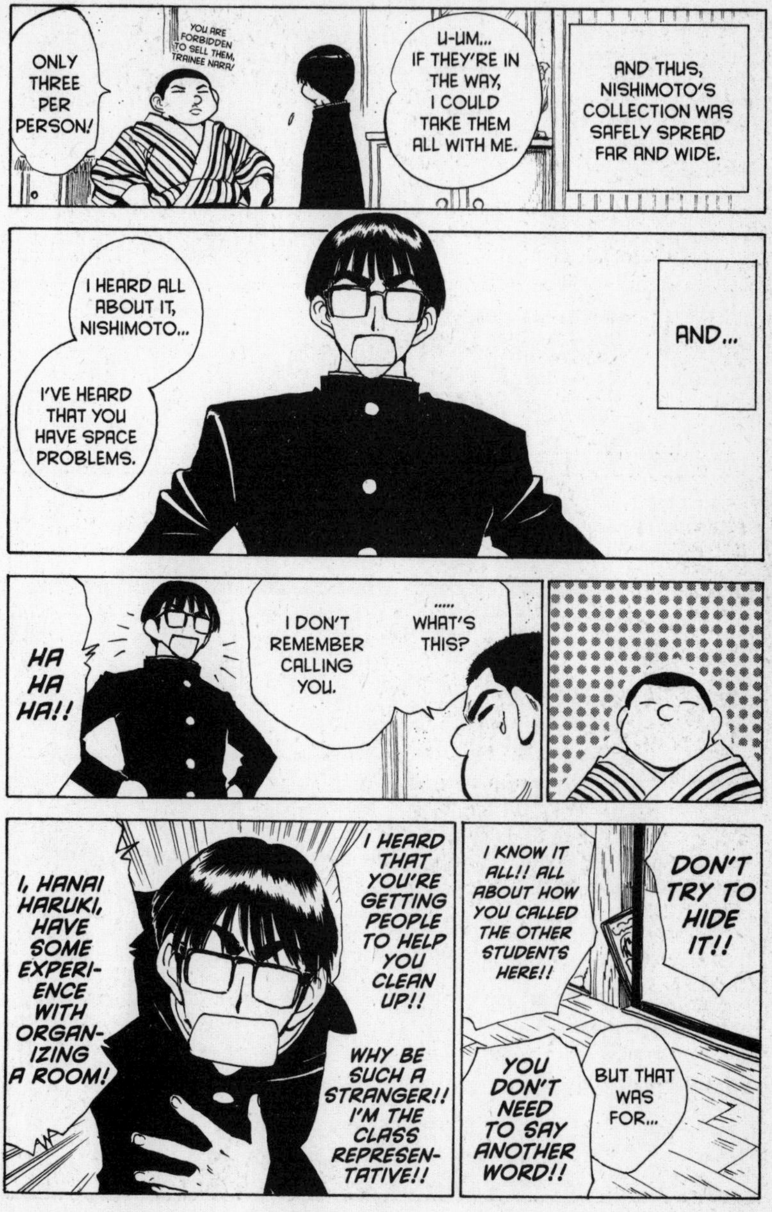
AND THUS, NISHIMOTO'S COLLECTION WAS SAFELY SPREAD FAR AND WIDE.
U-UM... IF THEY'RE IN THE WAY, I COULD TAKE THEM ALL WITH ME.
YOU ARE FORBIDDEN TO SELL THEM, TRAINEE NARA!
ONLY THREE PER PERSON!
AND...
I HEARD ALL ABOUT IT, NISHIMOTO...
I'VE HEARD THAT YOU HAVE SPACE PROBLEMS.
..... WHAT'S THIS?
I DON'T REMEMBER CALLING YOU.
HA HA HA!!
DON'T TRY TO HIDE IT!!
I KNOW IT ALL!! ALL ABOUT HOW YOU CALLED THE OTHER STUDENTS HERE!!
BUT THAT WAS FOR...
YOU DON'T NEED TO SAY ANOTHER WORD!!
I HEARD THAT YOU'RE GETTING PEOPLE TO HELP YOU CLEAN UP!!
WHY BE SUCH A STRANGER!! I'M THE CLASS REPRESENTATIVE!!
I, HANAI HARUKI, HAVE SOME EXPERIENCE WITH ORGANIZING A ROOM!

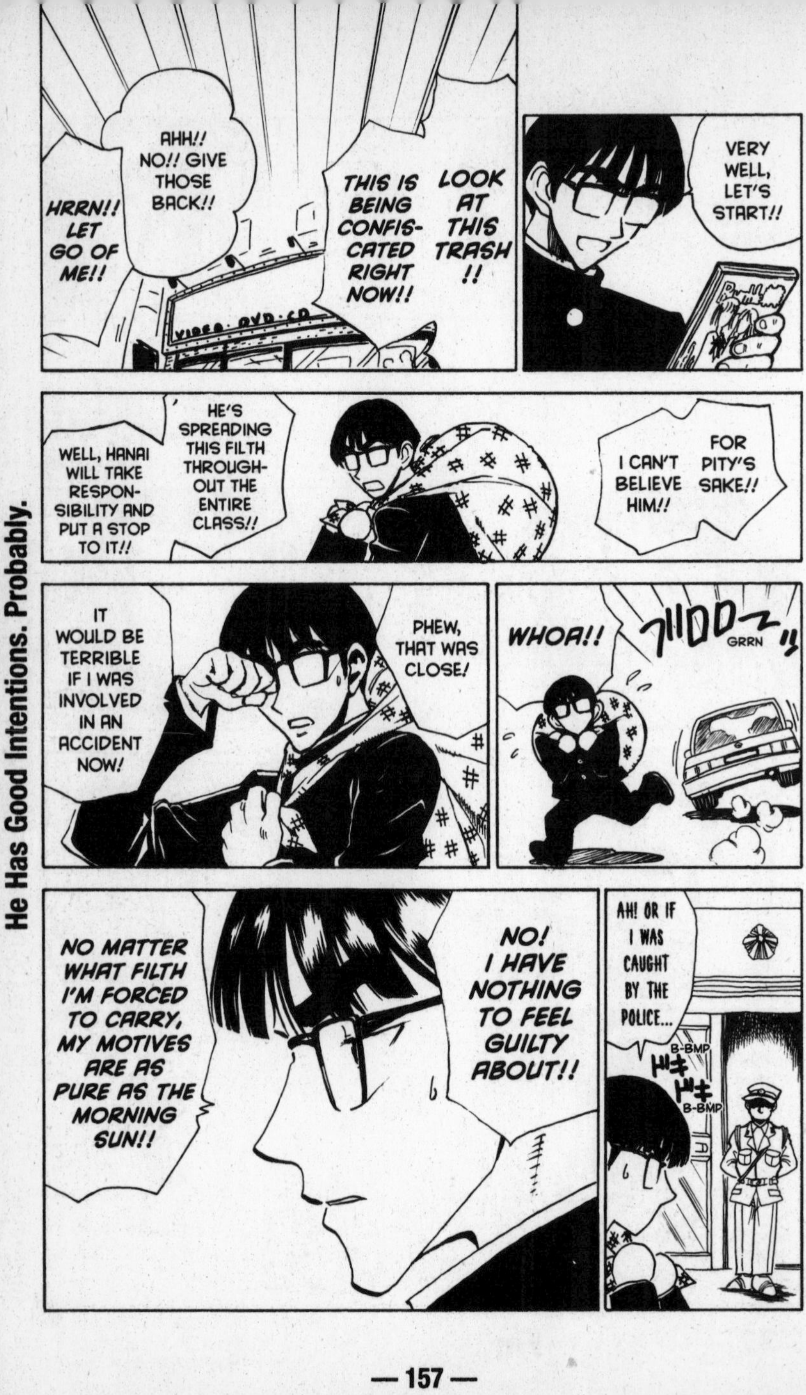
VERY WELL, LET'S START!!
LOOK AT THIS TRASH!!
THIS IS BEING CONFISCATED RIGHT NOW!!
AHH!! NO!! GIVE THOSE BACK!!
HRRN!! LET GO OF ME!!
VIDEO·DVD·CD
FOR PITY'S SAKE!!
I CAN'T BELIEVE HIM!!
HE'S SPREADING THIS FILTH THROUGHOUT THE ENTIRE CLASS!!
WELL, HANAI WILL TAKE RESPONSIBILITY AND PUT A STOP TO IT!!
GRRN
WHOA!!
PHEW, THAT WAS CLOSE!
IT WOULD BE TERRIBLE IF I WAS INVOLVED IN AN ACCIDENT NOW!
AH! OR IF I WAS CAUGHT BY THE POLICE...
B-BMP
B-BMP
NO! I HAVE NOTHING TO FEEL GUILTY ABOUT!!
NO MATTER WHAT FILTH I'M FORCED TO CARRY, MY MOTIVES ARE AS PURE AS THE MORNING SUN!!

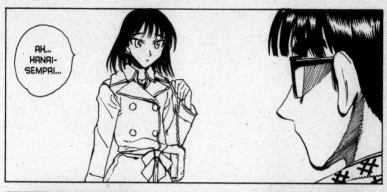

AH... HANAI-SEMPAI...
.....!!
WH— ?!
NO!! YOU'VE GOT IT WRONG!!
WAIT, YAKUMO-KUN!!
THIS IS JUST TRASH!! AND BESIDES, IT ISN'T EVEN MINE!!
I SHOULDN'T HAVE READ HIS MIND!
ピューーッ
VYUUM
WAIT UP, PLEASE?!
YO, HANAI!
HUH? WHAT'S THIS?
HE LEFT THIS HUGE BAG BEHIND.
I WONDER WHAT'S IN IT.

A Curse on Any Who Steals My Collection.

♭32 .... **Fin**

TO BE CONTINUED IN VOLUME 12.
VISIT DELREYMANGA.COM
FOR RELEASE INFORMATION.

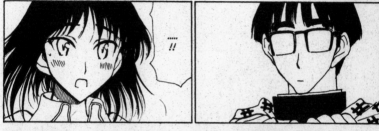

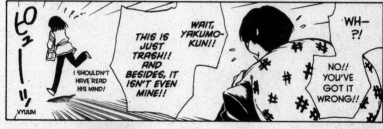

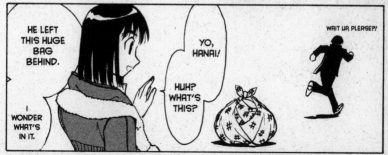

Sees Someone She Hasn't Seen in a Long Time.

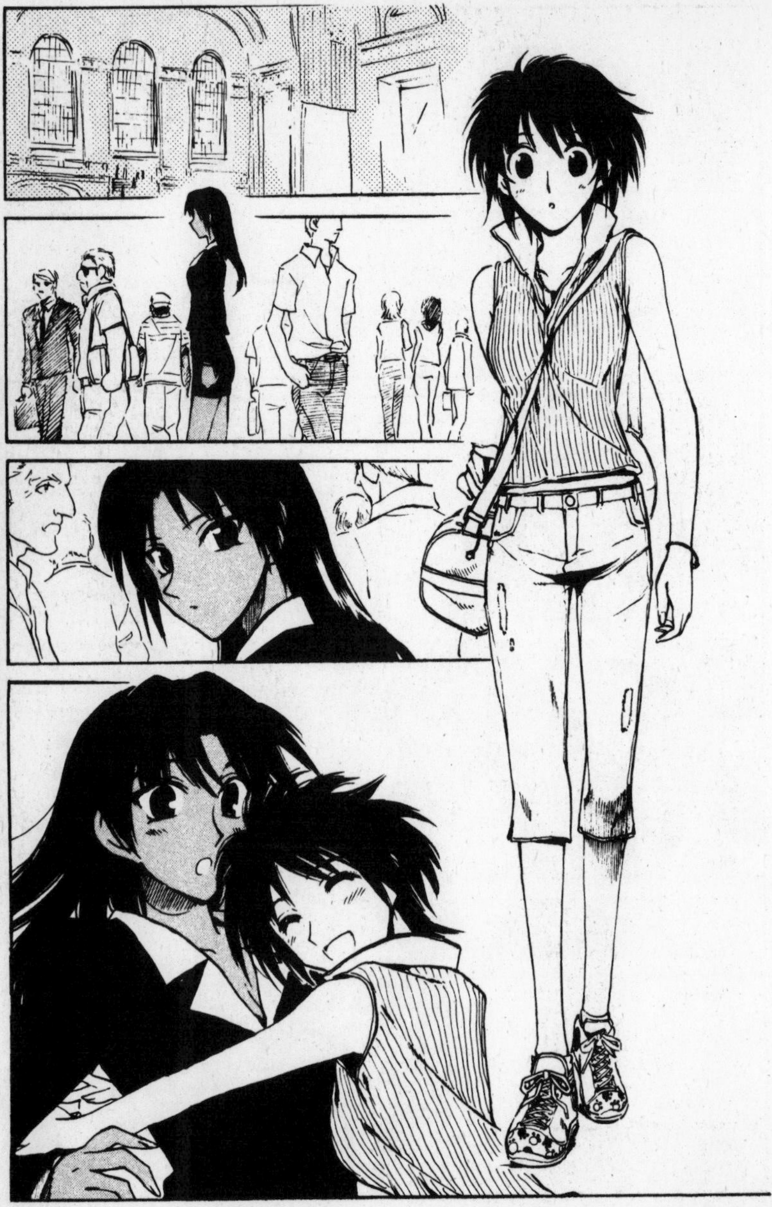

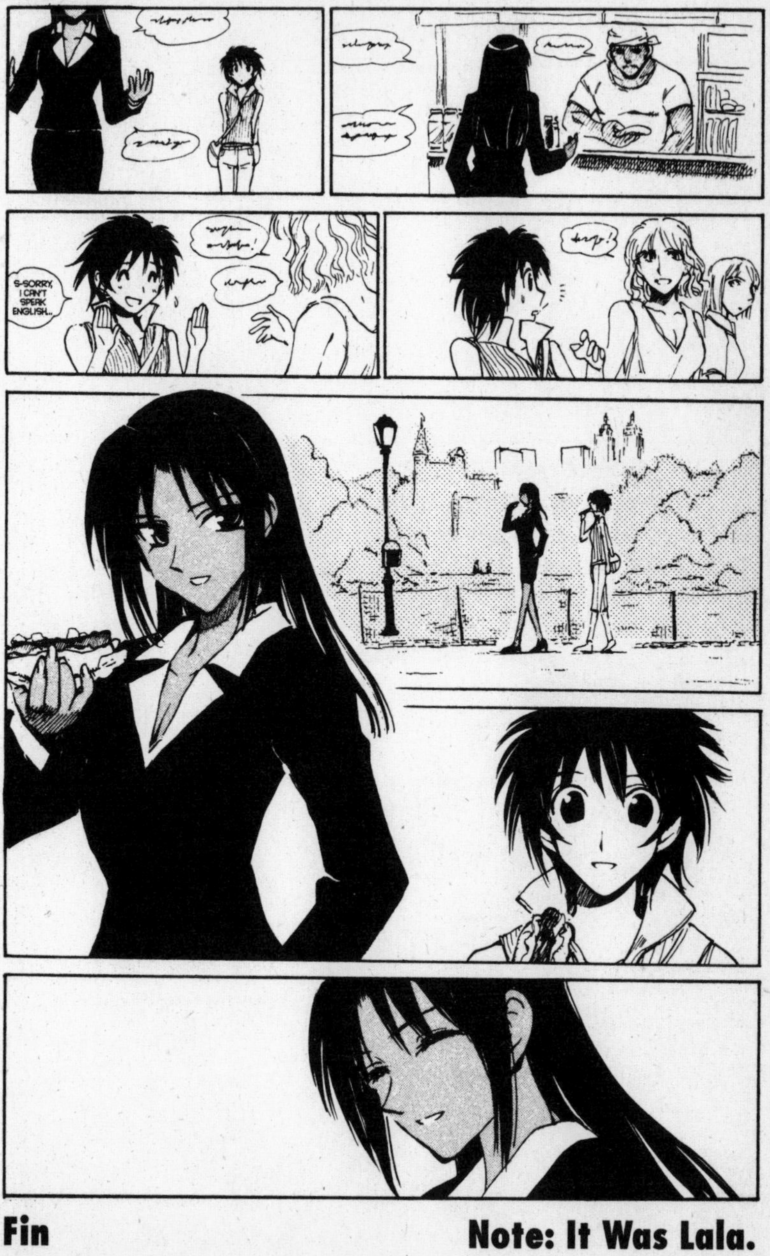
S-SORRY, I CAN'T SPEAK ENGLISH...

Fin

Note: It Was Lala.

About the Creator

Jin Kobayashi was born in Tokyo. *School Rumble* is his first manga series. He has answered these questions from his fans:

What is your hobby?
Basketball

Which manga inspired you to become a creator?
Dragon Ball

Which character in your manga do you like best?
Kenji Harima

What type of manga do you want to create in the future?
Action

Name one book, piece of music, or movie you like.
The Indiana Jones series

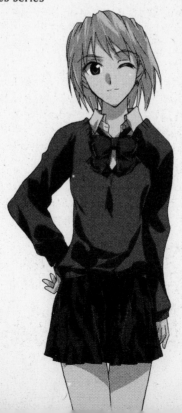

Translation Notes

Japanese is a tricky language for most Westerners, and translation is often more art than science. For your edification and reading pleasure, here are notes on some of the places where we could have gone in a different direction in our translation of the work, or where a Japanese cultural reference is used.

A man and a woman eating Chinese food together, page 27

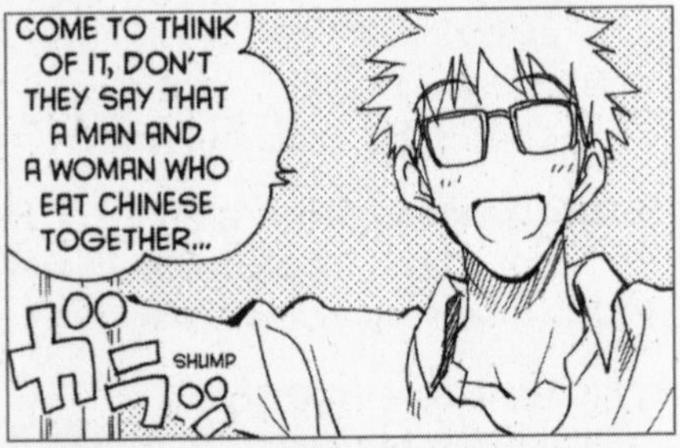
COME TO THINK OF IT, DON'T THEY SAY THAT A MAN AND A WOMAN WHO EAT CHINESE TOGETHER...
SHUMP

There is a saying that a man and a woman eating *yakiniku* (Korean barbecue) together must have a very tight relationship. That's because there is a lot of garlic in *yakiniku*, and if a man or woman doesn't mind the smell of garlic on their partner, they must be very close. Tani-sensei is intentionally or unintentionally mistaking Chinese food for *yakiniku* in his statement.

Kôhai, page 29

As explained in the honorifics section, older students or more experienced employees in a workplace are sempai, and their younger, less experienced counterparts are kôhai. Sempai are supposed to guide their kôhai, and the kôhai in turn are supposed to respect their sempai. This makes for sempai who have very parental feelings for their kôhai.

Natto and *hijiki*, page 42

Both *natto*, a viscous bean-based snack, and *hijiki*, a type of edible seaweed, are considered low-cost, healthy foods in the Japanese diet. They are thought to be very Japanese, since most foreigners shy away from them.

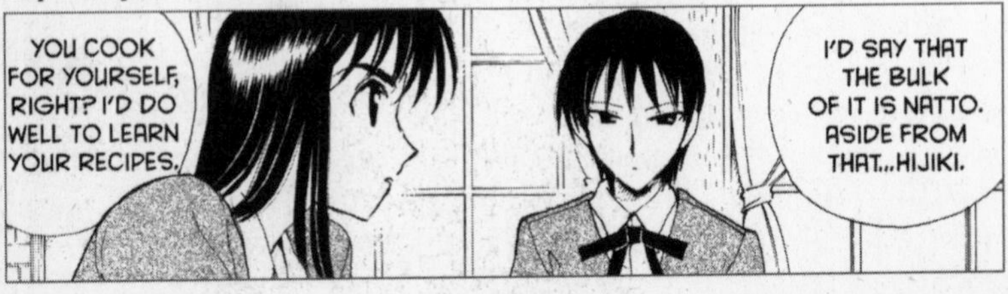
I'D SAY THAT THE BULK OF IT IS NATTO. ASIDE FROM THAT...HIJIKI.
YOU COOK FOR YOURSELF, RIGHT? I'D DO WELL TO LEARN YOUR RECIPES.

Beneath the Wheel, page 51

Beneath the Wheel is German author Hermann Hesse's most popular book in Japan. It tells the story of a gifted young man who is sent into a too-strict school system that rewards his achievements with harder and more impersonal studies. He then meets a rebellious poet who helps him begin to see that there may be more to life than academics and testing. But the soul-crushing school environment has already done its damage on the young main character. It is an indictment of the overly strict turn-of-the-20th-century German school system, but Japanese readers seem to relate to its message.

Penne pasta, page 52

Tenma got it right for a change. Penne means "pen" in Italian. The pasta is tube-shaped and comes to a point as if it were a quill pen.

Arrabbiata, page 53

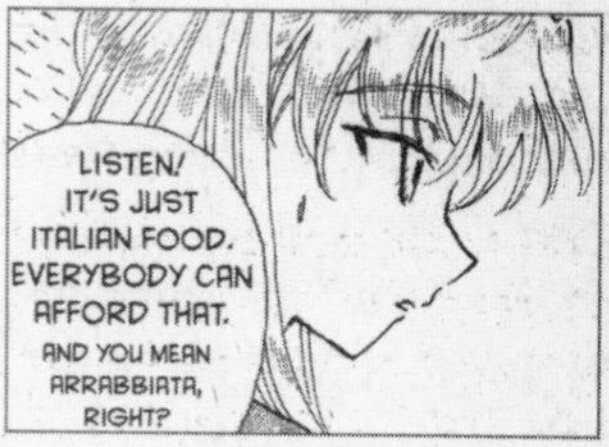
LISTEN! IT'S JUST ITALIAN FOOD. EVERYBODY CAN AFFORD THAT.
AND YOU MEAN ARRABBIATA, RIGHT?

Arrabbiata has nothing to do with Arabia. It means "angry" in Italian, and the dish is called that because the Roman penne pasta recipe comes out very hot and spicy.

Yakisoba and G-pen, page 53

Yakisoba is a fried noodle dish mixed with meats and vegetables. A G-pen is a manga artist's quill pen.

Teachers: Money? Glory?, page 58

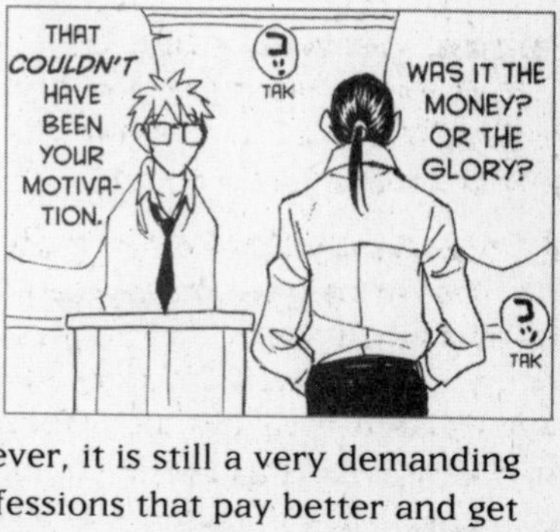
WAS IT THE MONEY? OR THE GLORY?
TAK
THAT *COULDN'T* HAVE BEEN YOUR MOTIVA-TION.
TAK

Tôgô Masakazu's statement may seem strange to American readers, considering the relative low status and pay of teachers in the States, but in Japan, it is possible for a teacher to have chosen the profession for those reasons. Teachers in Japan are better paid and better respected than their North American counterparts. However, it is still a very demanding profession, and there are other professions that pay better and get more respect—so most Japanese teachers' motivation is the desire to teach.

Nabe, page 63
An autumn and winter treat in Japan, *nabe* is a large pot (the word actually means "pot") in which various meats and vegetables are boiled. The food is taken from the pot in the center of the table, dipped in a sauce, and eaten. The warmth of the stove, smell of the cooking foods, and communal atmosphere make for a uniquely Japanese experience that most diners look forward to with great anticipation.

Imonikai, page 64
The kanji that make up the word *imonikai* mean "boiled potato party," and that's pretty much what this is. It's an outdoor party where potatoes and other root vegetables are stewed and served. Because stewing and *nabe* (see above) have a lot in common, it's a natural combination to mix the two into one big *nabe*-based party.

Habañero, page 65
Indeed, the habañero chile, grown from Texas down to South America, is one of the hottest chiles around.

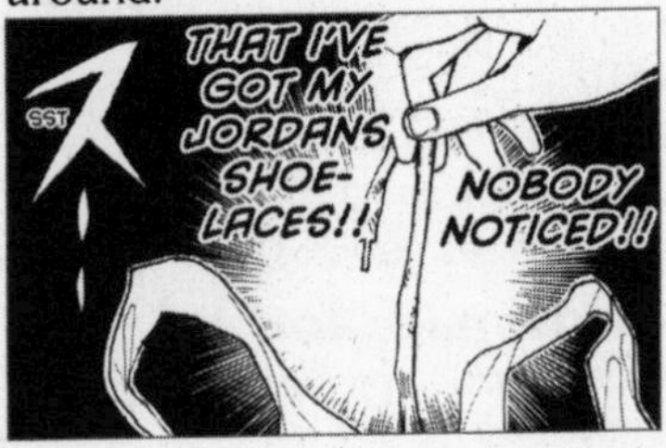
NOBODY NOTICED!!
THAT I'VE GOT MY JORDANS SHOE-LACES!!
SST

Udon noodles, page 65
Thick white flour-based noodles that go well with stews like *nabe*. And they do look something like white sneaker shoelaces.

Ton-shiru, page 67
Ton-shiru is a *miso* soup that is cooked with pork. It tends to have a richer flavor than normal *miso* soup.

Jômon period, page 68
The Jômon period represents prehistoric Japan between 13,000 BC and about 300 BC. It is marked by the hunter-gatherer existence of its inhabitants and the pottery that they left behind.

The Gods of Cookerly, page 75
No, this isn't a typo. Or...at least it isn't a typo on the part of Jin Kobayashi, Kodansha, or Del Rey. *The Gods of Cookerly* is a Hong Kong cooking show from the '90s that came to Japanese cable television in 2004 and 2005. Kobayashi-sensei spelled the English title exactly as it appeared on the show.

Fukujin-zuke, page 83
Sliced vegetables pickled and served with soy sauce.

Boripro, page 90

The Boripro agency in Tenma's dream world is Horipro in ours. It's one of the top talent agencies, representing long-time successes such as Akiko Wada and leading actors and actresses such as Kyôko Fukuda. Representation by them is a fast track to success in the entertainment world.

Nii-chan, page 100

Although Shûji is Harima Kenji's cousin, he still calls Kenji *nii-chan* ("brother"—see the honorifics section). In the Japanese original, he also called him the slightly less respectful and less cute *aniki*, which means the same thing as *nii-chan*. But this translation used *nii-chan* for those situations, since there was little difference in meaning and the different word would add an additional foreign word to an already long list of relationship words.

The menu, page 106

Hinaiji-dori is a bird native to the Aomori region of northern Japan. Satsuma is a region in Kyûshû in southern Japan. Sanriku refers to the seas off Aomori and Iwate prefectures in northern Japan. And the town of Himi is in Toyama prefecture in central Japan on the coast of the Sea of Japan. Although the food is grown or caught in Japan, it is cooked using Western methods, and so the establishment is considered a Western restaurant rather than a Japanese restaurant.

Cards, page 108

Credit cards are popular in Japan, but not nearly so ubiquitous as in the States. They are not accepted in most restaurants and small businesses outside of large city centers, and rejected even in many urban businesses. Carrying a good amount of cash is a good idea when traveling around Japan.

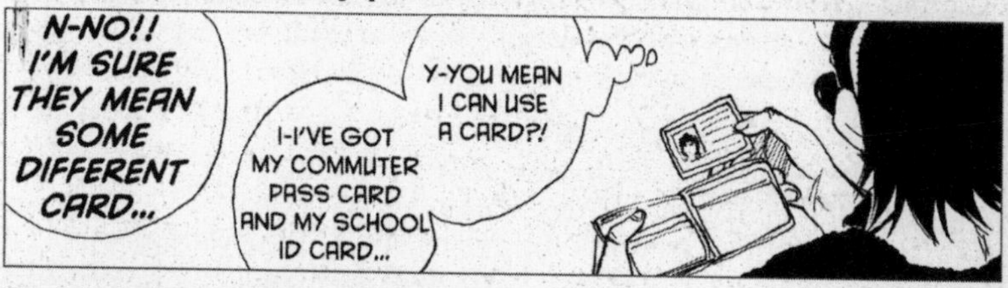

Y-YOU MEAN I CAN USE A CARD?!
I-I'VE GOT MY COMMUTER PASS CARD AND MY SCHOOL ID CARD...
N-NO!! I'M SURE THEY MEAN SOME DIFFERENT CARD...

Hold-back Sensei, page 111

To be held back a year in school is called *ryûnen* in Japanese, so the fact that Hold-back Sensei's name, Ryû Nenji, has *ryûnen* in it is no coincidence.

Write on Your Ears, page 120

This is a reference to a famous Japanese ghost story about a ghost that haunted a Buddhist temple. To make sure that the ghost couldn't see him, a monk wrote sutras all over his body, but he forgot to write on his ears. The ghost couldn't see the parts of the monk's body with sutras, so it only saw a couple of ears hanging in the air. It ripped the ears off the invisible monk's body and took them away with him. So if you are writing on your body to protect yourself from ghosts, don't forget your ears!

Semesters, page 121

The Japanese school year consists of three semesters: Spring, from the opening of school in late March or early April to summer vacation in mid-July; Fall, from the end of summer vacation in late August or early September to the end of December; and a short third semester from early January to the end of the school year in late February or early March.

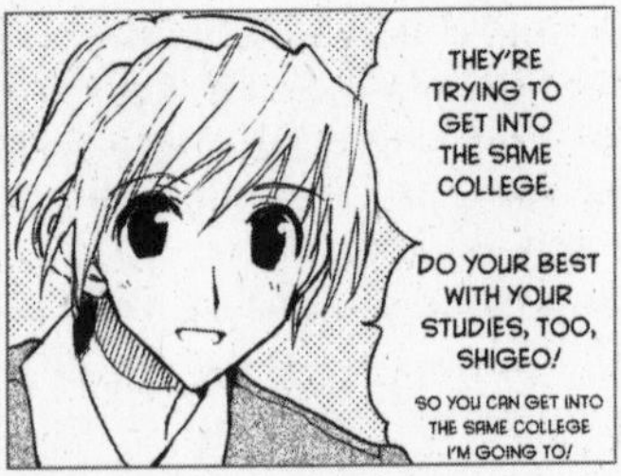
THEY'RE TRYING TO GET INTO THE SAME COLLEGE.
DO YOUR BEST WITH YOUR STUDIES, TOO, SHIGEO!
SO YOU CAN GET INTO THE SAME COLLEGE I'M GOING TO!

Getting into college, page 123

Entrance into most schools depends on passing tough entrance exams. However, a few students can qualify due to sporting or academic achievements or for other special reasons.

Sorry to barge in, page 127

This is a standard Japanese phrase, *Ojama-shimasu!*, which means, "I am about to be a bother." It's the polite thing to say whenever entering someone's house as a guest.

Ii kuni tsukurô and numbered mnemonics, page 127

The Japanese writing system allows for several different readings of its numbers. Many of these readings can be fashioned into sentences such as *ii kuni*. The two "i"s represent two 1's, and *ku* (9) and *ni* (2) combine to make the number 1192. So a large number of mnemonics have been developed to allow students to remember dates, math formulas, and other figures that come up on exams. *Ii kuni tsukurô* is one of the most well-known history mnemonics.

Filet, lobster, and eclair, page 127

The pun was a little different in Japanese since the words for fulcrum, load, and effort are different in Japanese from their English counterparts. The Japanese words used the kanji 'ten,' which means "point," and Tenma

substituted sound-alike words using the kanji *ten*, which means "store." which So Tenma's answer in Japanese was "Main store, branch store, and sales department." Not quite translatable as a joke... So this English translation changed the words to a different Tenma obsession, food.

Soon I May Go to See You, Jiko-chû, page 146

Starting with *Seka-chû* (*Sekai no Chûshin ni Ai wo Sakebu*, which literally translated means "Cry Out 'Love' from the Center of the World," but by author request was published in English under the name *Socrates in Love*) and continuing with *Ima Ai ni Yukimasu* (translated as "Be with You") and *Densha Otoko* (*Train Man*), there has been a rash of novels about idealized love that have gone on to become hits in all forms of pop-culture storytelling such as movies, TV dramas, manga, and other media. *Jiko-chû* and *Soon I May Go to See You* are the *School Rumble*–world equivalents of *Seka-chû* and *Be with You.*

Chôno, page 148

The Chôno they're probably referring to would be the *School Rumble* version of top pro wrestler Masahiro Chôno (known in the West as Masa Chono). His usual theme music when he enters the ring is called Crash, a combination of the songs "Martial Arts" by Royal Hunt, 'Victory' (Nine Inch Nails Remix) by Puff Daddy & The Family, and "No Way Out" by Puff Daddy & The Family. Also, the first kanji in his name (chô) means butterfly, so having a theme song named "Butterfly" would be natural.

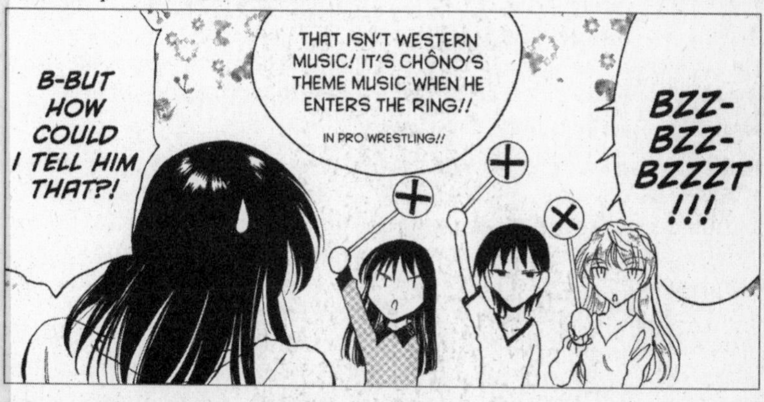
BZZ-BZZ-BZZZT!!!
THAT ISN'T WESTERN MUSIC! IT'S CHÔNO'S THEME MUSIC WHEN HE ENTERS THE RING!!
IN PRO WRESTLING!!
B-BUT HOW COULD I TELL HIM THAT?!

Chanelle poison, page 155

This fragrance is probably the *School Rumble*–world equivalent of a cross between Chanel's perfume products and Christian Dior's Poison perfume.

Watch out! It's Volume 12!

School Rumble

On sale from Del Rey Manga, April 28, 2009.

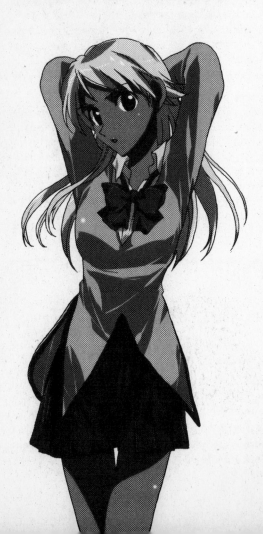

TOMARE!

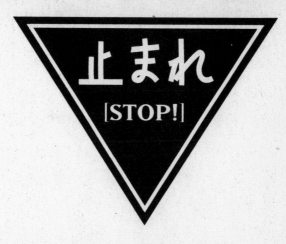

止まれ

[STOP!]

You're going the wrong way!

Manga is a completely different type of reading experience.

To start at the *beginning*, go to the *end*!

That's right! Authentic manga is read the traditional Japanese way—from right to left. Exactly the *opposite* of how American books are read. It's easy to follow: Just go to the other end of the book, and read each page—and each panel—from right side to left side, starting at the top right. Now you're experiencing manga as it was meant to be!